The Anglican Communion and Homosexuality

The Anglican Communion and Homosexuality

A Resource to Enable Listening and Dialogue

Edited by
Phil Groves

First published in Great Britain in 2008

Society for Promoting Christian Knowledge
36 Causton Street
London SW1P 4ST

Scripture quotations are taken from various versions.

British Library Cataloguing-in-Publication Data
A catalogue record for this book is available from the British Library

ISBN 978–0–281–059638

1 3 5 7 9 10 8 6 4 2

Designed and typeset by Kenneth Burnley, Wirral, Cheshire
Printed in Great Britain by Ashford Colour Press

Produced on paper from sustainable forests

Contents

List of Contributors

We are grateful for the time and energy put into this project by the writers listed below. They have taken time out of busy lives to offer their expertise. They are only responsible for the sections in their names and did not have the opportunity to engage with one another during the process of writing. They were asked to present as positively as they were able many diverse opinions, and so, even in those sections attributed to them, it should not be assumed that they are in agreement with all they have written and argued. They have presented what is being said to enable you to listen and reach your own conclusions, allowing yourself to be guided by God.

The Very Revd Dr Victor Atta-Baffoe (West Africa)
Victor Atta-Baffoe had his theological education at St Nicholas Seminary, Cape Coast, Ghana (LTh); Trinity College, University of Toronto, Canada (STL); Episcopal Divinity School, Cambridge, Massachusetts USA (MA); Yale University Divinity School, New Haven, Connecticut, USA (STM), King's College London, University of London (PhD). He is the Dean of St Nicholas Seminary, Cape Coast, Ghana. He is a member of the Inter-Anglican Doctrinal and Theological Commission, Chairman of the African Network of Institutions of Theological Education Preparing Anglicans for Ministry (ANITEPAM), served on the Inter-Anglican Theological and Doctrinal Commission, and is a member of the Anglican Covenant Design Group. He is married to Dorcas and has three children.

The Rt Revd Terry Brown (Melanesia)
Bishop Terry has been Bishop of Malaita, Solomon Islands, South Pacific in the Church of the Province of Melanesia for the past 11 years. He was born in the USA but he had his theological training in Canada, from which he first went as a missionary to the Church of Melanesia in 1975. For six years he taught at the provincial theological college, Bishop Patteson Theological College. He then returned to Canada to do his doctorate in church history. For 11 years he was Asia/Pacific Mission Co-ordinator of the Anglican Church of Canada, based in Toronto, and travelled extensively throughout the Asia/Pacific region and beyond. Finally, in 1996 he was elected Bishop of Malaita, returning not as a missionary but under local conditions of service with his fellow bishops. He is now Senior Bishop of the Province. Bishop Terry's interest in the area of the Church and homosexuality is general, covering areas of scripture, theology, history, science, ethics and culture, and is rooted in his own personal life, his interest in history and anthropology and his experience of mission

and ministry in many cross-cultural situations – the proclamation of the Gospel and living it faithfully but also sensitively in terms of those who have very different views from one's own.

The Revd Sue Burns (Aotearoa, New Zealand and Polynesia)

Sue is the Director of the Anglican Studies Programme at the College of St John the Evangelist, Auckland. In her previous role as Ministry Educator for the Diocese of Waikato, she was responsible for planning and facilitating respectful conversations on sexuality and homosexuality across the dioceses of Aotearoa, New Zealand and Polynesia. She regards it as a privilege to have met with the participants in each setting of these conversations. Before emigrating to Aotearoa/New Zealand she completed ministry training at Trinity College, Bristol, having graduated with an honours degree in Biblical Studies from the University of Sheffield. It was through the study of biblical hermeneutics in Sheffield that she responded consciously to God and also began a lifetime of interest in language and interpretation. She delights in conversation and holds a Masters in Counselling and professional membership as a counsellor. She is currently enrolled in a PhD which includes theological reflection with the narratives and identities of people who are migrating.

The Revd Canon Dr Adrian Chatfield (England)

(Adrian has acted as a consultant to the editor, edited Chapter 6 and facilitated the conversation recorded in Chapter 7.)

Adrian Chatfield is currently Director of the Simeon Centre for Prayer and the Spiritual Life at Ridley Hall in Cambridge, and involved with the development of new forms of training ordinands for a range of pioneer ministries. A Trinidadian by birth and upbringing, he has exercised his priestly ministry in the Dioceses of Trinidad and Tobago, Exeter, Southwell and Nottingham, and Christ the King in South Africa. His book and study course on global Anglicanism, *Something in Common*, was commissioned by SPCK and the Centre for Anglican Communion Studies to address the breadth and variety of perspectives in the Communion, and aims to portray Anglicanism from a non-Eurocentric point of view.

The Revd Dr David de Pomerai (England)

David de Pomerai is currently Associate Professor in the School of Biology at the University of Nottingham, where he has been lecturing in genetics and animal development for almost 30 years. He has published two books and some 80 scientific papers on a variety of research topics, most recently dealing with nematode indicator genes that respond to environmental stress. He was recently the recipient of a UK–IERI Major Award to promote research co-operation between the UK and India. He was ordained in 1993 after studying part-time on the East Midlands Ministry Training Course (EMMTC), where he obtained a distinction. His interests in faith and science are combined in a long-running taught course on bioethics, which examines the ethical and social implications of several recent developments in the biological sciences (cloning, genetic engineering, etc.). He is also a longstanding member of the Society of Ordained Scientists. He is currently serving as an Associate Minister in the parish of Walton-on-Trent, Croxall, Rosliston and Linton with Castle Gresley, and also acts as Science Adviser in the Diocese of Derby, England.

The Revd Dr Canon Ian Douglas (USA)
Angus Dun Professor of Mission and World Christianity at the Episcopal Divinity
School in Cambridge, Massachusetts. Ian is a member of the Design Group for the
2008 Lambeth Conference of Anglican Bishops, a Consultant for Theological
Education in the Anglican Communion (TEAC), a past member the Inter-Anglican
Standing Commission on Mission and Evangelism, and a former missionary in
Haiti. He serves on the International Editorial Board for the *Journal of Anglican
Studies* and is a founding organizer of the Anglican Contextual Theologians
Network. Ian is a member of the Executive Council of The Episcopal Church, and
was recently elected as The Episcopal Church's clergy member of the Anglican
Consultative Council. In addition he is Convener of the Episcopal Seminary Con-
sultation on Mission and a founder of Episcopalians for Global Reconciliation. He
publishes and speaks widely on mission, world Christianity and contemporary
Anglicanism. Ian is married to Kristin Harris and they are the parents of three,
almost grown, children.

The Revd Samson Fan (Hong Kong)
Samson was ordained to be a deacon in 2001 and priest the following year. He is
now the vicar of St Thomas' Church in the Diocese of West Kowloon, Hong Kong.
He has been involved in theological education in Ming Hua Theological College. He
has published books for young people about myths and Western culture, ways of
thinking and an introduction to ten important contemporary thinkers. He is now
studying for a Masters degree at the Chinese University of Hong Kong; his Masters
thesis is on Bishop Gore and the Anglican Incarnational Theology. He is particularly
interested in the history of Christian thought, especially the development of Anglican
theology.

The Revd Dr Griphus Gakuru (England)
Dr Griphus Gakuru is currently vicar of All Saints' Church, Stechford, in the Diocese
of Birmingham. Originally a science teacher by profession, he was ordained deacon in
the Anglican Church of Uganda in 1988. After serving as curate-in-charge of a parish
and part-time visiting tutor at Bishop Tucker Theological College, Uganda (now
Uganda Christian University), he studied at Cambridge University, where he graduated
with an MPhil and then a PhD in Old Testament Studies, and at University College
London where he obtained an MA in Philosophy and Religion. Dr Gakuru was
Visiting Lecturer in Old Testament at the Universities of Birmingham and Liverpool
Hope in 1987/8 and 2000/1 respectively. He is married with three children.

The Revd Dr Professor Joseph Galgalo (Kenya)
Joseph is the Associate Professor in Systematic and Contextual Theologies at St
Paul's United Theological College, Limuru, Kenya. He is also a priest of the Anglican
Church of Kenya and involved in theological education and ecumenical formation at
various levels. Joseph serves as a member of the Inter-Anglican theological and
Doctrinal Commission, the Archbishop of Canterbury's Panel of Reference, and the
Education and Ecumenical Formation Commission of the WCC.

The Revd Dr **Andrew Goddard (England)**
(Andrew has written the introduction and short introductions to each of the chapters.)

Andrew studied Philosophy, Politics and Economics at Oxford before completing a theology doctorate on the life and work of Jacques Ellul. He is a member of the Theology Faculty at Oxford University where he taught Christian ethics at Wycliffe Hall. In recent years he has played a significant role in the Anglican Communion debates on homosexuality and the nature of communion. He is the author of several Grove booklets on issues of human sexuality including *God, Gentiles and Gay Christians* and co-authored *True Union in the Body?* with Peter Walker. He is the editor of *Anvil*, the Anglican evangelical theology journal, and is a Fellow of the Anglican Communion Institute. He is on the Faith and Order Advisory Group of the Church of England, the leadership team of Fulcrum and active in the Evangelical Alliance. Andrew and his wife Elisabeth have two children.

Dr Paula Gooder (England)
Paula Gooder studied theology as an undergraduate and graduate student at Oxford University. After gaining her doctorate on 2 Corinthians 12.1–10 she taught at Ripon College Cuddesdon, Oxford and then at the Queen's Foundation, Birmingham. Her research areas include the writings St Paul (with a particular emphasis on 2 Corinthians), biblical interpretation and the development of ministry in the early Church. Paula is Canon Theologian of Birmingham Cathedral and an Honorary Lecturer at the University of Birmingham. She is a Reader in the Church of England and a member of the General Synod of the Church of England. She has published on a wide range of topics including *Only the Third Heaven? 2 Corinthians 12.1–10 and the Heavenly Ascent Tradition* (Continuum, 2006); *Exploring New Testament Greek: A Way in* (SCM, 2004) and *Hosea-Micah* (BRF, 2004). She is currently working on a book for SPCK called *Searching for Meaning: A Practical Guide to New Testament Interpretation*. Paula's experience comes from many years of reading and exploring methods of biblical interpretation, particularly of interpreting the Pauline Epistles and of wrestling with questions of how they can be best applied and used within the churches today.

Revd Canon Phil Groves (Anglican Communion Office)
Phil Groves is the Facilitator of the Listening Process on human sexuality in the Anglican Communion. His role includes monitoring the work being undertaken on the subject of human sexuality in the Anglican Communion and developing the process of mutual listening, including 'listening to the experience of homosexual persons' and the experience of local churches around the world. Phil was previously a vicar in the Church of England. Prior to that he was for seven years a lecturer at a Provincial Theological College in Tanzania where he was installed as an honorary canon of All Saints Cathedral Mpwapwa. He developed and taught a course on Anglicanism for the Church of Tanzania and is currently researching a biblical model of international partnership. He has published a Grove Booklet entitled *Global Partnerships for Local Mission*. Phil is on the Council of St John's Nottingham and is a Trustee of the Church Mission Society.

Professor Glynn Harrison (England)
Glynn Harrison is Norah Cooke Hurle Professor of Mental Health in the Department of Psychiatry, University of Bristol. He is a consultant psychiatrist interested in
early interventions for young adults and the evaluation of interventions to enhance
evidence-based practice. He researches the epidemiology of mental disorders, and is
interested in the relative contributions of biological and social/environmental risk
factors. He has acted as an Adviser to the World Health Organization and the UK
Health Department and he is currently President of the International Federation of
Psychiatric Epidemiology. He is a Diocesan Lay Minister and a member of the
General Synod of the Church of England.

The Rt Revd Dr John Holder (West Indies)
Bishop John Holder trained for the ordained ministry at Codrington College,
Barbados and continued his studies at the University of the South, USA. He completed
a PhD at King's College London in 1984. His specialities are in Old Testament
hermeneutics and the writings of Second Temple Judaism. In the 1980s and 1990s he
held a number of academic posts in the West Indies and was a visiting Professor in
Seminaries in the United States. During this time he was also active in parish ministry
in several parishes in the Diocese of Barbados. He was consecrated Bishop of
Barbados in 2000. Bishop John's academic publications have focused on the Old
Testament, but have reflected his concern for Christian ministry in the Caribbean.
He has also published biblical reflections and is a contributor to *Light for Our Path*.
His biblical reflections are based on his academic scholarship but aim to be accessible
for those who do not have an academic training. In his role as Bishop he is involved in
the life of Barbados and chairs the Religious Advisory Committee on National Affairs,
a body which offers advice to the Barbadian Government. He is also a member of the
Privy Council. He is the Chair of the Barbados Christian Council and of the Inter-faith
HIV/AIDS Commission. In 2004 he published a study guide to enable his pastors to
engage with critical areas of pastoral concern entitled *The Bible in the Anglican Tradition: The Bible and Human Sexuality*. He has served the global Anglican Communion,
and from 2001 to 2006 he was a member of the Advisory Group to the Anglican
Observer to the United Nations. In 2006 he attended the St Augustine's Seminar which
met to plan the 2008 Lambeth Conference.

The Very Revd Dr John Kevern (USA)
Dr Kevern is the Dean (Principal) of Bexley Hall Episcopal Seminary in Columbus,
Ohio, USA and also an Associate Professor of Historical Theology. Fr Kevern read
French as an undergraduate and theology at the General Seminary in New York, culmi-
nating at a doctorate at the University of Chicago with a thesis on Hans Urs von
Balthasar. He has had many years of parish experience, both in Chicago and in country
towns in upstate New York. He has also been a member of parishes in the Diocese of
Gibraltar (Church of England in Europe) and the Anglican Church of Canada, having
lived in Paris, Berne, Montreal and London. For these reasons, he has a high interest in
intra-Anglican affairs and the Communion generally. Fr Kevern was previously the
head of Affirming Catholicism in the USA, serving at the request of Bishop Griswold.
He also served for ten years as the secretary to the American Lutheran-Episcopal
dialogue, which produced the covenant leading to full communion. This experience of

'covenant making' also contributes to a desire for intra-Anglican covenant making. Dean Kevern very much enjoys teaching church history and liturgy at his theological college, and finds the formation of future Anglican priests to be one of the most gratifying careers one could possibly have.

The Revd Professor Jaci Maraschin (Brazil)
Born in Brazil, Jaci is a retired priest of the Igreja Episcopal Anglicana do Brasil and professor of the Anglican Institute of Theological Studies in São Paulo. He has published articles and books in the area of Liturgy and Culture and lectured at the Trinity Institute and Union Theological Seminary in New York. At the last two Lambeth Conferences he acted as theological consultant. He was a member of the Inter-Anglican Theological and Doctrinal Commission and of the second phase of the Anglican–Roman Catholic International Dialogue (ARCIC II). As a musician and hymnwriter he has published song books and CDs. Jaci holds academic degrees in music, philosophy, theology and sciences of religion. He has a doctorate from the University of Strasbourg, France, and undertook post-doctoral work at Union Theological Seminary and Columbia University in New York. For many years he was member of the Faith and Order Standing Commission of the WCC and worked in the Music and Liturgical Team for the World Assembly of the WCC in Canberra, Australia, 1991. Jaci is married to Ana Dulce and has two daughters.

Ms Janet Marshall (Canada)
Janet Marshall is a congregational development consultant and adult educator who works extensively with churches and judicatories to help create healthy communities of faith. Janet is co-founder of *Potentials,* an ecumenical centre for the development of ministry and congregations. Her work includes developing resources, and the design and facilitation of processes for listening and learning, visioning and planning, conflict mediation, leadership development, amalgamations, organizational renewal, and making difficult decisions. She is co-author of *Hearing Diverse Voices: Seeking Common Ground*, a programme of study on homosexuality for the Anglican Church of Canada, and *God, Kids and Us: The Growing Edge of Ministry with Children and the People Who Care for Them*, and author of *A Journey Just Begun*, a parish visioning resource. She is currently working on *Amalgamations and Mergers: Last Gasp or New Ministry?*

The Revd Canon Dr Michael Nai-Chiu Poon (South East Asia)
Michael is the Director of the Centre for the Study of Christianity in Asia and lecturer in church history at Trinity Theological College, Singapore. He is an honorary canon in the Diocese of Singapore, and chairs the Global South Anglican Theological Formation and Education Task Force. Michael was deaconed in 1986 and priested in 1987 in Hong Kong. He was the General Secretary of the Missionary Area of Macao before moving to Singapore in 2004. Michael grew up in a Methodist family. He is married to Kwai Fan. They have three children.

The Revd Debbie Royals (USA)
Debbie was born in Tucson, Arizona. She is from the Pascua Yaqui Tribe on her mother's side and part Cherokee on her father's side. She is the mother of two sons and a grandmother. She attended the University of Arizona studying nursing and worked

as a nurse and health-care administrator for 25 years prior to attending seminary. She attended seminary at the Church Divinity School of the Pacific and completed a Master of Divinity in 2005 and a Master of Arts in Religion and Society at the Graduate Theological Union in 2006. Her thesis, 'Bridge-maker: Developing/Imagining a Native American Narrative Theology for Ministry' offers an objective view of the systems that inform the development of Native ministry. Debbie's ministry in the Church includes Native American ministry development, writing curriculum for Native Ministry and the Church, spiritual direction, and the development of an appreciative focus on diversity training. She has published several articles in the *First People's Theology Journal* relating to the spirituality of indigenous people. She believes that the 'listening process' offers the hope for reconciliation and witness of the Anglican Communion to the world. As an indigenous woman theologian she understands that our relationship with our God and Creator seeks to bring into balance our whole selves; therefore, connecting sexuality and spirituality are essential. Her partner, the Revd Kay Sylvester, serves as priest in the Diocese of Los Angeles.

The Revd Canon Charley Thomas (Central Africa)
Charley is the son of the late Very Revd Canon K. T. Thomas, an Indian missionary to East Africa and Zambia for 40 years. His wife is Dr Rachel C. Thomas and their children's names are Molly, Tony and Jolly. Even though he was born in Kerala, India, he was educated in Tanzania, India, Zambia and the United Kingdom. He is a graduate in Theology, Mission Studies, Anglican Communion Studies and has attended numerous workshops and conferences in Globalization, WCC-Focus on Africa, Contextual Theology, Evangelism and Development, Canterbury Summer School, ALPHA, Inter-Faith Exposure, All Africa Conference of Churches, General Assembly, Peace and Conflict Resolution, etc. He was ordained to the diaconate in Central Zambia and to the priesthood in Bath and Wells. He was on secondment as Director of Ecumenical Theological Education by Extension in Zambia (1992–2001); and as Director of Mindolo Ecumenical Foundation (2001–2007) and is Dean Designate of the Cathedral of the Holy Cross, Lusaka, Zambia (October 2007). As an Indian resident in Africa for over 40 years and having trained in three continents, and with family in Africa, America, Europe and Asia, he believes he has been called to a ministry of cross-cultural reconciliation. As an Anglican priest and the son of one, he has grown up in the Anglican Anglo-Catholic, evangelical, charismatic and modernist traditions. Fifteen years of ecumenical ministry have had an impact on his life, preparing him to listen to views and voices that are not necessarily his, but have played an important role in his formation. He believes he can make a contribution to the 'listening process' and the healing process of the Anglican Communion.

The Revd Janet Trisk (Southern Africa)
Janet is a South African and a lecturer in Systematic Theology and Spirituality at the College of the Transfiguration, Grahamstown, South Africa. She is ordained and served for five years in parish ministry. She represented the ACSA at the ACC meeting in 2005. Before training for the ministry, Janet was a lawyer. Her academic interests include women's theologies, the construction of identity and Christian anthropology. She holds a Masters degree from the University of Cape Town. Her doctoral studies keep getting postponed by activities such as this study process!

Acknowledgements

So many people have worked so hard in the development of this book and we would like to thank all of them. The following list is a way of thanking those who have responded to my request to give their valuable time and assist by assisting in the identification of writers, encouraging people to make contributions, giving a critical assessment of the text, helping with practical arrangements, being prepared to meet with writers and the editor. Inclusion in this list does not imply an endorsement of any part of the text, nor the text as a whole.

Michael Ade, Donald Alcock, Bishop Daniel Allotey, Chris Ambidge, Clare Amos, Bishop Marc Andrus, President Bishop Mouneer Anis, Archbishop Phillip Aspinall, Professor Richard Bauckham, Christina Beardsley, Mario Bergner, John Clinton Bradley, Alix Brown, Richard Burridge, Lynne Butt, Gregory Cameron, Phyll Chesworth, Brian Cox, Colin Coward, Archbishop John Chew, John Clark, David Craig, Louie Crew, Bishop Michael Doe, Duncan Dormor, Karen Evans, Michael Fuller, Bishop Carol Gallagher, Kathy Galloway, John Gibson, Giles Goddard, John Goldingay, Caro Hall, Bishop John Howe, Jeffrey John, Primus Idris Jones, John Kafwanka, Isaac Kawuki-Mukasa, Graham Kings, Archbishop Paul Kwong, Roy McCloughry, Ruth McCurry, Dawn McDonald, Bishop Mark MacDonald, Davis Mac-Iyalla, Archbishop Thabo Makgoba, Professor Dale Martin, Jeremy Morris, Professor Oliver O'Donovan, Bertrand Olivier, Steve Schuh, Chris Sugden, Jenny Te Paa, Martin Reynolds, Charles Robertson, Bishop Gene Robinson, Terrie Robinson, David Runcorn, Susan Russell, Archbishop Carlos Touche-Porter, Kevin Ward, Flora Winfield, Donald Whipple Fox, Gill Young.

We would like specifically to thank all those who responded so generously to a bipartisan appeal for funds made by Brian Cox and Louie Crew to enable the writers to travel across the world to meet together.

We would like to thank those who made contributions for publication. We are seeking ways to publish many of these texts on line.

The following theological institutions gave practical assistance by responding to requests to host individuals and meetings involved in writing the book: Ripon College, Cuddesdon, Oxford; General Theological Seminary, New York; The Queen's College, Birmingham; Ridley Hall, Cambridge; Westcott House, Cambridge.

Introduction

Andrew Goddard and Phil Groves

Introduction

This book seeks to help you and fellow Anglicans around the Communion as we continue to explore together the complex mystery of human sexuality and the shape of faithful Christian discipleship in this area. Its purpose is to offer clear and accurate resources to bishops, clergy and lay people from men and women across the Communion with a wide variety of experience and expertise. The hope is that these resources will help us listen to one another – as individual Christians, within local churches and across the Communion as a whole – and listen to God. This introduction provides an orientation both to the subject of sexuality within the Communion and to this book – its purpose, its theological basis, its process of composition and its structure. It is hoped that it will enable you to get the most from the book whether you read it through from beginning to end or, perhaps more likely and more helpful, focus on specific chapters of interest to you in your context.

Anglicans and Sexuality

The current teaching of the Anglican Communion on sexuality is expressed in the 1998 Lambeth Conference Resolution 1.10. This states that the Conference 'in view of the teaching of Scripture, upholds faithfulness in marriage between a man and a woman in lifelong union, and believes that abstinence is right for those who are not called to marriage' and describes homosexual practice as 'incompatible with Scripture'. This resolution has been regularly reaffirmed by the other Instruments of Communion since 1998 and the full text appears at the end of this introduction. The focus of this book is particularly related to two aspects of that resolution of the bishops:

- 'We commit ourselves to listen to the experience of homosexual persons'.
- This conference 'requests the Primates and the ACC to establish a means of monitoring the work done on the subject of human sexuality in the Communion and to share statements and resources among us'.

These commitments to listen and to share statements and resources were made alongside the statement of the teaching of the Communion on sexuality and are important because of:

- the ongoing discussion on this subject in many societies, the Anglican Communion, and the wider Church.
- the diversity of views within and between different Anglican provinces,[1] and
- the need for 'all our people to minister pastorally and sensitively to all irrespective of sexual orientation' and to assure homosexual persons 'that they are loved by God and that all baptized, believing and faithful persons, regardless of sexual orientation, are full members of the Body of Christ'.

The discussions – as this book makes clear – cover a wide range of issues. On all of these there is a spectrum of views within the Communion. Any attempt to summarize the nature and importance of these complex questions is difficult. However, the following description of what is being discussed and why it is important may provide a helpful sense of the 'big picture' and guide you as you approach the more detailed studies that follow:

There are a number of people who identify themselves with those whom the bishops called 'homosexual persons' at the 1998 Lambeth Conference. They are people of great diversity, but they have in common that they are attracted to people of their own sex. Many of them, in so far as they know themselves, their loves, their sexual desires and their intimate relationships, also believe that they are not fitted for marriage to someone of the opposite sex. Some have embraced marriage or remained single but have known, or still know, same-sex attraction. Others are in some form of same-sex relationship.

In many places, as through much of human history, such matters are still not openly spoken about and those with this experience find it difficult or impossible to speak. However, in Western (and increasingly in non-Western) societies, some of these people now identify themselves publicly as 'gay' or 'lesbian'.

All these people, including those who are Christians, are asking for more understanding and an end to what they experience as exclusion and oppression. Some are asking for pastoral care and friendship as they seek to live in conformity to traditional church teaching. Others conscientiously believe they will flourish best and will grow in love of God and neighbour if they commit themselves to share their life with someone of the same sex in some form of special, loving, covenantal, sexual relationship similar to marriage. Some are asking for such relationships to be blessed by the Church especially in those countries where there is now the possibility of legal recognition for such relationships in civil partnerships or same-sex marriage.

The Church, for the sake of its pastoral ministry and its mission, has to work out a faithful Christian response to this new situation and to the people most affected by it. Those concerned are not only those who are described as homosexual persons but also their families, their friends and their brothers and sisters in Christ.

The Archbishop of Canterbury has voiced one of the major questions this raises in the following terms:

This is not and should never be a question about the contribution of gay and lesbian people as such to the Church of God and its ministry, about the dignity and value of gay and lesbian people. Instead it is a question, agonizingly difficult for many, as to what kinds of behaviour a Church that seeks to be loyal to the Bible can bless, and what kinds of behaviour it must warn against – and so it is a question about how we make decisions corporately with other Christians, looking together for the mind of Christ as we share the study of the Scriptures.[2]

These resources aim to help us as Anglicans, together with other churches, make such decisions and seek together the mind of Christ. It is an official book of the Anglican Communion. As explained below, it has been called for and supported by all four Instruments of Communion. It is designed to enable dialogue and discussion as we move together in mission and ministry. It is not an official statement or authoritative document of the Communion and makes no claim to any such authority. It is, however, set in the context both of decisions already made by the Communion on these matters, notably Lambeth 1998 Resolution 1.10, and of repeated statements on the need for ongoing study and discussion from all the Instruments.

The Lambeth Conference

The initial call for the sort of work you will find in this book came from the 1978 Lambeth Conference. In Resolution 10 the bishops called for 'theological study of sexuality' and specifically for 'deep and dispassionate study of the question of homosexuality, which would take seriously the teaching of Scripture and the results of scientific and medical research'. This resolution was reaffirmed in Resolution 64 of the 1988 Lambeth Conference when the conference added that it 'urges such study and reflection to take account of biological, genetic and psychological research being undertaken by other agencies, and the socio-cultural factors that lead to the different attitudes in the provinces of our Communion'. A minority of provinces have undertaken such studies but this is the first response on a Communion level.

The bishops present at the 1998 Lambeth Conference not only clearly reaffirmed traditional church teaching but also called for there to be a monitoring process. They asked that the significance of the Kuala Lumpur Statement be recognized (it is also reproduced at the end of this chapter) and for concerns raised about the authority of Scripture to be included in that process.

The Anglican Consultative Council

The Windsor Report in 2004 urged 'all provinces that are engaged in processes of discernment regarding the blessing of same-sex unions to engage the Communion in continuing study of biblical and theological rationale for and against such unions' noting that 'this call for continuing study does not imply approval of such proposals' (para 145). It also reminded (para 146), 'all in the Communion that Lambeth Resolution 1.10 calls for an ongoing process of listening and discernment, and that Christians of good will need to be prepared to engage honestly and frankly with each other on issues relating to human sexuality. It is vital that the Communion establish processes and structures to facilitate ongoing discussion'. In 2005, ACC-13 responded in Resolution 12:

In response to the request of the bishops attending the Lambeth Conference in 1998 in Resolution 1.10 to establish 'a means of monitoring the work done on the subject of human sexuality in the Communion' and to honour the process of *mutual* listening, including 'listening to the experience of homosexual persons' and the experience of local churches around the world in reflecting on these matters in the light of Scripture, Tradition and Reason, the Anglican Consultative Council encourages such listening in each Province and requests the Secretary General:

a. to collate relevant research studies, statements, resolutions and other material on these matters from the various Provinces and other interested bodies within those Provinces;
b. to make such material available for study, discussion and reflection within each member Church of the Communion;
c. to identify and allocate adequate resources for this work, and to report progress on it to the Archbishop of Canterbury, to the next Lambeth Conference and the next meeting of this Council, and to copy such reports to the Provinces.

As a result of this, the post of a facilitator was created to work within the Anglican Communion Office. Following his appointment to that post Canon Phil Groves collected information and saw the need for a book to enable the mutual listening which ACC-13 had envisaged. The Standing Committee of the ACC (which meets jointly with the Standing Committee of the Primates) received the draft proposal for this book and gave their support. The proposal included a theological basis, as well as an outline of the structure.

The Primates' Meeting

The same proposal was taken to the Primates Meeting a few days later in Dar in February 2007. They discussed it at length and unanimously supported it. The Primates were clear in their charge to Canon Groves. They wanted high-quality materials to enable understanding of 'the experience of homosexual people'. They were especially keen to receive a comprehensive summary of what science was saying about homosexuality. They wanted a reflection on Bible and tradition and a consideration of culture. They also looked forward to some materials on methods of listening so that practical action could be enabled around the Communion.[3] They approved the theological basis of the proposal.

The Archbishop of Canterbury

The Primates made some minor recommendations informally and these were incorporated into a revised proposal which was presented to the Archbishop of Canterbury who endorsed the proposal.

The Book's Purpose

The aim of this book is to enable you to begin or to continue listening to those identified as 'homosexual persons' and to discover and engage with the diversity of responses found among Anglicans. It seeks to give you resources for these tasks. It is hoped these will help you gain a deeper clarity and understanding of your own position, encourage you to speak for yourself, and enable you to understand the opinion of others.

The book is not seeking to be a document around which we can agree a common statement. It does not attempt to 'solve' the theological disagreements over homosexuality or the divisions these have created within the Communion. Although the book includes a large amount of material it does not make any claim to be complete, final or definitive. All you will find in each chapter is a brief summary of the subject matter.

Each reader will come to the book in a different context. As you read, remember that what you are reading will be being read and used across the globe by fellow Anglicans whose backgrounds, experiences and levels of knowledge about sexuality are quite different from yours. For some, many of the ideas here will be new. For others, much will be familiar. The hope is that you will find:

- your questions being asked and explored;
- your own answers being given accurately and positively;
- the answers you disagree with being explained in a way that deepens and clarifies your understanding so you are better equipped for ongoing dialogue with Christians who hold these views.

The intention is to encourage you in thinking, listening and speaking. Despite the size of the book, much is left unsaid and there will be times when you think it fails to reach its goals. If you find blanks or failings then you can respond in various ways:

- If there are questions you do not find being asked here, then ask them.
- If you believe a point has been made badly, then make it yourself or find someone you know and respect to make it.
- If you don't understand how someone can take a view expressed, try to seek out people who can help you learn more.

This book is neither an end nor a beginning when it comes to fulfilling the commitments we have made as Anglicans to listen, study and learn about sexuality. It is another step on the way which seeks to enable us to learn and work together as we serve the mission of God.

The hope is that you will want to engage further, read more, ask more questions, perhaps write or speak to help others and, above all, continue listening to God and to fellow disciples of Jesus.

The book will be supported with an internet site where you can pose questions, clarify understandings and enter into dialogue. The site will be supported for one year after publication of this book. You can contact the Facilitator for the Listening Process by email – listening@anglicancommunion.org . Further details will be available from the Anglican Communion Website – www.anglicancommunion.org/listening.

The Book's Theological Basis

ACC-3 meeting in 1976 spoke about the Communion in these words:

> As in the first century, we can expect the Holy Spirit to press us to listen to each other, to state new insights frankly, and to accept implications of the Gospel new to us, whether painful or exhilarating.[4]

Throughout the following 30 years of our Communion we have often found new insights to be both painful and exhilarating. In the 1980s and 1990s the churches in places where Anglican Christianity was comfortably part of their culture were greatly challenged by the dynamic churches of Africa and Asia to move from ministry to mission. At first they often found the call to engage in evangelism hard to hear. It was painful to accept their failure to live out mission. However, when they responded and took mission in their own context seriously, these churches have been rejuvenated. The developments of 'Fresh Expressions of Church' and the desire to break the bonds of extreme poverty have enabled churches in Europe and America to reconnect with the Mission of God. This is exhilarating!

The issue of how to respond to new understandings of human sexuality leads us once again into cross-cultural challenges. The prime task for all of us is to hear and obey what God is saying to us. We can only do this by listening to each other. As the Archbishop of Canterbury has quoted with approval: 'Only the whole Church knows the whole truth.'[5]

The Church of Uganda has asked to be listened to in this manner. In its Position Paper published for ACC-13 they say: 'We also believe the Church of Uganda has a mission to the Anglican Communion to share the treasure of the Scriptures and to call other parts of the Communion to recognize and to submit to the Authority of Scripture as the place of transformation into abundant life.'[6] This is an uncomfortable message for some, but a reminder from a Church – which has faced political violence and oppression with love and forgiveness and borne the brunt of AIDS/HIV with loving service – that its witness was founded on living out what it read in the Bible.

The Episcopal Church of the USA has also called for the kind of uncomfortable listening envisioned at ACC-3. Also at ACC-13 they offered *To Set Our Hope on Christ*.[7] In this report they sought to explain why 'in good faith and in loving obedience to the saving Word of God, many Christians in the Episcopal Church have come to a new mind about same-sex affection, and of how this has led us to affirm the eligibility for ordination of those in covenanted same-sex unions.'[8] They too believe that their insight is 'in loving obedience to the saving Word of God'. This too is painful for many to hear.

ACC-3 also reflected on partnership in the Church of the New Testament. They said:

> Christian partnership did not then mean that the partners, although united in their missionary goals, were always in accord on how they were to carry out this mission – witness the disagreement between Peter and Paul in Galatians 2. Rather they were asked to face each other, and the roots of their disagreement and agree-

ment, so openly that both could go forward in mutual love and respect into further creative activity.[9]

Significant missiological thinkers have argued that this is the biblical way. Andrew Walls has described our time as an 'Ephesian Moment'. We are at a point in time when the Western guardians of 'standard' Christianity have encountered new expressions of Christianity from Africa, Asia, America and beyond.[10] The original 'Ephesian Moment' was a brief time in history when Jewish Christians came together with Gentile Christians under the guidance of Paul who insisted that 'In union with him [Christ] you too are being built together with all the others to a place where God lives through his Spirit' (Ephesians 2.22).[11] Walls argues that 'the Church must be diverse because humanity is diverse; it must be one because Christ is one.'[12] The original 'Ephesian Moment' came to an end as the gentile church dominated the Jewish minority which was forced to conform to gentile Christianity or to find its Jewish identity outside the church. In the present age we see the Church as more diverse than it has ever been with not only people of every nation and ethnic group, but also women and the poor taking roles that were previously the preserve of white men with university education.[13]

Francis Bridger, a founding member of the British Evangelical Anglican group Fulcrum echoes this perspective. He reflects on the nature of Trinitarian theology and says:

> The theological method of the Evangelical centre is marked by a faithfulness to Scripture and the historic creeds on one hand and an openness to the breadth of Christian traditions on the other. This does not require that we assign equal validity to all theological perspectives (for all, including Evangelicalism, must stand under the scrutiny of Scripture). However, it does demand that we listen with respect to voices other than our own. Fundamental to this is a recognition that theology arises out of communities of faith which possess their own historical trajectories and which have found themselves having to address their own particular problems: it is not a system of ahistorical propositions that stand independent of the contexts which have produced them. Theological truth does not drop out of the sky: it is always and everywhere the outcome of community struggle and reflection.
>
> If the Trinity is central to all theology, then it follows that relationality lies at the heart of a Trinitarian theological method and that this in turn demands a willingness to enter into, and a desire to sustain, relationships with others who name the name of Christ and are seekers after truth *even if we profoundly disagree with them.*
>
> The Evangelical centre, therefore, finds itself committed, as a matter of fundamental principle, to encouraging dialogue even across heated differences. Moreover, it believes that the discernment of truth and the mind of God is more likely to arise out of a process of mutual respect and charitable assumption than out of polarization and demonization. However wrong-headed we may think Christian brothers or sisters, they are not Amalekites to be smitten hip and thigh.[14]

Being biblical is about how we walk and talk together. Sometimes this will mean shocking one another, but we should always be ready to speak and to listen rather than simply defend formulas and structures.

Desmond Tutu has articulated these same concepts under the title of *Ubuntu*:

> Ubuntu is very difficult to render into a Western language. It speaks to the very essence of being human. When you want to give high praise to someone we say, 'Yu, u Nobuntu'; he or she has Ubuntu. This means that they are generous, hospitable, friendly, caring and compassionate. They share what they have. It also means that my humanity is caught up, is inextricably bound up, in theirs. We belong in a bundle of life. We say, 'a person is a person through other people' (in Xhosa Ubuntu ungamntu ngabanye abantu and in Zulu Umuntu ngumuntu ngabanye). I am human because I belong, I participate, and I share. A person with Ubuntu is open and available to others, affirming of others, does not feel threatened that others are able and good; for he or she has a proper selfassurance that comes with knowing that he or she belongs in a greater whole and is diminished when others are humiliated or diminished, when others are tortured or oppressed, or treated as if they were less than who they are.[15]

In a debate which has become intensely polarized the form of the materials we seek to offer will attempt to follow biblical patterns enabling us to listen to one another with love and mutual respect. This is Scriptural, our Anglican tradition and the only reasonable way forwards.

The Book's Composition

The work of Canon Phil Groves as Facilitator for the Listening Process has made clear to him that good process in listening is vitally important. He has identified four practical elements which he brought into the composition of this book: common ground, safe space, the acknowledging of shared vulnerability and good human resources.

1. Common Ground in Mission

The foundation for dialogue is common ground. ACC-3 talked of common ground as being our common mission. This remains the basis for our shared life today and as a Communion is stated in the Five Marks of Mission.[16]

Our mission is to all people. The first four marks are relevant to how our mission is carried out including mission to gay and lesbian people, their families, their friends and those with whom they work. All the Churches of our Communion are agreed on the need to proclaim the Good News of the Kingdom, to teach, baptize and nurture new believers, to respond to human need by loving service and to seek to transform unjust structures of society.

Our mission is also, and has always been, even when we did not know it, *with* gay and lesbian Christians who are our partners in the gospel. This acknowledgement does not require acceptance of same-sex partnerships or partnered gay clergy. Most of the gay and lesbian people who have served the Church in mission and ministry, both lay and ordained, have not accepted such partnerships for themselves nor seen them as valid expressions of a holy life for others. The open acceptance of same-sex partnerships as moral in more and more cultures within our Communion demands however that we engage with lesbian and gay people in a new way. Our commitment to listen emphatically does not require that we must end up accepting the position of those to whom we are listening. It does mean that we seek to hear God speaking to us and discover his way. It does require that we respect those with whom we disagree and be open to learning new ways to speak to and about them.

It is on this common ground of mission that we begin our conversations.

2. Safe Space – Allowing All to be Heard

Some voices are easy for us to hear. But Jesus valued the voices of the quiet, those considered insignificant in the eyes of the world in which he lived. For him it was women, children, the disabled, the poor and those who were labelled as 'sinful'. The challenge has been to hear those voices, the voices of those who are often not heard. Today this may be due to their ethnicity, their gender, their lack of education or because they are regarded as 'sinful'. That does not mean that we ignore those who are educated, church leaders and men, but it does mean they are not to be heard to the exclusion of others.

The Lambeth Conference made a commitment to 'listen to the experience of homosexual persons'. Such people have a huge range of experiences and many have responded to the Good News of the Kingdom with joy and follow God with commitment. For such people to be heard we need to create safe ground where they will not be open to ridicule, abuse or emotional and even physical violence. Such violence is the experience of gay and lesbian people in every culture and the Instruments of Communion have consistently committed themselves to opposing it.

No voice has been consciously edited out in the process of writing this book. The voices of 'conservatives' from around the world were actively sought, even if it will mean pain for those who are 'liberal' in their outlook. The voices of 'liberals' were actively sought, even if that is likely to cause pain to those who are 'conservative'. Among those identified by Lambeth Conferences as 'homosexual' there are a great variety of identifiers and different views. The most common terms in English are 'gay' and 'lesbian'. 'Gay' can be an identifier for both men and women and where it is used this way within the text we hope it is clear. 'Homosexual persons' would also include bisexual men and women, many of whom live in faithful monogamous relationships, either straight or gay. Transgender people and those who are intersexed are not gay or lesbian but some do recognize themselves as also being identified by the texts of the Communion as 'homosexual persons'. A common shorthand for this group of diverse individuals is LGBT. Others find these labels to be a political act and the claiming of an identity which they reject. They often describe themselves simply as experiencing same-sex attraction (SSA). They may speak of being 'ex-gay' or 'post-gay' or refuse all such labels. In compiling this book we have sought out all these voices.

All shades of opinion have therefore been sought. Following Jesus, we have especially sought to hear the voices of those who would otherwise be silenced and not just the loud voices that can sometimes dominate in the media.

3. Vulnerability

The polarized arguments over the issues surrounding human sexuality have made us all feel vulnerable. Some fear the ending of the faith as we know it. Others fear not being accepted. Some fear being split in two with conflicting loyalties. Some fear to ask questions and some fear to answer them. These fears can only be answered by trusting in God to care for our Church and for all who come to him. However, we need to admit our own vulnerability and accept the vulnerability of others. It is important to do this while reading. We ask you not to seek arguments you can defeat but to allow God to inform you so you are strengthened in your walk with him.

Again the Bible gives us the ultimate model. Jesus accepted the vulnerability of being human. His fears in Gethsemane were answered by his trust in God who rescued him from despair and death. We need to accept that all are vulnerable and trust God who can bring reconciliation in any context.

4. Human Resources

The process leading to this book was convened by Canon Groves who has been entrusted with the task on behalf of the Instruments of Communion as described earlier. The contributors were chosen in order to present the spectrum of views held in the Communion. Taken together, therefore, the hope is they present the spectrum of opinions. They were not asked to represent particular parties or viewpoints. In many ways the authors are ordinary Christians and it is not claimed that they are the greatest experts in their field in the Communion. What they have brought are the skills to understand and present the expertise of scholars and the experience of real people.

As you will soon discover, each chapter is very different from all the others. This reflects the diversity of the contributors and the range of material being covered. As a group of women and men the authors reflect the geographic diversity of the Communion as well as its theological diversity. There are bishops, clergy and lay people within the group. There is a mix of expertise. For example, some would describe themselves as theologians but several would not. The voices of homosexual people are also present in the text although they may not always be specifically identified as such.

One common thread that runs through the book is that the contributors for each chapter worked in pairs. Given the huge distances between most of them it was a significant logistical task to bring them together. It was, however, accomplished in most cases although writing a unified text was impossible for some who could not physically be brought together and had to communicate electronically. For some writers, joint writing was a joy. For others, there were significant challenges to be overcome in the writing process itself and a cross-cultural struggle is present in the result.

Finally, the Christian literature on human sexuality is huge and growing but we hope we have engaged with the most significant texts in what follows. However, many of the standard books are from a Western point of reference. One of the distinctive contributions of these resources is that reflections from across the Communion have been actively sought out and included. The book also contains submissions in various forms – more academic texts, personal testimonies, practical guidance for listening processes, dialogue between the contributors – based on the authors' own research and conversations together and their decision about how best to present the fruit of this to the wider Communion.

The Book's Structure and Content

The book's eight chapters are presented in four parts. Obviously it is possible to read the book from start to finish, as one would read a novel. However, there is no need to do this and it is expected that most readers will dip into different chapters at different times. The book is therefore designed in such a way that each chapter makes sense when read on its own. It is, however, helpful to understand the structure and rationale of the book as a whole, the connection between its different sections, and the variety of its styles and diversity of its authors.

The book opens with the two related issues which we have already seen provide the common ground and particular focus for the whole book and for the Listening Process of which it is part – mission and listening. In relation to mission, two perspectives are offered – one from Ian Douglas in the US and one from Michael Poon from Singapore. Each author then responds to the other, giving an example of respectful dialogue across differences in cultural and theological perspective. The chapter on listening is quite different from any other in the book. Much more than presenting an argument or a set of viewpoints, it provides you with a hands-on practical 'how-to' guide. This is jointly authored by two very experienced facilitators from quite different contexts, one from Canada (Janet Marshall) and one from Zambia (Charley Thomas).

To be authentically Anglican, both our mission and our listening need to be directed by the authorities of Scripture, tradition and reason. These three areas therefore provide the structure and focus of the resources in the second section. In many ways these introduce us to the theological heart of the current debates. Those holding the views on sexuality expressed in the Communion's current teaching need to be able to show how that teaching is authorized by these sources. Those calling for the Church to modify this stance need to explain 'from within the sources of authority that we as Anglicans have received in scripture, the apostolic tradition and reasoned reflection'[17] how and why they have reached that different understanding.

Among these three sources Anglicans have held to the primacy of Scripture and any changes would need to persuade the Communion that they are compatible with Scripture. The Bible is examined therefore first and at greatest length. The editor, Phil Groves, provides an introduction to the subject of the place of Scripture, seeking common ground in the Anglican understanding of the nature and authority of Scripture which is explored through reference to the Thirty-Nine Articles. The book of Jude then guides a reflection on false teaching before two different perspectives on sexuality present their understanding of biblical teaching. The final sections look at some of the challenges faced in interpreting the Bible and how the Bible helps us when we have to consider whether a development in Christian thought and practice is faithful to Scripture. In the light of this overview focused more on method, a West Indian bishop, John Holder, and a lay biblical scholar from England, Paula Gooder, provide extensive resources on biblical texts. They help us engage with the specific teaching of the Old Testament and the New Testament in relation to sexuality as a whole and with particular reference to homosexuality.

The chapter on the witness of tradition captures the international and non-Western perspective of the resources more than any other chapter. It brought together Jaci Maraschin from Brazil and Samson Fan from Hong Kong, for both of whom English is not their first language. They set our current sexuality discussions in a broader historical and theological context by highlighting the distinction between tradition and traditions and helping us think through the relationship of tradition to both Scripture and reason. We are then enabled to consider current debates about the validity of blessing same-sex unions by looking at other areas where Anglicans have embraced and/or resisted changes to our traditions in recent decades.

The fifth chapter introduces one aspect of the work of reason by setting sexuality in the context of wider culture (another aspect of reason, that of science, is the focus in the final chapter). One of the major challenges in the Communion is undoubtedly the quite different cultures which Anglicans serve and the very varied understandings of sexuality and sexual ethics found within these. Our guides here are a bishop from Melanesia (Terry Brown) and a Ghanaian theologian (Victor Atta-Baffoe) with some additional material provided by Griphus Gakuru, a Ugandan priest working in England and John Kevern of the Episcopal Church in the USA. They begin by introducing us to different models of how Christians have understood the relationship of Christ to culture. These models are then made more concrete as we are provided with a taste of cross-cultural experience through introductions to the cultures of Uganda, North American Indigenous Peoples, South Africa and England and also to Anglican responses within them. The insights of anthropology and the different uses to which these have been put in Christian mission are then sketched before this approach is applied more directly to recent controversies. That application takes the form of highlighting some central features of Western culture and how these mould both 'liberal' and 'conservative' Western stances on sexuality. An African perspective on these deeper Western cultural forces and world views is then provided in order to shed light on some of the tensions over sexuality. Finally, the authors introduce the great variety of forms of homosexuality found within and across the cultures represented in the Communion.

Following the more academic contributions of Part Two, the next two chapters comprising Part Three have a different focus and so a different format and tone. The learning resources on Scripture, tradition and reason are provided to facilitate and give theological tools for wise listening and discriminating dialogue. It is such listening and dialogue that are displayed, exemplified and encouraged in chapters six and seven. As noted above, Lambeth 1.10 called on us to 'listen to the experience of homosexual persons'. Some readers will already have done this but many will have no experience and perhaps no opportunity to do so in their context. Sue Burns (from Aotearoa, New Zealand and Polynesia) and Janet Trisk (of Southern Africa) have engaged in that listening task and their contribution enables us to listen in on what they have heard and in particular to deepen our understanding of how questions of identity relate to sexuality. They provide extensive quotations from the wide range of people they listened to and in guiding us as we read they model how we can listen thoughtfully and prayerfully to often challenging and disturbing testimonies.

Challenging, disturbing, thoughtful and prayerful dialogue across cultural and theological difference was the experience of Joseph Galgalo, a Kenyan theologian committed to the Communion's teaching on sexuality, and Debbie Royals, an indigenous woman theologian whose partner is also a woman priest in the Episcopal Church. They were brought together to contribute resources on the relationship of sexuality and spirituality. The fruit of their week together is shared in yet another different style as we are invited to listen in on a dialogue between the two of them covering a wide range of subjects which they had explored in their time together.

The final section contains a single chapter, which is probably the most technical of all the material in the book, that covers areas less familiar to most readers. As noted above, successive Lambeth Conferences have asked for scientific study to assist Christian thinking and the Primates particularly requested these resources. Biologist David de Pomerai and psychiatrist Glynn Harrison each produced very significant accounts of the scientific research and literature. These focus on the fields of biological and genetic factors in relation to homosexuality and possible interventions in the forms of counselling or therapy. For those who would find the scientific detail of their work too complex, they have provided helpful executive summaries of their work.

Conclusion

These resources were neither commissioned as an academic exercise, nor as an attempt to reach a consensus within the Anglican Communion. They are not intended to be the last word in the debate on human sexuality in the Christian tradition. Their aims are both more modest and more far-reaching:

- to give voice to the widest possible range of perspectives, positions and responses;
- to allow deeply dissenting and divided views to dialogue with, and to interrogate one another within a safe space;
- to listen to voices from across the many cultures in the Communion without privileging any specific voice;
- to listen to voices which are often silenced by the narrow rules of Western academic discourse.

The varied formats and styles of the book may prove frustrating to some. This variety is intended to echo our ongoing conversation, in which the variety of responses is not tidied up in the interests of literary or academic excellence. We are committed to listening with respect, however softly spoken or stammering some of the contributions may seem.

In short, this book is not meant to provide readers with ready answers, or with a sense of satisfaction that their perspective has been vindicated. The essays are tools, which aim to give readers a sense of godly dissatisfaction that more needs to be said. The debate cannot end here. Our *koinonia* demands further listening, deeper respect and the willingness to continue on this journey of exploration and encounter with the *other* to whom we so often choose not to listen.

Notes

1 The subsection report on sexuality commended in the resolution states 'We must confess that we are not of one mind about homosexuality'. The final report of the International Anglican Conversations on Human Sexuality – convened by Archbishop Carey – admitted that they as a commission had not been 'able to reach a common mind regarding a single pattern of holy living for homosexual people'. It encouraged further conversations and stated that: 'It is important that bishops have the opportunity to better understand other positions than their own' (International Anglican Conversations on Human Sexuality (Ohio: Forward Movement, 2002), 13 and 17. Available online: http://www.anglicancommunion.org/listening/resources/conversations_on_human_sexuality.pdf).

2 'The Challenge and Hope of Being an Anglican Today: A Reflection for the Bishops, Clergy and Faithful of the Anglican Communion', letter sent by Archbishop Rowan Williams to all Primates in the wake of the deliberations on the Windsor Report at the 75th General Convention of the Episcopal Church of the United States held in 2006.

3 From the Primates Meeting Press briefing 16 February 2007: 'Canon Groves outlined preliminary proposals for the kind of approach being considered for the Lambeth Conference; he is working on developing high quality materials which will deal with the experience of homosexual people; what science can tell us about homosexuality, the legal and cultural contexts around the Communion, reflection on Bible and tradition in those specific contexts as well as training materials to develop skills in listening and facilitating listening.' Available online: http://www.anglicancommunion.org/acns/news.cfm/2007/2/16/ACNS4250.

4 ACC-3 page 55.

5 http://www.anglicancommunion.org/acns/articles/41/50/acns4161.cfm.

6 http://www.aco.org/listening/world/docs/doc6.cfm.

7 http://www.episcopalchurch.org/53785_71881_ENG_HTM.htm.

8 Ibid. page 6.

9 ACC-3 page 55.

10 Andrew Walls, 'The Ephesian Moment – At a Crossroads in Christian History' in *The Cross-Cultural Process in Christian History* (Maryknoll, New York: Orbis, 2002), 78.

11 Ibid., 76.

12 Ibid., 77.

13 Ibid., 81.

14 Francis Bridger 'Revisioning the Evangelical Centre' Fulcrum Newsletter, February 2006 available online: http://www.fulcrum-anglican.org.uk/news/2006/newsletter05.cfm?doc=87

15 Desmond Tutu, *No Future Without Forgiveness* (London: Rider, 1999), 34–5.

16 http://www.anglicancommunion.org/mission/fivemarks.cfm.

17 The Windsor Report, para 135.

Chapter 1

Listening and Mission

Ian T. Douglas and Michael Poon

Introduction

Mission is the central theme of this book. God's mission of reconciliation and the proclamation of good news to all people is the task of the Church in this and every generation. The passion of the debate over human sexuality is rooted in a common desire for service to God's mission. As the authors of *True Union in the Body?* note at the very beginning of that work:

> The call to bless same-sex unions arises because some (mainly in the West) believe this is an appropriate and loving response to people who seek the Church's support, and so should be an important feature of the Church's pastoral practice and a vital part of the Church's contemporary mission. Many, however, see it as a major challenge to the Church's identity, potentially overturning her traditional understanding of scriptural teaching about human sexuality and faithful Christian discipleship. Especially in the non-West there is the added fear that it effectively undermines the Church's mission in their context and denies the gospel.[1]

One of the most telling parts of the 1998 Lambeth sexuality debate was during discussion of the amendment (Resolution V.35) proposed from the West Africa Region which stated 'homosexuality is a sin which could only be adopted by the church if it wanted to commit evangelical suicide'. In response, Bishop Roskam of New York said, 'If affirming homosexuality is evangelical suicide in [Africa], to condemn it is evangelical suicide in my region.'

Given a shared passion for mission and yet such differences over sexuality, it is important to begin by thinking about listening and mission. The two essays that follow set out guiding principles on these themes. The first is by **Ian Douglas**, a missiologist well respected in The Episcopal Church USA. The second is by **Michael Poon**, a leading theologian of the Global South who is the chair of the Global South Theological Formation and Education Task Force. Ian and Michael worked independently and then shared their essays with one another. They have then written a brief response to one another as a way of modelling conversation among fellow Anglicans. These appreciate difference yet seek commonality in service to God's mission together.

Ian Douglas explains recent developments in Christian thinking about mission and explores the Bible's teaching about mission. He shows that both of these lead us to focus on the mission of God (*missio Dei*). At the heart of God's mission, he argues, is reconciliation and restoration of relationships. Today, we find ourselves in more and more relationships because we live in a globalized world and Anglican Communion. Drawing on studies of identity and identity politics he shows that ease of communication and travel can hide from us the complexity of who both we are and who other Anglicans really are. We can also forget the ways we are usually both powerful and powerless in different ways in all our relationships. Often, instead, we view ourselves and others in simple categories based on theology, colour, sexuality, nationality, gender etc. These single identities can then become the cause of increased conflict based on these differences. Part of the mission of God is therefore to restore these broken relationships. To do this, he argues, we need to learn to share our common experiences and feelings with one another and to listen to one another across our differences. This can help us discover and show the unity we have in Christ who is both human and divine and in whom we are reconciled to God and one another.

Michael Poon draws on the work of a historian and a missionary to help us recover the importance of listening and mission. These dual callings are rooted in the Word become flesh. They therefore should take place in face-to-face loving human encounters in which we connect with people in their lived reality. He is concerned that the revival of the language of *missio Dei* threatens to abstract us from this local, concrete inter-personal activity. It can also give us a sense of privilege as agents of God's mission which can then become part of a centrally imposed ideology and set of policies. He warns that the 'Listening Process' on homosexuality risks falling into similar traps especially if we fail to listen to the past and the different meanings of homosexuality in different cultures (a matter explored more fully in Chapter 5).

These two writers share a conviction that listening and mission belong together and are both to be shaped by the mystery of the Incarnation. They find themselves agreeing that, in the words of Dr Poon: 'listening and mission are ways in which the Christian community engages the world' and that 'listening and mission are ways of being present in the real world in its broken and gifted experience' and 'can only be acts of love'. They offer, however, different understandings of what this means in practice and of the value of focusing on the mission of God (*missio Dei*). Douglas focuses on the impact of globalization and the need – especially when meeting people from different contexts – to understand our varied and complex identities. He believes that through sharing our response to these differences (especially their impact on our personal, interpersonal, institutional and cultural power) we may engage in genuine listening and share in God's reconciling mission. Poon calls for us to focus not on abstract categories and processes or on the impact of globalization on these but rather on the concrete. It is here, he believes, that tensions such as those Douglas identifies are resolved. By loving our neighbour through listening to them and being fully present to one another we can discern how our differences become distinctive contributions to the life and mission of the Church.

Ian and Michael thus have disagreements – which two theologians do not! – but there is also significant common ground. This basis of common ground is vital for the rest of the book as we enter into areas where there is deep division which matter so much because we have so much common ground.

PART 1:
THE MISSIOLOGICAL SIGNIFICANCE OF LISTENING IN A GLOBALIZED WORLD OF IDENTITIES AND DIFFERENCES

Ian T. Douglas

The 1998 Lambeth Conference of worldwide Anglican bishops took up the difficult matter of human sexuality in its Resolution 1.10; and this resolution has become one of the best known, and contentious, resolutions of the 13 Lambeth Conferences. The resolution began by stating that the Conference 'in the view of the teaching of Scripture, upholds faithfulness in marriage between a man and a woman in lifelong union, and believes that abstinence is right for those who are not called to marriage'. The resolution next recognized that there are persons in the Church 'who experience themselves as having a homosexual orientation', and committed the bishops 'to listen to the experience of homosexual persons', assuring them 'that they are loved by God and that all baptized, believing and faithful persons, regardless of sexual orientation, are full members of the Body of Christ'. The resolution then went on to reject homosexual practice as incompatible with Scripture and advised against the legitimizing or blessing of same-sex unions and the ordaining of individuals involved in same-gender unions.[2]

While the resolves about the incompatibility of homosexual practice with Scripture and the proscriptions against blessings and ordinations are regularly quoted as establishing some kind of norm for sexual behaviour in Anglicanism, the call to 'listen to the experience of homosexual persons' has been slow to be engaged with fully across the churches of the Anglican Communion.[3] Only in the last few years has the Anglican Communion begun to 'listen to the experience of homosexual persons' in any kind of facilitated and organized manner. Such listening, however, is important work; important not only for the future of the Anglican Communion but also for the future of what God would have Anglicans be in the world today. There is thus profound missiological significance to listening, in general, and the Listening Process, in particular.

This paper seeks to place the act of listening, and the Listening Process in the Anglican Communion, within the wider perspective of God's mission. It will begin by tracing the theological shifts in mission thought over recent decades and then offer a brief reflection on the nature of God's mission in biblical perspective. Having traced the framework for mission today, we will then move on to consider how service to God's mission is affected by the contemporary dynamics of globalization. The forces of globalization make more pronounced and even hurtful the differences between nations, peoples, cultures, and, yes, even Christians.

Yet the same forces of globalization that exacerbate differences in the world, and in the Anglican Communion, also drive nations, peoples and cultures closer together than ever before in the history of humankind. It is in the midst of globalization, where differences are exacerbated as nations, peoples and cultures are brought into closer proximity, that the act of listening becomes missiologically significant. The power of identities and identity politics in this globalized world often drive individuals and groups of individuals into hurtful and violent interactions. A methodology of appreciating commonalties and differences in the multiple identities that an individual and/or group inhabit is needed if listening across differences is to be fruitful. Listening across differences in the hope of finding new solidarities and new levels of understanding and commonality is thus the vocation of Christians, of Anglicans, in the world today. It is in such a listening process that we are given the promise to become servants of God's reconciling love for all people through Jesus Christ in the power of the Holy Spirit.

The Changing Landscape of Mission Thought

From the late eighteenth century to the middle of the twentieth century mission was generally understood as a unidirectional activity from older sending churches in the West to dependent 'missions' in Africa, Asia, Latin America and the Pacific. Within Anglican historical experience these missionary activities were supported by either voluntary missionary societies, like the Society for the Propagation of the Gospel or the Church Mission Society in the Church of England, or by missionary agencies that were organizationally linked to a particular Anglican church, such as The Domestic and Foreign Missionary Society of the Episcopal Church in the United States. Mission in the wake of the Enlightenment thus made sense.[4] It was something that the churches of Europe and North America did. Conversion of 'the heathen', the spread of churches, and the advance of Western 'civilization' went hand in hand. The abuses, and contributions, of missionaries and the close connection between mission and imperialism in Africa, Asia, Latin America and the Pacific are well documented and need not be rehearsed here. Throughout the nineteenth century and for the first half of the twentieth century the Western churches thus had their missions, *missiones ecclesiarum*. These missions, as dependent outposts of European and North American Christianity, sought to extend the church models and cultural world views of the Enlightenment.[5]

In the middle of the twentieth century, significant shifts in the theological and ecclesiological terrain of an emergent global Christianity began to shake the ground of missiological thought. Quakes occurred and fissures opened up between older established models of mission and new understandings of mission in the emerging post-modern, post-colonial world. It is almost axiomatic to say today that the Body of Christ has become a truly global reality as never before. The growth of the Church in the 'Global South' has occasioned in the last five decades a profound reappraisal of what the nature of mission is. In the late 1940s and early 1950s discussion in ecumenical councils turned from the role of the churches' missions to wrestling with the nature of the mission of the Church, the *missio ecclesiae*.[6] Mission was seen less as something done by voluntary associations of Christians, often as a side interest of the churches, and more as the central calling of the Church. Such theological shifts led individuals such as Emil Brunner to state: 'The Church exists by mission as fire exists by burning' and Stephen Neil to proclaim: 'The age of missions is at an end; the age of mission has begun.'[7]

The predominance of this ecclesiocentric view of mission in the immediate post-Second World War era was short-lived. While the International Missionary Council promoted the coterminous nature of Church and mission, individual theologians and missiologists were beginning to look beyond the Church for the locus of God's action in the world. Increasingly the Church was seen as adjunct to God's saving action in the wider struggles of the world. The *missio ecclesiae* (the Church's mission) was to give way to the *missio Dei* (the mission of God).

In his article 'The Call to Evangelism', printed in the *International Review of Missions* in 1950, Johannes Hoekendijk led the charge against prevailing definitions of mission. He criticized church-centred mission theology as leading to a form of evangelism whose goal it was to maintain and extend the bridgehead of the Western Enlightenment church. Hoekendijk said:

> To put it bluntly; the call to evangelism is often little else than a call to restore 'Christendom', the *Corpus Christianum*, as a solid, well-integrated cultural complex, directed and dominated by the Church. And the sense of urgency is often nothing but a nervous feeling of insecurity, with the established Church endangered; a flurried activity to save the remnants of a time now irrevocably past.[8]

In short, Hoekendijk argued that 'Evangelization and *churchification* are not identical, and very often they are each other's bitterest enemies.'[9] Hoekendijk wanted to move mission from an ecclesiological to an eschatological point of departure. For him, the goal of evangelism, the goal of mission, was not to extend the Church as the *Corpus Christianum* but rather to participate with God in God's new creation, to work for God's *shalom*. Hoekendijk was the first of his generation to suggest that it was God's mission in the world to bring about God's *shalom*, God's Kingdom, God's Reign.

Most contemporary missiologists would affirm that the mission of God, the *missio Dei*, is God's action in the world to bring about God's Reign through the life, death and resurrection of Jesus Christ in the power of the Holy Spirit. The Trinitarian God has effected a new order, a new *shalom*; one in which all of creation can find new life and new hope. Unlike earlier proponents of the *missio Dei*, today's mission thinkers stress that the Church, as the Body of Christ in the world, does have a central role to play in the saving work of God. The Church is called and uniquely empowered by the Holy Spirit to participate with God in God's mission of restoration, reconciliation and redemption.

God's mission is thus profoundly evangelical. It is fundamentally about sharing and making real the good news that God in Jesus offers new hope, new life, and healing for all people. The mission of God, the mission of Jesus, and the mission of the Church is indeed one of restoration, reconciliation and redemption. Jesus was sent by God 'to bring good news to the poor . . . to proclaim release to the captives and recovery of sight to the blind, to let the oppressed go free, to proclaim the year of the Lord's favour' (Luke 4.18–19). God's mission, manifested in Jesus and empowered by the Holy Spirit, is not static but a centrifugal force of movement outward.[10] Jesus demonstrated in word and deed that the Reign of God, realized in the sending of God's Son, must continue to expand to the ends of the earth. 'As you have sent me into the world, so have I sent them into the world' (John 17.18). Two by two, Jesus' disciples are sent to bear his mission, God's mission, in the world. Being sent in God's mission has as much efficacy for the baptized today as it did in apostolic times. Participation in God's mission, therefore, is at the heart of the baptismal call. Baptism is thus a commission, co-mission, in God's mission. Just as God sent Jesus into the world, and Jesus sent his disciples to the ends of the earth, we too are sent in mission. The imperative is clear.

Christians today, in the many contexts in which we find ourselves around the world, are thus called to share the good news of Jesus and the story of what God is up to in the world. Being able to speak our truth of God's mission, particularly as it is given to us in the Bible, is fundamental if we are to be a light to the nations in a world of globalization and difference.

God's Mission in Biblical Perspective

So what does Holy Scripture say about mission? How do we Christians understand and proclaim and make real the *missio Dei* in the light of the truth of the Bible? To begin with, the word mission, per se, is not found in the Bible. Yes, the seventy are sent out, and there are various references in St Paul's epistles to sending, but mission as it has been historically understood by the Church, namely the sending of specific individuals to faraway places to convert others, is glaringly absent. The reason why we do not find the word mission, as such, in the Bible is because all of Holy Scripture is the story of mission, is the story of God's mission. The whole Bible, Hebrew Scripture and the New Testament, is a revelation of God's mission in the world. Notice how we say God's mission, not the Church's mission, or your mission, or my mission but God's mission. For ultimately it is God's mission that our Lord Jesus came to bear witness to, it is God's mission that the Church proclaims in the world today, and it is God's mission that we share in by virtue of our baptisms. So what is this mission? What is God's mission in the light of Holy Scripture?[11]

In the opening chapter of Genesis we learn that God is the God of all creation. Out of God's love, God brought everything into being, the heavens, the earth, all living creatures including humanity, and 'it was good'. At the very start of the biblical story we learn that God is a God of the whole cosmos, a universal God, who watches over and cares for all of creation.[12] The story continues, however. No sooner had this universal, loving God created humankind, than we turned our backs on God. In our sinfulness, we chose to live unto ourselves. We became alienated from the love and power of God and we became alienated from each other. In the 'Outline of the Faith', also known as the Catechism, found in the back of the *Book of Common Prayer* of The Episcopal Church, sin is described as 'the seeking of our own will instead of the will of God, thus distorting our relationship with God, with other people, and with all creation'.[13] Sin is less about actions and more about a state of separation, separation from God, separation from each other, and separation from all creation. Sin is about isolation, division and broken relationship.

But God did not want humans to be alienated from God and from each other. The loving creator chose to rebuild the bonds of love that had been severed through human sin. God's mission was to reconnect with humanity and heal the divisions that separate us. The central element of God's mission, the *missio Dei*, is God's desire to restore to unity that which had become broken; to reconcile a divided world, to heal a hurting humanity.

To fulfil this mission, God chose a particular people as an entry point into the world. Through Abraham and Sarah and their descendants, God began a new relationship with humankind. God says to Abraham:

Behold, my covenant is with you, and you shall be the father of a multitude of nations . . . I will make you exceedingly fruitful; and I will make nations of you, and kings shall come forth from you. And I will establish my covenant between me and you and your descendants after you throughout their generations for an everlasting covenant, to be God to you and to your descendants after you. And I will give to you, and to your descendants after you, the land of your sojournings, all the land of Canaan, for an everlasting possession; and I will be their God. (Genesis 17.4–8)

The whole of Hebrew Scripture is the telling and retelling of the quest for relationship between God and God's chosen people.

To help define this relationship, God gave the Law. The Law stood as God's assurance of God's love and faithfulness. In Exodus 19 God promises Moses and his people:

If you will obey my voice and keep my covenant, you shall be my own possession among all peoples; for all the earth is mine, and you shall be to me a kingdom of priests and a holy nation. (Exodus 19.5–6)

The Law stood as God's assurance of love and faithfulness. In the giving of the Law, God sought to establish Israel as the leadership of a new world order. By following God's commandments, the chosen people would stand as a beacon of hope in a world separated from God.

God's covenant with Israel was not, however, an exclusive arrangement. The new relationship begun with Abraham, and clarified by the Law, was intended for all of humanity, a light to the nations. God's covenant was to be the vehicle by which all the peoples of the world could be joined both to the almighty Creator and to each other. Israel's role in God's mission was to serve as a centripetal force pulling all of humanity back into relationship with God.[14] Abraham and Sarah's descendants thus were to be agents of reconciliation between God and an errant humanity. All the nations were to come to God through the Covenant. The prophets, especially the servant songs of Isaiah, testify to this calling. In Isaiah 42 God says to his chosen people:

I am the Lord, I have called you in righteousness, I have taken you by the hand and kept you; I have given you as a covenant to the people, a light to the nations, to open the eyes that are blind, to bring out the prisoners from the dungeon, from the prison those who sit in darkness. (Isaiah 42.6–7)

And again in Isaiah 49:

It is too light a thing that you should be my servant to raise up the tribes of Jacob and to restore the preserved of Israel; I will give you as a light to the nations, that my salvation may reach to the end of the earth. (Isaiah 49.6)

The servant songs of Isaiah proclaim clearly that God's mission in the world is to bring salvation to the ends of the earth, to set free those who are oppressed, to open the eyes of the blind (Isaiah 42.6–7); to heal the separation between God, humanity and all of creation; to restore to unity with God all the peoples of the world and all of creation. In Isaiah we find the affirmation of Israel's commission, or co-mission, with God.

The story of God's mission, however, does not end with the covenant of Abraham and his people. It goes on. As Christians we affirm that, because of God's love for the world and desire to be united with all of humanity, God took a decisive and unique step. In the incarnation of Jesus Christ, God enters the world anew and takes the responsibility for God's mission directly upon himself.

> For God so loved the world that he gave his only Son, that whoever believes in him should not perish but have eternal life. God sent the Son into the world not to condemn the world, but that the world might be saved through him. (John 3.16–17)

In Jesus, God creates a New Covenant, a new means by which all the world could be joined to the Creator. Jesus was sent into the world to be the way, the truth, and the life (John 14.6). As the human form of the creator God, Jesus' mission is coterminous, one and the same, with that of the Creator. His mission is God's mission.

> Jesus said to them: 'I am the bread of life; he who comes to me shall not hunger, and he who believes in me shall never thirst . . . For I have come down from heaven, not to do my own will but the will of him who sent me; and this is the will of him who sent me, that I should lose nothing of all that he has given me, but raise it up at the last day. For this is the will of the Father, that everyone who sees the Son and believes in him should have eternal life; and I will raise them up on the last day. (John 6.35, 38–40)

The ultimate act of Jesus' self-giving participation in God's mission is his sacrifice upon the cross and victory over death. The joining of Jesus' pain and suffering with our pain and suffering on the cross is where we are passionately connected with God, with one another and with all creation. On the cross is where this new relationship, this right relationship, with God and each other is effected. In Jesus' resurrection three days after the agony of the cross, we are given the promise of restored life in him. Jesus' atonement for the sins of the world is our 'at-one-ment': our 'at-one-ment' with God, and our 'at-one-ment' with each other through the power of the Holy Spirit.[15] In Jesus' death and resurrection we are given the means by which we become one with each other and with God. In the death and resurrection of Jesus the divisions between God and humanity are overcome, and the promise of reconciliation is made real.

The reality that Jesus takes on God's mission in his incarnation, life, death and resurrection is not, however, a departure from the mission that God entrusted to Israel. Jesus did not come to break down the Law but rather to fulfil it. Jesus testifies to his fulfilment of the Isaiah prophecy in the fourth chapter of Luke:

> The Spirit of the Lord is upon me, because he has anointed me to preach good news to the poor. He has sent me to proclaim release to the captives and recovery

of sight to the blind, to set at liberty those who are oppressed, to proclaim the acceptable year of the Lord. (Luke 4.18–19)

Over and over again, Jesus demonstrates his solidarity with, and preferential option for, the poor, the sick, the outcasts and those at the periphery of society. The Gospels are a living testimony to Jesus' life and ministry as the source of God's salvation for the world. In Jesus the Reign of God is made real and tangible in our broken world.

Although Jesus is the fulfilment of the Law and prophets, there is, however, a difference between God's mission as it was entrusted to the Jews and how it was realized in Jesus the Christ. Whereas Israel represented a calling of humanity to union with God, Jesus turned the direction of God's mission around. Instead of a centripetal force, God's mission, realized in Jesus and empowered by the Holy Spirit, becomes a centrifugal force, a going out. Jesus demonstrates in word and deed that the Reign of God, made real in the sending of God's Son, must continue to expand, to move out to the ends of the earth. 'As you have sent me into the world, so I have sent them into the world' (John 17.18). Jesus thus sends out his disciples, empowered by the Holy Spirit, to be the bearers of his mission, God's mission, in the world.

And Jesus called to him the twelve and began to send them out two by two and gave them authority over unclean spirits . . . So they went out and preached that people should repent. And they cast out many demons, and anointed with oil many that were sick and healed them. (Mark 6.7, 12–13)

And to the seventy Jesus said:

Go your way . . . Whenever you enter a town and they receive you, eat what is set before you; heal the sick in it and say to them, 'The Kingdom of God has come near to you.' (Luke 10.3, 8–9)

Notice here that God's mission, fulfilled in the incarnation of Jesus and then furthered by the sending out of the disciples in the power of the Spirit, is multiform. There is loving service, feeding the hungry, healing the sick, and setting free the oppressed. But these acts of love are always coupled with the proclamation of the Kingdom of Heaven. In other words, God's mission to unite all of humanity to one another and to God is realized through acts of love and justice combined with the proclamation of Jesus as the Christ, the Saviour of the world. The wholeness of God's mission is discovered in the combination of the Great Commandment, to love one another as God has loved us (John 16.12–17), with the Great Commission, to make disciples of all nations baptizing them in the name of the Father and the Son and the Holy Spirit (Matthew 28.19). Proclamation without loving service is empty words, and good works without naming Jesus as the Christ are simply honourable deeds.

The movement of God's mission in heralding and making real the Reign of God to the ends of the earth is exemplified in the life and writings of Paul. We cannot develop here the complete mission theology of Paul but it is worth highlighting two fundamental aspects of his role in God's mission. The first is that Paul and his coworkers reached out to the Gentiles with the Good News of Jesus Christ. It is true that in the Gospels we are given evidence of Jesus' mission to the Gentiles, see for example our Lord's healing of the Centurion's slave (Luke 7.1–10) and his curing of the Syrophoenician woman's daughter (Matthew 15.21–28). But it is in the life and ministry of Paul that God's mission expands beyond Jerusalem. The second important aspect about Paul's mission theology is the full development of the Church as the Body of Christ in the world today. In his letter to the Ephesians, we find Paul's testimony that all who follow Jesus Christ, Jew and Gentile alike, are united with God the Creator. Paul says:

> And Jesus came and preached peace to you who were far off and peace to those who were near; for through him we both have access in one Spirit to the Father. So then you are no longer strangers and sojourners, but you are fellow citizens with the saints and members of the household of God, built upon the foundation of the apostles and prophets, Christ Jesus himself being the cornerstone, in whom the whole structure is joined together and grows into a holy temple of the Lord; in whom you also are built into it for a dwelling place of God in the Spirit. (Ephesians 2.17–22)

As followers of Jesus Christ today, as the Church, we too share in this household of God and thus are called to preach peace to those who are far off and to those who are near. The calling of the Church, the calling of every Christian, is to participate with God in the restoration of unity between ourselves and God, and ourselves and each other; to participate in the *missio Dei*. It is the work of the Church to herald and effect the new order where alienation, division and separation give way to inclusion, reconciliation and unity. As the Body of Christ in the world today, we are called to work for the restoration to unity of all people with God and each other in Christ. The mission of God is to restore all people to unity with God and each other in Christ.[16] The eminent missiologist David Bosch has thus summarized:

> Mission is, primarily and ultimately, the work of the Triune God, Creator, Redeemer, and Sanctifier, for the sake of the world, a ministry in which the church is privileged to participate. This is the deepest source of mission . . . there is mission because God loves people.[17]

Our vocation as followers of Christ is dependent upon, and judged against, how faithful we are to the mission of God, to the making real of God's reconciling love in the world. As Christians, we are called to live beyond ourselves, trusting that God will use us to effect God's restoration to unity, God's reconciliation of division, and God's redemption of creation to wholeness and oneness in Christ.

Challenges of a Globalized World

Globalization is a term that raises many different images and ideas depending on the context in which the word is used.[18] For many, globalization often means the worldwide spread of a neo-liberal economic system undergirded by unbridled access to a single global economic market. In such an understanding of globalization, the rich seem to profit at the expense of the poor, and the gulf between those who have and those who have not continues to grow with no seeming end in sight. Many see economic globalization, the global reach of the free-market system with no checks and balances, as an evil that is fundamentally corrupt and unsustainable.

But globalization need not be framed in such dire circumstances. Globalization can also be considered as a morally neutral term. Simply understood, globalization is the process by which anything, any movement, any phenomenon becomes global. The Harvard economist Richard Parker has argued articulately that globalization as a phenomenon 'is at least half a million years old, and began when our prehistoric ancestors walked out of Africa, into the Middle East, Europe, and Asia – and eventually Australia and the Americas'.[19]

Parker believes that the process of the worldwide growth and spread of humanity is an inevitable and not necessarily negative phenomenon. He does argue, however, that over the last 500 years, which he describes as the era of 'Europeanization', there have been incredible abuses of the peoples and lands in what were considered the colonies of European and North American nation-states.[20] The project of European and North American colonization that subjugated the peoples of Africa, Asia, Latin America and the Pacific led to a superimposition of Western economic, cultural, political and, yes, religious norms on the variety of peoples across the face of the earth. Unfortunately, the same forces from the West that undermine the voices and self-determination of the peoples of Africa, Asia, Latin America and the Pacific often continue unchecked in the 'post-colonial' era of unbridled free-market economics.

The handmaiden of 'Europeanization' and Western colonial reach has been the emergence of instant global communication, and the technologies that support such, over the last century and a half. While worldwide immediate communication might have emerged with the advent of the steam printing press and/or Samuel Morse's invention of his 'Morse Code' in the nineteenth century, the advent of digital communication with the internet and the World Wide Web over the last few decades has only exacerbated the process of globalization in recent years.[21] Today, no corner of the world is untouched by digital communication and the spread of information technology. Such technology has linked economic markets together, with billions and billions of dollars or Euros flowing immediately between time zones, leading to one global market that never sleeps. The loss of the bipolar world of the Cold War, and the demise of socialism as a viable economic and social alternative, has meant that an unconstrained capitalist free-market system has emerged as the single unchecked and unfettered global economic system.

A result of the new global digital information flow and the single market economy is a worldwide cultural hegemony that can assert a normative, singular cultural norm of flavour, taste, and desire around the world. The result has been a growing homogeneity of society and a creeping cultural hegemony that discounts diversity and plurality of voices. The sociologist George Ritzer has described this homogenization process and loss of local cultural expressions as the 'McDonaldization' of society.[22] McDonaldization uses as a metaphor the proliferation of the chain of hamburger restaurants known as McDonald's, beginning first in the United States and now spreading increasingly around the world. The McDonald's restaurant chain claims as part of its marketing programme that it has sold 'billions and billions' of hamburgers around the world. In the McDonaldized world, all people eat the same hamburgers and drink the same milk shakes, no matter where they might live. Today the same McDonald's hamburger or Gap jeans can be found in the streets of Baltimore, Buenos Aires, Berlin, Brussels, Beijing, or Bombay. This fact is not lost on faithful Anglican pilgrims who might notice that the store abutting the main gate to the Close of Canterbury Cathedral is none other than a Starbucks coffee shop.[23]

In the McDonaldized world, those at the margins, those without power, suffer most, particularly indigenous peoples. It is they who must struggle to reassert their own ways of understanding the world; who must fight for their own means of production and sustenance. In the McDonaldized world the local, the vulnerable, the particular are always vulnerable to the interests and power of the global. And so today we see the push back of local voices and peoples against the forces of globalization. The reassertion of the local is not limited to indigenous peoples in far-flung places such as Aotearoa who assert their treaty rights to ancestral lands in New Zealand, or India's refusal to let Coca-Cola into their country in order to protect their national soft drink industry. No, the push back of the local against the global can be seen anywhere individuals refuse to give up their identity and their power for fear of losing what is most precious and of value in their own context and cultural ways of making meaning.

The push back of the local can either be a healthy form of resistance to globalization or, at the worst, can lead to a new tyranny of the local where all possibilities and opportunities for new growth and access in the global world are sacrificed on the altar of the single identity politics of the local.[24] The negative forces of the local against the global are not limited to young anarchists throwing rocks through storefronts at meetings of the World Trade Organization, for even the atrocities of 9/11 can be seen as a response of the local against the global. Were not the targets of the terrorists what they considered the symbols of globalization, namely the political and economic institutions of the World Trade Center, the Pentagon, and the United States government? No, the push back from the local can be healthy or can be malignant. Like the forces of globalization themselves, the push back from the local can be either life-affirming or destructive depending on the circumstances and the context.

In the globalized world we thus see the twin competing phenomena of the worldwide reach of a mono-economic, mono-cultural reality and the concomitant push back of local, particular peoples and their cultures.[25] The challenge of globalization is: how can the realities of a single economic and cultural system, driven by the worldwide capitalist market and facilitated by digital communication, co-exist with a myriad of localities, such that the voices and cultural realities of any one people are not lost? In other words: how can the global live with the local, and local live with the global, without either one or the other seeking to superimpose itself on the other with a destructive and life-denying result? What are the possibilities for the global and the local to co-exist, and even thrive together, such that both the global and the local can better inform and add to the life-affirming possibilities of the other?

Rabbi Jonathan Sacks, the Chief Rabbi of the United Hebrew Congregations of the Commonwealth, has spoken and written articulately on the challenges and possibilities of globalization, specifically as they relate to religious communities. He stresses the fact that the global/local dynamic of globalization at one and the same time drives peoples and different religions together while simultaneously exacerbating differences, thus driving groups apart.

It has become ever more clear that we face great dangers in the coming century, and that we are not adequately prepared for them. On the one hand, globalization is bringing us closer together than ever before, interweaving our lives, nationally and internationally, in complex and inexplicable ways. On the other, a new tribalism – a regression to older and more factious loyalties – is driving us even more angrily apart. One way or another, religion is and will continue to be, part of these processes. It can lead us in the direction of peace. But it can equally, and with high combustibility, lead us to war. Politicians have power, but religions have something stronger: they have influence. Politics moves the pieces on the chessboard. Religion changes lives. Peace can be agreed around the conference table; but unless it grows in ordinary hearts and minds, it does not last. It may not even begin.[26]

The forces of globalization, which bring peoples closer together while exacerbating differences amongst groups, that Rabbi Sacks is speaking about, albeit from an inter-religious post-9/11 perspective, also affect the life of the Anglican Communion, particularly with respect to conflicts related to human sexuality. Never before have Anglicans lived so closely together, with new networks of communication and relationship emerging in ways unimagined even a decade ago.[27] At the same time, divisions in the Anglican Communion have never been so deep. The alienation and discord over deep differences with respect to human sexuality in general, and the place of gay and lesbian people in the Church, in particular, threaten to tear the Anglican Communion apart. The question before the Anglican Communion in this time of globalization is: will our differences over human sexuality, in the words of Rabbi Sacks, lead us in the direction of peace or to war? Is there a way forward for the Anglican Communion such that neither the global nor the local annihilates the other? Can we live together in the greater proximity of this globalized world where differences are exacerbated; and how can the Listening Process contribute to our common life in Christ given the challenges of globalization?

Identities and Differences

The challenges of globalization, between the global and the local, the drawing together of peoples while exacerbating differences, are played out in the politics of identity. Rabbi Sacks has said most adroitly that while the twentieth century was driven by conflicts over ideology, the twenty-first century will be characterized by conflicts over identity, or identities. Identity politics, the way by which individuals or groups seek to assert some aspect of who they are or see themselves to be, can be empowering and life-affirming while at the same time oppressive and hurtful. Identity politics, driven by the forces of globalization, is the arena in which the conflicts over human sexuality in the Anglican Communion are being fought. If the Anglican Communion is to engage with the Listening Process in an authentic manner across the differences that exist in the Communion, then 'unpacking' the power of identities and identity politics is important to the process.

Identity, the way by which a person or group of people define themselves based upon some aspect of their personhood, is a powerful force for both the individual as well as for the social group to which an individual belongs. The variety of personal and social identities that exist are as broad and rich as the fullness of God's good creation. Some of the more easily defined identities include: gender, ethnicity, national origin, age, geography, race, class, economic status, sexuality, religion, theological commitments, and, particularly within the Anglican Communion, provincial membership and clerical status. The identity or identities that an individual or group inhabits can be a positive force of social cohesion, and relationship building. The Nobel prize-winner economist Amartya Sen has recently written:

> The sense of identity can make an important contribution to the strength and the warmth of our relations with others, such as neighbours, or members of the same community, or fellow citizens, or followers of the same religion. Our focus on particular identities can enrich our bonds and make us do many things for each other and help to take us beyond our self-centred lives.[28]

But it is equally true that identity and identities can be divisive and serve to alienate individuals or groups of individuals from each other. Akin to the forces of globalization, the same power that draws people together can be turned around and focused negatively on those who might be different, other, or the stranger. When disproportionate power exists between individuals and/or groups then the differences in identity or identities that exist between them can result in violent attacks by one on the other. Stories of violence perpetrated by an individual and/or group who have power over those who are different are rife through history and continue almost unabated in the globalized world today. We need not spend time elucidating conflicts driven by identity differences, but recent violence in such places as Afghanistan, Israel/Palestine, Iraq, Northern Ireland, Pakistan, Rwanda, Sudan, and the inner cities of the United States comes to mind. And even in the Bible, identity differences often result in oppressive and sometimes violent circumstances, whether it be the people of Israel enslaved in Egypt, or the followers of Jesus who claim to belong to Paul, or to Apollos, or to Cephas (1 Corinthians 1.12).

The power inherent in identity or identities, and the way it gets meted out in various social circumstances, is the realm of identity politics. Identity politics presupposes a social construction of reality where individuals and groups have power and authority to assert an identity or set of identities, and/or are disenfranchised and oppressed because of the same. Whether one is empowered or disempowered by one's identity is based upon the power differential in the social circumstance. Generally speaking, those who enjoy the most power, be that because of majority status, historical circumstance or some other social dynamic, are considered privileged in the power differential; while those who are disempowered are seen as being 'targets' of oppressive actions and structures.

Dr Valerie Batts, an anti-racism and multiculturalism consultant and theorist, speaking out of her context in the United States as an African-American woman, has charted some of the non-target and target groups that function in America. For example, on the variable of race, the non-target (privileged) group would be those who are considered white, and the target group would be people of colour (African, Asian, Native, Latino/a Americans.) Similarly, on the variable of socio-economic class, the non-target would be those of the middle and upper classes while the target groups are the poor and working classes. And the same would be true on the variable of gender, with men being non-target and women being target. These are just a few of the many different identity variables discussed by Batts.[29] In these power dynamics of non-target and target groups it is very important to note that there are multiple identities at work for any one individual or group at any one time, be they along the variables of race, class and gender, or innumerable others such as education, religion, age, physical or mental ability, sexual orientation, language, etc. Thus every person 'enjoys' both non-target and target status at the same time depending upon the variable considered.

For Christians, the embodying of non-target and target status at the same time is powerfully manifest in Jesus the Christ. Jesus lived in the power and the possibility of being fully God while he also embodied the finiteness and finitude of being fully human. On the cross, Jesus' most powerful and freeing self-offering of God for the sake of the world occurred as he was the most oppressed, most debased, most persecuted. It is impossible for Christians who believe that Jesus is fully divine and fully human, and for whom Jesus in his death on the cross provides new life, to deny that both non-target and target variables can co-exist in one individual and/or group.

Batts emphasizes that, in addition to individuals and groups inhabiting multiple identities at any one time, the power dynamics of non-target and target status are also played out at multiple levels concurrently. At the *personal* level, how one sees her/himself in the world and before God, with respect to the identities she/he inhabits, has a bearing on their psychic, emotional, and spiritual well-being. At the *interpersonal* level, the differences between two individuals with respect to power and status affect the outworking of the relationship. At the *institutional* level, the power and status enjoyed by an individual or group has a direct bearing on, and is a result of, the place that they occupy in an organization. Similarly, in the wider context at the *cultural* level, what a culture chooses to privilege, or not, has a direct bearing on an individual's or group's non-target or target status.[30] So the power of identity and identities is not only informed by multiple variables, but they also function at multiple levels concurrently, those of the personal, interpersonal, institutional, and cultural levels.

Perhaps a few hypothetical examples taken from current realities in the Anglican Communion might be helpful here to show how multiple identities at various levels function. Let us consider the somewhat pronounced example of a white, lesbian, celibate, lay-woman from the United States who is gainfully employed and speaks only English, and a heterosexual, married, bishop in an African Anglican Province for whom English is not his first language. The woman from the United States enjoys the non-target, privileged status of: being white, a United States passport holder, with economic security and an education in a Western English-speaking context. Yet, at the same time, she inhabits the target status of being a lesbian, a woman, and a lay-person (in Church circles). Let us now consider the African bishop. He enjoys the non-target, privileged status of being a heterosexual, married, male, bishop in a growing Anglican church. At the same time he is a target in that, historically speaking, he has the experience of marginalization because he is an African whose people and country has been colonized by the West, for whom English is not a first language, and who continues to struggle under dire economic realities today.

As the woman from the United States and the African bishop meet in an inter-Anglican gathering, perhaps at a link/companion diocese consultation or at a meeting of the Anglican Consultative Council, all of their different identity variables, at the four levels of the personal, interpersonal, institutional and cultural, affect their interactions. While the woman from the United States might feel secure and maybe even powerful in her status as an American, English-speaking person who can easily negotiate her way through Western-arranged meeting processes and agendas, she might feel insecure or marginalized as a woman, as a lay-person, or as a lesbian. In a similar vein, but with a different set of variables, the African bishop might feel secure in the meeting as a man and a bishop coming from a growing and vital Anglican church. But he might also feel constrained or disempowered in a meeting that is conducted in English or that presupposes that he and his church cannot fully participate because of their financial limitations. The reality of the non-target and target status of these two faithful Anglican leaders is experienced in how they each see themselves in the international meeting (the personal level), as they come to share stories and know each other over tea (the interpersonal level), when they are speaking on behalf of their diocese or church in plenary sessions of the meeting (the institutional level), and when they are seen as representatives of the West or of the Global South (the cultural level). The question is: what is the possibility for genuine understanding and mutual responsibility and interdependence in Christ between the lay-woman and the Bishop when all of these identity variables and levels are operative?

Before considering the possibilities for understanding across the differences that exist between individuals and groups, it is worthwhile to look at what it is that most impedes such mutuality and interdependence. Given the multiple identity variables involved for any individual or group in the non-target/target power dynamic, combined with the multiple levels in which power is exercised, it is difficult to see how a dualistic either/or presentation of identity politics can be sustained. And yet the Anglican Communion seems to be at a crisis point where the divisions over human sexuality are so pronounced that they threaten the very existence of the Communion as a family of churches. In order to perpetrate these battles over human sexuality, the many identities at the multiple levels that any individual or group inhabits must be diminished to a single identity politic.

A single identity politic, by definition, elevates one identity variable to a place of predominance and exclusivity while significantly under-appreciating, or even denying, the other identities inhabited by a person or group. When one identity variable is focused on, it is very easy to construct a dualistic either/or scenario that pits one side off against another. With two sides clearly determined and articulated along the one identity variable, it is then easy to demonize or vilify the other as different or less deserving of full respect or dignity. Objectifying the other as 'different' and 'less than' becomes a precursor to perpetrating violence and even warfare. Sen sees single identity politics, or the 'illusion of singular identity' or 'unique identity', as the root cause of violence:

It is not remarkable that generating the illusion of unique identity, exploitable for the purpose of confrontation, would appeal to those who are in the business of fomenting violence, and there is no mystery in the fact that such reductionism is sought. But there is a big question about why the cultivation of singularity is so successful, given the extraordinary naïveté of that thesis in a world of obvious plural affiliations. To see a person exclusively in terms of only one of his or her many identities is, of course, a deeply crude intellectual move . . . and yet, judging from its effectiveness, the cultivated delusion of singularity is evidently easy enough to champion and promote. The advocacy of a unique identity for a violent purpose takes the form of separating out one identity group – directly linked to the violent purpose at hand – for special focus, and it proceeds from there to eclipse the relevance of other associations and affiliations through selective emphasis and incitement.[31]

While Sen is writing out of the conflicted multi-religious context of South Asia, his analysis might well describe current tensions in the Anglican Communion over human sexuality. Those who reduce the complex and plural realities of the Anglican Communion today to the single identity politic of human sexuality are then in a place to characterize the other with such violent words as 'homophobic' or 'less than human' depending on where one stands with respect to the place of gay and lesbian people in the church. Such hurtful and violent characterizations do not build up the Body of Christ.

So how do we get beyond the confines and spectre of violence in single identity politics? Returning to the work of Valerie Batts and the multiple identity variables she emphasizes in her process of multicultural change, it is useful to re-emphasize that every human and every social group embodies many different identities. The more that we can live in the multiple identities and the simultaneity of both our non-target and target variables in our personal, interpersonal, institutional, and cultural transactions, the more free we will be from the trap of singularity. This calls for an awareness of, an appreciation of, and ownership of both our own non-target and target identities as well as the non-target and target identities of the other. Embracing the multiple non-target and target identities that I and the other inhabit is a first step in overcoming the confines and violent possibilities of single identity politics.

It is important, at this juncture of articulating our multiple identity variables, that we neither rank the variables nor compete with the other about who has more non-target or target variables. Such ranking or competition is simply another more subtle form of single identity politics that fundamentally denies the multiplicity of identities any person or group inhabits. The key point is that each person or group fundamentally inhabits both non-target and target identities, and that they are able to identify and articulate what these identities are for themselves.

While appreciating differences and multiple identities for myself and for the other can be a cognitive exercise that calls for mindfulness and awareness, a second and possibly more important step is necessary if we are to move to a place of genuine appreciation and reconciliation with those who are different. This step requires us to be in touch with how we *feel* about the many different identities we inhabit.[32] What does it feel like to be a target of oppressive structures? How do we process the pain and hurt that we experience when disempowered or abused? Conversely, and this is sometimes more difficult than identifying the feelings associated with our target identities, what does it feel like to have power and privilege? Can we identify the feelings associated with being non-target?

Once we are able to identify our feelings associated with our non-target and target identities, we are then able to connect effectively with those who inhabit different non-target and target identities. Specific non-target and target variables will obviously be different from individual to individual, or group to group. But the assertion here is that the feelings associated with each non-target and target status will be the same as the way the dynamics inherent in having power or being disenfranchised are strikingly similar despite the particular identity variable at play. We are thus challenged to share what it feels like to be privileged *and* oppressed, non-target *and* target, even if the variables are different. In the sharing of the commonality of these feelings across the various variables we inhabit is the possibility of building solidarities across differences. Like Jesus who wept at Lazarus's tomb and yet drew on his power to raise his friend, we Christians are called to be in touch with our feelings of hurt and pain *and* our power and possibility if we are to serve the fullness of God's mission in the world.

Returning now to the example of the American lay-woman and the African bishop, how would the awareness and appreciation of multiple identity variables, and the effective sharing of common emotions related to these variables, build understanding and solidarity across the differences they inhabit? Imagine if the American lay-woman could share with the African bishop what it *feels* like to have power as a Western English-speaking person, or one who is economically secure, or who is white, or one who holds a United States passport. And imagine if the bishop could share what it *feels* like to have power as a man, or one who is married, or one who is a bishop in a growing and vital church. Similarly imagine if the American lay-woman could share what it *feels* like to be disempowered as a woman, or as a lesbian, or as lay-person; and if the African bishop could identify what it *feels* like to be targeted as a historically colonized African, or a person who lives in economically dire conditions, or for whom English is not a first language in inter-Anglican meetings where English is the prime language of discourse. While these two Christian leaders experience different sources of power and oppression based upon the different non-target and target identities they inhabit, the feelings associated with being privileged and disempowered are very similar. Sharing their feelings of power and privilege, or oppression and disempowerment, allows for the finding of commonality and solidarity as a sister and brother in Christ in the midst of their profound differences.

Clearly, if the American lay-woman and the African bishop are to discover their commonalties in their differences then there needs to be a theological, or even a missiological, rationale for being vulnerable and open to one another. Key to this open and trusting exchange is the willingness to listen to the other, and the desire to see the face of Christ in the other. In meeting Christ anew in the other, through a listening process where individuals and groups can share the possibilities and pain of their non-target and target identities, is the promise of the restoration and reconciliation at the centre of God's mission.

The Missiological Significance of Listening

This paper began by briefly tracing the changes in mission thought over the last century with an emphasis on current understandings of the *missio Dei*, the mission of God. A brief review of Holy Scripture as offering a meta-narrative on the nature of God's mission followed. The operative missiological assertion of these first two sections is that God's mission in Jesus Christ, empowered by the Holy Spirit, is to restore all people and all creation to unity with God and each other in Christ; to reconcile an alienated and divided world wracked by sin to a wholeness and oneness intended by God in creation.

The context in which God's mission is being played out today, in the Church and in the world, was then considered. Particular attention was paid to the forces of globalization which at one and the same time drive individuals and groups closer together as never before in the history of humankind while at the same time exacerbating differences and tensions that exist between peoples. The differences and tensions that exist between individuals and groups were looked at from the perspective of identity variables and identity politics. A model of discovering commonalties in the midst of differences in identities was offered. Basic to this model was an appreciation of the fact that any individual or group inhabits many different identities, some of which offer privilege and power, and some of which engender oppression and disempowerment. It was posited that in the eyes of God all of our many differences can be bridged in solidarities across differences as we share how it feels to be both a non-target and target in our personal, interpersonal, institutional and cultural interactions.

So what does all of this discussion of mission, globalization, and identities have to say to the Listening Process in the Anglican Communion? First, listening to one another and listening to God is fundamentally an exercise in faithfulness to the mission of God. If the Bible calls us to follow in the footsteps of a God who seeks to restore all people to unity with God and each other in Christ, then listening to the other in the promise of restoring unity in a divided world is profoundly missiological in nature. The missiological significance of listening is that in listening across differences we are participating in the hope of a restored and reconciled world intended by God.

Listening across differences is brutally difficult in a world torn apart by the forces of globalization and single identity politics. We Christians believe, however, that in Christ God is reconciling the world to himself. In Christ the seemingly irreconcilable identities of one who is fully human and fully God have been brought together in a reconciled reality for the redemption of the world. As the Body of Christ today, the Church is thus called to live in the same fundamental reality that our profound differences are indeed already reconciled and that unity with God and each other in Christ is assured. The process of listening across our differences models for the world the promise of our unity in Christ. The process of listening across our differences is a testimony to the world that the Trinitarian God, Father, Son and Holy Spirit, has effected restoration and reconciliation for all people and for all creation. As Anglicans, the world over, let us then offer the Listening Process as an act of faithfulness to God's mission of restoration and reconciliation.

Notes to Part 1

1 *True Union in the Body?* (Grove Books, 2003), para 1.2.
2 *The Official Report of the Lambeth Conference 1998* (Harrisburg, PA: Morehouse Publishing, 1999), 381–2.
3 The descriptive word 'homosexual' is used here in reference to Resolution 1.10 because that is the language of the resolution. Generally speaking, people whose sexual orientation is described as 'homosexual' prefer their own self-description as gay and lesbian people.

4 David J. Bosch, *Transforming Mission: Paradigm Shifts in Theology of Mission* (Maryknoll, NY: Orbis Books, 1991), 262–74.

5 This overview of mission thought has been presented in various forms over the last decade. Much of this material was originally published in Ian T. Douglas, 'Baptized in Mission: Ministry and Holy Orders Reconsidered', *Sewanee Theological Review* 40 (Michaelmas 1997), 431–4.

6 The meetings of the International Missionary Council in Whitby, 1947, and Willingen, 1952 were particularly concerned with the missionary nature of the Church.

7 Stephen Neill, *A History of Christian Missions* (New York: Penguin Books, 1964), 572.

8 Johannes C. Hoekendijk, 'The Call to Evangelism', *International Review of Missions* 39 (April 1950), 163.

9 Ibid., 171, italics in original.

10 See Johannes Blauw, *The Missionary Nature of the Church* (Grand Rapids, MI: Eerdmans, 1974).

11 This biblical overview of mission was written by Ian T. Douglas and originally published in Sabina Alkire and Edmund Newell, *What Can One Person Do: Faith to Heal a Broken World* (New York: Church Publishing, 2005), 44–50.

12 Grant LeMarquand has appropriately pointed out that God's mission did not begin with the Fall but with creation. God's mission in creation was to extend the love that is of the essence of God for the whole cosmos. Grant LeMarquand, 'From Creation to New Creation: The Mission of God in the Biblical Story', in Ian T. Douglas (ed.), *Waging Reconciliation: God's Mission in a Time of Globalization and Crisis* (New York: Church Publishing, 2002), 9–34.

13 From 'An Outline of the Faith: Commonly Called the Catechism', in the *Book of Common Prayer* of The Episcopal Church. *The Book of Common Prayer* (New York: The Church Hymnal Corporation, 1979), 848.

14 See Donald Senior and Carroll Stuhlmueller, *The Biblical Foundations for Mission* (Maryknoll, NY: Orbis Books, 1984), and especially for Old Testament resources: Christopher J. H. Wright, *The Mission of God: Unlocking the Bible's Grand Narrative* (Downers Grove, IL: IVP Academic, 2006).

15 Martin L. Smith, SSJE, *Love Set Free: Meditations on the Passion According to St John* (Cambridge and Boston: Cowley Publications, 1998), 5–13.

16 In the 'Catechism' in the *Book of Common Prayer* of The Episcopal Church it is asked: 'What is the mission of the Church?' I would prefer to rephrase the question as: 'What is the mission of God in which the Church is privileged to participate?' The answer given to the original question is: 'The mission of the Church is to restore all people to unity with God and each other in Christ.' *The Book of Common Prayer*, 855.

17 Bosch, *Transforming Mission*, 392.

18 This discussion of globalization is drawn from: Ian T. Douglas, 'Called to Reconciliation: The Challenge of Globalization and the Anglican Communion', in Barbara Braver (ed.), *I Have Called You Friends: Reflections on Reconciliation in Honor of Frank T. Griswold* (Cambridge, MA: Cowley Publications, 2006), 149–64.

19 Richard Parker, 'Globalization, the Social Gospel and Christian Leadership Today', in Douglas (ed.), *Waging Reconciliation*, 79.

20 Ibid., 82.

21 Ibid., 81.

22 George Ritzer, *The McDonaldization of Society: An Investigation into the Changing Character of Contemporary Social Life* (Thousand Oaks, CA: Pine Forge Press, 1993).

23 Starbucks is a chain of shops that sells coffee and teas. As an emerging global chain of stores, Starbucks mimics the globalization of tastes and commodities as described in Ritzer's *The McDonaldization of Society*.

24 The classic study of this tension between the local and the global is: Benjamin Barber, *Jihad vs McWorld* (New York: Ballantine, 2001).

25 Christopher Duraisingh describes these twin phenomena as the centripetal and centrifugal forces of globalization. Christopher Duraisingh, 'Encountering Difference in a Plural World: A Pentecost Paradigm for Mission', in Douglas (ed.), *Waging Reconciliation*, 174–5.

26 Jonathan Sacks, *The Dignity of Difference: How to Avoid the Clash of Civilizations* (London: Continuum, 2002), 5.

27 The best single study of how new networks of communication and co-operation have emerged as a result of the forces of globalization in the Anglican Communion is: Miranda K. Hassett, *Anglican Communion in Crisis: How Episcopal Dissidents and Their African Allies Are Reshaping Anglicanism* (Princeton: Princeton University Press, 2007).

28 Amartya Sen, *Identity and Violence: The Illusion of Destiny* (New York and London: W. W. Norton, 2006), 2.

29 Valerie Batts, 'Is Reconciliation Possible? Lessons from Combating "Modern Racism"', in Douglas (ed.), *Waging Reconciliation*, 41. Much of the power analysis in this section has been developed through collegial work with Dr Batts.

30 Ibid., 51–2.

31 Sen, *Identity and Violence*, 175.

32 The power of feelings in building solidarities and understanding across differences is emphasized in the process of multicultural changes as developed by Dr Valerie Batts.

PART 2:
MISSION IS ANTITHEORETICAL:
LISTENING AND THE DISCLOSING OF THE PRIMAL VISION

Michael Nai-Chiu Poon

Two seminal works from seemingly unrelated disciplines inspire the title of this essay. One is Prasenjit Duara's 'Why is History Antitheoretical?', and the other is John V. Taylor's *The Primal Vision*.[1] Professor Duara's writings focus on questions of nationalism, imperialism and transnationalism with specific reference to the social and cultural history of modern China. Bishop Taylor served as a Church Missionary Society missionary to Uganda from the 1940s, and succeeded Max Warren as the Society's General Secretary from the early 1960s.

Historians and missionaries share a common task. They are attentive to the past *and* to the present. In short, good historians and missionaries are listeners. Insights from these two eminent scholars – the one a historian and the other a missionary – may well serve to introduce our present subject matter – on listening and mission in the twenty-first century.

Listening and mission are ways in which the Christian community engages the world. They are two aspects of the same divine calling: to awaken hope and breathe life to the world. Too often they are reduced into methodological and programme-oriented considerations, as if they are matters that are obvious and intuitive. The purpose of this essay is to invite us to reflect on our own suppositions, and so rediscover a distinct Christian vision for our listening and mission practice.

This self-reflexive exercise is not merely of academic interest, best left to the professional theologians, experts, even bishops! Rather, it is a personal undertaking and urgent task for the whole Christian community at the beginning of the third millennium. We may suppose all along that the world around us welcomes our engagement. We may have assumed so far that others want to be listened to by the Christian community, and that others agree such listening and mission efforts by

Christians would lead to positive changes. To be sure, such an outlook may have once held true in the time of Christendom. But this is no longer so. In the context of the present-day debate on the European identity, Roman Catholic theologian George Weigel considers whether the human rights charter provides the best guarantee for Europe's future:

> Christianity is not merely a nonfactor in the development of contemporary European public life but has functioned historically as an obstacle to the evolution of a Europe at peace, a Europe that champions human rights, a Europe that governs itself democratically. From here it is but a short step to the conviction that even to mention Europe's Christian heritage [in the new Constitution of the European Union] is to invite a regression to the intolerance, obscurantism, and fratricide of yesteryears.[2]

If human rights agencies are the torchbearers of the future, should not the Christian community stand aside? Should not the cathedral (as represented by the Cathedral of Notre-Dame in Weigel's article) give way to the cube (that houses the International Foundation for Human Rights at La Grande Arche in Paris)? For, according to this line of reasoning, what can Christians contribute? Lambeth 1998 confidently resolved: 'We commit ourselves to listen to the experience of homosexual persons and we wish to assure them that they are loved by God and that all baptized, believing and faithful persons, regardless of sexual orientation, are full members of the Body of Christ . . .' (Resolution 1.10c). Yet the point is this: Who wants to talk to the church? Who wants its assurance if it is an obstacle to human progress?

The hostile and dismissive situation in which present-day Christians live should inform our listening and mission activities. To affirm confidently that *our* listening and mission do matter *for the world*, we need to rediscover the distinct Christian grounds for such undertakings. We embark on this journey with a historian as a guide.

*   *   *

Drawing from his research in contemporary China, Duara provides a penetrating analysis of issues in the writing of history. History writing can become ideologically driven for nation-building purposes. 'History becomes the most important pedagogical technology in identity formation.' Duara reflects on his own education in India. 'The early stages of our education, the historical pedagogy of the nation-state involves not a grammar or methodology of history but the learning, often rote learning, of its content. One of its principal goals is to instil all love, pride, shame, resentment, or even vengeance for the nation, not to understand the grammar that could question its categories.'[3] Further, national histories pretend to provide a definitive account of our past, and 'bar inquiry into history as a means of constituting and organizing knowledge'. These national histories often are linear and evolutionary. Thus history writing is important for the nation because it is future oriented and 'performative': it propels the nation 'into a desired future direction'.[4]

Duara then discusses three sets of issues as to how we make sense of temporality: on periodization (how we divide periods in history), causality (the cause and effect of history), and the spatial–temporal vectors (the terms by which we organize our space and time and so our identity) in national histories.[5]

He ends with these words:

> Without a critical self-reflexivity, [our notions of history] can be made to serve as a tool of power. Without thinking through the problem of how space and time are conceived and produced in history, we become passive agents of powers such as the nation-state that control the meaning of such categories . . . But the historian also has a special relationship with the real and the particular . . . because it is in the distinctive unfolding of the real that theory has its true reason for existence. Historians of our time face the double challenge of thinking theoretically while remaining aware that every interpretation seeks to close a source whose generativity is inexhaustible.[6]

Duara's criticism of national histories is illuminating for mission discourse. One only has to replace nation-building with *missio Dei*, the often unchallenged paradigm for mission in the present day. The one is concerned with the building of nations; the other with labouring for God's Kingdom. As the writing of history in nation-building can structure realities, so the instruments attendant to a *missio Dei* ideology can dictate the terms by which Christians interpret their identity, their space–time boundaries, and the grammar of their discourse among themselves and with the wider world.[7]

The end of the Second World War marked a watershed for historians and Christian churches in the Western world. The rapid rise of new nation-states and the retreat of Western missionaries often went hand-in-hand. Whereas historians began in earnest to move to a more geographically centred approach to history writing, thus opening fresh lines of enquiry and reinterpretation of the past,[8] Christians lagged behind in opening up to more radical rethinking in how churches from different geographical places can collaborate in mission.

It is important to remind ourselves of the history of how the concept of *missio Dei* was (re-)introduced in mission discourses after the Second World War. The model supposedly served as a reminder that mission is not merely an institutionally and ecclesiastically centred undertaking. Mission issues from the mission of the triune God. Karl Hartenstein put it this way: Mission is a 'participation in the sending of the Son, in the *missio Dei*, with an inclusive aim of establishing the lordship of Christ over the whole redeemed creation'.[9] The context of the above quotation is significant. It came out of Hartenstein's report on the historic Willingen 1952 World Mission Conference called by the International Missionary Council. Missionary societies urgently needed to reassess their positions and strategies amid radical political changes. The expulsion of missionaries from China, and the Korean War, highlighted the crisis at the time. The 'younger churches' outside of the traditional Christian lands were not strong enough to stand on their own, especially in the face of the sociopolitical instabilities in the new nation-states. Missionaries and churches from the West perpetuated their presence in the younger churches by providing them with material and personnel support to counter the perceived Communist threat.[10] Some Christian leaders from younger churches did speak up for a more geographically centred approach to the reconfiguration of world Christianity.[11] But as it turned out, *missio Dei* became the cardinal model and justification for the continuing engagement of Western churches in the wider world.

Notice that the *missio Dei* reorientation lends itself to two conceptual shifts. There is first a shift from the earthbound church to the God who can be interpreted along transcendental lines. Mission becomes detached from its ecclesial anchor. It is no longer seen as a *human* act of discipleship in *response* to God in the space–time before the Second Coming. Rather, the church regards itself as God's privileged agent who does not have 'to learn obedience' through sharing in human suffering (contra Hebrews 5.8). 'The initiative in mission is God's, not ours,' so MISSIO declares.[12] This confession can also be used to absolve ourselves from the need for self-criticism, since it is after all *God's* initiative, and not ours. The second shift is from church-centred activities that are anchored in geographical and particular realities (e.g. *this* church-planting, *that person's* conversion, *this* school and *that* social services centre: the particulars that filled the pages of missionary journals and letters) to the abstract 'establishing the lordship of Christ over the whole redeemed creation'. So *missio Dei* is prone to ideological shaping.

To be sure, *missio Dei* becomes performative and future oriented. Each instance of perceived injustice becomes a pointer for the church's intervention and bringing in the 'new'. Looking to the Anglican Communion, from ACC-8 in 1990, Anglicans define the mission of the church by five central tasks: (1) to proclaim the good news; (2) to nurture new believers; (3) to respond to human need; (4) to transform unjust structures; and (5) to safeguard the integrity of creation.[13] However, there was little reflection on the theological and missiological significance of particular provinces that are grounded in particular geographical places across the Communion.

Indeed, *missio Dei* can be pursued apart from geopolitical considerations. They are merely 'contexts' – the particular settings – for implementation of central policies.[14] One can launch God's mission from headquarters (conveniently situated in technologically sophisticated locations). Instead of needing to engage the world in its particularities, the world (now recast as ethnic and cultural balances) can come to the centre.[15] From such a centre, one can be most effective in devising and launching programmes to the rest of the (underdeveloped) world. So, in an ironic way, the *missio Dei* ethos perpetuates the civilizing mission model. It in fact hardens the model by assuming, itself, the role of being God's agent and vanguard of his Kingdom, and not merely as representatives of missionary societies and bearers of civilizational advances of the Western world.[16]

*   *   *

Duara's observation that 'the historian also has a special relationship with the real and the particular' applies with especial relevance to our present discussion. Put in Christian terms, *the* incarnation underpins the gospel, and indeed life itself: 'The Word became flesh, and made his dwelling among us' (John 1.14). Fundamental to this is that Jesus Christ, the Word, came to the human world in a particular time and particular place. This constituted and affirmed his presence: 'No one has ever seen God, but God the One and Only, who is at the Father's side, has made him known' (John 1.18). John V. Taylor discovered the 'world of presences' through his years of personal encounters in Africa. He marvelled:

The primal vision is of a world of presences, of face-to-face meeting . . . [The Christian] has nothing to offer unless he offers to be present, really and totally present, really and totally *in* the present. The failure of so many 'professional' Christians has been that they are 'not all there'![17]

He went on to underline 'listening' as the particular way of reconnecting ourselves to the world of presences:

[H]ow much of the mission of his Church seems to be contrived in 'routines and possessiveness'! . . . Those who have lost the capacity for listening, who cannot be there for others, are unable even to be truly present to themselves.[18]

Ronald Owen Hall, one of the most distinguished and controversial of missionaries and a bishop in South China, drew similar lessons from his years of engagement in China. At the height of the Sino-Japanese War, he wrote a small classic, *The Art of the Missionary*, a primer for Western missionaries preparing themselves for service in the new China after the War. In it, he complained that former missionaries often hid themselves behind the 'concession area' (the safe zones in China where those from Western powers could conduct their affairs outside of China's jurisdiction). He said:

We live largely in an area which is unreal and has no roots in the real life in China. To live in an unreal world is fatal to true Christian living anywhere . . . To break out into the real life of the people is the task of the modern missionary.[19]

Listening and mission are ways of being present in the real world in its broken and gifted existence. So we approach our proximate neighbours with the mind of Christ, and commit ourselves to engage, to be reconciled, and to share with one another in building a common life – for us and for our children – at where we live. In so doing, we redeem the past and create new possibilities – beyond our control and expectations – for our children in their generations. In committing ourselves to such practical and concrete tasks, we at the same time reject a false ordering of the world and of ourselves along ideological lines. Such ideological ordering can come in several forms: the periodization of time according to post-missionary and post-colonial categories; the labelling of the human person and societies according to preconceived cultural, ethnic, sociological and psychological models; and the enforcement of a set vocabulary that manipulates conversation along predetermined lines.[20] The human person remains elusive. Again in Duara's words, in understanding a human person, we face 'the double challenge of thinking theoretically while remaining aware that every interpretation seeks to close a source whose generativity is inexhaustible'.

So, listening and mission are, and can only be, acts of love. We listen, and can only listen, in the concrete. Oliver O'Donovan's analysis of the love-command is helpful. 'Who is my neighbour?' (Luke 10.29). The neighbour is contingent; so the love-command cannot be rendered in terms of an undifferentiated 'respect for persons' or 'equal regard':

[Jesus' response in the Parable of the Good Samaritan] counters the limiting structures of racial and communal proximities precisely by challenging them with a proximity of a different sort, the contingent nearness into which we constantly find ourselves thrown with all sorts of people.[21]

✳   ✳   ✳

I end with an observation about homosexuality. 'To commit ourselves to listen to the experience of homosexual persons and we wish to assure them that they are loved by God' (Resolution 1.10c) is a Christian radical act of discipleship if and only if this takes place in the concrete. It cannot be reduced into a diocesan, provincial or Communion-wide programme. We meet and listen in the concrete proximate relations: among our friends and family members not of our choosing. There we do not simply face a 'homosexual', as if he/she is part of a victimized class or a sociological unit. Still less do I and (he/she) know fully what homosexuality is about. Indeed, we can learn much from the medical sciences and other disciplines on what homosexuality is. Yet what often is ignored is that the homosexual experience may carry different meaning to different people in different places. How lexical meaning changes and is transformed across cultures and places is an issue of huge interest in historical studies. Similar efforts should take place in the listening within the Communion.

In the real world, we come to one another with legacies of sin and disorder, and bound in webs of injustices and wrongs. We come too with the divine promise and primal vision: '"The first man Adam became a living being"; the last Adam, a life-giving spirit . . . Flesh and blood cannot inherit the kingdom of God, nor does the perishable inherit the imperishable' (1 Corinthians 15.45, 50). In listening, we together take responsibilities for our journeys, and open ourselves to new ways of seeing our common lives.

There is still one wider challenge. Listening does not only take place in this time–space. We listen to the past, and have a duty to pass on to the future. The Psalmist declares: 'O my people, hear my teaching; listen to the words of my mouth . . . I will utter hidden things, things from of old – what we have heard and known, what our fathers have told us. We will not hide them from their children; we will tell the next generation the praiseworthy deeds of the LORD, . . . so the next generation would know them, even the children yet to be born, and they in turn would tell their children' (Psalm 78.1–4). Listening binds us to traditioning; the reflective transmission of the faith that was once delivered to the saints to our children's generation. In this age we often forget we are sons and daughters of our parents. Often we live as if there is no tomorrow. If listening is an act of love that always hopes (1 Corinthians 13.7), Christians would do well to listen too to their forebears and recover their sense of confidence in the world – that God will continue to work his purposes out through the Church for the sake of the world. There is a bright future for Christianity, and so for the world. The present malaise in the Communion, to borrow Weigel's words, is 'a failure of self-confidence'. 'That broader failure is no less surely tied to a collapse of faith in the God of the Bible.'[22] This failure is expressed, Weigel laments, in the failure among Europeans to create a successor generation! Do Anglicans today have the confidence to commend our own faith to our children? How can we be deaf to the cries of children from broken homes and marriages when we claim we can hear the pleas from homosexuals?

We return to the challenges Weigel poses at the beginning of this essay. What are our grounds for mission and listening? Listening and mission are rooted in the incarnation of the Word. The late fourth-century church fathers discovered this soteriological principle in the discussion on the Person of Jesus Christ: 'What is not assumed is not saved.' Listening and mission flow out of this Christological understanding of personhood. Without this anchor, our listening and mission would be in a sorry state. The listening *project* would be like the last rites attendant on the passing of the Christian era, hailing the goddess of human rights from afar: 'Behold, the cube of human rights, *salvator mundi*! The cube must increase, the cathedral decrease' (contra John 1.29, 3.30).

Dear Ian,

We share many concerns in our essays. I agree with you that listening must be underpinned by missiological reflections. Again, the shifts in mission theology and ecclesiastical terrains in the second half of the twentieth century need more attention within the Communion. I agree with you too that the mystery of Incarnation holds the key to working our way forward in what it means to 'listen to the experience of homosexual persons'.

At the same time, I invite you to explore beyond the horizons within which you place your analysis. I am unsure whether the global-local paradigm offers a helpful way in seeing the plights in the present world. Identity politics also put people within a geopolitical, socio-economical and gender-political grid. But that homogenizes people. A human person defies social representations. Your illustration of the meeting between an American lay lesbian and an African bishop in an inter-Anglican gathering is revealing. Both might have a better feel of the other. But I wonder whether you would wish for more concrete outcome. The settings of the meeting – an inter-Anglican gathering – are rare and artificial. Each may return home with the warm feeling that despite their differences they still belong to the 'Anglican Communion'. They may still live in their worlds, entrapped by their social identities. This is why in my essay I avoided using the word 'local' – which may carry the nuance of being 'limited'. I prefer the word 'concrete'.[23] Listening needs to take place in the concrete. There we are called to build a common home; and in doing so rediscover that the 'differences' are in fact 'distinctives' – broken and yet charismatic – for promoting the common welfare. Indeed, the concrete is where the tensions between local and global, and conflicts between social representations are resolved. The concrete discloses the universal and binds us to personal responsibilities. In loving and listening to our neighbour, in becoming committed to rebuild a world together, we love Jesus.

I invite you too to go deeper in our levels of communion. Your interpretation of Christ is revealing: 'In Christ the seemingly irreconcilable identities of one who is fully human and fully God have been brought together in a reconciled reality for the redemption of the world.' The point is how this statement should be interpreted. The Chalcedonian definition understood Christ as 'one Person *in* two natures'. The unity of Christ is not to be sought in the sphere of nature, but in the Person. This Christological understanding invites us to understand Christ – and the world – not primarily in the worlds of identities. We do not simply live in our own virtual worlds. If we can rediscover all differences are distinctives, and that there is a face that defies social and historical categorization behind every meeting, then listening would indeed be acts of love that draw us closer to the God who meets us face to face.[24]

Your brother in Christ,

Michael

Advent 1, 2007

Response by Ian T. Douglas to Michael Nai-Chiu Poon's:

'Mission is Antitheoretical: Listening and the Disclosing of the Primal Vision'

Dear Michael:

It is an honour and a pleasure to be asked to respond to your article: 'Mission is Antitheoretical'. Reading your paper, I am intellectually and missiologically enlivened and challenged by your words. At the same time I am drawn more deeply into the experience of listening to you as an Anglican Christian brother who speaks powerfully and honestly out of a context so very different from my own. The opportunity to engage you in person through our exchange of papers is not only an act of listening but also, I would argue, an act of mission. So I thank God and I thank you for this opportunity.

I so much appreciate your opening affirmation that 'listening and mission are ways in which the Christian community engages the world.' I agree with you completely on this point. Too often the radical acts of listening and mission are divorced from the everyday realities in which we Christians live and instead are domesticated within the inner life of the Church. In this later sense listening becomes a nice cover for some nice Christians to talk with other nice Christians in the hopes of creating a nice church where we can all just get along. In such a domesticated ecclesial-centric understanding of listening the radical call to conversion, being turned inside out by God in Jesus Christ in the power of the Holy Spirit for the sake of a hurting and divided world, is avoided in our efforts to make 'nice.' Similarly when mission becomes primarily about the Church, the radical call to proclaim and serve a crucified Christ in the pain and hurt of the world is easily overlooked. So, thank you for making the point that listening and mission are for the sake of the world first and not primarily for the sake of the Church.

In your review of the *missio Dei,* you probably will not be surprised that I take some exception to your conclusions that such a missiology can be interpreted along transcendental lines and is prone to ideological shaping. These conclusions might be true if the *missio Dei* lacks a well-developed Trinitarian foundation. But any sound Christian *missio Dei* missiology must contend with the fact that God became fully human in Jesus who lived, died and rose again for the sake of the world. The miracle of God's mission in Jesus is that what God did uniquely in a first century wandering Aramaic speaking Jew has universal implications for all people in all contexts through history, today, and into the future. And by the power of the Holy Spirit, the particularities of Jesus become our particularities in all of our various global contexts. So I would argue that a fully developed Trinitarian *missio Dei* missiology that is grounded in our particular flesh and blood realities undercuts a disembodied transcendentalism. At the same time our common participation in God's mission in Jesus through the Holy Spirit drives us, in all of our differences, into a larger universal Body of Christ, (the Church catholic) and thus challenges the sanctity of our contextual ideological proclivities.

In the end then, I am in full accord with your assertions that 'listening and mission are ways of being present in the real world in its broken and gifted experience' and 'can only be acts of love.' I hope and pray that our brief exchange here, as we speak out of the contextual particularities of Cambridge and Singapore in the hope of discovering a greater commonality in Christ, models the 'missiological significance of listening' for the sake of the world.

Your brother in Christ's mission,

Ian

Notes

1 Prasenjit Duara, 'Why is History Antitheoretical?', *Modern China*, 24.2 (1998), 105–20; John V. Taylor, *The Primal Vision: Christian Presence amid African Religion* (London: SCM, 1963).

2 George Weigel, 'The Cathedral and the Cube: Reflections on European Morale', *Commentary*, 117 (June 2004), 35. See also Andrew Targowski, 'Universal-Complementary Civilization as a Solution to Present-day Catastrophic International Conflicts', *Dialogue and Universalism*, 15.7–8 (2005), 73–99.

3 Duara, 'Why is History Antitheoretical?', 107. It is remarkable that the four instruments of unity are promoted as orthodoxy in the Anglican Communion, with the Archbishop of Canterbury as the focus of the Communion. The four instruments as *instruments* are of recent origin. Crises (like national crises) serve as an occasion for instilling the Communion (or state) ideology. Those who question such an account of Anglicanism (and of the state) are sometimes regarded as those who do not promote the common good of the Communion (or as unpatriotic).

4 Duara, 'Why is History Antitheoretical?', 107–9.

5 So take, for example, the issues we face in writing a history of a particular diocese or province. How do we decide which are the major events in the time-line? How do we label such events? How do we see our beginnings? How do we draw the continuities? Do we include the histories of other dioceses and other nations in our accounts? History is not merely a matter of adding information. There is no one true and exhaustive account to history.

6 Duara, 'Why is History Antitheoretical?', 118.

7 See also my criticism of Brian Stanley and Samuel Escobar in 'Till They Have Homes: Christian Responsibilities in the 21st Century', *Global South Anglican*, <www.globalsouthanglican.org/index.php/weblog/comments/till_they_have_homes>.

8 As a case in point, Paul A. Cohen is among those who have embraced a China-centred approach in writing China's history. See e.g. his discussion on the China-centred approach in *Discovering History in China: American Historical Writing on the Recent Chinese Past*, 2nd edn (New York: Columbia University Press, 1996), ix–xxiii, 149–98.

9 Quoted in Tormod Engelsviken, '*Missio Dei*: The Understanding and Misunderstanding of a Theological Concept in European Churches and Missiology', *International Review of Mission*, 92 (2003), 482.

10 See, e.g., S. R. Anderson and C. Stanley Smith, *The Anderson–Smith Report on Theological Education in Southeast Asia Especially as It Relates to the Training of Chinese for the Christian Ministry: The Report of a Survey Commission, 1951–1952* (New York: Board of Founders, Nanking Theological Seminary, 1952).

11 The East Asia Christian Conference Assembly was a main critic in the World Council of Churches' 1961 Delhi Assembly. K. H. Ting was a prime mover in advocating a more geocentric approach to mission during his time with the World Student Christian Federation in the early 1950s. See his unpublished draft, 'Missions in the Light of Ecumenism' in Yale Divinity School Library Special Collections, RG 42, Series III, Box 372, Folder 372. A revised version of the essay appeared as editorial 'The Missionary Concern of the W.S.C.F', *The Student World*, 45.1 (1952), 1–8. See also Harold E. Fey, 'Confessional Families and the Ecumenical Movement', in *The Ecumenical Advance: A History of the Ecumenical Movement*, vol. 2 1948–1968, ed. Harold E. Fey (London: SPCK, 1970), 115–42, esp. 126–8.

12 The Anglican Consultative Council, *Anglicans in Mission: A Transforming Journey. Report of MISSIO, the Mission Commission of the Anglican Communion*, eds Eleanor Johnson and John Clark (London: SPCK, 1999), 21.

13 Anglican Consultative Council, *Mission in a Broken World: Report of ACC–8 Wales 1990* (London: ACC, 1990), 101.

14 In this way, one imagines that a programme formulated at a central location can be implemented in all places. One only has to devise appropriate strategies at each locale to sell the same product. Cf. Oliver O'Donovan's essay, 'The Loss of a Sense of Place', in *Bonds of Imperfection: Christian Politics, Past and Present*, eds Oliver O'Donovan and Joan Lockwood O'Donovan (Grand Rapids: Eerdmans, 2004), 296–320. 'What has made mobility possible is technology, and technology creates homogeneity, since it depends upon mass-production of interchangeable parts; homogeneity in turn numbs our sense of how one place differs from another, and so weakens our connection with the place we belong to, our 'home' (296–7).

15 My purpose here is not to criticize those from the Southern Hemisphere who choose to reside and work in the West. The point is simply that their lives become detached from the ecclesiastical realities of their original homeland that once gave them the credibility to serve as theologians from that particular region. The theologies they produce (on topics relating to their original homeland) suffer from lack of concrete engagements with the present realities, and so become idealist and abstract.

16 Cf. Adrian Hastings' comment on America: 'What none of us anticipated at that time was that the gravest nationalist threat to Christianity by the late twentieth century might come from the United States, essentially a rehash of the traditional Christian imperialism of Western European countries. It is just the latest example of a self-appointed "chosen people" carrying forth a gospel message reshaped by its own values and bonded to its own political expansion.' 'The Clash of Nationalism and Universalism within Twentieth-Century Missionary Christianity', in *Missions, Nationalism, and the End of Empires*, ed. Brian Stanley (Grand Rapids: Eerdmans, 2003), 32.

17 Taylor, *The Primal Vision*, 197.

18 Taylor, *The Primal Vision*, 199.

19 R. O. Hall, *The Art of the Missionary: Fellow Workers with the Church in China* (London: SCM, 1942), 62, 65.

20 For example, how do we see the Anglican world? The post-missionary and post-colonial vectors continue to define Communion in terms of East–West/North–South exchanges, and brush aside the South–South interactions that have existed long before the end of the colonial and missionary era. The traditional Anglo-Catholic, evangelical and liberal traditions are no longer useful categories in understanding the present Communion. The term 'Global South' does not refer to a homogeneous reality; it is open to abuse.

21 Oliver O'Donovan, *Resurrection and the Moral Order: An Outline for Evangelical Ethics* (Grand Rapids: Eerdmans, 1986), 240. See his earlier remarks on moral learning: 'Whether in deliberation, in reflection or in abstract moral exploration, the consideration of particular cases involves learning about the moral law, which is to say, about the created order itself . . . The particular discloses to us aspects of the generic to which we have not previously been sensitive' (*Resurrection*, 191, 195).

22 Weigel, 'The Cathedral and the Cube', 38.

23 So I also avoid the term 'listening process'. It lends itself to becoming a programme implemented in controlled environment.

24 Cf. the title of C. S. Lewis's novel *Till we have Faces*.

Chapter 2

Listening and Dialogue

Janet Marshall and Charley Thomas

Introduction

Mission is the central theme of this book, as we noted earlier, and part of the common ground across divisions over sexuality. In addition, in the last chapter Michael Poon and Ian Douglas agreed that listening and mission are acts of love and 'ways in which the Christian community engages the world . . . ways of being present in the real world in its broken and gifted experience'. As we prepare to approach issues of sexuality, which will be the focus of the following sections, we do so in the light of the commitment of the bishops of the 1998 Lambeth Conference to 'listen to the experience of homosexual persons' and of ACC-13's commendation of mutual listening. In relation to both mission and sexuality, therefore, a central question is: 'How can we best listen to others and learn to dialogue with them?' This chapter is a very effective guide to the tasks of listening and dialogue written by two experienced practitioners.

Janet Marshall and **Charley Thomas** come from quite different parts of the Communion – Canada and Zambia respectively. In this chapter they provide guidance for those wanting to engage in listening and dialogue about difficult and controversial subjects. They offer some very useful ways of facilitating listening and dialogue processes. This help and down-to-earth advice comes from their extensive experience of facilitating listening processes, primarily for mission. The principles they offer us come from both a commitment to learning and also from practical experience. They can be applied to all kinds of situations and we hope you will be able to apply them whether you are running a Church Council or a Synod.

Listening and dialogue may seem easy but in reality it is something we often find very hard. Evidence for this is that there are countless training programs and consultants who make their living by helping people listen and speak to each other respectfully, honestly and constructively. It is even more difficult when what we are trying to talk about is a difficult or taboo subject, perceived as causing conflict, and when we speak from a variety of different cultures. Such is the case in our Anglican conversations about the place of gay and lesbian people in the life of the Church. The good news is that the necessary skills can be learnt and implemented even in the most difficult circumstances.

After introducing some biblical and theological reflections on the call to listen, the chapter highlights the challenge of cross-cultural listening. Particularly in relation to an issue like sexuality, we need to learn how to disagree in a loving, Christian manner, and here the example of Paul's advice to the Philippian church and some Mennonite principles are examined. An important distinction is then drawn between debate, on the one hand, and listening and dialogue on the other. Janet and Charley commend and focus on these last two as ways forward. To help with this they offer concrete, practical guidance on how to listen in a dialogue group in a receptive, encouraging and reflective manner. Such 'deep listening' helps us understand others and to speak for ourselves in the group. It also enables us to be hard on issues but soft on people. Good dialogue also requires good facilitation and so guidance is offered here on the role of the facilitator and the importance of agreed group norms. Tips are given as to how to facilitate well and how to respond to particular challenges that can arise. The final section focuses on how to encourage listening rather than dialogue, using the example of the 'Sharing Circle' from North American indigenous peoples.

This chapter precedes detailed discussion about sexuality because, as Christians, listening to God and to others is a fundamental Christian discipline and a basic expression of our faithfulness and love. It is one of the ways in which we obey the commandments to love the Lord our God with all our heart, mind, soul and strength and to love our neighbour as ourselves (Matthew 22.37–39).

As you read through this chapter and even more as you put its many principles and tips into practice, you may find helpful the following words from Dietrich Bonhoeffer, the distinguished German theologian writing about life in Christian community at another time of great conflict in the Church:

> The first service one owes to others in the community involves listening to them. Just as our love for God begins with listening to God's Word, the beginning of love for other Christians is learning to listen to them. God's love for us is shown by the fact that God not only gives us God's Word but also lends us God's ear. We do God's work for our brothers and sisters when we learn to listen to them. So often Christians, especially preachers, think that their only service is always to have to 'offer' something when they are together with other people. They forget that listening can be a greater service than speaking. Many people seek a sympathetic ear and do not find it among Christians, because these Christians are talking even when they should be listening. But Christians who can no longer listen to one another will soon no longer be listening to God either; they will always be talking even in the presence of God. The death of the spiritual life starts here, and in the end there is nothing left but empty spiritual chatter and clerical condescension which chokes on pious words. Those who cannot listen long and patiently will always be talking past others, and finally no longer will even notice it. Those who think their time is too precious to spend listening will never really have time for God and others, but only for themselves and their own words and plans.
>
> For Christians, pastoral care differs essentially from preaching in that here the task of listening is joined to the task of speaking the Word. There is also a kind of listening with half an ear that presumes already to know what the other person has to say. This impatient, inattentive listening regularly despises the other Christian and finally is only waiting to get a chance to speak and thus to get rid of the other. This sort of listening is no fulfilment of our task. And it is certain that here, too, in our attitude toward other Christians we simply see reflected our own relationship

to God. It should be no surprise that we are no longer able to perform the greatest service of listening that God has entrusted to us – hearing the confession of another Christian – if we refuse to lend our ear to another person on lesser subjects. The pagan world today knows something about persons who often can be helped only by having someone who will seriously listen to them. On this insight it has built its own secular form of pastoral care, which has become popular with many people, including Christians. But Christians have forgotten that the ministry of listening has been entrusted to them by the One who is indeed the great listener and in whose work they are to participate. We should listen with the ears of God, so that we can speak the Word of God.[1]

Loving God and Others Requires Listening

As the people of God we are often asked to listen. Every time we gather as a community to worship we are invited to hear the good news of the gospel. We are called to listen intently to those life-giving texts that build our relationship with God and others. We listen to sermons and to the teaching of our scholars and spiritual leaders. Over and over again Scripture bids us listen: 'Let anyone with ears, listen' (Luke 14.35). We listen to grow in understanding and faith.

Historically as a Communion our listening has been selective. Our Church has a long history of blocking voices from being heard. The churches of the Global South repeatedly complained of not being heard through the Partners in Mission process of the 1970s and 1980s and this is a situation that sadly continues to this day. The list of the excluded is long: it has included the voices of children, youth, women, the elderly, ethnic minorities, gay men, lesbian women and their families and friends, single people, widows, orphans, single parents, prisoners and ex-prisoners, people with physical or mental disabilities and the silent – either those who have no forum for expression or those who choose to be silent. These voices and perspectives are too easily overlooked or not heard.

> People were bringing little children to him in order that he might touch them; and the disciples spoke sternly to them. But when Jesus saw this, he was indignant and said to them, 'Let the little children come to me; do not stop them; for it is to such as these that the kingdom of God belongs.' (Mark 10.13–14)

Christ through his ministry among us reached out to make relationships with those who were silenced and marginalized.

We are complicit in creating a culture of silence when we withhold acceptance of or permission to express views which challenge our Christian cultural norms. We are complicit when we accept the suppression or the silencing of diverse or different voices. When we choose to suppress our true selves, our silence becomes a sacrificial guilt offering to a Church that will not listen.

> 'You shall love the Lord your God with all your heart, and with all your soul, and with all your mind.' This is the greatest and first commandment. And a second is like it: 'You shall love your neighbour as yourself.' On these two commandments hang all the law and the prophets. (Matthew 22.37–40)

Loving as you love yourself presupposes existing love of oneself. Love of self does not, however, excuse blindness to the ways we have fallen short of God's will for us. We have all fallen short of the glory of God, we are sinners together. We need more sinners to join us in our churches – that together we may be challenged to live out that honest and healthy love of self and love of our neighbour. Only thus can we most fully offer ourselves to Christ's transforming love.

Listening to those whose difference challenges us is an act of Christian love. In order to listen fully to one another, with open hearts and minds, we all must be willing to lay aside our presuppositions and judgemental attitudes. This letting go is a sign of our love, our humility and repentance. Listen to the words of our Saviour Jesus Christ: 'I give you a new commandment, love one another. If you have love for one another, then the world will know that you are my disciples' (John 13.35).

Jesus and the Canaanite Woman

Just then a Canaanite woman from that region came out and started shouting, 'Have mercy on me, Lord, Son of David; my daughter is tormented by a demon.' But he did not answer her at all. And his disciples came and urged him, saying, 'Send her away, for she keeps shouting after us.' He answered, 'I was sent only to the lost sheep of the house of Israel.' But she came and knelt before him, saying, 'Lord, help me.' He answered, 'It is not fair to take the children's food and throw it to the dogs.' She said, 'Yes, Lord, yet even the dogs eat the crumbs that fall from their masters' table.' Then Jesus answered her, 'Woman, great is your faith! Let it be done for you as you wish.' And her daughter was healed instantly (Matthew 15.22–28).

Here we have an example of a brief dialogue between Jesus and someone marginalized both by her sex and her cultural identity as a Gentile. This encounter and Jesus' reaction to the woman's challenge, challenge us in turn in our encounters with difference and diversity.

At first, Jesus does not respond to the woman, despite the fact that she is shouting for him. His first reaction is to disregard her. It is only through her persistence that Christ begins to pay attention, despite the disciples' encouragement to send her away, but the conversation is not easy. Coloured by cultural judgement and condemnation, Jesus calls her a 'dog' – not simply a person less worthy than the people of Israel, but someone less than human. Nevertheless, the woman persists through reproach and insult because she understands and trusts in the power of God's mercy. The resulting exchange reveals Jesus as a leader of humility, courage and transforming mercy. Through listening and dialogue Jesus recognizes the veracity of the woman's faith despite all that should keep her separate from him. The result is an encounter that overcomes prejudice and, even more significantly, leads to the expansion of Jesus' own sense of the limits to his ministry. Breaking with tradition, Jesus reaches beyond his own sense of purpose for his ministry, defined as: 'I was sent only to the lost sheep of the house of Israel'. He risks his reputation by engaging the Canaanite woman in dialogue and in so doing, points to a future where 'Israel's Messiah will ultimately bring blessing to the whole world'.[2]

Here is a model for us. Such mutual listening, though opposed at that time by the disciples, sets the stage for their future cross-cultural mission. Jesus' example reveals how by listening it is possible both to serve and to lead. This might define our ministries as we overcome any significant prejudice we might hold against those to whom we listen.

In similar ways to the Canaanite woman, the silenced or marginalized people within our churches continue to seek our attention and try to bring their voices into dialogue. Despite years of prejudice, marginalization or worse, they persist in asking the Church to hear and to respond to their voices. Christ shows himself willing to extend the boundaries of his ministry in response to the faith of the stranger, and this is a challenge to our churches.

As Anglicans we are responsible to one another, linked through service and leadership. We are not called to protect ourselves and remain in our safe comfort zones. Rather we are called to step out in faith, into the unknown, following in the apostolic tradition, confident of our relationship with Christ. In our world today – where we easily cross continents and cultures – we encounter God in others: people speaking to us differently, unexpectedly and from unfamiliar places. Our mission leads us to listen and respond.

These encounters can be difficult and challenging. We need to learn to listen to each other in an attitude of Christian love. We do not need to agree. We do not need to accept all we hear from one another. We do need to learn to agree and disagree in love: to struggle with each other, as Jesus and the Canaanite woman did, and through this struggle, be open to the unexpected.

So in listening and responding to those who are different from us we are called to an inclusive, humble, servant leadership. The Anglican orders of deacon, priest and bishop are a model that reminds us that all who have been ordained remain deacons no matter what additional responsibilities may be given. The servanthood and humble leadership of the deacon is not just a liturgical expression, but a lifestyle demanded of us, even within the exercise of priestly or episcopal office. This lifestyle includes listening and building bridges within our Anglican Communion, ecumenically and between churches and those on the margins.

Mission and Listening Across Cultures

The God of mission is a God of justice, a listening God who listens to those in trouble (Psalm 116.1). Listening is an essential mission activity. Mission is to reach out to the world with the love of Christ in word and deed. For many years the focus of mission was to reach out to other cultures. In the process we were challenged to listen to contextual voices from those cultures and to seek to communicate a relevant gospel. We were challenged when we listened.

Today our mission activity is challenged to participate with God in listening to the voices of our own context and that of our neighbours. These voices include those of youth, orphans, widows, people living with AIDS, people of diverse sexual orientation, and the differently-abled. As the Anglican Communion we have responded to many of these challenges, especially that of HIV-AIDS, not enquiring about source or cause. We simply respond in love.

At the request of Lambeth 1998, we are being called to listen to the voices of homosexual persons, and we encourage you also to listen to them, their family members, and others who care about them. These are Anglicans who have suffered discrimination, exclusion, physical abuse and mental anguish. As we consider how to respond we will disagree and we know only too well the destructive potential of these disagreements: destructive potential for our personal relationships, for our churches and dioceses, for the Anglican Communion, and the relationships and reputation of our Anglican Church in the wider world. Therefore, in accepting the bishops' request, we take up the responsibility to listen and speak with one another with respect, opening our hearts and minds truly to hear each other and in these encounters discern God's guidance.

Listening: A Story of Testimony and Cultural Challenge

At a training centre in Africa, a volunteer from the West testified during Chapel. She spoke of how her father had left her mother, for a man friend, and how she herself was struggling with her sexual orientation. She said this tearfully and with much pain.

The congregation – which included over twenty clergy – took the training centre to task and demanded to know their position on the 'gay and lesbian issue'; and why the pulpit was being used for the promotion of homosexuality. In response, the centre administration asked how many clergy had spoken to the volunteer, counselled her or prayed with her. None had.

The use of the pulpit for testimony was a common practice at the centre. This particular testimony, however, upset them because it was a cry for help and a plea for acceptance, rather than a thanksgiving. It was the testimony of a hurting person struggling with her sexuality and spirituality. The presuppositions and judgemental attitude of the clergy needed a divine intervention.

The question the leadership posed to the angry congregation was: 'Can the testimony of those who distress us be part of God's work among us?' After an open discussion, there was more pastoral openness in accepting the person, even though people's positions regarding homosexuality had not changed. The listening process challenges our pastoral response.

This example of cross-cultural testimony is a reflection of what many in our churches are experiencing at this time within the Communion. The story emphasizes the necessity for our cultures to create successful listening experiences. Every culture occupies a particular place in the world. Each place is a product of particular history and geography, a product of the struggles and successes, of faiths, politics and institutions that co-exist, as well as the nexus of relationships within which the people of that culture live.

Our particular culture determines our perspective, and forms the basis from which we build assumptions and stereotypes of others. How we understand what we see, hear and experience is shaped not only by what is there to be seen and heard, but also by the cultural perspective from which we view it. There is no view from nowhere.

Between cultures attitudes differ widely. A North American will perceive a testimonial disclosing personal issues of sexuality differently from an African. However, both may be comfortable with the concept of testimony. Someone from another culture may not have an issue with the sexuality, but with the concept of someone laying himself or herself emotionally bare in such a format. Within cultures there will be differences also. It cannot be assumed that any culture does not have its own unbreakable rules. It is sometimes argued that North Americans have an 'anything goes' culture, but this is not true. For example, in North America regulations or even laws exist which prohibit employers dating employees and priests from dating parishioners. Such things are counted as sexual harassment in the workplace and regarded as sin. In other cultures a congregation might look with joy on a single man or woman becoming engaged and married to a parishioner.

Agreeing and Disagreeing in Love

In order to listen to one another with respect, honesty and integrity – to open one's heart and mind to hear both those with whom we agree and those with whom we profoundly disagree – we need to be able to agree and disagree in love. This is easier said than done, but in Scripture we find guidance to help us remember that this is something we can do as Christians, following the example of Christ. The following is a set of commitments developed by the Mennonite Church to help us embrace the attitude and practice of agreeing and disagreeing in love.[3]

'Making every effort to maintain the unity of the Spirit in the bond of peace' (Ephesians 4.1) both as individuals and as the body of Christ, we pledge we shall . . .

In thought:

Accept conflict	Acknowledge that conflict is a normal part of our life in the church. *Romans 14.1–8, 10–12, 17–19; 15.1–7*
Affirm hope	Affirm that as God walks with us in conflict, we can work through to growth. *Ephesians 1.15–16*
Commit to prayer	Admit our needs and commit ourselves to pray for a mutually satisfactory solution (no prayers for my success or for the other to change but to find a joint way). *James 5.16*

In action:

Go to the other . . .	Go directly to those with whom we disagree; avoid behind-the-back criticism. *Matthew 5.23–24; 18.15–20*
In the spirit of humility	Go in gentleness, patience and humility. Place the problem between us at neither doorstep and own our part in the conflict instead of pointing out the others'. *Galatians 6.1–5; Philippians 2*

Be quick to listen	Listen carefully, summarize and check out what is heard before responding. Seek as much to understand as to be understood. *Proverbs 18.13; James 1.19*
Be slow to judge	Suspend judgements, avoid labelling, end name calling, discard threats and act in a non-defensive, non-reactive way. *Romans 2.1–4; Galatians 5.22–26*

Reconciliation in the Philippian Community

In the Christian community in Philippi we read of two significant leaders in dispute. Paul urges the Christian community to work proactively to bring the two women together in order to seek resolution and reconciliation (Philippians 4.2–3). They are to resolve their own conflict with the aid of a facilitator and Paul does not impose a solution from outside. His solutions to the problems of division in Philippi are those of the Mennonites outlined above. He accepts that there is conflict, he knows that both names are written in the book of life – thus affirming hope – and he prays for the community. He tells them to go to one another (for which blogging and internet debates are no substitute) and he commends the spirit of humility as the way of Jesus Christ. They are to listen to one another without arguing and should consider the interests of others, being slow to judge.

Dialogue, Debate and the Role of Expertise

In order to engage with each other helpfully when addressing an issue as significantly contentious as our current disagreements concerning the place of gay and lesbian people in the life of the Church, we first need to recognize the effect different methods of engagement might have on relationships in our communities. We need to ask ourselves how the ways we engage in moral argument can sustain our communities both at home and within the wider Communion. How might these discussions instead fracture us or undermine the possibility of community? To address these questions, we need to look at the differences between dialogue and debate and how each might affect community life and relationships.

Debate and dialogue are two very different types of process. While both strive to clarify meaning and reveal truth, our churches tend to privilege debate. When faced with the need to address a difficult subject, we more often talk about 'debating the issue'. Synods and parish vestries and annual meetings are styled as parliamentary debates. We seem to feel more confident when we believe we are working out our differences in what appears to be a rational, intellectual forum. However, in this chapter another way of addressing our differences is being encouraged – dialogue.[4]

In dialogue there is a capacity to share a more full and inclusive account of a community's moral struggle. Community relationships, even in the most fractious of environments, can be respected and upheld within dialogue. Debates are oppositional. Disputes in the argument are fuelled by conflicts and disagreements within a community and are often rooted in misunderstandings of a truth. Each side seeks to create a persuasive version of the truth, amassing evidence in ways that make the best case, in order to persuade others of its veracity. Debaters then attempt to clarify truth by glossing over what is erroneous, inadequate or incomplete. Debates offer discernment through persuasion.

At their best, debates acknowledge that no one side may have a complete understanding of meaning or account of both meaning and truth. However, through a disciplined process of intellectual argument, debaters aim to achieve a more trustworthy account of both. At its best, this process gleans a greater overall sense of the truth from the input of all participants in the process.

But when sustaining community within the context of a complex and conflicted argument about its moral life is at stake, debating is problematic, particularly as a single mode of discourse. Debating encourages us to believe that our problems, no matter how complex, have solutions. By clarifying what is true or right, the conflict will be resolved. The volumes that have been written on the subject, the current history of our Church, and the thirty years of debate about homosexuality that have taken place in the Communion (as well as the content of this book) taken together raise serious doubts that a solution is on the horizon waiting to be debated into shape.

Even more troublesome, the primary goal of the debater is to persuade – to win the argument – rather than to work with others to discern a more complete meaning and truth. The effect of trying to persuade others of our perception of truth is to incite those who disagree with us to gather more evidence to support their argument. Sides become entrenched, and volley information back and forth at each other without any sign of heightened understanding or resolution. Debate discourages the search for greater understanding and the prayerful watching for the work of the Spirit amongst us. In debate, we are more likely to stand our ground poised to attack with the next piece of rhetoric or the next study that affirms what we already believe.

Debates elevate assertion, suspicion, competition and partisan affiliations. Those identifying with the winning side will certainly comply with any resulting decisions. The losers will be faced with unenviable choices: compliance with something they feel is wrong, or withdrawal from the community, or becoming entrenched in a longer-term process of protest. There is also a risk of those on the losing side becoming further marginalized, silenced and excluded from their communities, and sometimes being persecuted.

In practice then, debates have a tendency to take little account of community. All too often, debates are experienced as a process resulting in winners and losers, with no allowance for the middle ground of opinion. The result is the alienation and fragmentation of communities.

Dialogue is a process of discourse where people learn to talk and think together. Theologian Martin Buber used the word dialogue in 1914 to describe 'true turning to one another',[5] the purpose of dialogue is to identify common meaning, insight and understanding. With dialogue, disagreements are seen as being rooted in the nature of relationships within the community and how the community responds to these relationships. As such, the discernment of truth, meaning and the moral good is work that needs to be done within communities of people who are able to think together: to listen, to learn, to speak.

At its best, dialogue invites people into a disciplined process of challenging listening and discussion that respects both the intellectual and emotional dimensions of community life.

The larger story of communities feeds dialogue: the history, the stories of those who have lived before us, the knowledge and witness of current experience, people's hopes and concerns for those unborn – all these are part of dialogue. Dialogue builds up community because it is cast in terms of listening with sensitivity to the voices of many. It pays attention to community and to relationships, building ownership of the products of its process of discernment.

The rational process of debate can be faulted for over-privileging the persuasive speaker and the intellectual approach. It can be exclusive of all except expert opinion; dialogue can sometimes be faulted for over-privileging experience and failing to ensure intellectual rigour. Dialogue has been used as a forum for voices and perspectives that often go unheard within debate, sometimes to the exclusion of experts. Similarly, experts sometimes choose not to participate, eschewing dialogue as a soft approach which undervalues the status of their offering. Neither option on its own is healthy or helpful.

Dialogue must engage the best of critical thinking – encouraging and inviting scholars and experts to come to the table: to listen, talk and learn together. In this way, dialogue recognizes that many types of expertise are needed for community discernment. A variety of experts, each providing their own particular perspectives and witness, can achieve as full an accounting as possible.

Eyewitnesses provide expertise through their first-hand experience of life as gay or lesbian people, as do their families, friends and colleagues, their parish priests and even their bishop. Character witnesses are able to attest to the effects of particular situations and decisions on the lives of people and their cultures, on the community and its relationships, on our churches and the wider Communion. Academic expert witnesses bring scholarly and intellectual expertise to help us interpret Scripture, history, and the other texts and sciences that inform the discussion.

Successful dialogue will often begin with participants preparing themselves for the discussion. This preparation includes a time of prayer, reflection and learning, and events might include a Eucharist, reading Scripture and prayer. Some dioceses have held learning sessions, hosted by their bishop, where experts in fields such as biblical scholarship, medicine or psychology, make presentations and are available for question and answer sessions. Two credible and trustworthy experts, are invited from each field, each representing a different opinion of how the texts or data is interpreted, thus an honest accounting of differences is presented. This book explores information and opinion similar to that, which would be presented in these sessions. Reading it could be another way to prepare for dialogue.

The challenge to those who facilitate dialogue is to invite all, recognizing that each participant, no matter how learned or able they may be, will bring their particular perspective, which can be informed or enhanced through dialogue with others. The challenge to those who dialogue is to recognize that no single expert, regardless of their expertise, has the solution. We are not used to this type of exchange where as participants we need to accept with humility that only God alone has true perspective. That gift has been granted to none of us. In order to find our best way forward we need to suspend any convictions that our stance might be unerringly true, and really believe in our need of the insights of others. We will be asked to re-examine our assumptions, to re-evaluate our opinion of those who disagree with us, and to look again at the validity of how we characterize our differences.

> God chose what is foolish in the world to shame the wise; God chose what is weak in the world to shame the strong. (1 Corinthians 1.27)

In order to do this healthfully and helpfully dialogue, like debate, requires rules of discourse. Standards need to be set to define what is acceptable and unacceptable in discussion. An experienced facilitator is required, a person able, through skill and impartiality, to create an atmosphere for fair and productive listening and discussion. Taking into account the existence of different models for dialogue and discussion from the diversity of cultures in the Anglican Communion, the following sections of this chapter present one such model and guide for convening, participating in and facilitating dialogue sessions.

Participating in Dialogue

Listening

Effective dialogue begins with the participants' ability to listen to each other. Listening is a skill and a discipline, and like other disciplines listening requires self-control.

- To be a good listener we have to put our own needs on hold and concentrate our attention on others.
- As a skill, listening is only effective when it involves both hearing and understanding that which is being said.
- To listen effectively we take in both the content and the emotions being communicated by the speaker: we hear the whole message – from the mind and the heart.

This is what is called active or deep listening. Hearing becomes listening only when we exercise the discipline of our undivided attention and develop our skills of actively listening and attending to the whole of what is being said.

> In everything do to others as you would have them do to you; for this is the law and the prophets. (Matthew 7.12)

At its most basic, deep listening is simply putting Jesus' commandment into practice as you listen to others. It helps us to live this ministry by listening to others, as we would have them listen to us. Reciprocal and respectful, it invites open and honest engagement with matters of importance.

Through this type of listening we are able to share the gift of our pastoral and intellectual curiosity with others, whether we agree with them or not. In a listening process or a listening group we also ask this of others as we share our own thoughts, ideas, beliefs and stories. We seek insight from others and we ask that others seek insight from us. As such it is only through active listening that successful dialogue becomes possible.

A good listener tries to understand thoroughly what the other person is saying. In the end he may disagree sharply, but before he disagrees, he wants to know exactly what it is he's disagreeing with. (Kenneth A. Wells)

Listening as a Participant in a Group

Here are some guides for listening in a group.

To listen as actively as I can:

- I do not participate in side conversations.
- I never interrupt the person who is speaking.
- I turn off all electronic equipment (cell phones, computers, pagers, BlackBerries, etc.) and put them away.
- I show my interest in the speaker through my posture and facial expressions.
- I keep my expression and posture interested, engaged and calm, even when I very strongly agree – or disagree – with the speaker.
- When it is my turn to speak, I first demonstrate how I have listened to others by paraphrasing what they have said. I do this using my own words and ask 'Have I understood you correctly?' when I have finished my paraphrase.
- I avoid making statements that suggest or assert that I completely understand what another is saying.
- If anyone in the group behaves in ways that block or impede listening, I support the group facilitator as they ask for these behaviours to stop.

This means that as an active or deep listener in a dialogue we will be *receptive, encouraging, and reflective*. We will strive for understanding of others in the group and take responsibility for our own behaviours and thoughts during the dialogue. Let us look at these behaviours in more detail.

To be a *receptive* listener:

- I adopt a comfortable and open posture and facial expression.
- I avoid crossing my arms.
- I avoid judgemental or confrontational body language – pointing fingers, shaking fingers, pursing lips or scowling.
- If culturally appropriate I look at the speaker and make eye contact if the speaker looks at me.
- I avoid closing my eyes and I do not fall asleep.

As an encouraging listener I will help draw the speaker out. This is a particularly helpful and pastoral approach with those who are shy, reticent, or unaccustomed to being given the opportunity to speak in this type of process.

To be an *encouraging* listener:

- I sit forward, leaning slightly towards the speaker.
- I keep an open facial expression, occasionally smile or nod my head. This way I can affirm that a person is contributing without necessarily affirming what the person is saying.
- I ask for more information. I can ask a speaker if they could say more about what they are thinking to help me understand.
- I thank the previous speaker before I begin to speak.

As a reflective listener I will show my understanding of how others are feeling. I will appreciate the emotional effect of the conversation on my fellow participants, and in doing so, help them evaluate their own feelings after hearing them reflected back to them.

To be a *reflective* listener:

- I can acknowledge the speaker's feelings or the emotional state of the group. For example: 'You seem very upset . . .' 'You seem to care a great deal about . . .'
- I can also reflect the emotions of the whole group. For example: 'As a group we seem to be finding this very difficult.' 'I am sensing that the group is very frustrated. Am I right about this?'

To strive for *understanding*.

I can paraphrase in order to check my interpretations and perceptions of what is being said by others. I can:

- Restate facts and ideas shared by others. This is particularly helpful when trying to add to a discussion that was begun by others in the group.
- Remember to observe and name the emotions being shown or shared when paraphrasing.
- Paraphrase using my own words. This is always more effective than merely parroting back what a person has said.
- When paraphrasing, it is very helpful to conclude with a question to those I am paraphrasing such as 'Did I get that right?' This affirmation from a previous speaker is a public acknowledgement that I am listening effectively.

I can also ask for clarification to seek better understanding of what is being said. I can:

- Ask questions, framing them so they focus on my perceptions and understanding of what was said rather than asking people directly what they mean by . . . This will invite clarification without putting the person on the defensive. For example: 'I heard . . . do I understand you correctly?' not 'Did you mean to say . . . ?' or 'I am not clear about what you meant when you said . . . ?' rather than 'You weren't very clear . . . '
- Address these types of questions to individual speakers or to the whole group. For example: 'I am hearing that as a group we are saying . . . does this mean?' rather than 'We agree that . . .'

To take *responsibility*:

Finally, as an effective listener I will also show self-awareness in what I add to the dialogue. I will take personal responsibility for my ideas, thoughts and feelings. I can:

- Use 'I' statements. Speak only for myself and not for others in the group.
- Uphold the standards of intellectual credibility by being precise rather than vague. For example: 'I think that . . .' rather than 'Many people say . . .' or 'My research has found that . . .' rather than 'The research says . . .'
- Acknowledge my feelings. For example: 'I am finding this very difficult . . .' 'I feel angry when . . .' 'I rejoice that . . .'

There are three basic problems in human communications that 'I'-statements help overcome: *credibility, trust and respect*.

Being Hard on the Issues, Soft on the People

Taking ownership for your own ideas and thoughts builds credibility in the content of the dialogue. Appealing to the beliefs and ideas of others generally may feel as though you are rallying an argument with more weight behind it than your own ideas alone; however, when you say 'many people think . . .' or 'someone I know said . . .' you are merely being vague. People who already agree with you will continue to do so, but others will not be convinced.

Being precise is especially important when speaking from a perspective of scholarly expertise. Expert participants can give an important gift to a dialogue, inviting the group to hold themselves to higher standards of critical thinking and discernment by making careful distinctions between what is accepted as fact, what is still open to debate, and what is the participant's own best opinion – which may or may not be right.

I-statements build trust within a group. When you demonstrate honest and open self-awareness, people are more likely to believe that you are able to understand them, too. Speaking for oneself helps sustain a respectful dialogue by avoiding statements that sound accusatory or blaming. Statements such as 'You think that . . .' or 'You seem to believe . . .' may result in the listener becoming defensive and argumentative.

Group participants who take ownership for themselves invite others to do the same. Authentic and credible listening and dialogue happens within groups where each participant speaks from their own perspective and each is heard.

There will be times when as a member of the group you will feel the need to challenge ideas expressed within a dialogue. There are ways of doing this without closing down the group or alienating participants. This requires challenging the issues without criticizing or judging people.

Begin by stating how you are feeling about the issue you are finding difficult. This way you acknowledge up front its effect on you. For example: 'I am very upset by the idea/belief/opinion that . . .' or 'I find it very difficult to hear that . . .'

Then focus on the problems you have with the issue, rather than the person. For example: 'I am troubled by what I am hearing you say . . .' rather than 'You are a heretic to believe something like that . . .' or 'you are homophobic to believe . . . .'

As you are speaking, avoid directly addressing the person or people with whom you disagree. Instead address your comments to the facilitator. Another idea is to imagine putting the issue being discussed in the middle of the group, rather than locating it with specific people, and address your comments to the centre of the group. This also sets up a helpful dynamic for the dialogue as it models how these difficult conversations are the work of the whole dialogue group, not simply the particular individuals who at this point are actively disagreeing with each other.

Sometimes there are cultural issues that do not allow for some dialogue member's ideas to be challenged openly. For example, in some cultures it is considered impolite for a younger person to disagree with what is said by an elder. You will need to rely on the facilitator to help the group find sensitive and appropriate ways to draw out all opinions.

Cultural Practices

It is important to recognize that different cultures will have very different practices of social interaction: that which is polite or rude, acceptable or unacceptable, hospitable or excluding. If participating in, or facilitating, a multicultural or cross-cultural group, or a group whose culture is not your own, you will need to know these things and practise them within the group. Some social practices to be aware of are as follows.

- Making eye contact
- How close you stand to a person you are speaking with
- Volume of speech
- Cross-talk, and speaking over each other
- What to do with your hands
- Comfort with silence
- The need for group fellowship – the value of relationship building before beginning to dialogue

Facilitating Dialogue

Dialogues need a facilitator. Someone needs to take the role of managing the group interactions so that it functions effectively. Communication is complex at the best of times. There are many challenges to our ability to communicate effectively with each other. Language and cultural differences can make it extraordinarily difficult to achieve communication that is clear and mutually understood across cultures. Within cultures, status, class, gender, age, etiquette, social protocols, and taboos can make communication very difficult. A good facilitator is essential to help a dialogue group listen and speak together as openly and effectively as possible.

The social constraints affecting how we communicate may frustrate us, but working in ways that challenge these constraints may feel very uncomfortable. The challenge is to acknowledge this discomfort and find ways of facilitating conversation that alleviate resentment. People may become resentful when asked to interact in ways other than those usually accorded to their status.

Setting up a dialogue includes preparing group members for open conversation that may challenge their sense of status. It is through skilful facilitation that this can be negotiated so that a group may become a place where people with different roles and status, and diverse beliefs and opinions, can share openly. For dialogue to be effective:

- It is possible for all participants to contribute.
- No single individual dominates the conversation.
- Different opinions are expressed and heard sensitively and respectfully especially when there are different age groups and genders in the group.
- The value of listening and dialogue is shared, helping mitigate the discomforts of the challenges of this type of process to people's status.
- Assumptions are allowed to surface and be tested.
- Mutual understanding is built.
- People feel heard.

What Does a Facilitator Do?

To understand facilitation it is important to see the two aspects to a group's interactions: content and process.

- Content is what is being discussed. It is all the thoughts, ideas, beliefs, data and feelings about the subject of the group's meeting.
- Process is how the subject is being discussed. It is the interaction itself: the methods used to generate and sustain listening, dialogue and decision-making. It is the format used for group interaction; it is the group dynamic.

A facilitator's responsibility is to manage the process – they are the process leader. Here are some guides for facilitating a dialogue.

- Stay neutral on the topic at hand. Do not express any opinions, ideas or information about the subject of the dialogue.
- Be impartial, showing no favouritism to any individual or stance. Do not take sides.
- Be responsible for how the group interact with each other, the structure and process of the dialogue.
- Help the group set and agree to norms and expectations for the dialogue. Then hold participants accountable to what they have agreed.
- Ensure that each dialogue member has the chance to speak, and that no one dominates the conversation.
- Never give advice or offer solutions to problems the group is facing.
- Ask questions for clarification.
- Restate, paraphrase and summarize what the group is saying, the ideas, facts and the feelings, regularly throughout the group discussion.
- Keep the group on topic and on track. Direct the group back to the topic when they are sidetracked.
- Help the group open up and test assumptions that are implied but not openly stated.
- Manage conflict when it arises.

Facilitation, like listening, is a skill with specific behaviours, tools and techniques that can be learned. These will help groups function well even when dealing with difficult and contentious issues. The following is a description of some of these behaviours and techniques.

Neutrality and impartiality

To be effective, a facilitator must be experienced and trusted not only by dialogue participants but also by the bishop or whoever is convening the dialogue process. This is the only way they will be able to manage the process without being seen as having a desired outcome other than effective dialogue itself. As someone with no personal stake in the outcome of the dialogue, and able to disregard personal opinions on the subject, a facilitator can operate effectively, eliciting assumptions, clarifying meanings and negotiating communication blocks.

A facilitator can establish their impartiality by letting the group know from the outset that they will not add any content to the discussion. Neither will they share ideas, beliefs, thoughts or feelings about the subject at hand with the group. They will however share thoughts and feelings about how the group process is going, and how participants are working together.

During the dialogue, the facilitator avoids all temptations to offer opinions on the topic being discussed; instead, they will ask open questions. This can be particularly helpful when attempting to bring assumptions to the surface and to clarify participants' meaning. For example:

'You have been using the word ＿＿ a lot to describe ＿＿ . I am not familiar with this. Can you help me understand what you mean?'

'Is it common for people to refer to ＿＿ as ＿＿ . Where does this come from?'

'You have talked about fearing that ＿＿ might happen if the church proceeds in this way. Tell me more about this – what specifically do you fear happening?'

The facilitator avoids becoming defensive, and does not become emotionally involved in the outcome of the group's work. The worst that can happen is that the group becomes unable to engage in dialogue. This may be because of an inappropriate choice of process for the group, and something else needs to be tried, or that the timing is not right for this kind of discussion. Either way, the facilitator's task is to name the situation and help the group decide how to move forward.

Place and space

One of the first and very practical responsibilities of a facilitator is to find a good and safe space for the dialogue group to meet. The location and layout of the meeting place will greatly affect group interaction.

The location of the group meetings needs to be safe and neutral. For example, holding the meeting in an office next to the bishop's office or within a church hall of a church that is well known for its stance on the subject will make it difficult for some to speak openly. Helpfully, in some cultures there will be a traditional meeting place, such as the Zambian *insaka*, where people come to hear each other.

The set-up of the room is important. Circles are often associated with listening and sharing. Use of a table may depend on the cultural norm. If the group is ready and willing to be open and vulnerable, a circle without a table can symbolize this.

Setting expectations

A facilitator needs to work with the dialogue group to establish appropriate expectations for the conversation they are about to have, both in terms of the scope of discussion and the effect it may have on participants. Much of this is done in preparation for the first meeting of the dialogue group, and at the beginning of the dialogue session. The bishop can be very helpful in setting expectations, showing support to the dialogue group in achieving them, and communicating both expectations and support widely.

A dialogue group has neither agenda nor minutes, but it does have a specified purpose and a question or a small set of questions that may help get the conversation started. The purpose and the questions to be addressed will be set clearly at the outset of the process. Often it is possible to communicate these to dialogue participants prior to the first meeting. The facilitator takes time at the start of the dialogue to ensure that all members of the group have a shared understanding of the purpose and goals of the process, making it clear that the key purpose is to listen actively and respectfully to each other – to ideas and thoughts as well as people's feelings. The basic principles of listening as a participant in dialogue (as outlined in the previous section) are reviewed.

If the conversation is likely to be difficult, the facilitator acknowledges this at the start of the process, and names what might be expected from a dialogue where people are going to disagree, or where people may bring diverse emotional responses to the table. For example:

'We can expect that this conversation will be very difficult for some people in this room and we will have different reactions to this.'

'We can expect that there may be times when our feelings and emotions get the better of us. We will need to pay attention to the emotional impact of our dialogue for some members of our group.'

Setting group norms

Group norms are a code of conduct that will guide people's behaviour during the dialogue. Established by the group itself at the beginning of a dialogue process they help create the conditions for full participation and build a co-operative and supportive climate for the conversation. Norms are set, noted, and agreed to by group members. Later the facilitator can make use of them should it become necessary, asking people to abide by their own rules for healthy conduct.

When establishing norms, a facilitator can ask each group member to identify what they need from the others in order to feel comfortable and to participate fully in this dialogue. They can ask what guidelines or rules should the group establish to help ensure that no one feels unable to participate openly and safely in the conversation? If this is an unfamiliar practice, the facilitator may start the group with a short list to discuss and add to. Some examples of norms are commitments to:

- listen actively to each other
- speak respectfully to each other
- speak only for ourselves using 'I' statements
- challenge issues, not people – there will be no personal attacks
- honour privacy and confidentiality – things shared within this room will stay within this room
- talk about differences calmly
- not participate in any recrimination, retaliation or repercussion outside of this room as a result of this conversation

The facilitator will write the list of possible rules or norms on paper and post it where the whole group can see it, asking the group if all can agree, and are willing to be held accountable to each norm. When the group has created its list of norms, they are asked to agree to abide by them, and when failing to do so, look to the facilitator to help them get back on track. The posted list is displayed for the whole group to read at each meeting of the dialogue group. We offer two examples.

Example 1. Guidelines for Discussion produced by the Human Sexuality Task Force, Diocese of Nova Scotia

- We expect that the full range of issues of human sexuality exists within the Church;
- We acknowledge that gay and lesbian persons are in the Church;
- We will always assume that gays or lesbians are present;
- While we disagree on issues we will use language which respects the dignity of others;
- We will respect the right of people to 'name' themselves and their experience;
- If we ask a question, we will be prepared to respond to it ourselves;
- We will respect people's privacy;
- We will respect people's integrity as people of faith.

Tips for applying these Guidelines

- Speak for yourself. Use 'I' statements. Avoid generalizations.
- Don't argue – but don't be obstinate either! (Don't defend a position just for the sake of argument.)
- Respect each other's sincerity.
- Discuss the issues. Don't name people outside the group.
- Don't interrupt – don't monopolize – encourage, but don't force others to speak.
- Use language of respect.

Example 2. Adapted from the Anglican Diocese of Toronto Dialogue Guidelines, 2004
The issues that will be discussed today are very personal. Some of us may well feel that the discussion touches on our very being and most deeply held beliefs. Some of

us may feel quite vulnerable from time to time. Some people have expressed concern at how safe they will be at these diocesan educational events. Those concerns are real and deserve to be addressed.

Our baptismal covenant calls on us to seek and serve Christ in all persons, loving our neighbours as ourselves. We have promised to strive for justice and peace among all people and to respect the dignity of every human being.

Each of us must tread carefully at these events, therefore, respecting sisters and brothers in Christ whose views do not coincide with our own. A wide spectrum of feelings and opinions will be voiced from the podium and in the conversations around us. We will hear views expressed with which we agree and views with which we may have real difficulty. The presenters are aware of these sensitivities and will conduct themselves accordingly. To help us make the most of today's gathering we all agree to honour the following group norms:

1. We will respect people's integrity as members of this community of faith.
2. We will assume that as people of faith we are all sincere in our beliefs, including our reverence for Holy Scripture.
3. We will assume that lesbian and gay persons are present.
4. We will not use language known to be offensive to others.
5. We will respect the right of people to 'name' themselves and their experiences.
6. We will ask no questions that we are not prepared to answer ourselves.
7. We will speak in the first person.
8. We will respect the privacy of others.

Here are some group norms written for each individual to agree for the sake of the dialogue:[6]

1. I accept with gratitude the call to live my life in the fellowship of the Christian Church on earth.
I will receive and celebrate this as a joyful and also painful mystery that is nothing less than divine gift. '. . . something has been given, which we are struggling to articulate and respond to . . . you are here because God wants you to be here. And God's wanting you to be here has been mediated to you by centuries of mixed but exciting and imaginative witness within this tradition. Be thankful for that witness, and how it has made the reality of God's welcome complete for you'. (Rowan Williams). To be a Christian means belonging to a diverse and varied community. It means sharing my life with people who have very different views to mine. It means learning to differ in Christian love, respecting opinions other than mine and always seeking to understand the experiences of faith and life that lead people to the convictions that shape their discipleship. I will therefore experience the church as a place of joyful unity and painful conflict. This will be so because it is a community of forgiven sinners not finished saints, and because the questions matter deeply and passionately, and because we will always 'see dimly' in this life.

2. I will seek to offer a hospitable place in which to welcome those I meet.
All our meeting is in the love and mercy of Christ – even (above all) with our

enemies. Henri Nouwen says this involves both receptivity and confrontation. 'Receptivity without confrontation leads to bland neutrality that serves nobody'. Receptivity is no way involves becoming neutral. 'Confrontation without receptivity leads to an oppressive aggression which hurts everybody'. Confrontation is the loving and respectful task of offering ourselves as an 'articulate presence . . . showing our ideas, opinions and lifestyle clearly and distinctly. An empty house is not a hospitable house. Real receptivity asks for confrontation'.

3. I will listen first – and so hope to earn the right to be listened to.
This is a basic courtesy and also enables me to start from a position that is open rather than defensive. So I will listen to understand before asking to be listened too in order to be understood.

4. I accept the possibility that listening to others will change my own beliefs.
Unless we are open to this possibility then we will not be listening in fact. The very act of listening makes possible new understanding and appreciation – and therefore requires an openness to change.

5. I will accept the possibility that I may be wrong.
'I beseech you, in the bowels of Christ; think it possible you may be mistaken'. (Cromwell to the General Assembly of the Church of Scotland, 1650).

6. I will avoid bad arguments.
All the arguments need examining carefully – my own as well as those I argue with. We sometimes have a tendency not to examine too closely arguments that support our own position. This is especially true if we are insecure about our own conviction on an issue. Bad arguments can be used to make us feel more secure or comfortable in preconceived positions. Bad arguments undermine the seriousness of the debate. Bad arguments are usually 'closed' and therefore reinforce our own prejudices. Bad arguments will not help us to know and celebrate what is true. The best protection against bad arguments is the honest recognition that we are prone to accept them – especially where the issues at stake make us insecure or fearful.

7. I accept responsibility for my own beliefs and opinions.
Real debate cannot happen without truthful offering of what I think. There can be an isolation involved in offering our own convictions in a place of conflicting debate. I must learn to live with this. My security is in Christ not in the strength of privately held convictions.

8. I accept responsibility (in so far as I can influence it) for the way I am heard and experienced by others as I offer my beliefs to others.
It is possible to champion what is true and good but to do so in such a way that it bruises, wounds and alienates others. We communicate many important things before we speak a word. I may need to ask if I do this to others. We are told that only 7 per cent of all communication is verbal. 'The last thing we realize about ourselves is our effect' (William Boyd).

9. *I will argue with the best of my opponent's beliefs and practice, not with the worst.*

10. *I will not impute disreputable personal motives or characteristics as a way of discrediting those I disagree with.*
This is a dishonouring and manipulative way of trying to influence an argument. It has no place in the search for Christian truth.

11. *I will not publicly criticize individuals or groups I disagree with unless I am willing to express my views to them personally if love and wisdom require it.*

12. *I affirm that 'all truth is public truth' (Newbigin).*
This means that the way the Church negotiates its own life and conflicts is actually a part of its apologetic and missionary vocation in the world. The process is part of the content. But in a media-driven age serious public debate is particularly difficult. Sustaining public interest requires debate to be brief, to polarize and over-simplify the issues. As far as I am able I will not use public pronouncements or court media attention as weapons in Christian debate.

13. *I will not use money as a means of influencing Christian debate.*
Responsible stewardship of my financial resources will rightly reflect my theological convictions and concerns. But the Gospel nowhere supports the use of money as a means of manipulating debate or gaining power in the process of difficult decision-making.

14. *I accept that there will be people and groups with whom I cannot be reconciled and where communication is no longer possible.*
In this event I will confess my part in the divisions of the Church and humanity and seek forgiveness to begin again. I will pray for my enemies and bless them. In even our deepest divisions we will meet in the *breaking* of the bread.

15. *I understand this to be the way Christ meets us. It is therefore the way of the cross.*
I accept this and ask for grace to live faithfully in the way of Christ.

Facilitation Techniques

During the course of the dialogue there are many techniques a facilitator can use to draw out the group and help them have the best discussion they can.

Questioning

Questions are a facilitator's most important tool in helping the group seek deeper meaning and understanding. Questions help people challenge their assumptions, aid contextualization and challenge the intellectual and emotional information being shared. Group members need not agree with each other; the goal is greater mutual understanding. This is an important distinction for a facilitator to keep in mind when facilitating a dialogue on a subject as difficult as that of homosexuality and the Church.

Being neutral and impartial, the facilitator is able to ask questions that others in the group can or will not. They can ask people to work on articulating more clearly what they mean. For example:

- I hear the group talking about homosexuality being a choice. What do you mean by choice? What is your experience of choice within your own sexuality? What can you say you have chosen? What is more instinctual? How do you think this is the same or different for people of different sexual orientations?

Questions can be used to help the group achieve a higher standard of critical discourse, challenging them to be specific and careful when considering their sources. For example:

- You have been talking about a lot of studies that support your point of view. What studies specifically are you referring to? Does the whole group have access to these materials? Is there anyone here with the expertise to adequately access the validity of these studies? Are there also studies that offer a different perspective? How do we assess the authority or veracity of studies such as these?

When a group moves to recommending action, questions can help achieve a greater sense of understanding of the potential consequences thereby supporting thorough and thoughtful responses.

- What are the benefits of taking the actions you are suggesting? Who will benefit? Who will be disadvantaged?

Engaging and Curbing

A facilitator will need to draw some speakers out, supporting those who are reticent or unaccustomed to speaking in a dialogue. Ways this can be achieved are to watch for people who look as if they would like to speak but who have not been able to break into the conversation. Invite them to speak next. Similarly, a facilitator will want to invite people whom they notice have not contributed much to the dialogue to speak, rather than waiting for them to jump in. You might ask: 'John, do you have anything you would like to add?' or 'Sally, we haven't heard from you yet, what are you thinking about this?'

Other speakers will require a firm hand, to help them recognize when they have spoken long enough. A facilitator will need to find a number of ways politely but firmly to interrupt people who are taking up an excess of airtime. In church dialogues, sometimes a group participant begins what sounds rather like a sermon, which will need to be stopped sooner rather than later. Similarly, the facilitator will notice those feeling the need to respond to every speaker. This pattern can be interrupted and redirected. In some cultures, it may be expected that an elder will respond to each speaker. In these situations, the facilitator will need to have talked with the elders beforehand, to agree the guidelines for facilitation and to have the elder's full support for the method.

Clarifying

There are times when it is helpful for the facilitator to ask the group for clarification. This is in order to seek better understanding of what is being said and check that all participants are interpreting or perceiving what is being said in similar ways. The facilitator can watch for expressions of confusion on people's faces, and when these are apparent, seek clarity. For example: 'I am seeing a lot of confused faces. Could you please say more?' or, 'I am not sure that everyone in the group understands what is being said. Could we take some time to clarify what we are trying to communicate, and where these ideas come from?' Sometimes it is helpful for the facilitator to admit their own confusion. 'You have completely lost me. Could you please say more about this idea – help me understand it better.' The chances are that if a good facilitator has lost the thread of the conversation, then so have others in the group, but they may be too embarrassed to say anything.

Reflecting

Since a facilitator is responsible for managing the group process, they will need to be aware of the emotional elements of the group's interaction, demonstrating that they understand how the group is feeling and appreciate the emotional effect of the conversation or the topic. In doing this they help to evaluate and manage their own feelings.

The facilitator does not hesitate to name the emotional temperature of the group from time to time, acknowledging that some anxious behaviour is normal and to be expected. 'We knew this would be difficult, it's not surprising that some members of the group are finding this really frustrating.' Specific, observable behaviour and reactions of group members can be remarked on without making any accusations or pointing out specific people. 'Some members seem to be quite upset by the last comment.'

When the group is working well, managing to discuss their differences calmly, challenging issues rather than people, the facilitator will affirm their behaviour. If the facilitator feels the tension rising, it may be helpful to name when the group is going into contentious and fractious ground. 'It is clear that this conversation is beginning to get quite difficult for the group.' When this is the case, it can be helpful to remind people of the group norms.

Any sign of a personal attack will require immediate intervention by the facilitator who will explain that they are observing a personal attack rather than a focus on the issues under discussion. People will be reminded of their commitment to the agreed norms for their dialogue. 'Jane, I have just heard you ask Susan how she can think of herself as a Christian. Please remember our agreement to not make personal attacks on people during this dialogue.'

'Christopher, I have been noticing that you have been making your disapproval clear by shaking your head and making noises as people you disagree with have been talking. I need to remind you of our agreement to listen openly to others, even when we disagree and to keep our body language neutral.'

In these situations it is helpful to acknowledge again how difficult the dialogue is for the person you are confronting and reaffirm that it is also difficult for others. 'Susan, I know this is a difficult process for you – as it is for everyone else in the group.'

Summarizing

A particularly helpful technique for facilitators is occasionally to summarize the group's dialogue. Not only does it show that they are paying close attention to the group's conversation, following both the content and the emotional dimensions of the process, but it also gives the group a sense of the overall progression of their dialogue. It is helpful for others who may be trying to pull the pieces of the conversation together and endeavouring to understand what the group's conversation has achieved so far. Hearing back what they have been talking about allows the group to interact once more with the content of their conversation apart from the associated personalities.

Summarizing can be particularly helpful to overcome lulls in the conversation and help find new points of energy and engagement. It is always a good idea to conclude the group discussion with a summary of what has been said, the feelings people have expressed and the general mood of the group as it completes the process.

When summarizing, the facilitator goes over the high points of the discussion so far, and names any emerging themes acknowledging contrary opinions. When the group has expressed divergent thoughts without common themes, they are voiced. Where there are unresolved issues or incomplete conversations these are noted and named as unresolved.

Facilitator Challenges and Responsibilities

Creating a safer space for listening and dialogue

For many, being part of a process that concerns the place of gay and lesbian people in the life of the Church will be very difficult. For gays and lesbians within our churches, coming forward to tell their stories publicly is risky. For some this represents serious risk, particularly in countries where violence against homosexual people is common or in societies where homosexuality is illegal. Even within contexts that many would consider tolerant of gay and lesbian people, choosing to become a public witness in this debate is experienced as personal risk.

What can be done?

No situation is completely safe where people are willing to dialogue about deeply personal thoughts and feelings touching on some of their most important and deeply held beliefs. We can only create a safer environment where this vulnerability may be appropriately respected and honoured. For many situations, one of the best things we can do to create safety for ourselves and our dialogue partners is to be disciplined in our approach to setting group norms; abiding by them in group session and also after the dialogue is over.

Having the bishop publicly support and agree to these norms is essential, especially where there is fear of recrimination within the church. In some situations it may be important for the group's norms to include the promise of anonymity so that, while the content of the dialogue may be made public, only a very few people actually know who the participants were.

Where it is not possible for gay and lesbian people to participate the group can still acknowledge that there will be those among them who have friends, family members or colleagues who are homosexual. Or, the group members can recognize that, while there is no safety for homosexual people here, we all have lesbian and gay sisters and brothers in Christ within the wider church.

Where it is not possible personally to include their voices, a video, DVD, or audio-tape can be used. There are many of these available featuring gay and lesbian people speaking from a variety of experiences and points of view.

Drawing out the voices of all participants

The facilitator will need to be aware of cultural issues that may not allow for some members of the group to question or challenge ideas coming from others.

What can be done?

A flip chart can be used to write down what is being said in the dialogue, without attaching names to comments. When summarizing the dialogue, the facilitator will go through the list of themes and comments inviting further reflections from the group. For example: 'It has been suggested that . . . I wonder if there are other possibilities, other thoughts about this . . .' Comments now will be directed towards the facilitator.

A number of dialogues may be held in groups defined by age and gender. People often share fully and openly when dialoguing with a group of peers.

Taking time to get to know each other

For some cultures getting down to the business at hand quickly is expected and com-fortable. Others need time to establish relationships and a rapport within the group before they are comfortable addressing the topic, especially when it is controversial and personal.

What can be done?

It is helpful for the facilitator to become aware of the cultural norms and design a process appropriate to these needs and comforts. In a situation where rapport needs to be established before substantive discussion can take place, planning for the group to meet a few times, perhaps over a meal to facilitate social time is helpful, as is designing a number of group building conversations and times to share family stories. The facilitator will pace the introduction of the topic carefully and gently, being prepared to learn that the group is not ready yet, and to withdraw the question and try again later.

It is remarkable how dialogues, even when they are very difficult, will proceed more easily when people have had a chance to interact socially beforehand. Knowing each other as people first makes it much more difficult to stereotype or dismiss them later when finding you disagree substantively about an issue.

Discussing the undiscussible

People can be very reluctant to speak openly about the subject of sexuality. For many talking about sex is taboo – socially unacceptable, uncomfortable and even repugnant.

What can be done?

Each person can be given an identical index card or piece of paper and pen. Without discussion or collaboration, each is asked to write one 'undiscussible' statement that they believe the group needs to deal with on their card. They are asked to describe it well enough to be clear to all in the room. Where literacy is an issue, cards can be prepared by the facilitator in advance through individual conversations with each participant. The cards are collected, shuffled and then read out, the statements listed on flip chart paper for all to see. Any common themes underlying those things that are so difficult to discuss are identified.

Before engaging with the subject of the undiscussible statement, ask the group:

- Why do we think it is so difficult to deal with this openly?
- What blocks us from dealing with this in an up-front and open manner?
- What is the threat behind these undiscussible statements?

By this you are enabling them to confront what is uncomfortable.

Managing anger

If someone in the group becomes angry, or a confrontation begins between two or more people, it is the facilitator's job to intervene quickly.

What can be done?

The facilitator will need to stop the argument and slow down the process. This will give group members the chance to listen, take some deep breaths and think. It will give some time to help people move from reaction – fight or flight – back to a place where they can resume a reasonable and respectful interaction.

The facilitator must never join the argument, nor get defensive. They interrupt the argument as and when they can, summarize the substance of the argument, asking if they have understood it correctly. The group process does not proceed until agreement has been obtained from those involved in the outburst that the facilitator has understood what they have been fighting about.

Next there is a time of reflection on all the emotion within the group: anger, upset, withdrawal, shame, and embarrassment, not just the emotions of those actually involved in the confrontation. Reflection led by the facilitator will make the point that those caught up in their own anger are having a significant and negative effect on the rest of the group.

Referral to the group's norms will take place again, and people will be asked if they are willing to live by this code of conduct. A particular point will be made of asking those who are most angry if they will be able to go forward within the conditions of the group norms.

It is less likely that there will be a need to manage anger if the facilitator has done a good job of intervening at the first signs of group members breaking the group's norms. Calling people on inappropriate or disrespectful behaviour, early and consistently as needed, will make angry outbursts far less common.

Asking someone to leave the group or ending a dysfunctional group process

Should someone choose to refuse to abide by the group's norms, and persist in disrupting and upsetting the group by demonstrating behaviour that the group has agreed is out of bounds, the facilitator will need to ask this person to leave the group. This usually only happens after two or three interventions have been made with no change in behaviour.

.

What can be done?

The facilitator will describe what they have clearly observed, for example, that this person is unwilling or unable to respect the group norms and as such is indicating that they do not want to participate in this type of listening group. Firmly but respectfully they will be asked to leave the group so the others can continue. Once the person has left, the conversation and emotional dynamic so far will be summarized, a time of prayer offered, and the dialogue resumed.

The person will not be allowed to make a parting speech. Too often what is said will be potentially very damaging and hurtful to people in the group and, once the person has left, there will be no way for the group to hold that individual responsible for the pain they have inflicted. So once the person has agreed to leave, they say nothing more. If they try to speak, they will be firmly and respectfully stopped; it will be observed that the choice was theirs – to stay and say their piece in a way that respected the guidelines set by the group itself, or to withdraw. They have chosen the latter.

If the person who is being disruptive has status such that the group cannot continue without their presence, the group's process will need to end early. It will be articulated that the group is not able to continue without this person's presence, and it is not possible to continue within the guidelines set by the group with the person there. The group will be asked to explore and discuss what this might mean.

The group's discussion and the emotional dynamic will be summarized and the time concluded with prayer.

Who Can Facilitate?

There are no hard and fast rules about who will be the best facilitator for your situation but there are a few things to consider as you make this decision. Not everybody can comfortably or effectively function as a facilitator. For example, people with strong opinions, feelings or biases about the topic or subject of the group's interactions will probably find it extremely challenging to lead the group without adding their input.

There may be skilled facilitators within your diocese who have the trust of the bishop and would be willing to put their ideas and opinions aside for a few hours to help the group. It can be a good idea to have pair of facilitators (just as Jesus sent his followers out in pairs). Co-facilitators can bring different gifts and skills to bear, especially when the subject of the group is difficult and potentially conflicted. One facilitator can lead the group process while the other pays close attention to the group dynamic – such as emotions being displayed, who is silent, and who is dominant. They then can intercede to redress any issues they have observed.

It is said that the success of a group process depends 40% on the facilitator, 40% on the participants and 20% on what happens between the two. Recruiting a skilled and trusted facilitator is one of the most important things you can do to ensure a healthy and helpful dialogue.

The Role of Bishops

It will be rare that the bishop can facilitate a group process within their diocese. Their role as leader will have a profound effect on who can participate and how the group feels it can interact. It is not reasonable to expect that a bishop can or should be neutral on some subjects of concern to their diocese. However, there are no hard and fast rules here. Both cultural identity and specific situations should be the guide when determining whether the bishop can or should facilitate.

Even if they do not participate in the dialogue group itself, there are key roles for the bishop. A dialogue needs a convenor. The bishop has the authority to convene, that is, to promote and sponsor the process. Their task is to find someone who they trust, with the gift of facilitation, to function in that role. The bishop must openly support the dialoguing process. Agreeing and publicly stating their intention to abide by the group's norms can go a long way towards creating a safer environment for the dialogue and its participants. The bishop can also provide access to resources for participants in order to help them prepare. Resources include print materials such as this book and the many others on this topic, annotated bibliographies, web-based resources, audiovisuals, and even hosting particular learning events with speakers. At the conclusion of the dialogue process, the bishop can receive a report, summarizing the content of the discussion. In those particularly dangerous contexts where it is not safe for gay and lesbian people to be identified openly, the report can be submitted without the participants names attached.

Should a bishop participate in the dialogue in places where it would be unseemly or unusual for members of a group to disagree openly with their bishop the following will help the group to function as effectively. First, the bishop will need to be clear with the group from the start that the purpose is for all members of the group to listen to each other, rather than only listening to the bishop.

The bishop will need to give assurance to members of the group and give permission for them to share openly in his/her presence without fear of future reproach or recrimination. This need to be said early in the process, the bishop should not be the last to speak, and they can monitor how often they speak, making sure that there are others who speak more often than they do.

There are also cultural situations where a dialogue group will judge the significance of the process by the input of the bishop. If the bishop is seen not to participate honestly and openly, no one else will. The bishop will need to be clear with the group about his or her beliefs, ideas and struggles. The honesty of the bishop in these situations will set the bar for how honest others are expected to be.

Similar issues for group participation are present for rectors within their parishes.

Just Listening – Without Dialogue

When dialogue is most difficult, or when it is not yet time to talk, the best thing can be to offer an opportunity for people to listen to one another without interaction. When the leadership feels that the issues are too contentious to have any healthy or helpful dialogue, but where it is important to hear and learn from each other, a pure listening process, such as that held during the General Synod of the Anglican Church of Australia (October 2007), is an option.

Listening without discussion or debate will challenge some cultures where it will feel wrong not to be invited to respond. It may even feel as if the voices are being affirmed when they are not challenged through discussion and debate. Where this is the case, the bishop will need to be committed to this process and share their commitment to it openly.

Where listening to lesbian and gay people is most difficult and dangerous, either a DVD or video presentation can be used; alternatively, gay and lesbian people from outside the diocese may be invited to come and speak to a group. For situations where it is too risky for gay and lesbian people to be identified, a sound recording could be used.

Listening to each other: The Sharing Circle – An Aboriginal Process of Listening[7]

The Sharing Circle is a process of listening that comes from North American indigenous peoples. For these indigenous people, the Circle is a sacred symbol. From their history as peoples whose voices were often ignored and silenced, this process is a gift that highlights the importance of all voices being heard.

For groups needing to listen to each other and speak about difficult and contentious issues, the Circle breaks the normal patterns of communication we experience in these discussions. In some cultures stronger, more confident voices often dominate, and other quieter voices are silenced; hierarchy and status often play a defining role in who gets to speak, and who is listened to. The Circle offers the possibility for all, including quieter voices, to share and to be heard. It gives a value to listening and encourages listening through a disciplined format.

In a Circle, people speak without being interrupted. As each person shares, they are offered the undivided attention of all other participants. There is no cross-talk or debate during the Circle. This is symbolized by the use of a 'talking stick', an object such as a beautiful stone held by the person who speaks. Only the person holding the talking stick is permitted to speak. The process discourages argument and supports healthy dialogue by respecting the need for the group to hear all voices without interruption before any discussion begins. We are not prepared to dialogue with each other until we have heard from each voice in the group.

Guiding Principles

Sharing   Everyone in the Circle shares by speaking and actively listening. There should be no pressure placed on anyone to speak. A person may pass, and then be offered a chance to speak after the others in the circle have spoken.

Gift   Each person's participation in the Circle is a gift of value and is to be appreciated and received as such.

Respect   In the Circle, members receive each others' gifts with respect, neither judging nor belittling the gift that each person makes. The person is listened to and allowed to speak without interruption.

Equality   The Circle is not hierarchical. No person, and the gift they share, is more important than another. Each person's gift is necessary to complete the Circle.

Sacredness   The Circle is sacred space, made up of sacred relationships. It is an altar upon which members of the Circle offer themselves to each other and to the Creator. The language one uses and the way that one relates to others in the Circle reflect this sacredness.

The Circle Process

- People sit in a circle. This works best without tables. If at tables, people are asked to clear the space in front of them, putting away all equipment, clutter or anything else that may distract.
- Arrangements ensure that the group will not be disturbed during the process.
- The facilitator will need a 'talking stick'. A beautiful stone works well because as it is passed from person to person, it absorbs the warmth of people's hands. Participants can feel the touch of others in this warmth.
- The facilitator introduces the process and its principles. Participants agree to these and to their part – sharing and listening without interruption.
- A prayer of invocation is offered asking the Holy Spirit to be present in what is said and what is heard. Often a candle is lit in the centre of the circle.
- The facilitator sets the topic or question for reflection and sharing. She/he passes the talking stick to the person next to them who through this act is invited to speak.
- As each person finishes what he or she has to say, they pass the talking stick to their neighbour who then shares.
- Should a person choose to pass, they simply indicate this by saying 'pass' and hand the talking stick to their neighbour.
- When the talking stick returns to the facilitator, they offer any who have passed the opportunity to share. The talking stick is passed to them in turn.
- People speak only once. No one has a second turn to speak.
- When everyone else has shared, the facilitator is the last to speak.
- The Circle finishes with prayer.
- People leave in silence.

Modelling listening and dialogue

People who hold different perspectives are invited to form a panel for presentation. The panels should include representation from the variety of voices. The choices include: heterosexual people who hold very different positions; someone who holds a moderate view; a gay man or lesbian woman who is celibate; a gay man or lesbian woman who is living in a committed relationship; someone who has a story of being healed or has chosen not to live as a gay man or lesbian woman. Each is invited to tell their story and share their position while being watched by an audience of listeners. The panel then models active listening and dialogue by holding a discussion session in front of an audience.

For this to work well, members of the panel need to commit themselves to the principles and practice of active listening and respectful dialogue.

Final thoughts

And it came to pass, as Moses entered into the tabernacle, the cloudy pillar descended, and stood at the door of the tabernacle, and the Lord talked with Moses. And all the people saw the cloudy pillar stand at the tabernacle door: and all the people rose up and worshipped, every man in his tent door. (Exodus 33)

Each person stands in his own tent door, in the presence of God; the Israelites come to the threshold but no further. The tabernacle of God's fullness is 'afar off'. They face towards the place where those who encounter God are transformed but they do not encounter God. They do not encounter each other. These people are fragments of a lost wholeness.

In some ways this is a picture, an image of how we fail to encounter one another by not listening. We each stand at our own threshold. On one side is all the security and certainty of our own worldview, our culture, background, education, religious faith, experience, and the nexus of relationships within which we live. On the other, there is the vulnerability and challenge.

But Jesus describes himself as the gateway – the threshold. He waits for us in places of choice, promising that the encounter with others will draw us, not just into individual gain but into the fullness of God in all creation. While our quest for understanding is limited, God is all in all, and has always known us. To God all hearts are open, all desires are known and from him no secrets are hidden. We come to fullness only through Christ in whose pure love we are all known. So we are called to listen to each other; to learn from each other and from Scripture in compassion and curiosity, while the Spirit, with sighs too deep for words, will pray us into community.

Notes

1   Diterich Bonhoeffer, *Life Together*, 98-9.
2   See N. T. Wright, *Matthew for Everyone (Part 1)* (London: SPCK, 2004), 201.
3   General Conference Mennonite Church and Mennonite Church (1995). 'Agreeing and Disagreeing in Love — Commitments for Mennonites in Times of Disagreement (General Conference Mennonite Church, Mennonite Church, 1995)'. *Global Anabaptist Mennon-*

ite Encyclopedia Online, <http://www.gameo.org/encyclopedia/contents/A41.html>.

4   For more on the ideas underlying this section see Eric Beresford 'Community and Diversity: The Role of Perspective in Debates about Human Sexuality' in Catherine Sider Hamilton (ed.), *The Homosexuality Debate: Faith in Search of Understanding* (Toronto: ABC Publications, 2003).

5   Peter Senge et al., *The Fifth Discipline Fieldbook* (New York: Doubleday, 1994), 359.

6   David Runcorn, 'Some Principles for Meeting with People Whose Beliefs Differ From Mine' (October 2003). These thoughts have borrowed widely but were inspired initially by a briefer statement of principles in the introduction to Gareth Moore, *A Question of Truth* (London: Continuum, 2002).

7   Much of this description is taken from the Anglican Church of Canada, National Aboriginal Day of Prayer 2007 .

Chapter 3

The Witness of Scripture

Phil Groves, John Holder and Paula Gooder

Introduction

This second section comprises three chapters which turn our attention to the authoritative sources for Anglican theology and ethics: Scripture, tradition and reason. Because of its primacy among these and its centrality in debates about sexuality, the first and longest of the three chapters is focused on Scripture. This falls into three distinct parts. Each of these has its own main author although **Phil Groves, John Holder and Paula Gooder** worked together on the chapter as a whole.

Part 1, by the Listening Process Facilitator, **Phil Groves,** opens the chapter with reflections on what it means to live under the authority of Scripture. The authority of Scripture is confessed by people across the spectrum of views on sexuality but it is clear that there are also quite different understandings of what this means in practice. This presents a challenge to us because, as the Archbishop of Canterbury explained in his Advent Letter of 2007, a full relationship of communion will mean:

The common acknowledgment that we stand under the authority of Scripture as 'the rule and ultimate standard of faith', in the words of the Chicago-Lambeth Quadrilateral; as the gift shaped by the Holy Spirit which decisively interprets God to the community of believers and the community of believers to itself and opens our hearts to the living and eternal Word that is Christ. Our obedience to the call of Christ the Word Incarnate is drawn out first and foremost by our listening to the Bible and conforming our lives to what God both offers and requires of us through the words and narratives of the Bible. We recognize each other in one fellowship when we see one another 'standing under' the word of Scripture. Because of this recognition, we are able to consult and reflect together on the interpretation of Scripture and to learn in that process. Understanding the Bible is not a private process or something to be undertaken in isolation by one part of the family. Radical change in the way we read cannot be determined by one group or tradition alone.

This chapter therefore begins by seeking common ground as Anglicans across our differences on the Bible's teaching on homosexuality. This is found by looking at what the 39 Articles teach about Scripture and its authority in the Church. Although the Articles have a varied status across the provinces of our Communion they are an important part of our common Anglican heritage. The guide to their teaching on Scripture which is provided here is based *On the 39 Articles* by Professor Oliver O'Donovan, a study first published in 1986 and reprinted for the 2008 Lambeth Conference.

In our listening and learning about sexuality, many Anglicans are concerned about faithfulness to Scripture, the dangers of false teaching, and how doctrine and ethics develop over time. Having attempted to find common ground in the Articles, the chapter proceeds to look at these issues through a study of Jude. This short letter's emphasis on standing firm for the 'faith once delivered to the saints' has often been appealed to in the course of recent discussions about sexuality. Then we are asked to consider what the issues were in the early Church that led to Jude writing this letter and to explore what parallels might legitimately be drawn with our discussions of sexuality today.

The scene has now been set by examining how our thinking is shaped by our understanding of the authority of Scripture and what it means to guard the faith. We therefore turn next to explore how those in favour of same-sex relationships and those opposed to them both appeal to the Bible in making their case. A biblical overview of these two views is presented. In the light of these it is asked what we mean when we claim that a view is compatible or incompatible with Scripture.

Underlying different understandings of what is compatible with Scripture are often different ways of interpreting the Bible. The section therefore turns next to the discipline of hermeneutics – how we interpret the Bible. Some key issues are outlined by looking at some of the challenges we face as we seek to understand and apply the Bible today.

Finally, the section returns to the question of faithful development in Christian thinking and practice and concerns about inclusion of outsiders and the role of experience in biblical interpretation. These issues are examined by looking at a key biblical example. The early Church welcomed Gentiles and decided not to apply aspects of the Jewish law to them. This is often appealed to in debates about the sort of welcome to be given to those who identify as gay and lesbian and discussions about what the Church expects of them in terms of holy living. It is central to the account (*To Set Our Hope on Christ*) given by The Episcopal Church (USA) to ACC-13 in response to the Windsor Report. Different understandings of how the Council of Jerusalem in Acts 15 reached its conclusions are therefore explained in order to help us understand whether and how this might help us in our dialogues today about sexuality.

In **Parts 2 and 3** we move on from a general introduction to consider the wider background and teaching of the Bible in relation to sexuality. Here we are guided by **John Holder** from Barbados (writing on the Old Testament) and **Paul Gooder** a biblical scholar based in England (who writes on the New Testament material). The original plan was for them simply to provide a guide to the main controversial texts. However, after study, prayer and consultation with Phil Groves, they decided to attempt to place the debate about homosexuality in the context of biblical understandings of sexuality more widely. Between them they take us on a journey through the Old and New Testaments.

John Holder combines his gifts as an Old Testament scholar and a bishop who lives the Bible in his context. He shows how sexuality has been the subject of human reflection and discussion, including religious reflection and discussion, for millennia.

He sets the Old Testament in the wider context of Ancient Near Eastern beliefs. Israel's neighbours viewed the gods as sexual beings and related both fertility and sexual experience closely to religious devotion. The creation narratives set the scene for the development of themes, which emphasize both the blessing and ambivalence of sexuality.

God's people are seen to celebrate sexuality as a good gift of God, particularly linked to procreation. However, the Old Testament also warns against and illustrates the dangers of misusing this gift in various ways. Although sexual imagery is sometimes used for Yahweh and his relationship with Israel, the emphasis is on God transcending sexuality. Against this backdrop, the few negative texts relating to homosexuality are examined and by setting them in their original context some of their complexities are highlighted.

Paula Gooder guides us through the material on sexuality found in the New Testament from the Gospels and Acts, through the Pauline tradition before concluding with a look at other texts. What she describes reveals a continuation but also a development of the Old Testament's engagement with sexuality. One of the most important innovations is the prominence given to celibacy.

In the Gospels, God's transcendence over sexuality is again emphasized in the accounts of Jesus' virgin birth. Jesus' strong teaching on adultery, divorce and re-marriage is explored, as is his discussion of marriage in heaven. This teaching needs, however, to be put alongside his attitude to those, particularly women, who are seen as sexual sinners. Finally, both Jesus and the early Church in Acts (notably again in Acts 15) warned about sexual immorality (*porneia*), and the scope and significance of this prohibition are examined. Paul, too, warns against any acceptance of *porneia* in the Christian community, particularly in his most concentrated discussion of sexuality in 1 Corinthians 5—7. Here, there is not only further teaching on divorce (1 Corinthians 7) but also a vice list which includes words traditionally understood to refer to homosexuality. The debates over the meanings of these terms and the different interpretations of the fuller discussion of homosexuality in Romans 1 are carefully explained to help you understand these texts and some of the disagreements that exist between scholars on how to interpret them. The chapter concludes with brief discussion of some texts in the Pastoral Epistles (another vice list which includes a reference to homosexuality and advice for the conduct of church leaders), 2 Peter, Jude and Revelation.

Although a lot of ground is covered in what follows, neither John nor Paula expects what they have written to be the final word. Once again it must be stressed that their work is simply a resource, not an authoritative statement. It is offered in the hope it will send you back to read your Bible with a fuller and wider understanding, and send you out to dialogue about this and study the Bible with fellow Christians.

PART 1:
THE AUTHORITY OF THE BIBLE
IN THE ANGLICAN TRADITION
Phil Groves

1. Setting Common Ground

When asked to define the 'Anglican Way' by the 1988 Lambeth Conference, the Inter-Anglican Theological and Doctrinal Commission began with a statement about the authority of Scripture:

> Anglicans affirm the sovereign authority of the Holy Scriptures as the medium through which God by the Spirit communicates his word in the Church and thus enables people to respond with understanding and faith. The Scriptures are 'uniquely inspired witness to divine revelation', and 'the primary norm for Christian faith and life'.[1]

They continued by saying that the Bible is to be interpreted in each generation and in every context, not so that we alter Scripture, but so that its teaching is understood in our time and place:

> The Scriptures, however, must be translated, read, and understood, and their meaning grasped through a continuing process of interpretation. Since the seventeenth century Anglicans have held that Scripture is to be understood and read in the light afforded by the contexts of 'tradition' and 'reason'.[2]

These twin principles of the authority of Scripture and the importance of context for understanding Scripture are a shared starting point for many Anglicans. This first section will set out these two widely accepted principles of Anglican understandings of Scripture from the perspective of the 39 Articles of Religion.[3]

1.1 Scripture in the 39 Articles

The English Reformers defined themselves as being distinct from the Roman Catholics by stressing the priority of Scripture in life, worship and theology. Prior to the Reformation, reading the Bible had been the sole preserve of those who could read Latin. As it was only those who had been educated by the Church who could do so, the Church was, to a certain extent, able to control theology.

The placing of an English translation of the Bible for public reading in every church was a significant act in the reformation of the Church in England. The regular reading of the Bible by the consistent use of the Lectionary was fundamental to Cranmer's liturgical reforms. The ordered reading of the Bible every day was the focus of Morning and Evening Prayer, which Cranmer intended to be said by every Christian, not just clergy. The reduction in the number of Saints' Days enabled a regular reading through the Scriptures on Sundays. It appears that the reading of the Bible was more important to the Reformers than preaching or interpretation. For the Reformers, the reading of the Bible was a liberating act: they believed 'false' doctrines would be exposed when ordinary people had access to the Bible, the true source of all theology. This belief remains at the heart of Anglican approaches to Scripture.

The place of the Scriptures in Anglican theology has been enshrined in the 39 Articles, particularly in Articles 6–8 and 20. The Articles assume that intrinsic to being Anglican is an acceptance of the prime authority of Scripture in the formation of theology, in worship and in how we live.

This section is a selective summary of Chapter 4 of Professor Oliver O'Donovan's book *On the Thirty Nine Articles*.[4] O'Donovan provides us with a commentary on the Articles. As with all the books we invite you to engage with critically, we hope it will make you think.

1.1.1 Articles 1 to 5

The first five Articles state the common ground of historic Christianity and place the Anglican Church within a Trinitarian tradition. God is known as Father, Son and Holy Spirit and it is the Word of God who saves us, who died, rose again and who sent his Holy Spirit. Salvation comes from the Word made flesh, that is, God with us in the person of Jesus Christ. 'It is Jesus who contains all things necessary to salvation, who is the locus of God's self giving and self revelation. God incarnate in a man, not a book.'[5]

In our generation the contrast with Islam will be familiar to many of us. For Islam the Word of God is undeniably the Koran. For Christians reading John 1 the Word is the incarnate Son – God made flesh – who lived among us. This is not to deny or reduce the authority or sufficiency of Scripture, but to frame its purpose. 'The Scriptures are a *way of access* to the knowledge of God's saving deeds in Christ . . . an authoritative sphere where Christ is made known [to us].'[6] John Stott agrees: 'The reason why Christians love the Bible is that it speaks to us of Christ. We are not bibliolaters, we do not worship the Bible. But we worship Christ, and the Bible points us to him.'[7]

1.1.2 Article 6

Article 6. Of the Sufficiency of the Holy Scriptures for Salvation

Holy Scripture containeth all things necessary to salvation: so that whatsoever is not read therein, nor may be proved thereby, is not to be required of any man, that it should be believed as an article of the Faith, or be thought requisite or necessary to salvation. In the name of the Holy Scripture we do understand those canonical Books of the Old and New Testament, of whose authority was never any doubt in the Church.[8]

Article 6 begins by stating that the Scriptures contain all things necessary for salvation. Here it is salvation which is the focus, not the Scriptures themselves. As Rowan Greer has commented, 'The function of Scripture to contain all things necessary to salvation must surely mean that its chief purpose is to form Christians and to guide them toward the destiny prepared for them by God and revealed to them through Christ.'[9]

If the Scriptures are sufficient in themselves, we need no special knowledge passed from bishop to succeeding bishop in an unbroken chain to the apostles, as the Reformers sometimes unfairly represented the Catholic understanding of Apostolic Succession. Bishops are to guard the faith through being faithful to Scripture, not by having special knowledge.

The Articles define the canon of Scripture, but only list the Old Testament books. In the Reformation the New Testament canon was not in doubt, it had emerged from the patristic Church, which placed weight on 'apostolicity' when discerning which books to include and which to omit. They did not imagine that the authors were all apostles themselves, but that they had had access to that inner circle and so had an intimate connection to Jesus. The information the apostles passed on then is sufficient for us now to gain our salvation in Christ. The 39 Articles, therefore, understand that while it is Jesus who saves us, we have no access to him except through the witness of the apostles in the Bible.

The Reformers found that their reading of the Bible challenged longstanding beliefs and practices within the Church – such as the veneration of relics and beliefs in purgatory and transubstantiation. They did not, however, reject the role of tradition understood as 'the life of the contemporary Church, in so far as it is in continuity with that of immediately preceding generations'.[10]

In terms of doctrine, the English Reformers were inclined to favour traditions common to the universal Church and of patristic antiquity. They asserted the freedom of the Church to challenge tradition, but stressed the obligation of the Church with respect to Scripture. They qualified the Church's freedom only as far as it is necessary to safeguard the freedom of the individual believer not to have improper burdens imposed on his or her conscience, faith or vocation.

1.1.3 Article 8

Article 8. Of the Three Creeds
The Three Creeds, Nicene Creed, Athanasius's Creed, and that which is commonly called the Apostles' Creed, ought thoroughly to be received and believed: for they may be proved by most certain warrants of Holy Scripture.

Article 8 accepted the Great Creeds that had developed from ongoing doctrinal debates, especially over Christology, through the early Christian centuries. By doing so the Reformers rejected voices that called for the abandonment of all theology and practice that was not in precise accord with Scripture. More radical Reformers in Britain and Europe argued from Scripture for reconsideration of many doctrines and practices. For example, some argued that baptism was for believers alone and some of the most radical argued that the Trinity as classically expressed was a later imposition on the original doctrines. In contrast, the English Reformers allowed for theological developments, which, they argued, were developed from Scripture and not denied in Scripture. They realized 'that to restrict theology to the actual words of Scripture was to inhibit its critical task'.[11]

O'Donovan argues that, for the Reformers, the sense of Scripture was more important than the words of Scripture. This was not to play down the words, because without the words Scripture is nothing, but words alone lose their meaning over time and can be manipulated to support all kinds of opinions. He argues that 'the task of biblical exegesis is to restore and maintain the clear outline of the scriptural sense, assisting the reader to hear the words of Scripture with the force which they had at their first uttering, so that they are effective in bringing to critical examination the ideas and speculations which prevail at any given age'.[12] Such an approach does not allow proof texts to end theological debate.

1.1.4 Articles 7 and 20

Article 7. Of the Old Testament
The Old Testament is not contrary to the New: for both in the Old and New Testament everlasting life is offered to Mankind by Christ, who is the only Mediator between God and Man, being both God and Man. Wherefore they are not to be heard, which feign that the old Fathers did look only for transitory promises. Although the Law given from God by Moses, as touching Ceremonies and Rites, do not bind Christian men, nor the Civil precepts thereof ought of necessity to be received in any commonwealth; yet notwithstanding, no Christian man whatsoever is free from the obedience of the Commandments which are called Moral.

Article 20. Of the Authority of the Church

The Church hath power to decree Rites or Ceremonies, and authority in Controversies of Faith: and yet it is not lawful for the Church to ordain any thing that is contrary to God's Word written, neither may it so expound one place of Scripture, that it be repugnant to another. Wherefore, although the Church be a witness and a keeper of Holy Writ, yet, as it ought not to decree any thing against the same, so besides the same ought it not to enforce any thing to be believed for necessity of Salvation.

The relationship between the Old Testament and the New was a key debate for the Reformation theologians. Article 20 declares that the Church has no authority to expound one place of Scripture in a manner that it be 'repugnant' to another. Two immediate difficulties were in their minds. First, it was argued that, for example, the words of vengeance in the Psalms are contradictory to Jesus' words of forgiveness; second, that some of the laws of the Old Testament were set aside by Jesus. They refused to allow either that the Old Testament could be set aside, or that the Bible was too complicated for lay people to read and understand. The Reformers insisted upon the ordinary readability of Scripture, all of which had a unity and coherence.

Modern critical methodologies have often stressed the diversity of Scripture and sought understanding through investigating differences. That there is diversity and difference is not denied in the Articles but these are the realities of a developing theological pattern. O'Donovan illustrates it in this way:

> If we wish to understand what it means to say that Jesus is 'the Christ', we must come to grips with the history of the Messianic idea in the Old Testament. That is the way in which the Holy Spirit has expanded the concept of the Christ for us. But the history of the idea in the Old Testament is a history of change and transformation.[13]

The actual character of the Bible that we have before us is the record of an emerging theological idea, made real by being lived out in a society whose history is woven together with that of the idea. The biblical God makes himself known by acts in history and his revelation takes the form of history. O'Donovan argues that to omit the words of vengeance in the Psalms is to reduce the power of the words of forgiveness which come from the mouth of Jesus.

Article 7 does recognize the discontinuity between the Old and New Testaments, especially in the rejection by Jesus of the ceremonial laws, but the dominant theme is one of continuity. The opening phrase declares that the Old is not contrary to the New, for in the Old and the New Testament everlasting life is offered to humanity by Christ. The article finishes with the statement that no Christian whatsoever is free from the obedience of the commandments which are called moral (by which is meant especially but not solely the Ten Commandments).

Common Ground?

We hope that by engaging in a study of the 39 Articles we will have found common ground. However, having attempted to build the common ground we are immediately aware of an issue of contention. Some will see the words of the Articles in making a distinction between commands that are moral others that are ceremonial as closing all discussion on the acceptability of blessing same-sex unions. They argue that the commands in Leviticus 19 and 20 are moral and so permanent. Others argue that these commands are specifically among the ceremonial laws and only by a profound injustice to Scripture do we place them among the moral laws. There are those who understand both arguments and so take issue with the neat classification of laws as either ceremonial or moral.

Having attempted to build the common ground this last paragraph will immediately alert the reader to an issue of contention. Some will see in these words a closing of all discussion on the acceptability of blessing same-sex unions. There are those who take issue with the Reformers' neat classification of laws that are ceremonial and others moral, but there are also those who argue that the Levitical commands on homosexuality are specifically among the ceremonial and that only by a profound injustice to Scripture do we place them among the moral laws as well as those who consider them plainly to be moral. There is no denying that there are significant differences between some Anglicans, but we hope that by engaging in a study of the 39 Articles we will have found common ground.

Conclusions

1. Understanding Scripture is not an end in itself; the aim is to know God, Father, Son and Holy Spirit.
2. The Scriptures give us sufficient and authoritative revelation of God in Jesus Christ.
3. Interpretation is required to find the sense of Scripture, not purely the meanings of words.
4. The Scriptures reflect a development in walking with God by the nation of Israel and by the apostolic community.
5. Theological development is a good and necessary task. Therefore, the Reformers accepted the historic creeds and the requirement for the development of traditions in continuity with the Scriptures.

1.2 Scripture, Theology and Ethics – A Reflection on the Letter of Jude

1.2.1 Introduction

The emphasis on the sufficiency of Scripture for salvation was immediately relevant to the prime theological concerns of the Reformation – issues such as justification, purgatory and the real presence in the eucharist. In the last century the same emphasis was relevant to the concerns of that generation such as the debates on the divinity of Jesus. The application of the Articles in doctrinal debate was immediately apparent.

The question of morality – of how we should live – has a relation to theological concerns, but many argue it is not the same as with these other doctrinal matters. The single-chapter book of Jude is a very useful text to frame the questions before us as we seek to reflect on how we should live and proclaim the good news in relation to theology.

Please read the whole letter and allow time to think about it before reading this section.

Richard Bauckham – one of the major commentators on Jude – argues that Jude was a Jewish Christian who used the Hebrew Bible when referring to the Old Testament and who was also a very able writer in Greek. He claims that there is no reason to dismiss the traditional assumption that Jude was the brother not only of James, but also of Jesus.[14] The letter of Jude is consciously in continuity with the Old Testament and also consciously develops Jewish traditions. References to the Old Testament and to the writings of Second Temple Judaism are carefully woven into the letter.

The letter was sent to a specific congregation and was not a general open letter for all. The initial greetings, written in a Jewish style, are followed by a carefully crafted sermon with a doxology as a conclusion. At its heart is the sermon that the community would have heard had Jude been able to be with them. As such it is not a generalized attack on heresies, but a 'message for a specific situation in which a specific group of false teachers were troubling a specific church or group of churches'.[15]

The intended readers would have understood all the references and the cultural allusions and they knew the false teachers in their presence. We read with our own cultural assumptions and we have some idea of what happened next. We know that the antinomian forces did not win the day in the Church. The community it was addressed to, like all first Christian communities, were open to the real possibility that Christ would return in their lifetime. We know he did not return and so, with hindsight, our understanding of the text can be different to theirs. If we accept the common ground principles set out above, we are called to read Jude as authoritative in our lives. This requires us to take seriously how it might have been understood then, but also what God is saying to us now in our time and place.

1.2.2 Structure

Jude 3 sets out the central theme of the letter: 'I find it necessary to write appealing to you to carry on the fight for the faith which was once and for all delivered to the saints.' This verse is followed by an analysis of their situation in dialogue with both Scripture and works of Second Temple Judaism (4–19). The theme of Jude 3 is then delivered in three direct verses (20–23).

1.2.3 The Opponents

Jude sets out the context of the letter by referring to people who claim to be of Christ but who are opponents of the gospel:

> For certain people whose condemnation was written about long ago have secretly slipped in among you. They are godless people, who change the grace of our God into licence for immorality and deny Jesus our only sovereign and Lord. (Jude 4)

These people were probably travelling charismatic preachers who rejected all moral authority. They are often identified by the term 'antinomian' – those who denied the relevance of any moral law or authority. They preached freedom from the Law on the grounds that they were forgiven from their sins and could do as they pleased. This was a denial of the lordship of Christ in their lives.

Jude weaves references to both the Old Testament and to the apocalyptic works of

Second Temple Judaism into his condemnation of his opponents and he presumes all the references are known by his audience. These sinful preachers blame the angels for bringing the law and thereby place themselves above that law (8–10). Jude condemns them, as their contempt for the law is contempt for God himself. The reference to Sodom and Gomorrah implies that they were engaged in and encouraging sexual licence (7).[16] Scholars disagree over whether the context implies a direct reference to homosexuality,[17] or if the primary reference is to all forms of sexual lust as part of a rebellion against the divinely established order, especially lust between humans and angels.[18] These wandering preachers received food and money for their ministry and in offering a message that the community wished to hear they would have received more gifts (11–12).

Legitimate Parallels?

Parallels have been drawn between Jude's opponents and those who argue for the acceptance of lesbian and gay relationships. However, the parallels are not immediately obvious. The message of Jude is that any church seeking to be in continuity with apostolic teaching should be vigorously opposed to anyone who argues that there should be no moral restrictions. Jude is clear in saying that antinomian teaching is wrong. In reality, however, people teaching such ideas are rare.

It cannot be assumed that those who support the blessing of same-sex unions and the ordination of clergy in same-sex partnerships are antinomian.

Paragraph 135 of the Windsor Report asked TEC (The Episcopal Church) for a contribution to explain, using Anglican sources of authority, 'how a person living in a same gender union may be considered eligible to lead the flock of Christ'.[19] In response they published *To Set Our Hope on Christ* in which it was made clear that they were not suggesting an antinomian direction for the Church.[20]

To Set Our Hope on Christ condemns a list of sexual sins such as promiscuity, prostitution, incest, pornography and adultery and sets up a moral structure for gay and lesbian relationships which they argue should be 'exclusive, life-long, unions of fidelity and care'.[21] Other proponents of the blessing of same-sex unions have proposed that any recognized Christian gay partnerships should be 'permanent, stable and faithful'.[22] If the opponents of Jude were antinomian they would have rejected such categories. A true antinomian would argue that 'All things are permissible for me' (see 1 Corinthians 10.23). That was not the stand of TEC.

This does not mean that the arguments presented by those who would seek to revise the teachings of the Church are right, but that they are not the same as those made by the antinomians. The application of a single proof text is not enough to condemn their teaching or action.

1.2.4 'Fight for the Faith which was Once and for All Delivered to the Saints'

Please read Jude verses 3 and 20–23.

Jude argues that if as Christians we base our life on 'the faith once and for all delivered to the saints' then we will not slip into antinomianism. O'Donovan argues that all ethics are based in the gospel: 'There can be no change of voice, no shift of mood, between God's word of forgiveness and his word of demand, no obedience-without-gift, no gift-without-obedience. The gift and the obedience are in fact one and the same. They are the righteousness of Jesus Christ, encompassing and transforming our own lives, past, present and future.'[23] The unqualified inclusive welcome to Christ is met with an uncompromising call to obedience to him. Our knowledge of God in Christ (theology) is intimately related to how we live as disciples of Christ (ethics).

Some contend that Jude is referring to a fixed body of orthodox doctrine passed down from the apostles and which is unalterable. Historically this has not been the Anglican understanding. A further discussion on this is in Chapter 4 of this book, but we have already seen that in endorsing the historic creeds the Reformers said that this was too simplistic an approach.

In contrast, the American Unitarian Association used Jude 3 as the basis for their rejection of the Trinitarian Creeds.[24] They argued that there can be no theological development from the closing of the writing of the Scriptures and therefore that Trinitarian formulations were unbiblical and false. The Anglican Reformers maintained that there was an essential gospel and fixed points on the journey (such as the creeds), but that the journey continued towards knowing more about God.

Jude does say that there is an essential gospel. This is in continuity with Paul's theology. N. T. Wright has proposed an understanding for 'the gospel' as Paul understood it:

When Paul refers to 'the gospel', he is *not* referring to a system of salvation, though of course the gospel implies and contains this, nor even to the good news that there now *is* a way of salvation open to all, but rather to the proclamation that the crucified Jesus of Nazareth has been raised from the dead and thereby demonstrated to be both Israel's Messiah and the world's true Lord. 'The gospel' is not 'you can be saved, and here's how'; the gospel, for Paul, is 'Jesus Christ is Lord'.[25]

There is an essential uncompromising truth at the centre of the faith once delivered to the saints, but not a fully formed systematic theology or comprehensive code of ethics. Truth is in the person and work of Jesus which is more powerful than can be contained in words.

To say that Jude and Paul were not referring to a fixed, defined, unalterable body of doctrine and ethics is not to say that doctrine and ethics are insignificant. Jesus was clear that his emphasis on fulfilling the law went beyond the mere following of rules and did not mean an abandonment of rules. Jude recognizes that we are called to a real commitment. He identifies the sins of the false teachers: they are greedy and grumbling, they follow their own desires and boast about themselves. These are sins, but they do not represent an exhaustive list.

Jude's challenge to the community to whom he wrote – and to us – is to stand firm by building up our most holy faith by prayer in the Holy Spirit and to keep ourselves in God's love. Jude proposes that the relationship between us and God is the key to our resisting antinomianism.

John makes the same link between our salvation and how we live in his first letter:

We love because he first loved us. If anyone says, 'I love God', yet hates his brother, he is a liar. For anyone who does not love his brother, whom he has seen, cannot love God, whom he has not seen. And he gives us this command: Whoever loves God must also love his brother. (1 John 4.19–21)

The relationship of love offered by God to us requires that we act in love. Acting in love is not an abandonment of ethics but a heightening of ethical demands. Such demands cannot be entirely covered by ethical codes and require levels of flexibility for their fulfilment. They do not result in the abandoning of ethical codes but in the interpretation and application of any codes in the light of the command to love God and neighbour. The loving of a fellow Christian can involve a word of encouragement or forgiveness as well as not stealing their goods or spreading lies about them.

1.2.5 Conclusion

Jude is proclaiming that Christian individuals and communities who build their lives on the foundation of the gospel will 'embody the moral implications of the Gospel which the antinomian teachers are subverting'.[26] He never denies the law of Moses, but it is their relationship with Christ, not only adherence to law, which will enable his listeners to stand firm.

Common Ground

Anglican common ground is based on an understanding of the Scriptures as sufficient for salvation and authoritative in theology, worship and ethics. The continued authority of Scripture across succeeding generations and in every place is in concord with theological development of the tradition, which is always required and always subservient to the authority of Scripture. This common ground is vital for our life together, as has been stated clearly by the Archbishop of Canterbury:

So a full relationship of communion will mean:

The common acknowledgement that we stand under the authority of Scripture as 'the rule and ultimate standard of faith', in the words of the Chicago-Lambeth Quadrilateral; as the gift shaped by the Holy Spirit which decisively interprets God to the community of believers and the community of believers to itself and opens our hearts to the living and eternal Word that is Christ.[27]

2. Points of Disagreement

There are deep points of disagreement in the Anglican Communion; to argue otherwise would be false. The bishops of the Communion at the Lambeth Conference voted overwhelmingly for a view that the only proper context for sexual expression was in marriage which was defined specifically as between a man and a woman. They rejected all homosexual practice because it is 'incompatible with Scripture'.

In 1999 the then Archbishop of Canterbury, George Carey, convened a group from around the Communion to continue conversations on the topic of sexuality and on homosexuality in particular. They agreed on the status of the Scriptures but could not agree on a common pattern of holy living for homosexual people based, they stated, in differing approaches to the Scriptures.[28]

As the present teaching of the Church on human sexuality rests on its 'compatibility' with Scripture those who wish to challenge the teaching of the Church need to show that any development of the tradition is 'compatible' with Scripture.

2.1 Compatible with Scripture?

What does it mean to be 'compatible' and 'incompatible' with Scripture?

For a teaching to be *incompatible* with Scripture it would need to be something which either contradicts Scripture, goes against the general thrust of biblical witness or goes beyond what Scripture can legitimately be claimed to support. It would therefore be said that something can claim to be *compatible* with Scripture if:

1. it is in not contradiction to Scripture;
2. it goes with the general thrust of biblical witness and it can be supported by Scripture even if the biblical witness is only indirect.

The concept of being compatible with Scripture is very important for Christian ethics as we seek to live morally in all of our life, not just in accordance with specific commandments laid out in the Bible. Some ethical decisions are clear. When in a shop we know that we should not steal a chocolate bar. At times we may be tempted to steal and the living out of the ethic may not be easy for us, but what is right and what is wrong is clear to us. However, we are constantly presented with new ethical dilemmas for which there is no direct reference in the Bible, and at times what is right and wrong may not be clear. For example, there is no direct biblical teaching on the right use of the motor car in an age where we are concerned about global warming. Our ethical response in this context cannot be merely to look for a biblical command, but to seek the general thrust of biblical witness and an option which can be supported by Scripture.

Some regard 'homosexual practice' as coming in the first category. They regard all 'homosexual practice' as condemned by specific biblical texts. They may recognize the challenge involved in following clear rules, but not the difficulty of knowing what is right and wrong.

Others regard only specific 'homosexual practices' as observable in the texts. They argue that loving relationships of fidelity and care are either not present or hidden by false interpretation. They believe there are clear rules to be followed, but these are relevant to abuse and idolatry, not to the blessings of permanent, faithful and stable unions.

To illustrate some of the dilemmas we offer two readings of Scripture to see how those supporting opposing views on the acceptability of homosexual practice and same-sex relationships. Those in each group believe their views are compatible with Scripture. These readings are very brief and we ask you to look further into the supporting literature to gain a fuller understanding.

2.2 Two Readings of Scripture

To illustrate some of the dilemmas we offer two readings of Scripture. Each one is a summarized account of longer arguments. We ask you to read each one in its own right and to ask yourself if it has any merit, not to play one against the other. You may already have a firm opinion of your own on this matter and it is possible that it is different from either of the summaries, but we ask you to see the strengths as well as the weaknesses in these summaries as they stand.

We are not asking you to give up a firm view, or arguing that both readings can be 'true', but we hope that in undertaking this exercise you will have greater clarity in formulating and explaining your own understanding of Scripture as well as appreciating the views of others. We hope parts 2 and 3 of this chapter will as a consequence be of further use to you in this task.

2.2.1 A Traditional Reading of Scripture

This reading of Scripture is in line with the tradition of the Church, especially that expressed in Lambeth 1.10. It is a witness of the Scriptures consonant with a view that rejects homosexual practice of any kind, and maintains that marriage between a man and a woman in lifelong union remains the only appropriate place for sexual relations. It is in line with a number of publications and resolutions, notably those of Archbishop Akinola of Nigeria and the Anglican Church of Uganda.[29]

The Bible is a continuing and developing revelation of God to humans in the form of a story with six acts or epochs, in each of which we see a consistent line in God's plan for our sexual activity.

Act 1: Creation
Genesis 2 portrays the creation of male and female as of central significance to humanity. The man finds delight in the woman who is different from him and this is a pattern for normal sexual relationships. Marriage is a created order.

Act 2: The Fall
In Romans 1 Paul shows that sexual desire is disordered within the general corruption of the whole of nature. Homosexual acts are part of the consequence of our human idolatry. What feels right to us is often part of our fallen nature and the argument that 'God made us this way' fails because each of us is the product of fallen nature and not of the nature God intended.

Act 3: The Life of Israel
Good same-sex covenantal friendships, like David's friendship with Jonathan, existed within the life of Israel, but such relationships were loving within the strict bounds and clear framework which forbade homosexuality. This contrasted with the culture of all the surrounding societies. The story of Sodom is rightly seen as irrelevant in this context, because it involved abuse and violence that no Christian would condone. However, the Levitical covenant set down the prohibition of same-sex relationships as a requirement of godly living.

Act 4: The Ministry of Christ
It is true that in the Gospels Jesus never expresses his thoughts on the issue of homosexuality, but he modelled a faithful, single and abstinent life developing close

personal friendships with men and women, and with one beloved disciple in particular, without any hint of a sexual relationship. His teaching on sexual conduct only strengthened Israel's traditional understandings. He quickly corrected false interpretations of the Old Testament and he was eager to challenge traditional boundary markers. That he did not challenge this one is significant. He did reaffirm marriage and made significant use of the story of Adam and Eve, setting it up as normative for married relationships. We as Christians are called to live as he taught and lived.

Act 5: The Era of the Church
As Paul took the gospel to the Gentiles he relaxed Jewish norms on food laws and circumcision. On matters of sexual conduct there was no compromise. Homosexual conduct, accepted in Gentile culture, was to be rejected as contrary to God's purpose for humanity. There might be significant questions about some key texts if Greek terms used by Paul are about abusive relationships and not about the kind of same-sex unions presented to us today. However, the defining text remains Romans 1.18–32. This text is about Gentile culture as a whole, not about individuals. While Paul did not have our scientific understanding of orientation, he saw the desire for homosexual relationships as a symbol of the sinfulness of all humans following the Fall. A significant part of Romans 1.26 is the inclusion of female same-sex activity. This provides strong evidence that Paul is not just talking about oppressive sex (older men frequently used younger men for sexual pleasure). Rather it is derived from an understanding of what it means to be made 'male and female' in the 'image of God'. Homosexual activity is clearly called idolatrous and sinful.

Act 6: The Ultimate New Creation
The New Testament vision of heaven talks of a resurrected body and no marriage. This encouraged the call to celibacy in the Early Church. It did not promote the idea that sexual activity had no eternal consequence.

Summary
The opposition to same-gender sexual activity is not reliant on individual proof texts but part of the core biblical witness of humanity's relationship with God.[30]

___

How is this compatible with Scripture?
This reading does not contradict Scripture and is in line with the biblical tradition. Its strength rests on the claim that the Scriptures are not silent on homosexuality and that there is a direct correspondence between homosexual activity known in the time of the Old Testament and of Paul and gay and lesbian relationships in our time. It admits Scripture is silent in places, most notably there is no direct teaching from Jesus, but argues that the teaching is both in line with the general thrust of the biblical witness and can be supported by Scripture.

2.2.2 An Alternative Reading of Scripture
Many sincere and devoted Bible readers have come to understand the Scriptures differently from the summary outlined above which supports the traditional prohibi-

tion against homosexuality. Initially these readers may have been moved to re-examine the tradition by the obvious dissonance between the depiction of homosexuality in the Bible on the one hand, and the Christian testimony of loving and committed same-sex partners on the other. Or perhaps they were motivated by what they observed as the corrosive effect of the traditional interpretation on the faith and life of many Christian men and women who discover themselves to experience same-sex attraction. Inspired by a love for people and for Scripture, many Christians are studying the biblical passages about homosexuality again. They are asking new questions of the text and the of Church's traditional interpretation. Their conclusions not only challenge the traditional view but call the Church to a new understanding of its ministry among homosexual people today.

The Bible is the story of God reaching out to humanity in love and our flailing attempts to respond. The biblical writers illustrate the successes and failures of that relationship by drawing on our experience in human relationships, especially those that are most intimate. In this way we discover the kind of relationship God wants with us, and how those qualities are best reflected in our relationships with each other.

The few passages in the Bible that describe particular homosexual acts fit into this pattern, as do the positive biblical examples of love and commitment shared by couples of both the same and opposite sex. Together these contribute to a fuller understanding of God, and God's intention for us.

Homosexuality in the Old Testament
Israel's 'Holiness code' was designed to distinguish and separate God's people from their neighbours who had earned God's wrath with the 'detestable customs' of pagan idolatry, including child sacrifice and cultic prostitution. Under penalty of death, the Hebrew people were forbidden from incorporating pagan practices into their worship of God and from prostituting themselves – literally – in the worship of fertility deities.

While God repeatedly demonstrated covenant love and continuously called Israel to exclusive faithfulness, the Bible is replete with accounts of Israel's recurring infidelity and lapses into pagan religion, including homosexual cult prostitution, making it a dramatic symbol of the rejection of God for idolatry. Homosexual acts are not mentioned by Old Testament writers in any other context.

Homosexuality in the New Testament
This pattern continues into the New Testament. In the first chapters of Romans, Paul draws his Jewish readers into understanding that, like their Gentile neighbours, they have also fallen far short of God's intention. Paul recounts, first, the familiar story of the Gentiles' rejection of God and God-honouring worship. Their idol-making, idol-worship, and 'unnatural' sexual practices – by which they had earned God's righteous wrath. Paul then turns the spotlight and reminds his readers of their own idolatrous past, which was not an abstracted or secularized idolatry-of-the-heart, but a raucous and bawdy paganism of the kind known throughout the Mediterranean. Jews and Gentiles alike deserve God's wrath, Paul writes, and both are likewise saved and restored to right relationship with God by faith in Christ alone.

Homosexual acts appear in this text as a vivid example of idolatry. This is also the immediate context of Paul's two other references to male homosexual prostitution (as the Early Church Fathers agreed, Paul makes no mention of female homosexuality). Even Paul's unique vocabulary is taken from the Levitical prohibitions against 'detestable' pagan customs.

As in the Old Testament, references to homosexuality in the New Testament are rooted in the Hebrew experience of cultic prostitution and idolatry, a pagan culture from which God's people are called to be distinct and separate. Homosexual acts are not mentioned in any other context.

Marriage and Same-Sex Relationships as Biblical Metaphor

Throughout the Bible, sexual relationships are used as metaphors for our relationship with God, whether in faithfulness, commitment, and love (as in marriage) or in infidelity and betrayal (adultery and prostitution).

In the garden, on seeing Eve's likeness to himself, Adam declared, 'This is bone of my bone, and flesh of my flesh' and 'the two became one'. Paul uses this phrase to describe sex in both marriage and prostitution, and as a metaphor for the union of Christ and the Church and of Christ and the individual believer.

The image of 'two becoming one' also describes Jonathan's love for David, for 'the soul of Jonathan was knit with the soul of David, and Jonathan loved him as his own soul'. The texts are silent about a sexual union, but their covenant promises – as with Ruth and Naomi – are the most personally intimate of the Bible.

With the best examples of heterosexual marriage, these relationships between people of the same sex exemplify the most significant aspects of committed love, and add to these the virtues of equality and mutual love, respect, and support which opposite-sex relationships found difficult to express in Hebrew culture due to its particular understanding of sex and, especially, gender.

From Creation to the New Creation

The biological pairing of male and female is understandably important in the founding story of Abraham and his many descendants, but the theological significance of gender, procreation, and marriage diminishes as the biblical revelation unfolds.

In response to a question about divorce, Jesus affirmed lifelong commitment in marriage, but he also chose not to marry and often challenged traditional gender roles. The New Testament church likewise favoured singleness and valued equality, love, and mutual submission in marriage and in their shared community life, contrary to the cultural norms of their tradition.

The trajectory of the biblical story, then, is not a return to the Garden of Eden but toward the New Creation in which divisions of race, class, and gender are radically altered. At the resurrection, Jesus explained, marriage will be no more. There will be no 'male and female', for we will all be one in Christ.

Summary

The Bible witnesses to a triune God, a 'God-in-relationship', who made us for relationship and who sees that it is good for us to be in relationships that reflect God's own kind of love. Our personal relationships can be occasions for love and fidelity but also for unfaithfulness and betrayal. They can picture our union with Christ or our rejection of God for idolatry. Homosexuality, like heterosexuality, fits into this pattern. Rightly condemned in one context, the same act may be part of God's creative purpose in another.[31]

How is this compatible with Scripture?

This reading argues that the context of the homosexual behaviours described in the Bible is significantly different from the permanent, faithful, stable, loving relationships emerging in the present generation. In this way the blessing of loving committed relationships is not contradicted in the Scriptures, but affirmed. The thrust of the biblical witness, particularly in the life and teaching of Jesus, is supportive of the alternative interpretation. The biblical witness towards same-sex unions of fidelity and care is only indirect, but a positive response can be supported by Scripture.

Questions

We ask you to be careful with these summaries. They are just summaries and those who agree with their conclusions will want to add and qualify parts of them. There are also other readings which others would offer. Having read the two summaries, is it clear to you why the authors of each one think their belief is compatible with Scripture?

Both authors believe they love the Bible and are committed to 'the faith once delivered to the saints'. What evidence do you find for their belief?

What further information would you require to know if they are right?

A fuller account of sexuality in both the Old and New Testaments and a greater opportunity to examine more closely the specific texts in the summaries follows this part of Chapter 3. However, the argument is not simply about the content of the Bible, but how we interpret that content.

The commission was called together by Archbishop Carey following the 1998 Lambeth Conference. They said that their conversations brought them to the conclusion that Anglicans 'approach and interpret particular Scriptural passages in different ways'.[32] In other words, they came to different conclusions because they were using differing hermeneutical methods. We now turn to consider some issues in hermeneutics.

3. Hermeneutical Methods

Both of the readings of Scripture above are based in historical critical method. There is a significant difference between the results, but both are from Christians in the evangelical tradition and make the assumption that the best reading of the text is the natural reading of the original intentions of the authors taken in a harmonious sense.

Hermeneutics, the task of interpreting Scripture, is something we all do. Merely turning the symbols on the page into words which we understand is an act of interpretation. In the present context of division it is important that we understand the similarities and differences in our interpretative methods. We may assume that the way we were taught to interpret the Bible is the Anglican way, but hermeneutical methods are constantly being refined.

We will now consider the method endorsed by John Stott in one of his most popular works, *Understanding the Bible*.[33] Stott is a good place to begin because his books have been translated into many languages and have been used in theological colleges and Bible Schools around the Communion. This means that many Anglicans follow his three principles of interpretation. They also offer a clear approach which can give a basis from which to understand more recent developments.

John Stott – Three Principles of Interpretation

1. The Natural Sense[34]

God wishes to communicate with us and it is natural to assume that he will make it as easy as possible, so the complexity brought in by scholars or mystics is something to be avoided. The natural sense is not necessarily the same as the literal sense; the natural sense of a poem or a parable is often figurative. Stott is also aware of the desirability of reading the text in the original languages and he argues that: 'in reading the words and sentences of the biblical text, we must look first of all for their obvious and natural meaning'.[35] Stott calls this the *principle of simplicity*.

2. The Original Sense[36]

We are asked to seek the original sense. Stott calls this the *principle of history*. Central to Stott's understanding of the Bible is that it was a revelation in a historical context. He argues that: 'The permanent and universal message of Scripture can be understood only in the light of the circumstances in which it was originally given.'[37] He recognizes that it is possible to read the Bible in the natural sense and to misunderstand the meaning because the natural sense is our sense, not the sense of those who originally wrote.

He embraces historical critical method and suggests four vital tasks:

- to reconstruct the situation of the writing of the texts
- to take note of the literary genre of the text, for example asking if the text is poem, letter or 'Gospel'
- to seek the original meaning of words in Greek or Hebrew
- to seek to understand the cultural setting of the writer, recognizing it is different from our own.

3. The General Sense[38]

The historical critical method has been the dominant hermeneutical principle in biblical studies. The primary concerns have been to seek for the original sense of Scripture in the study of languages to reconstruct the historical setting, to understand the literary style of the text and to comprehend the cultural context of the text. The historical critical method is endorsed by many in the Communion.

Stott says that: 'the whole Bible emanates from one mind. It is the word of God expressing the mind of God and so possesses an organic unity.'[39] The Bible, then, needs reading as a whole within the *principle of harmony*. The reading of a text out of its context or the use of a 'proof' text is a false use of the Bible.

3.1 The Historical Critical Method

Of Stott's three guiding principles the *principle of history* has been to the fore in biblical studies on texts concerning homosexuality in the Bible. Stott himself notes the tension between what might be for us the natural sense and the original meaning for the authors who lived many centuries ago.

In seeking an ethical basis for living the historical critical method attempts to discover the meaning of the Bible in its own terms and to exclude experience as a hard category. N. T. Wright argues: '"Experience" is far too slippery for the concept to stand any chance of providing a stable basis sufficient to serve as an "authority" unless what is meant is that, as the book of Judges wryly puts it, everyone should simply do that which is right in their own eyes.'[40] Some historical critical scholars warn of placing 'experience' above all categories and reducing Scripture to a position where it is only allowed to be heard if it supports the prejudices of the interpreter.

Robert Gagnon – the writer of a comprehensive text entitled *The Bible and Homosexual Practice* – stresses the importance of the historical critical method.[41] He contrasts his approach with that of Christopher Seitz.[42] Both believe that the Bible teaches that all homosexual practice is wrong and that this should be the determining factor for ethical decisions for individuals and for the Church, but Gagnon argues that the rigorous study of the texts is the correct theological order, whereas Seitz bases his criticism of alternative readings of Scripture on the plain reading of the texts. Gagnon criticizes Seitz for not countering the claims of other historical critical scholars who, falsely in Gagnon's opinion, argue that the method can be used to endorse a liberal attitude to homosexuality.

It should be noted that it is not only conservative scholars who endorse the cultured context of the text. It can be claimed that Stott's *principle of simplicity* allows for the experience of the interpreter to influence the exegesis of a text. The natural reading depends upon the experiences which have led the interpreter to that reading and does not necessarily take into consideration the original meaning of the text. In contrast, according to the historical critical scholar the primary task is to discover the original meaning of the texts. These insights are then to be interpreted into the present world. The question asked is if that was the message then in that culture, what is the message now in our culture? This second task is not a simple task and even when there is agreement about the original meaning there is not always agreement about the present interpretation. A case study can illustrate the issues.

Case Study

Stott chooses a case study to illustrate the significance of the historical critical method. He considers 1 Corinthians 11.10 to be a controversial verse which, he argues, becomes clear and binding using his *principle of history*.[43] We are not attempting here to produce a definitive answer as to its meaning or the validity of its application, but to illustrate the complexity of the task for the historical critical method.

The text refers to the status of women. Stott assumes that the letter form is one with which we are familiar and that Paul is offering a logical argument. With the rise of rhetorical critical analysis this would not now go uncontested, but he is right not to look for the poetic or the allegorical meaning. He looks at alternative English translations of 1 Corinthians 11.10 and favours the NIV, where it says that a woman ought to wear 'authority' on her head, over the RSV, which interprets the verse and uses the word 'veil'. Stott argues that while Paul regarded it as vital for a woman to cover her head, this was a Greek sign of being under authority. In the context Paul is arguing that a woman should have her head covered, but Stott is keen to emphasize the meaning of such a head covering.

Stott argues that as head covers do not have symbolic significance for his target audience – modern Western society – the wearing of an article of clothing is neither here nor there. The significant message is that women should be under the authority of men.

His *principle of harmony* demands that, in line with Galatians 3.28, this authority is not a sign of superiority – male and female are equal – but that men have the responsibility for loving care for women.

For Stott the original meaning – the author's intent – is that men are in authority over women and he concludes that we are required to apply this in our context and challenge Western culture. We are not to demand that women wear hats, but assist them to understand that they are under authority in the home and in church.

There are several problems with the method:

1 Linguistic experts are not at all clear how we should translate the verse. Fee, a leading commentator on 1 Corinthians, regards it as one of the most difficult verses in the whole of the letter to translate and devotes five pages to it in his commentary, ending with a possible meaning of which he says 'we must admit we cannot be sure'.[44]

2 Even if we are agreed on the translation of the words, it does not mean that we agree on their meaning. For example, Fee, supported by Thiselton, argues that in endorsing head-covering Paul is asserting woman's freedom and autonomy, the opposite of Stott's understanding.[45] A woman who covers her head takes responsibility for herself.

3 All the voices heard so far are those of men. Stott, Fee and Thiselton are all men commenting on a text which applies to women. If we believe that men only can teach the faith, then this is fine and their interpretation can be deemed authoritative, but we will have predetermined the outcome prior to engaging with the text. White Englishmen brought up during the first half of the last century – such as Stott – were brought up to believe that men should be the head of the family and in authority in the church. Their assumptions may predetermine how this text is understood. We may not be hearing the text, but hearing the interpreter. '[As] feminist scholars have shown there is power behind many seemingly "natural" aspects of gender and sexuality. With this power comes hierarchy and with hierarchy, exclusion and eventually persecution.'[46] It is argued that the neutrality of the interpreter is a myth, we are all shaped by our experiences. Women must be present in the interpretative community to hear how the text is lived out and their voices prominent in interpretation and application of this verse.

4 This text may not be in harmony with Galatians 3.28. The Galatians reference concerns the fundamental baptismal relationship we have with God through Jesus, so there is every reason to believe it should take precedence over a confusing verse in a letter to a dysfunctional church.

The natural sense is not easy to discover, the original sense is disputed, the neutrality of the interpreter is challenged and the significance of the verse compared to others questioned. This means that the implications for present action are open to debate.

The verse itself and the subject matter in general have generated a huge amount of literature. We are making no attempt to offer any original insight, but an attempt to interpret this verse illustrates the complexity of hermeneutics and should make us wary of simple answers to any major hermeneutical question.

3.2 Alternative Methodological Approaches

The search for original meaning has been challenging. Reputable scholars with a thorough knowledge of Greek and Hebrew and of the historical setting do not agree on the original meaning of many verses. Scholars frequently come to consensus that some readings are illegitimate, but often there is considerable debate about the actual meaning of a verse.

3.2.1 Who Can Interpret?

In recent years the historical critical method has come under sustained attack. While it remains a dominant method, it is no longer obvious that it is the only, or even the right, approach to Scripture. Initially the challenge to the method came from African scholarship. LeMarquand describes how Mbiti in his 1963 thesis stepped beyond the narrow confines of Western biblical studies, seeking relevance and present meaning rather than objectivity and an account of past history.[47] African theology has continued to combine biblical scholarship with a keen awareness of context and to look for significance rather than valuing knowledge for its own sake.[48]

Since then questions of hermeneutics across the world have moved from the original meaning to focus on the interpreter and the interpretative community. Three reasons may be presented for that change.

First, the possibility of disinterested scholarship is questioned. The goal of the historical critical method is to find original meaning. Logically it was assumed that the best interpreters are scholars who have no self-interest in the result of their scholarship. They can be charged with the task of finding a neutral answer to the questions of meaning. However, it is argued that the interpreter inevitably brings their preconceptions into the reading of the text. Numerous examples of historical critics ending up with the answer they wanted by so-called disinterested scholarship can be given.

Second, the search for original meaning has led on to the search for the authentic voices behind the text. The result of the Bible being analysed like any other text has been to seek the authentic words of Jesus, to unscramble the editorial work which harmonized differing traditions in the Pentateuch and to seek the reality of the history behind the book of Acts. Some argue that it is not the text as we have it which is authoritative, but the actual words of Jesus himself or the unedited meaning of Paul. Historical critical scholarship – through the use of such methods as redaction criticism, source criticism, form criticism and tradition history – has sought to use the Bible as a window onto Jesus and Paul. The question asked is not 'What does the Bible say?', but 'What did Jesus say?' or 'What did Paul say?'

Richard Burridge writes: 'However, in recent decades there has been a reaction to this use of the gospels as 'windows' to look through at what lies behind the text. After all, we do not know who wrote them, or when, or for whom. What historical critics think they see *behind* the text may just be their own concerns reflected from *in front* of the text. Thus many modern literary approaches view texts as more like *mirrors* than windows.'[49]

Third, questions are asked about the ethical conclusions which have historically been supported by the historical critical method. Burridge's approach to the Scriptures was influenced by the realization that support for slavery and apartheid by some churches was based upon solid biblical grounds which cannot be simply argued away by better historical critical understandings.[50] He describes how important it was to have an inclusive interpretative community in which to read the Scriptures together in the process of changing the Church from supporting to opposing both slavery and apartheid.[51] Change in the official stance of the Church towards slavery only came when slaves were recognized as humans. The orthodoxy of the Dutch Reformed Church in South Africa was only challenged by processes of interpretation which included the formerly marginalized voices of black and coloured African Christians. In line with the interpretative method of Paul and the inclusive example of Jesus,[52] Burridge commends the work of Gerald West in including 'ordinary' readers alongside biblical scholars in the interpretative community in the South African context.[53]

Those proposing new methodologies point out that this is the way Jesus and Paul handled Scripture and that they are in accord with the Reformation principle of the open reading of Scriptures in church by an interpretative community.[54]

In the introduction to the alternative reading of Scripture outlined above, Steve Schuh points out the commitment in Lambeth 1.10 to 'listen to the experience of homosexual persons'. He recognizes that the motivation to reassess the traditional reading of Scripture comes not from the product of disinterested scholarship, but from positive experiences of gay and lesbian couples by people who are 'sincere and devoted Bible readers'. The argument is that the traditional understanding of Scripture is constructed by heterosexual men, reflects their preconceived ideas and, despite any claims to the contrary, is not disinterested scholarship.

The realization that interpretation has historically reflected the interests and perspectives of the interpreters and that the dominant voice in interpretation has been white men has given rise to black theology, feminist theology, theology from the perspective of the poor, Asian theology and African theology. Those who stress the significance of the interpreter suggest that any interpretation of significant verses by individuals or groups which exclude gay or lesbian people from their interpretative process will inevitably be 'heterosexist' in its result.

The approach of Burridge and West is to be widely inclusive so as to ensure the interpretative community is not dominated by single interest groups. This reflects the idea – often endorsed by Archbishop Rowan Williams – that 'Only the whole Church knows the whole truth' (Max Warren).

Such an approach will not necessarily lead to a reading which challenges traditional interpretation. However, by 'listening to the experience of homosexual persons' – that is including the voices of gay and lesbian people – there will be a significant change in the way the gospel is articulated. The result of such an interpretative community cannot be predetermined. Oliver O'Donovan puts it this way:

Our first and last duty in this sphere is to discern the light the gospel sheds on the gay movement of our time. The Church must learn to attest its faith in the gospel before this cultural phenomenon. The gay Christian must learn to attest the truth of the gay consciousness in the light of the gospel. What we commit ourselves to, when we commit ourselves to true debate, is no more and no less than this learning. But let nobody presume to announce in advance what we are going to learn before we come to learn it![55]

One of the sternest critics of the historical critical method is Dale Martin. He criticizes the belief that the Bible can be analysed as something separate from the experience of the interpreter:

The fact is, it is misleading to act as if Scripture can be set up as an independent source for knowledge apart from experience. Every time we read a text we are experiencing. Readings of texts are part of our human experience, not something separate from it that can then serve as a control over experience . . . We can never encounter the text 'outside' experience.[56]

Martin contrasts the hermeneutical methods as between those who approach Scripture as a historic document – where the original meaning and the intent of the author are considered to be authoritative – against an approach which treats 'Scripture as Scripture'. Like Burridge, Martin argues that scholars should ensure that texts are used in a way which is true to linguistic, historical and socio-cultural research. He opposes the anachronistic readings of texts even when they support his own conclusions. He describes his own approach as 'postmodern Christian historicism':[57] postmodern in its realism about the limits of what can be historically known but Christian in that he regards the Bible as more than a historical document but as Scripture: 'It [the Bible] is Scripture when it is taken as Scripture – Holy writing, the "word of God", "inspired" – by the church, the community of Christians, the communion of the saints.'[58] He proposes that to treat 'Scripture as Scripture' is to go beyond modernist reasoning:

We *are* accessing the meaning of Scripture when we attempt to read it in faith, when we read it aloud in Church, when we sing it in hymns, when we perform it in music, when we dance it, when we enact it in procession, when we stage it in the stations of the cross or the Easter vigil, when we construct it in stained glass or statuary.[59]

Conclusion

Hermeneutical method is of great significance to us all as scholars, preachers and followers of Jesus. Martin points out the significance of the historical critical method and values the insights it gives. Davidson, in his book *Flame of Yahweh*, draws upon feminist scholarship often being enlightened by the insights of new hermeneutical methods, but he himself sticks firmly to the historical critical method.[60] There is therefore significant interaction between those using differing methods.

This is reflected in the consideration of the full acceptance of Gentile Christians recorded in Acts 10—15.

4. Acts 15

The debate between those who see the authority of the Bible as being separate and above the category of experience and those who see the two as complementary has been formalized in a discussion of how the Church came to accept Gentiles without demanding that they become Jews.

To Set Our Hope on Christ includes a reading of Acts 10 to 15.[61] In Acts 10, Peter was determined in his commitment to Jewish cleanliness. His refusal to eat unclean animals, was in obedience to the biblical codes of Leviticus 11. A vision of God calling him to eat such meat led him to comprehend that the Gentile Cornelius and his family had received the Holy Spirit as Gentiles, not as Jewish converts. This recognition was not immediate, but followed a period of listening and discernment. The concept seemed strange and even contrary to the essentials of the faith to the community of God in Jerusalem and so Peter and Paul were summoned to give an account of themselves to a council of the Church.

> It was only after Peter told the story of how he had been led by the Spirit, how he had perceived God's grace upon Cornelius and the others, how the Holy Spirit had clearly fallen upon them, and that this was why he went ahead with the Baptism, that the rest of the Church was ready to consider the matter in greater detail. They did not automatically say Peter could do whatever he wanted.[62]

This was not a matter of non-essentials (*adiaphora*) but potentially church-dividing. The argument made by Peter and Paul was not based upon human rights, but on a recognition of the acts of God. The result was that the Church decided that they should not impose an impossible yoke on the new believers (Acts 15.10 reflected back in Acts 15.19).

The conclusion drawn by the writers of *To Set Our Hope on Christ* is that if the community of God discerns the presence of the Holy Spirit in the life of gay and lesbian couples living in faithful partnerships, then they should be accepted as gay and lesbian people and not forced into either heterosexual marriage or celibacy, and that those in gay or lesbian partnerships should be accepted for ordination: 'It seems to us that arguments such as that persons of same-sex affection can be ordained only if they remain celibate are thus rejected by implication. In the Anglican tradition, celibacy has been understood as a gift given to some, not a requirement for ordination.'[63] The argument is that it is *biblical* to accept the category of experience in discerning the appropriateness of accepting the blessing of same-sex unions and the ordination of clergy in such unions. It is argued that such a development is compatible with Scripture.

Others respond that the category of 'experience' is invalid.[64] They argue that any analogy is invalid based on the claims that this was a specific, unique work of God, that the apostles had specific authority not available to us today and that this is a fundamental revelation of the gospel, not an issue of ethics and church order.

Gagnon presents a case as to why the specific analogy is invalid by pointing out category confusions between the two propositions. He asserts the difference between accepting ethnicity – a hereditary reality only incidentally linked to sinful behaviour – and homosexual practice – which he claims is based upon a chosen 'self-definition directly linked to sinful behaviour'. The Council of Jerusalem is about welcoming people, the claims in *To Set Our Hope on Christ* are about affirming behaviour; the two cannot be equated.[65]

Andrew Goddard argues that Acts 15 does offer a good model for discussion of contentious issues and, while we cannot claim apostolic authority, we can follow their method as we constantly seek to reform the Church.[66] However, his conclusions are not the same as those in *To Set Our Hope on Christ*. He agrees with TEC that serious disputes are to be expected in the life of the Church, that those who hold differing views should listen to one another, that we should expect God to work in surprising ways and that it is those at the forefront of mission who are likely to bring testimonies new to us.[67] His fifth point, however, is his most important. He argues that the 'narratives of experience cannot be conclusive'.[68] He argues that a closer reading of Acts 15 points to the pivotal role of James in appealing to Scripture. James finds that 'the words of the prophets are found to be in agreement with what Peter and Paul have been saying'.[69] He argues that just as the conservatives need to hear the prophetic words of the 'Peters' and 'Pauls' so the revisionists need a 'James' to remind them of the significance of the Scriptures.

Goddard concludes that we need to take on board the missiological implications, rid ourselves of negative stereotypes of gay people and have the confidence to speak of gay Christians. He argues that we should not demand that gay people become straight: 'Whatever else may be required of them, they do not have to conform themselves to the heterosexual expectations which predominate in both church and society.'[70] However, he also considers Acts 15.20–21 as a vital part of the whole. Gentiles are accepted as Gentiles into the community of faith, but James sets out demands upon all Christians. These are linked to the Holiness code of Leviticus 17 and 18, the part of the Law which includes the prohibition on homosexual acts. Just as the Gentiles were called upon to accept these parts of the Holiness code, so gay Christians are called upon to live within that code and refrain from homosexual acts.

4.1 Conclusion

From Acts 10—15 there are three responses to experience which are offered as biblical:

1   Acts 10—15 shows that experience is a primary source for developing the Church.
2   Acts 10—15 is a singular event with no implications for the current debate.
3   Acts 10—15 is a significant event which shows the significant place of experience, but places it in the context where it is under the authority of Scripture.

Further study is required of these texts and you are encouraged to seek the arguments in full.

5. Conclusion

This section is a brief introduction to the complex issues raised in the copious literature on the Bible in the context of our contemporary discussions. We have looked at how Anglicanism regards the Scriptures as authoritative for doctrine and through a consideration of the 39 Articles, thought about what that means for Anglican theology. We have used the letter of Jude to think about how doctrine and ethics intertwine. From there we have considered what it means to describe something as compatible with Scripture. We have briefly considered hermeneutical methods and finished with a consideration of Acts 15 to enable us to consider the difficulties of formulating the relationship between experience and Scripture.

We hope you will have the tools to engage with the further two sections within this chapter. The first looks at human sexuality in the Old Testament and the second in the New Testament. We encourage you to listen to the Bible and to discover insights of other faithful Christians.

We can leave the last word to the Archbishop of Canterbury:

Our obedience to the call of Christ the Word Incarnate is drawn out first and foremost by our listening to the Bible and conforming our lives to what God both offers and requires of us through the words and narratives of the Bible. We recognize each other in one fellowship when we see one another 'standing under' the word of Scripture. Because of this recognition, we are able to consult and reflect together on the interpretation of Scripture and to learn in that process. Understanding the Bible is not a private process or something to be undertaken in isolation by one part of the family. Radical change in the way we read cannot be determined by one group or tradition alone.[71]

Notes to Part 1

1 The Virginia Report, Para. 3.6.
2 Ibid., Para. 3.7.
3 Not all churches of the Anglican Communion have adopted the 39 Articles, but they are said to be honoured throughout the Communion.
4 Oliver O'Donovan, *On the Thirty Nine Articles: A Conversation with Tudor Christianity* (Exeter: Paternoster, 1986).
5 Ibid., 50.
6 Ibid., 51. Emphasis his.
7 John Stott, *The Anglican Communion and Scripture* (Carlisle: Regnum, 1996), 49.
8 These words are followed in the article by a list of the canonical books of the Old Testament and a list of those books 'read for example of life and instruction of manners' but not 'to establish any doctrine'.
9 Rowan Greer, *Anglican Approaches to Scripture* (New York: Crossroad, 2006), xi.
10 O'Donovan, *On the Thirty Nine Articles*, 53.
11 Ibid., 54.
12 Ibid.
13 Ibid., 59.
14 For a full discussion see Richard Bauckham, *Jude, 2 Peter* (Dallas: Word, 1983), 3–18.
15 Ibid., 3.
16 A fuller discussion of Jude 7 is set out in a later section in this chapter.
17 For example: Robert A. J. Gagnon, *The Bible and Homosexual Practice: Texts and Hermeneutics* (Nashville: Abingdon Press, 2001), 87–8.
18 For example: Bauckham, *Jude*, 54.
19 The Windsor Report, Para. 135.
20 *To Set Our Hope on Christ* (New York: TEC, 2005), available online at: <www.episcopalchurch.org/documents/ToSetOurHopeOnChrist.pdf>.
21 Ibid., Para. 2.1.
22 Jeffrey John in *Permanent, Faithful, Stable* (London: DLT, 2000). John identifies the first use of this phrase in the unpublished Gloucester Report (1979) presented to the bishops of the Church of England.
23 Oliver O'Donovan, 'Good News for Gay Christians' .

24 American Unitarian Association, 'Tract One, 1827'.
25 Tom Wright, 'New Perspectives on Paul', 10th Edinburgh Dogmatics Conference, 2003, available at <www.ntwrightpage.com/Wright_New_Perspectives.htm>. Emphasis mine.
26 Bauckham, *Jude*, 117.
27 The Archbishop of Canterbury's Advent Letter 2007. He states also that full relationship of communion means commitment to 'Word and Sacrament' and to Mission. Full text available online: <www.anglicancommunion.org/acns/news.cfm/2007/12/14/ACNS4354>.
28 International Anglican conversations on Human Sexuality.
29 See Archbishop Peter Akinola, 'Why I Object to Homosexuality and Same-sex Unions', available online: <www.anglican-nig.org/Pri_obj_Homo.htm>. Also 'Church of Uganda Position Paper on Scripture, Authority, and Human Sexuality' (May 2005). Available online: <www.anglicancommunion.org/listening/world/docs/doc6.cfm>.
30 This reading is a summary of the argument in *True Union in the Body?* by Andrew Goddard and Peter Walker and is agreed by them to be a true and fair summary. You are encouraged to read the whole text for yourself.
31 This summary is of *Challenging Conventional Wisdom* by Steve Schuh and written with his full co-operation. You are encouraged to read the full text which is available online: <www.integritycanada.org/publications/Challenging_Conventional_Wisdom-Schuh.pdf>.
32 *Conversations on Human Sexuality*, 6
33 John Stott, *Understanding the Bible* (London: Scripture Union, 3rd edn, 1988).
34 Ibid., 165–70.
35 Ibid., 167.
36 Ibid., 170–5.
37 Ibid., 170.
38 Ibid., 175–82.
39 Ibid., 176.
40 N. T. Wright, *The Last Word: Beyond the Bible Wars to a New Understanding of the Authority of Scripture* (San Francisco: HarperCollins, 2005), 101.
41 Robert Gagnon in Dan Via and Robert Gagnon, *Homosexuality and the Bible: Two Views* (Minneapolis: Fortress, 2003), 41.
42 Robert Gagnon, 'A Comprehensive and Critical Review Essay of *Homosexuality, Science, and the "Plain Sense" of Scripture*, Part 2', *Horizons in Biblical Theology*, Vol. 25 (2003). Christopher Seitz, 'Sexuality and Scripture's Plain Sense: The Christian Community and the Law of God', in David L. Balch (ed.), *Homosexuality, Science and the 'Plain Sense' of Scripture* (Grand Rapids: Eerdmans, 2000), 177–96.
43 Stott, *Understanding*, 174–5.
44 Gordon Fee, *The First Epistle to the Corinthians* (Grand Rapids: Eerdmans, 1987), 518–22.
45 Ibid., 522. Anthony Thiselton, *The First Epistle to the Corinthians* (Grand Rapids: Eerdmans, 2000), 838–9.
46 Lisa Isherwood, 'Scripture for Liberation', in Andrew Linzey and Richard Kirker (eds), *Gays and the Future of Anglicanism* (Winchester: O Books, 2005), 50.
47 Grant LeMarquand, '"And the rulers of the nations shall bring their treasures into it": A Review of Biblical Exegesis in Africa', *The ANITEPAM Journal*, November 2006, 75–87.
48 See the methodological essays in Grant LeMarquand and Joseph Galgalo (eds), *Theological Education in Contemporary Africa* (Eldoret, Kenya: Zapf, 2004), 5–104.
49 Richard Burridge, *Imitating Jesus: An Inclusive Approach to New Testament Ethics* (Grand Rapids: Eerdmans, 2007), 23. Emphasis his.
50 Richard Burridge, 'Being Biblical? Slavery, Sexuality, and the Inclusive Community' (2007). Available online: <www.anglicancommunion.org/listening/world/docs/Eric%20Symes%20Abbott%20Memorial%20Lecture%202007.pdf>.
51 Ibid., 8–9.
52 Burridge, *Imitating Jesus*, 62–79.
53 Burridge, 'Being Biblical', 9.
54 Richard Hays, *Echoes of Scripture in the Letters of Paul* (New Haven: Yale University Press, 1989), 156.
55 Oliver O'Donovan in Bradshaw (ed.), *The Way Forward?* (London: Hodder and Stoughton, 1997), 24.
56 Dale Martin, *Sex and the Single Saviour* (Louisville: Westminster John Knox, 2006), 157–8.
57 Ibid., 162.

58   Ibid., 163.
59   Ibid., 165.
60   Richard Davidson *Flame of Yahweh: Sexuality in the Old Testament* (Massachusetts: Hendrickson, 2007), 2–6.
61   *To Set Our Hope on Christ*, Para. 2.10.
62   Ibid.
63   Ibid.
64   For example: Dave Leal, '. . . my argument is against the category of "experience" altogether'. Dave Leal, *Debating Homosexuality* (Cambridge: Grove, 1996). From the preface.
65   Robert Gagnon, *Two Views*, 43–4.
66   Andrew Goddard, *God, Gentiles and Gay Christians: Acts 15 and Change in the Church* (Cambridge: Grove, 2001).
67   Ibid., 10–11.
68   Ibid., 11.
69   Ibid.
70   Ibid., 18.
71   The Archbishop of Canterbury's Advent Letter 2007.

PART 2:
SEXUALITY IN THE OLD TESTAMENT

John Holder

Introduction

Two vital drives in humanity are the drive for self-preservation and the drive towards procreation – the preservation of the species. Nat Lehrman says; 'Human sexual behaviour is of vital concern to every single individual throughout his or her life. Aside from the instinct for self-preservation, it is the most forceful response we know'.[1] The desire for communal self-preservation places issues of human sexuality at the heart of every society.[2] The sexual drive is such a dominant force in human life that the good ordering of any society depends upon the ordering of sexual relationships by convention and law.

Sex is necessary, indeed absolutely vital for human survival among other creatures. Sexuality has fascinated human beings for millennia and continues to do so. It is still one of the most effective ways of catching our attention, and this power is put to very productive use by those who advertise and sell a wide range of products.

It is no surprise to see the numerous issues and concerns emanating from this vital human drive significantly affecting the flow of human history, and reflected in the literature of the world. The religious literature of humanity is no exception. As pointed out by Paul Gebhard, who says; 'many religions have incorporated sexual behaviour into their rites and ceremonies. The ancient and continuing interest of man in the fertility of food plants, animals and himself makes such a connection between sex and religion inevitable.[3]

Davidson argues that; 'A radical, even "tectonic," paradigm shift in modern critical scholarship in the last few decades now sees creation, and not just salvation history, as foundational to the rest of the Old Testament canon.'[4] Previously the creation narratives were often considered as a mere foreword to the event of the fall and the Song of

Songs frequently interpreted as an allegory for the relationship between Christ and his bride the Church. The effect of both feminist and non Western interpretations of the Old Testament has been to emphasize the significance of the dynamic reality of the Old Testament and the central place of sexuality in the stories of creation.

The Old Testament was not written in a world isolated from the cultures of the nations surrounding Israel. The wider environment of the Ancient Near East was the environment within which the Bible emerged and developed. Many of the ideas found in the pre-biblical material are reflected or objected to in the Bible.[5] It is helpful to explore the continuity and contradictions in themes between those of the wider Ancient Near Eastern (ANE) communities and the Biblical tradition.[6]

Please read Genesis 1 and 2 afresh in a single reading.

Reflect on the key themes of goodness.

You may wish to read Psalms 104 and 148 and praise God for his Creation.

Note on Language

The Old Testament does not use specific words for sexuality, neither acts nor parts of the body. Almost all references are in euphemisms – words that mean one thing, but are used for another. A common example is the verb to know – *yada* – which occurs nearly 1,000 times in the Hebrew text. Occasionally the context requires *yada* to be understood as sexual intercourse.

Euphemisms are often the clearest vocabulary for the subject addressed, frequently there are no other words used. However, they do cause some problems for those interpreting and communicating the text. Do you think the verb *yada* when used as a euphemism should be translated literally by 'to know' even though in modern English this does not imply sexual union? Should it be translated by modern euphemisms – such as 'to sleep with' – or should it be translated in direct language – 'to have sex with'? This is an example of issues which translators face. At times it may be impossible for a translator be sure if *yada* is referring to sexual union rather than friendship.

Some other examples of euphemisms are *yarek* – thigh or loin – or *basar* – flesh – both used for the male genital organs. *Basar* can also be the vagina, as can *nablut* – shame – and *erwah* – nakedness.[7]

1. Creation

Theologians and biblical scholars are increasingly recognizing that the story of Eden provides an interpretative foundation for the rest of Scripture (New Testament as well as Old Testament). There is a focus on sexuality in the narrative so this theme is of fundamental importance for human relationships with one another and with God.

In the opening chapters of Genesis the triangular relationship of God/man/woman is set in place to explain and inform subsequent narrative and legislation as it unfolds. The reader has the necessary framework to read the codes and recognize proper and improper behaviour.[8]

Background

In the ANE the nations also had creation myths which reinforced their self-understanding and reflected their customs and laws. The writers of the Hebrew Bible challenged the myths and practices of their neighbours. They encountered the same themes of the ambiguity of sexuality in its potential for great good and great evil. To understand the Hebrew Bible it is helpful to have an understanding of the myths of the nations which were consciously rejected.

Four common themes emerge from the study of the diverse myths of the ANE. First, in most cultures, the gods were themselves sexual beings. For example, Ishtar and Tammuz in Mesopotamia religion, Isis and Osiris in Egypt, Cybele and her young in Asia Minor were all creators by their sexual activity and in the Ugaritic myth Anat can sometimes appear as the consort of El.[9] It followed that sexuality as expressed in fertility was used to explain the work of the gods in the created order. In the Akkadian myth when Ishatar the god of fertility descends to the nether world the nation falls into chaos with domestic animals refusing to procreate and men and women losing the drive for sex.

Second, sexual activity is seen as placing humans in the realm of the gods. The link between the gods and sexuality is explored in one of the best-known pieces of ANE literature, the Epic of Gilgamesh, a poem from ancient Babylon. One of the chief characters of the Epic is Enkidu the son of the goddess Aruru who is half-beast, half-human. When the half-beast Enkidu encounters the woman Shamhat there is a seven-day sexual encounter which is dramatically transforming (note the seven-day cycle of completion). The transformation is such that Enkidu becomes human and is rejected by the other beasts with whom he had previously shared company. His sexual experience creates a condition that separates him from his fellows (see Genesis 3 and 4). Shamhat has the power of sex and uses it to assert control over Enkidu.

Third, Enkidu's sexual encounter has not only created a divide between himself and the wild animals but has also catapulted him into the realm of the gods (see Genesis 3.22 for parallel). But sexuality has also done something that is critical to the man-woman power relationship: It has given the woman the power of control. The sexual experience is here presented as a gateway to the world of the gods.

Fourthly, sexuality needs regulating for the good of society. Consequently there are laws which emerge from the myths in the nations within which Israel had its life.

The Old Testament creation stories have both continuity with and stand in contrast to those of their neighbours. The centrality of the significance of procreation (Genesis 1.28) is affirmed as is the requirement to follow the laws of God given the power of the human sexual drive. However, there are significant differences, which we will explore.[10] It is within this literary and religious context with its dominant sexuality themes that we can place the Old Testament discussion on sexuality. A common factor linking the discussion in Ancient Israel with that of its neighbour, is the human drive for preservation and procreation.

Creation in Genesis 1 and 2

So God created humankind in his image, in the image of God he created them; male and female he created them. God blessed them, and God said to them, 'Be fruitful and multiply, and fill the earth and subdue it; and have dominion over the fish of the sea and over the birds of the air and over every living thing that moves upon the earth.' Genesis 1.27–28

In Genesis 1.28 'To be fruitful and multiply and fill the earth' is a command and a blessing. Sexuality is a gift of Yahweh, which is to be put to work. It is given for one expressed purpose and this is procreation. This link between sexuality and procreation is critical to the biblical understanding of sexuality. However, unlike the gods of the myths of the ANE, it is not an activity in which Yahweh himself is involved. Procreation is the power Yahweh gives to humanity. Von Rad says; 'Man's procreative ability is not here understood as an emanation, a manifestation of his creation in God's image.'[11]

With sexuality comes power. This is the power to increase, to control and to manage. But it is not – as in the case of Enkidu in the Gilgamesh epic – the power to enter into the realm of the divine. As Eugene Maly puts it, the narrator shows: 'man's procreative power to be not an indication of his divine likeness (achieving a kind of immortality), but the result of a special divine blessing. By using this power man does not enter into the mythical world of the gods as in the... rite of sacred prostitution, but he fulfils a divine precept.'[12] There is therefore from the very start a clear indication that sexuality is not a door through which mortals can enter to become like Yahweh.

In Genesis 2.18–25 there is a reflection on the man–woman relationship. It is depicted as a mysterious relationship. It seems as if man and woman can be so close that the woman is like a rib, that is, part of the man. This mysterious relationship is the result of the creation of Yahweh (2.21). The man had no say in it at all – he was fast asleep when it occurred: out of *ish* (man) comes *ishshah* (woman). This connection results in such a powerful attraction to each other that the man readily leaves his primary household to start a new one with his woman, 'Therefore a man leaves his father and his mother and clings to his woman, and they become one flesh' (Genesis 2.24).

The Hebrew word for flesh – *basar* – can also be used as a euphemism for the male sexual organ,[13] which means sexuality is introduced into the discussion in 2.24, not after the fall. Clinging – *dabaq* – can also be read as a euphemism for sexual activity. As such therefore human sexuality is not a curse, as some have read into 3.16, but it is an integral part of Yahweh's great act of creation. It is a blessing of Yahweh. It is Yahweh who arranges things so that the man can have the woman as his companion. It all comes with a deep sense of innocence, 'And the man and his wife were both naked, and were not ashamed' (Genesis 2.25). The nakedness that can be the precursor to sexual activity is nothing to be ashamed of. It is part of the world created by Yahweh. This rings with a powerful positive understanding of human sexuality.

There is absent at this stage in this creation story the functional nature of sexuality that is present in the first creation story. There seems to be more an emphasis on companionship and support. Sexuality is a powerful magnet that draws the man and the woman to each other. The power of the passion keeps them together.

Sexuality in the Creation Narratives

Davidson in his book *The Flame of Yahweh* identifies ten significant themes in the creation narrative for Old Testament understandings of sexuality.

1. Sexuality as a Created Order
God is not a sexual being and is neither male nor female, but both male and female are made in his image (Genesis 1.26–28). In creating male and female God creates sexuality by forming man from the dust and building woman from one of the man's ribs.

2. A Heterosexual Human Duality and Marital Form
Davidson argues that the contention that the original being was androgynous (of no sex) or hermaphrodite (of both sex) cannot be maintained from the Hebrew used in Genesis 1.27. The male and female are blessed in 1.28 and he argues that 'The sexual distinction between male and female is fundamental to what it means to be human. To be human is to live as a sexual person.'[14] The creation narrative comes to a conclusion with the marriage of Adam and Eve as a paradigm for human living (2.23–25). The model of Eden is a heterosexual marriage.

3. A Monogamous Marital Form
The marriage of Adam to Eve also holds up the paradigm of a monogamous relationship. The Hebrew is specific in the use of the singular for both man and woman in Genesis 2.23 and 24 which leaves no doubt that the divine design for marital form is monogamy.

4. Equality of the Sexes without Hierarchy
Davidson argues that the language of Genesis 1.26–28 makes it clear that male and female have equal status. They are both blessed and have the same responsibility to 'fill the earth' and subdue it and both have dominion over the creation. Neither is superior or inferior to the other and neither is in a position of leadership or submission.

Davidson claims that the false assumption of male superiority is based upon misreading of the text. While the creation of the male in Genesis 2 comes before that of the female this does not imply superiority. In the myth of the contemporaneous (patriarchal) Akkadian community the female was created first, but was clearly intended to be inferior. The adjective used to describe Eve and commonly translated 'helper' in English is not an indicator of inferiority. Its use elsewhere in the Old Testament generally indicates a partner of greater strength to the one being assisted. In any case it is clear that the help Adam needs is that 'he has an egalitarian partner, a soulmate.'[15] His naming of her is a cry of discovery not of dominion, emphasized by the statement that she and he are of the one bone and flesh. That she is built by God of his rib is not of his doing and the linguistic link between rib and side implies that they are to be side by side in equality. The Bible stands in contradiction to the rest of the ANE literature, where creation myths make it clear that women are inferior to men.

5. Sexuality and Wholeness

Only the male and female together are the fully human image of God. Greek concepts of the difference between the physical and the spiritual (the body and the soul) have confused Western theology from understanding that humans are a single whole which includes the physical and psychological. Man alone is 'not good' and only complete in relationship in complementarity with another being who is like himself.[16] Being alone is the only thing described as 'not good' in the creation account. Davidson asserts that humans are social: 'sexuality is for sociality, for relationship, companionship, partnership.'[17] He argues that; 'Singleness, although not God's original ideal, does not prevent an individual from experiencing socialization, including healthy relationship/companionship between both sexes. God provides for those who are lonely.'[18] However, it is the marriage between Adam and Eve that is held up as the paradigm for being fully human.

6. Sexuality and Exclusivity

The marriage paradigm in Genesis 2.24 calls for a man to 'leave' (*azab*) his father and mother. *Azab* is a forceful term elsewhere translated as 'abandon' or 'forsake'. It is remarkable that it is the man who is to leave. This runs against not only the cultural assumptions of the nations of the ANE, but also of Israel itself. The couple to be married is to cut away all old ties, free to bind exclusively to one another. The exclusive relationship is connected to the monotheism of the Hebrew religion. Davidson says; 'Just as the one God (Yahweh Elohim) created the whole of humanity for fellowship with himself, so the man and the woman made in God's image were to be exclusively devoted to one another in marriage.'[19]

7. Sexuality and Permanence

Once he has broken with his parents Genesis 2.24 calls on the man to 'cling' (*dabaq*) to his wife and *dabaq* is often used in the Old Testament to describe the covenant relationship between Israel and God. Adam addresses God in describing Eve as the 'bone of my bones and flesh of my flesh' (2.23) in the form of a solemn covenant to the permanence of the married relationship that we stress in the utilization of the words 'For richer for poorer, in sickness and in health' in marriage services.

8. Sexuality and Intimacy

The final clause of Genesis 2.24 is that the two will become 'one flesh' a phrase which commends the sexual union. Davidson points out that the one flesh theology is not only about sexual intimacy, but the full union of the couple in all its dimensions. This is not a unity easily achieved and the use of the word 'become' one flesh makes explicit a developing unity. The unity is not endowed immediately at the point of marriage, but marriage is a relationship strengthened by the passage of time.

9. Sexuality and Procreation

In Genesis 1.27 and 28 the statement of humans being created in the image of God is made distinct from the blessing of procreation. Sexuality for the purpose of procreation is a special blessing, not part of what it means to be made in the image of God. The omission of any reference to procreation in Genesis 2.20–25, Davidson argues, shows that sexual love is valued as an expression of the relationship bond, without denying the significance of procreation.

10. The Wholesome, Holy Beauty of Sexuality

It is at the point where creation is complete, with human sexuality as a vital part of the created order, which God declares to be 'very good' (Genesis 1.31). Sexuality is not a mistake or something shameful, it is not a product of the Fall, but wholesome and with a holy beauty – a blessing from God. Adam's greeting of Eve is passionate and celebratory and they are not ashamed in their nakedness.

The creation narratives in Genesis 1 and 2 are the ideal: they offer a picture of how things are when everything is going to plan, Yahweh's plan. This picture is soon distorted and in Genesis 3 led into the world of harsh reality and, while the blessing of sexuality remains, it is distorted and becomes an ambiguous gift.

Questions

We have shown that the view of sexuality in Genesis 1 and 2 stands in contradiction to the general cultural and religious assumptions of the surrounding nations in the ANE. How do they compare and contrast with the assumptions of your culture, both historically and it the present?

Davidson argues that the picture of the perfection offered in Genesis is of a male or a female in a heterosexual marriage which is monogamous and where neither partner is superior or inferior. The image of human perfection is one of a relationship which is exclusive, permanent and intimate and which involves procreation. It is this relationship which is blessed with holiness.

Have you experienced such a relationship of perfection for ourselves or in others?

How do we respond pastorally and theologically to:

Single people who seem fulfilled in their singleness?
Single people who are seeking intimacy, but who are unable to find a life partner?
Married couples who are unable to have children?
People who have not been exclusive in their commitment, or whose partner has not been exclusive?
Those who are dominated by their husband or wife, physically beaten or emotionally repressed?
Divorced people?
Women who have had no option but to be in a polygamous marriage, or men who are culturally bound to take more than one wife?
Those who are not attracted to anyone of the opposite gender?

Those whose gender assignment is ambiguous – it is not physically clear if they are male or female?

How do we as Christians defend the significance of the paradigm of perfection in a fallen world?

2. The Fall

In Genesis 3.1–7 we have an account of the loss of innocence and in 3.8–23 we are given the consequences of this new development. In 3.1–7 the loss of innocence is connected to the acquisition of new knowledge by the man and the woman. The nature of this knowledge is given in a discussion between the man and Yahweh:

> But the LORD God called to the man, and said to him, 'Where are you? 'He said, 'I heard the sound of you in the garden, and I was afraid, because I was naked; and I hid myself.' He said, 'Who told you that you were naked? Have you eaten from the tree of which I commanded you not to eat?' (Genesis 3.9–11).

The dabbling of the serpent in these special matters of Yahweh that has provided new knowledge for the man and the woman which brings evil into the world, including the blessing of sexuality. The gift is contaminated. That the knowledge is linked to nakedness, which is linked to sexuality and suggests that the knowledge given transforms sexuality from being merely an innocent divine gift.

The role of the serpent in enticing the man and the woman away from the way of Yahweh may reflect a polemic against the Canaanite fertility religion in which the serpent was a primary cultic fertility symbol. As such therefore the serpent should be understood to represent an understanding of sexuality that is counter to that of Yahwism.[20] The good gift of sexuality is distorted by the man and woman embracing an understanding of sexuality which is in contradiction to the plan of Yahweh. That which was once the source of support and companionship now becomes a source of pain and creates a lopsided, unhealthy relationship between the man and the woman: 'To the woman he said, 'I will greatly increase your pangs in childbearing; in pain you shall bring forth children, yet your desire shall be for your husband, and he shall rule over you.' (Genesis 3.16). Sexual intercourse that was once generated by passion and created companionship is now associated with pain and domination.

The gift of sexuality is still good, which is recognized by the response of Eve in Genesis 4.1 – 'I have gotten a man with the help of the Lord'. Yahweh is still present and actively at work. But the result of procreation is not unquestionably good. Cain and Abel end up locked in a bitter conflict that results in the murder of one by the other (4.8). Something has gone drastically wrong with the gift of sexuality.

The Ambiguity of Post-Fall Sexuality

The Old Testament is full of examples of how the good gift of sexuality blessed by God becomes ambiguous in the living out. We offer some examples. This is not intended to be a complete survey and you will be able to consider other narratives for yourself. They are intended to be illustrative and are snapshots of famous people or events.

Abraham

In Genesis 12.1–3 Abraham is called to leave his country and his people, and in return God promises to bless him as the father of a great nation. As Abraham and his wife Sarah get older and older they respond in a manner which emphasizes the ambiguity of sexuality. The promise becomes entangled in a sexual arrangement of convenience, one that is devoid of intimacy, is not monogamous and a denial of the ideal relationship between the man and the woman in Genesis 2. Neither Sarah nor Abraham believes the promise and they are overwhelmed by panic:

> Now Sarai, Abram's wife, bore him no children. She had an Egyptian slave-girl whose name was Hagar, and Sarai said to Abram, 'You see that the LORD has prevented me from bearing children; go in to my slave-girl; it may be that I shall obtain children by her.' And Abram listened to the voice of Sarai. (Genesis 16.1–2)

The intention is to ensure the fulfilment of the promise and sexuality is being put to work for the right reason, procreation, but there is a illegitimate participant, the Egyptian slave-girl. There are good intentions, but the wrong means to an end. The gift that should be utilized between the legitimate participants, Abraham and Sarai, is being misused and abused and so places the promise in jeopardy.

Abraham's story offers a vision of the power of Yahweh to utilize human sexuality for his specific purpose beyond the rules of nature.

> Now Abraham and Sarah were old, advanced in age; it had ceased to be with Sarah after the manner of women. So Sarah laughed to herself, saying, 'After I have grown old, and my husband is old, shall have pleasure?' The LORD said to Abraham, 'Why did Sarah laugh, and say, 'Shall I indeed bear a child, now that I am old?' Is anything too wonderful for the LORD? At the set time I will return to you, in due season, and Sarah shall have a son.' (Genesis 18. 11–12)

Yahweh here is putting human sexuality to work for its purpose of procreation when all the signals from the body clock indicate that this is not possible. There is a story of redemption within the faithlessness of Abraham and Sarah as the nation of Israel is born.

Sodom and Gomorrah

The story of Sodom and Gomorrah is a complex story and deserves careful consideration. It has great significance in both the Old and the New Testament and it is to do injustice to the authority of Scripture to simplify it as being 'for' or 'against' homosexuality. The story is found in Genesis 13.5–13 and 18.16–19.29. We have to consider that we may not be considering just a historical story but traditional material used to explain a number of theological propositions.[21] We ask you to be aware of your own preconceptions about the text and to subject them anew to a fresh look. It may well be that you continue with the same opinion and we hope it is strengthened by the fresh look, or you may find a challenge, either further qualification or a full rethink. In any case it is important that we are faithful to Scripture.

Sodom and Gomorrah are accorded a dreadful reputation. In Genesis 13.13 we are told, 'Now the men of Sodom were wicked, great sinners against the LORD.' In a wider context, the story of the destruction of Sodom and Gomorrah, as it now stands, functions within the Patriarchal narratives to sustain what is a sub theme of sin and judgement. Most scholars attribute the story to the Yahwist who is using it to support his major theme of God's election of Abraham.[22] Lot in the story functions to stress Yahweh's power to remove evil. At the same time, the story allows the Yahwist to improve the image of Abraham by presenting him as a compassionate intercessor (Genesis 18.22–33).

Sodom in the biblical narrative

The Sodom story assumes a great importance in the Old Testament narrative, not simply because of the drama of the story itself but also because of the number of times it is referred to elsewhere in the Bible. References to the event begin even before it has occurred as early as Genesis 13, which describes Lot's decision to settle in the region of Sodom. The looming disaster is hinted at even here by the author who states that 'the people of Sodom were wicked, great sinners against the Lord' (Genesis 13.13). This is picked up again in Genesis 18.20–22, which acts as the bridge between the story of Abraham's three visitors and Sodom's destruction. This passage describes three visitors who came to investigate the nature of the outcry that had arisen against Sodom.

There is also extensive subsequent reference back to Sodom. Much of it refers to the absolute destruction of the city (Deuteronomy 29.23; Isaiah 1.9; 13.19; Jeremiah 23.14; 49.18; 50.40; Lamentations 4.6; Amos 4.11; Zephaniah 2.9). This tradition also continues into the New Testament period where Sodom and Gomorrah are held up as types of utter destruction (Matthew 10.15; 11.23–4; Luke 10.12; 17.29; Romans 9.29; 2 Peter 2.6; Jude 1.7; Revelation 11.8). Occasionally the story is also referred to, to illustrate the great sinfulness of a people who are now being addressed. So in Deuteronomy 32.32 the vine of the enemies of Israel is described as being like that of Sodom; or in Isaiah 1.10 Judah is addressed as 'Sodom' as an illustration of their great wrong. Likewise in Isaiah 3.9, Jerusalem is likened to Sodom in that her inhabitants do not hide the crimes that they commit. What is unclear in these passages is whether it is the content of the sin (oppression in chapter 1 and partiality in chapter 3 of Isaiah) which is to be liked to that of Sodom or the quality (i.e. it is excessive). On balance the latter seems most likely as the sins condemned in chapters 1 and 3 are different.

The most significant and extended reference to the Genesis 19 account can be found in Ezekiel 16, where Sodom is described as being guilty of pride, excess of food, and prosperous ease and not helping the poor and needy. The passage goes on in verse 50 to condemn them further for haughtiness and the abominable things or abominations that they did before God. One of the bones of contention in this passage is what is meant by 'abominations'. The word to_eba is the same one as is used in Leviticus (see discussion below) and some argue that it is a general word here used to describe the social injustice referred to earlier in the passage;[23] others that it is so general it is hard to know what it means[24] and others still to homosexuality[25] Gagnon argues that Ezekiel understands this passage is neither hospitality nor homosexual acts but 'human arrogance in relation to God'.[26]

One thing seems clear in these earlier and later references to Sodom in the biblical text which is that Sodom's sin is seen as wider than the events of Genesis 19. They had a reputation of 'great sinfulness' even before these events took place and it is this wide, general sinfulness that is most keenly remembered in the tradition. In a recent book, Michael Carden has argued that the story of Sodom and the parallel story of Gibeah were not seen as primarily about homosexuality until certain key Christian interpreters,[27] although others would disagree with this view.

The Men of Sodom in Genesis 19

The story itself starts at the beginning of Genesis 18, with the arrival of the three visitors. The way in which the story is framed emphasizes that this is essentially an account about good and bad hospitality. The focus of the debate on this passage is not on whether it is or is not about hospitality but whether it is *only* about hospitality, as some claim,[28] or whether it is about hospitality *and* homosexual relations,[29] or even about 'xenophobic aggression' which generated 'phallic aggression'.[30] In other words, what is the central theme of this story: hospitality and its abuse; homosexuality or arrogance which led to a xenophobia which found its expression in homosexual rape? As with many subjects, views on this passage can often be seen to be on a sliding scale with just hospitality at one end; just homosexuality at the other end and abuse of hospitality taking the form of homosexual rape in the middle.

The debate focuses around the meaning of the word *yada* – to know. Although Bailey attempted to argue that the verb has no sexual connotations here,[31] few modern scholars find his view persuasive,[32] as Lot's response to the men that they could 'know' his virgin daughters makes explicit a sexual undertone (if not overtone).[33] Where a number of scholars are agreed, it is that the story of the sodomite inhospitality is symbolized by their attempt to 'know' the visitors sexually,[34] where disagreement exists it is about whether this is a condemnation of homosexual practice *per se* or of the kind of social injustice that would pervert the demands of hospitality in this way. It should also be noted that there is disagreement about whether the crime here is to be seen as the attempted penetration of men, attempted rape, inhospitality or the unwitting or attempted sex with angels (making this the reverse of Genesis 6.1–4).[35]

What is clear, in this story, is that we have three models of hospitality at work: hospitality as it should be – between Abraham and the three visitors – (18.1–15); marred hospitality – between Lot and the three visitors – (19.1–4) and abuse of hospitality between the 'Sodomites' and the three visitors (19.5ff).

Gibeah and the Levite's Concubine

A very similar story to the Sodom one, can be found in Judges 19. This gives rise to a certain level of discussion about the nature of the relationship between the two. Scholars are generally agreed that literary dependence exists and that Judge 19 is dependent upon the earlier Genesis 19.[36] If this is the case, and the content of Judges 19 is shaped by a dependence on Genesis 19, then Judges 19 may be a piece of interpretation of the Sodom story. In which case the differences between the two become worthy of note.[37]

The story is introduced with what could be an idea of a 'free for all' society; there being no central authority (king) in Israel (Judges 19.1). It is into this type of society that the Levite brings his woman who is described as a *philenesh* – a concubine. This term is riddled with negative sexual motifs. The woman is one to whom the community has not conferred the necessary legitimacy to engage in sexual activity with one of its members, her partner. The rendering of *ishat* in 19.3 as 'husband' does not diminish the negative sexuality theme, since for all intents and purposes the word if read in relation to *philenesh* should probably be rendered 'her man'.

Judges 19.2 introduces the theme of conflict between the Levite and his concubine because his concubine was unfaithful to him. Or as the King James Version graphically puts it: 'His concubine played the whore against him, and went away from him unto her father's house to Bethlehem in Judah, and was there four whole months.' Drawing on fuller sources most English translations render this verse in terms of the anger instead of sexual unfaithfulness. The translation of the NRSV is '. . . his concubine became angry with him.' There is a strong sexual theme in the material, which the above translation does not capture.

The claim that the story of Sodom is about a failure of hospitality is strengthened by reference to Judges 19. The Levites, the priestly tribe, were marked by not having a land of their own and being reliant on the hospitality of the other tribes. The hospitality of Judah is contrasted with the inhospitality of Benjamin where no one will take the Levite in until an old man offers to supply him what he needs.

The differences include the words of the Ephraimite in Judges 19.24 which adds to Lot's words in Genesis 19.8 'Look, I have two daughters who have not known a man; let me bring them out to you, and do to them as you please; only do nothing to these men, for they have come under the shelter of my roof,' with the much more censorious 'Here are my virgin daughter and his concubine; let me bring them out now. *Ravish them* and do whatever you want to them; but against this man do not do such *a vile thing*.' (Judges 19.24).[38]

The old man regards the homosexual rape of a man as more vile than the rape of his own daughter and the man's concubine. 'Repugnance for male penetration of males must have been a significant factor in twice designating the demand for sexual intercourse with the Levite as a *nebala* much greater that that involved in intercourse with the old man's daughter and the Levite's concubine.'[39] The question for us is if the old man is right.

The Levite himself in reporting the crime accuses the men of Gibeah of trying to kill him and does not mention the threat of rape, putting the emphasis back on hospitality. Had his concubine not died in the merciless attack it is not clear that he would have reported them for their crimes (19.28). The story points to a complete failure of morality. The war with the Benjamites is a further sign of the lawlessness of the age and no delight is taken by the destruction of the tribe (21.2–3). The solution is for more killing (21.10–11) and the planned forced entrapment of the girls of Shiloh (21.20–22). The creation ideal of the equality of women and men is utterly destroyed and it is this context that the conclusion is drawn 'In those days Israel had no king; everyone did as he saw fit.' (21.25)

Conclusion

There is no ambiguity in the stories of Sodom or Gibeah – there is no goodness in either. Most gay and lesbian commentators do not deny that the men of Sodom wished to assault and humiliate Lot's guests in acts of rape and sexual violence.[40] Nor would they deny that the threat to the Levite was of homosexual rape regarded by the old man as a vile thing, more vile than the raping of a virgin and a concubine. This is immoral behaviour of a most vile nature. They do not deny that there is immoral homoerotic behaviour, but dispute that this requires all homoerotic love to be considered immoral.

Joseph

In Genesis 39.7ff sexuality is once more associated with power and domination. The sexual overtures made to Joseph by Potiphar's wife seem to reflect lust and an expression of her power over him. There are a number euphemisms for sexual intercourse used in the story. There is the verb *sikebah* – to lie – that is engage in sexual intercourse and the word *zahak* which can is traditionally rendered 'insult' but can also be rendered 'play' which as von Rad claims can mean 'erotic play' or 'fondling'.[41] The power of sex creates an innocent victim in Joseph who ends being punished for a crime he did not commit. His imprisonment is eventually the route to release and freedom and so there is an element of redemption.

Moses

The challenges posed by sexuality surfaces in Numbers 12. It is the story of Moses marrying a black woman, a Cushite, to the consternation of his brother and sister.42 That Aaron and Miriam do not accept their new sister-in-law could be interpreted to mean that for them, there should be no sexual crossing over into another race. If so, they understood that sexuality should function along strictly ethic and racial lines. The great gift of God is in danger of being highjacked to support a narrow racist position.

That there is the type of reaction from Yahweh in Numbers 12.9–15, where Miriam turns white as punishment for her rejection of her black sister-in-law, makes the important point that man-woman relationships and the great gift of sexuality should not be subjected to and be distorted by race.

Ruth

The relationship between Ruth and Naomi has been identified in recent years as a positive model of same sex relationships, particularly lesbian relationships. It is certainly true that it is described in intimate terms with Ruth 'clinging' – *dabaq* – to Naomi (Ruth 1.14, see Genesis 2.24). It could be a euphemism for a sexual relationship if it were not for the direction of the narrative: Naomi is seeking to assist her widowed daughter in law to find a husband not seeking to find acceptance of their relationship. Also *dabaq* is used three more times in Chapter 2 as Boac encourages Ruth to cling to his workers (2.8, 21, 23).

However, the story of Ruth and Boaz has its own ambiguity. As with Moses the marriage of Ruth and Boaz is another inter-racial marriage. On the instigation of her mother-in-law, some argue that the young Ruth sets out to entice older Boaz into sexual activity: 'When Boaz had eaten and drunk, and he was in a contented mood, he went to lie down at the end of the heap of grain. Then she came stealthily and uncovered his feet, and lay down' (Ruth 3.7). Frank Spina has pointed out that Ruth 3 is 'replete with double-entendres and sexual innuendoes'.[43] He argues Ruth uses her sexuality to gain a measure of control over rich Boaz and so attain a level of economic security for herself and her mother-in-law Naomi.[44] More recent commentators dispute the implication that there was sexual contact before the marriage, but it remains true that the act of lying at his feet entails and element of sexual suggestion.

The sexual intrigue that is present in the story of Ruth Naomi and Boaz, is a reminder of the story of Judah and Tamar. A younger woman uses her sexuality to conquer an older man and so secure a better position in life. There is no euphemism about the barter for the sexual favour. There is a request for a sexual favour and a favourable response (Genesis 38.16). We see once more the power of sexuality being used by a woman to her advantage. We can compare the story of Enkidu and Shamhat in the Gilgamesh epic. The perfection of the creation narratives included the absence of power and domination and these relationships demonstrate how that image is defiled.

Whatever the ambiguity, the blessing of fruitfulness is given by God on the interracial marriage of the faithful Ruth and generous Boaz as they conceive a son who became the grandfather of King David and the forefather of Jesus (Ruth 4.14–22).

David

Two episodes in the life of David illustrate blessing and ambiguity and there are parallels with the story of Ruth. Just as with Ruth and Naomi, the story of David and Jonathan has within it the elements of the paradigm of creation in its intimacy and faithfulness. The Bible says that 'Jonathan made David swear again by his love for him; for he loved him as he loved his own life' (1 Samuel 20.17). The relationship was based on genuine love and affection and this love is most marked in David's moving elegy for Jonathan after his death (2 Samuel 1.25–26). What is not clear is if the relationship had any sexual element.

Some writers have claimed it is an oblique or suppressed account of a sexual relationship.[45] Nissinen argues that it is possible to interpret this relationship as a homoerotic one, and cites as example Saul's outburst to Jonathan about David: 'Do I not know that you have chosen the son of Jesse to your own shame, and to the shame of your mother's nakedness?' (1 Samuel 20.30), which both contains the word *bahar* – choose – a word used to describe 'a permanent choice and firm relationship' and raises the question of his mother's nakedness thereby introducing a sexual connotation.[46] He also acknowledges, however, that the narrative can equally be understood as the 'intimate camaraderie of two young soldiers' and that the relationship may be no more than that. Davidson, following Gagnon, argues that the words describing the relationship are those of father to son and indicate political alliance not sexual intimacy.[47] To ask the question of whether David and Jonathan were 'gay' is to go beyond the expression of blessing in the intimate faithful relationship between the two of them. James Jones says of this passage: 'Here is the Bible bearing witness to love between two people of the same gender'[48] This may be as far as we can go.

Another story of sexuality in the life of David is clearly sexual and unambiguously sinful. The story of David and Bathsheba illustrates the negative power that can be generated by human sexuality (2 Samuel 11–12). As in the story of the Levite's concubine, there is a combination of power and sexual desire and these are directed at one who has no power to tame or control them. Sexuality is being used for all the wrong reasons.[49]

Bathsheba is the victim of the combination of David's power and his ill directed sexuality. The purpose of his sexual encounter with Bathsheba seems to be one of sexual gratification rather than procreation or the blessings of intimacy. That the union results in procreation is the irony of the story. Sexuality is not the private property of those involved in sexual encounters, even if the person is mighty king David. Indeed the holding to account of even the most mighty of kings for his actions is a very significant theme in the story.

There is another victim of the ill directed sexual desires. The victim here is Uriah, the husband of Bathsheba. In 1 Samuel 11.6–13, the narrator places in tension David the king who descends to deeper sin and Uriah, who displays his love and loyalty by refusing to have legitimate sex with his wife. They engage in an intriguing conversation and Uriah emerges far above David on the moral scale as David becomes entangled and trapped in his own sexuality.[50]

The depth of David's depravity is made known to the nation by a prophetic declaration. David subjects himself to humiliation and his contrition is recorded in Psalm 51. Yet even here the fruit of the procreation is the heir to a divine promise, the one who is to build Yahweh's temple.

Questions

We have considered the ambiguity of sexuality in the narratives and histories of the Old Testament. You may think of other examples and consider for yourself how the paradigm of Eden is upheld and how it is destroyed in those stories.

You might consider the story of Jacob and his wives Leah and Rachel in Genesis 29–30. How are the paradigms of Eden are broken? Does God bless the fallen relationships?

How do the stories compare to stories of sexual immorality in your society?

Stories of sexual immorality among church people (especially clergy) are popular in newspapers. How would the press treat the story of David and Bathsheba? How does God treat them?

None of us are without ambiguity in our own lives. You may wish to meditate on Psalm 51.

4. The Law

In all the societies of the ANE laws on sexual issues were significant. For the nation of Israel they were intended to remind the people of the blessing of God and to act against the ambiguity of the fall. The most famous law on human sexuality is the seventh command of the Ten Commandments: 'You shall not commit adultery' (Exodus 20.14).

The law in its entirety was to ensure holiness and the blessing of Yahweh so the people might live well in the land. Random examples of laws to confirm the blessing of sexuality include the rejection of cultic prostitution (Deuteronomy 23.18) and the uncleanness of 'discharges' – both male and female (Leviticus 15). We do not have the space for a full discussion of all the laws in this text, but it would be wrong to give the impression that the laws relating to sexuality were especially numerous, the law is richer and deeper than that. However, they are significant. The Holiness code of Leviticus is especially important for our study as the laws relating to homosexuality are within that code. You may wish to read the whole code – Leviticus 17–26.

The Holiness Code

It is in Leviticus 18.22 and 20.13 that we find the strongest condemnation of homosexual behaviour in the Old Testament. The practice is condemned in 18.22 and it is accorded the death penalty in 20.13. One is led to ask the question 'Why this harsh punishment?' We offer two considerations of these laws from our two writers that show their differing cultural perspectives. They are not in conflict with one another and are not set up to present differing conclusions, but to enable you to reflect on the text itself and come to your own conclusion.

John Holder

It is no coincidence that of the three legal codes in the Old Testament – the Covenant code (Exodus 21–23), the code of Deuteronomy (Deuteronomy 12–26) and the Priestly code (Leviticus 17–26) – the Priestly code is the only one to mention homosexuality and pronounce the death penalty on those who engage in this form of sexual activity. There are a number of reasons for this.

The first reason relates to the context of the final shaping of the priestly material in the Pentateuch. This occurred in Babylon, the very heart of an alien and probably hostile culture.[51] The Jewish community in Babylon was an exiled community having been plucked away from its roots in Palestine and set down against its will in an alien land. Babylon was the symbol of judgement and disgrace. In the midst of these conditions however, the exiled priests became the rallying points for survival and continuity. These concerns are reflected in the priestly material in several ways. They are reflected through the divine command to the community in the creation story in Genesis 1.1–2.4a. In 1.27–28a we read: 'So God created man in his *own* image, in the image of God created he him; male and female created he them. And God blessed them, and God said unto them, "Be fruitful, and multiply, and replenish the earth, and subdue it."'

It is against this text that we can read the strong prohibitions against homosexuality in Leviticus 18.22 and 20.13. This type of sexual relationship could be interpreted as a threat to the very survival of the Jewish community in Babylon. Following on the Yahwist creation story, homosexuality is proscribed against a background of heterosexuality being divinely ordained, and functions as the fulfilment of a divine promise and command. There was therefore no place for homosexual activity in an exiled community that was heavily conditioned by a possibility of annihilation. This community now obsessed with a sense of survival had to reproduce itself and keep on doing so. Homosexuality in this context was nothing short of self-destruction. It is no coincidence therefore that the prohibition against homosexuality now becomes part of the divine law delivered to Moses by Yahweh at Sinai, and the penalty of violation is death.

In order to legitimize and indeed strengthen a prohibition that was seen as crucial for the survival of the Jewish community in Babylon, the Priestly writers, as in the case of the Sabbath law, resort to the well established Sinai and legal traditions. They draw Moses into the picture as Yahweh's agent and as a pillar of support that the community dare not question. The law against homosexuality is pronounced and the community can only follow.

There are as well other elements of the priestly tradition that militate against homosexuality. This tradition is very concerned with order and symmetry. Things are to be done according to the inherited way and every detail of life is governed by the law. There is little room for any different approach. Undoubtedly there must have been many of these approaches that were tempting for the members of the Jewish community in Babylon. The law according to the priestly tradition, however, laid down the rules. There was to be no venturing into the attractive non Jewish world where cult prostitutes both male and female were common.

Homosexuality is deemed to be contrary to traditional sexual behaviour and would therefore be diametrically opposed to the priestly traditional approach to life. Given the Priestly understanding of life and the world, this type of sexual activity could not be accommodated or tolerated. The strict right/wrong, clean/unclean approach of Priestly thinking left no room for this. This Priestly factor, when applied to human behaviour in general and homosexuality in particular, leaves no room for moral deviation.

Paula Gooder

Probably the most significant discussion on homosexuality in the Old Testament, takes place around the Levitical prohibitions in chapters 18.22 and 20.13. These appear in the part of Leviticus (17–26) known widely as the Holiness code (H) the emphasis of which was a concern to encourage purity for Israelites as a whole and not just priests. Gerstenberger argues that Leviticus 18.22 and 20.13 are related and that the latter (20.13) was probably dependent on the former (18.22), as 18.22 simply mentions one of the characters involved and takes the form of a prohibition; whereas 20.13 mentions both characters and lays down the punishment for the breach of this prohibition.[52] The verses appear in a long list of prohibited sexual relations including banned family relationships (18.6–18 and 20.19–21); intercourse during menstruation (18.19 and 20.18); adultery (18.20 and 20.10); and sex with animals (18.23 and 20.15–16). Of course in Chapter 20 not all of these carry the same severity of punishment.

Mary Douglas understands this section of Leviticus as arguing for completeness –

anything that contravened 'different classes of things' could not by her definition of holiness be counted as holy because '(h)oliness requires that individuals shall conform to the class to which they belong'.[53] All the sexual prohibitions, therefore, in her eyes were about the avoidance of confusion (which she argues lies at the root of the Hebrew word *tebhel* normally translated perversion, e.g. 18.23). Furthermore, Nissinen points out that the context in which these prohibitions lies identifies them as actions which the Egyptians and Canaanites (18.3 and 20.23) did and so were part of the formation of the distinctive social identity of the Israelites.[54] There are some who would argue that the framing of these prohibitions, with the inclusion of the slightly odd mention of child sacrifice, refers to cultic worship that included sexual activity.[55] Gagnon, though not disputing that the condemnation of cultic worship stands as a general background to the whole of Leviticus, argues that this is not the sole context being prohibited here and that the prohibition stretches to all forms of homosexual activity.[56]

All of the sexual prohibitions in Leviticus 18 and 20 can be seen as attempts to form a separate and pure identity for the Israelites. It is interesting to note that Jacob Milgrom argues that this passage is only applicable to Jews and not to others.[57]

The phrase 'a man as with a woman' (literally 'you shall not lie a male lyings of a woman'), is thought by some to have given rise to the Pauline word *arsenokoites* in 1 Corinthians 6.9 and 1 Timothy 1.10.[58] The construction is complex, though made clearer by the companion verse 20.13 which says 'A man who lies with a male lyings of a woman'. Countryman adopts Douglas' interpretation here and argues that what is being referred to is a man who adopts a woman's role, thereby mixing kinds and rendering himself impure.[59]

Of even more significance in the word *to_eba* often translated abomination. The discussion here focuses around whether the word means something intrinsically evil or something that is ritually unclean. It is clear, especially in the light of Mary Douglas' careful work on the subject,[60] that the word contains an element of the prohibition of confusion and boundary crossing. The question is whether this word is simply an Israelite cultic word referring to impurity or whether, as Gagnon argues it is a word 'whose abhorrent quality is readily transparent to contemporary believers'.[61]

Questions

It is clear that male homosexual activity is prohibited in the Holiness code. Few Christians embrace the whole code. Some laws, such as the food laws, we are explicitly freed from by Jesus (19.26). Others, such as the prohibition on selling our daughters to prostitution (19.29), we all fully endorse as Christians. Laws such as the one prohibiting the wearing of clothing made of two kinds of material (19.19) are written as commands from God which we rarely consider.

Read a section of the Holiness code and consider which laws are significant to you and your church and which are not. Does the distinction between laws that are 'moral' and those that are 'ceremonial' assist you in thinking why some continue to have value and others we ignore? How do we decide which is which? Is it simply a case of marking those we like as 'moral' and those we do not like as 'ceremonial' or are there criteria for making the distinction?

---

5. The Prophets

Hosea

One of the most intriguing presentations of sexuality in the Old Testament is found in the book of Hosea. Hosea presents us with some radical and creative thinking that makes an unprecedented link between Yahweh and sexuality. Hosea is recommended to marry Gomer the prostitute who becomes pregnant and eventually gives birth to a son (Hosea 1.2–3). Once introduced, the theme is further strengthened and developed. One of the radical elements of this development is the allocation of sexuality to Yahweh who becomes the husband and lover of Israel. Sexual activity and Yahweh are not treated as incompatible.

The heavy sexual overtones in the book must however be read in relation to the conditions to which the prophet was responding. The book should be read as a response to the dominance of the Canaanite religion in the Northern kingdom. The Canaanite religion was a fertility cult with a strong sexual theme. This theme was closely related to the experiences of nature. The Canaanites sought to explain the cycles of nature though the use of sexual motifs: 'The god Baal was at the centre of this explanation. The growth of the crops, the rains and the various seasons were all explained through the activities of Baal. Baal was a god of fertility. But fertility has to do with sexuality, and so he was given a female consort Anat.[62]

Hosea responds to the Canaanite religion in two specific ways utilizing its dominant sexual motifs. First, he articulates Israel's violation of the covenant, that is, their worship of the Canaanite gods in place of or alongside Yahweh, in terms of sexual unfaithfulness:

Therefore your daughters play the whore, and your daughters-in-law commit adultery. I will not punish your daughters when they play the whore, nor your daughters-in-law when they commit adultery; for the men themselves go aside with whores, and sacrifice with temple prostitutes thus a people without understanding comes to ruin. (Hosea 4.13b–14).

Hosea also responds to the threats posed by Canaanite religion violating an earlier principle that keeps Yahweh free from sexual activity. Yahweh is here portrayed as Israel's husband who engages in sexual activity with her. God is the 'husband' of Israel: 'She did not know that it was I who gave her the grain, the wine, and the oil, and who lavished upon her silver and gold that they used for Baal.' (Hosea 2.8) Grain, wine and oil were the symbols of fertility and represent the sexual engagement of Baal and Anat.[63] Yahweh is now assuming the role of Baal and Israel is portrayed as his consort. We encounter some explicit sexual language that describes the fractured Yahweh–Israel relationship. Indeed there is talk of divorce (2.1) and a request:

Plead with your mother, plead, or she is not my wife, and I am not her husband – that she put away her whoring from her face, and her adultery from between her breasts, or I will strip her naked and expose her as in the day she was born. (Hosea 4.12–14).

Yahweh behaves like a jealous lover (2.9–13), but is still madly in love and will make a renewed effort to restore the broken relationship by taking his beloved out of the environment of temptations. He uses the language of a burning passion: 'Therefore, I will now allure her, and bring her into the wilderness, and speak tenderly to her.' (2.14) The word *mephateyah* – allure –also means seduce when used in the *piel* stem as it is used here. Yahweh sets out to seduce Israel in order to bring her back into their love relationship. There is, therefore, present in this verse a strong sexual motif that sees sexuality as a means of repairing a broken love relationship. This can be treated as a positive understanding of sexuality and can be placed alongside the negative understanding of Israel being seduced by the gods of Canaan.

In Hosea therefore, sexuality is not an experience that is alien to Yahweh. Like Baal, Yahweh is depicted as a sexual being who is passionately involved with his partner Israel. The relationship is a turbulent one, Israel is sexually promiscuous, Yahweh is angry and threatens her, but she remains his beloved, and he works to restore the relationship.

Ezekiel

The use of a sexual theme to articulate the Yahweh–Israel relation is also at work in Ezekiel. In Ezekiel 16 there is a reflection on the history of Jerusalem. As in Hosea with the Yahweh – Israel relationship, that of Jerusalem and Yahweh is portrayed as that between a man and a woman. Indeed, Israel is Yahweh's wife. Here, the imagery of Ezekiel is like that employed by Hosea: 'Both Hosea (Hosea 1–3) and Ezekiel (Ezekiel 16.23) represent Yahweh as the spouse of mortal women without feeling and need to fear that such representations would be misunderstood as having a mythical significance.'[64]

Yahweh is deeply in love with his lover. The language tells of the nature of this love:

> You grew up and became tall and arrived at full womanhood; your breasts were formed, and your hair had grown; yet you were naked and bare. I passed by you again and looked on you; you were at the age for love. I spread the edge of my cloak over you, and covered your nakedness: I pledged myself to you and entered into a covenant with you, says the Lord GOD, and you became mine. (Ezekiel 16.7–8)

This is explicit sexual language. 'The spreading of the cloak' which is often interpreted as a pledge of marriage may also be a euphemism for sexual intercourse.[65] Ezekiel like Hosea portrays Yahweh as a suitor going after the love of his life, a love he eventually wins and articulates the old covenant relationship in a new language, a language that is brim full of sexual motifs.

In Ezekiel 23 there is again the use of sexual imagery to articulate the Yahweh–Israel relationship Jerusalem and Samaria are depicted as two over-sexed sisters who were involved in several affairs before Yahweh made them his wife (23.1–4). Not that this bold move on his part brought an end to their sexual escapades. These continued (23.5ff). As in Hosea, there is the use of graphic sexual imagery to describe what for the prophet is a precious yet tortuous relationship.[66]

6. The Wisdom Tradition

Proverbs

The wisdom literature like the rest of the Old Testament engages in a number of reflections upon sexuality. It reflects on many of the challenges of life and offers the best advice for managing these challenges and living the life of the wise. The sages identify sexuality as one area that needs special attention given the challenges it poses for the young and indeed the wider society. The young are seen as especially vulnerable to the sexual wiles of older persons. In Proverbs 7.6–23 there is a reflection on this. There is a vulnerable young man who encounters a woman who is bent on seducing him. In 6.18 she issues an invitation to him: 'Come, let us take our fill of love till morning let us delight ourselves with love. For my husband is not at home.' (Proverbs 7.18).

Here we are a very long way from the original intention of Genesis 1. In this section of Proverbs it is just for pleasure (see Proverbs 6.23–26). We can compare the two other cases where this is the understanding of sexuality; Joseph and Potiphar's wife and David and Bathsheba. The advice of the sage is clear and straightforward. This type of sexual involvement is to be avoided (Proverbs 6.24–27).[67]

The Wisdom Traditions of Second Temple Judaism

In the book of Sirach, from Second Temple Judaism, there are also warnings about the need to be aware of the power of our sexuality that can lead to involvement with the wrong person. In Sirach 9.9 there is the advice: 'Never dine with another man's wife or revel with her at wine; lest your heart turn aside to her, and in blood you may be plunged into destruction.'

This power can also lead to incest (Sirach 23.16) and infidelity in marriage (23.18). He is fully aware of the challenges posed by a 'bad' wife who is a drunkard and is unfaithful (26.7–9), but he also praises the 'good' wife who values chastity (26.15). The sage is not averse to admiration of the 'shapely' legs of the opposite sex (26.18). Women are often cited in the wisdom tradition as the source of sexual infidelity and entrapment. The theme is present in the Wisdom of Solomon where the actions of the unfaithful wife also come in for criticism. Indeed, the understanding here is that these actions are so disastrous that they have devastating effect upon her offspring (Wisdom of Solomon 3.16–19).

What, however, is significant about the discussion of sexuality in the Wisdom of Solomon is the radical approach to the subject reflected in Wisdom of Solomon 3.13b–14. We have in these verses adoration for those who have not engaged in sexual intercourse. Even if these verses are read against the background of the tirade against the ungodly and their offspring (3.10–13a) and so reflects the dictum: better to have none (children) than some that may be corrupted. There is a positive endorsement of the virgin (3.13b) and the eunuch (3.14). The condition of 'childlessness with virtue' (4.1) is one that leads to immortality.

What we are seeing emerging here is an understanding that the absence of sexual engagement – that is celibacy – brings one nearer to the realm of the divine. This may be a resurgence of the old idea that in the divine realm there is no sexual activity, since God is non sexual. It leads us back to Genesis 1 and 6 where this point is made.

It points us forward to the New Testament where Jesus' entry into the world is one that is devoid of sexual activity.

Song of Solomon

But the Wisdom tradition is not all wary of sexuality. There is also the celebration of this important human experience. Indeed there is a celebration of what surely seems like erotic sexuality. This is to be found in the Song of Solomon. These love songs address human sexuality in a manner that we have not yet encountered in the Old Testament tradition. We can readily agree with Rowley that the poems are indeed love songs.[68]

This collection of poems has generated its fair share of controversy down the ages with several interpretations being imposed upon them. It was only accepted into the Jewish canon because of the traditional Solomonic authorship.[69] Song of Songs was accepted by the Church primarily because of the allegorical interpretation that was imposed upon the poems.[70]

There are two main characters in the poems, two lovers – a man and a woman. Much of the poem is taken up with address of the man to the woman (Song of Songs 1.9–11, 15–17, 4.1–7, 6.4–9, 7.1–9 and 8.13) and that of the woman to her lover (1.2–4, 7–8, 12–17, 7.10–13, 8.1–4 and 8.14). The poems start with the woman issuing an invitation to the man to engage her in a passionate kiss: 'Let him kiss me with the kisses of his mouth! For your love is better than wine.' (Song of Songs 1.2).

It seems here that the woman is making the first move even if this is treated as a dialogue between her and her female companions. This is a case of the passionate 'intoxicating effects of love'.[71] Indeed the passion seems to be getting out of control. Hence the urgency: 'Draw me after you, let us make haste. The king has brought me into his chambers. We will exult and rejoice in you; we will extol your love more than wine; rightly do they love you.' (Song of Songs 1.4). This seems like the anticipation of lovemaking.

The woman in Song of Songs 1.5 describes herself as 'black and beautiful'. Often this has been translated 'black *but* beautiful' but a more recent translation of this verse that takes us beyond the problem some have had in rendering the Hebrew conjunction *waw* as 'and' instead of 'but'. They ignore the LXX rendering of the conjunction as *kai*, which can only be rendered 'and'. The problem here seems to be more one of racial stereotyping than the limitations of Hebrew grammar. The difficulty of making 'back' and 'beautiful' complementary rather than opposites seemed to have been overcome at least by some translators.[72]

The verse introduces the issues of race and sexuality. Once more, as is the case of Moses, there is an interracial sexual relationship. There is no protest in this case. Indeed the man is fixated with his black lover. He paints a glorious picture of her beauty (Song of Songs 1.9–11 and 15–17, 4.1–7 and 6.4–9). The passion is very strong and there is a longing to engage in sexual intercourse: 'You are stately as a palm tree, and your breasts are like its clusters. I say I will climb the palm tree and lay hold of its branches. Oh, may your breasts be like clusters of the vine, and the scent of your breath like apples, and your kisses like the best wine that goes down smoothly, gliding over lips and teeth. (Song of Songs 7.7).

The passion is mutual with the sexual desire equally strong on both sides. The woman invites her lover to make love: 'Let my beloved come to his garden and eat its choicest fruits.' (4.16b). Sex is to be enjoyed and the two young lovers in the poems are doing just this. There has been a tendency by commentators to add some respectability to what is obviously a reflection of wild erotic sexuality by casting the lovers as man and wife. There is nothing in the text to support this. There is no need for this imposition of 'respectability'.

The poems should be taken as they are, and for what they are; the passionate poetry of two young lovers who enjoy making love to each other. We cannot assume that those responsible for preserving this material and guiding its entry into the canon were not aware of this. That the poems found their way into the canon indicates that those responsible saw no measure of incompatibility between the enjoyment of sex and the Word of God.

Wisdom and the Female

We also find in the Wisdom tradition what can be treated as the introduction of a female element into the concept of deity. As in the book of Proverbs, Wisdom is accorded female characteristics. Woman wisdom becomes Yahweh's able assistant. In Sirach and the Wisdom of Solomon she seems however to be more that an assistant. The characteristics given to wisdom in Sirach 24.1–7 are divine characteristics. Wisdom existed before creation as was an active participant in creation (24.3). There is a similar understanding of wisdom's role in creation (9.9). This and similar treatment of wisdom in the Wisdom literature comes very close to identifying woman wisdom as Yahweh's consort.

It is highly possible that given the dominant Greek environment in which Sirach and the Wisdom of Solomon emerged that there was a need for Judaism to respond to the attractive more sophisticated Greek religion in which there were dominant female deities. It is highly possible that this effort to add a female element to the traditional understanding of Yahweh was an effort to address what might have been regarded as one of the limitations of Judaism.

That there is no sexual engagement of Yahweh and Wisdom would indicate that there was a point beyond which Judaism was not prepared to go in its response to the challenges posed by Greek religion. Wisdom may be Yahweh's female companion, but her role seems to be primarily functional in assisting in the origin and sustaining of the universe.

Questions

How comfortable are you when the Song of Songs is read out in Church?

Is it good to encourage married couples to enjoy the sexuality blessed by God?

How can we do that?

Conclusions

Sexuality as understood in the Old Testament is a gift of God given to human beings. The creation narratives of Genesis 1 and 2 offer a picture of perfection of sexuality that is focused on procreation, but that procreation is pictured in the context of a loving relationship between one man and one woman. This relationship is faithful, permanent and reflects the exclusivity called for by Yahweh in his relationship with the nation of Israel. The companionship brings wholeness and is fully mutual with no superiority or inferiority on either side. It is also heterosexual.

However, following the fall, all the relationships in the narratives of Israel reflect an ambiguity as elements of evil enter into all the stories. Violence, lust, unfaithfulness and seduction distort the blessing of sexuality. Laws are required to maintain holiness and the prophets compare the unfaithfulness of Israel to prostitution. The Song of Songs reminds us of the original unambiguous goodness of sexuality in poems of love.

There are moving accounts of wonderful same sex relationships – such as between Ruth and Naomi and David and Jonathan – but it is unlikely that they were intended to be read as sexual in any way. Violent rape is condemned in the story of Sodom but, while all are condemnatory of such behaviour, scholars are divided over whether the story has any relevance to loving, faithful monogamous same sex relationships with most saying it has little significance. The status of Levitical laws is equally controversial as some point out how much of the Holiness code we ignore while others consider them valid for all time. Further consideration of the New Testament is now required.

Notes to Part 2

1 Nat Lehrmam *The Nature of Sex* (London: Sphere Books, 1970), 172
2 'Sex (contrary to anything your personal experience might suggest) is not necessary for individual survival. (But) it is necessary of course for group survival among humans and other creatures.' Dennis Coon *Essentials of Psychology. Exploration and Application* (Ontario: Nelson, 2000), 389
3 Paul Gebhard 'Human Sexual Behaviour' *Encyclopaedia Britannica Vol. 16* (Chicago: University of Chicago, 1983), 594
4 Richard Davidson *The Flame of Yahweh – Sexuality in the Old Testament* (Massachusetts: Hendrickson, 2007), 3. He argues that this is a growing consensus in both evangelical and liberal scholarship.
5 Walter Beyerlin ed. *Near Eastern Religious Texts Relating to the Old Testament* (London: SCM, 1978). G.R. Driver *Canaanite Myths and Legends* (Edinburgh: Clark, 1956), 12. George Fohrer *History of Israelite Religion*, Trans. David Green (London: SPCK, 1973), 42–80
6 J. B. Pritchard, ed., *Ancient Near Eastern Texts Relating to the Old Testament ANET* (Princeton: University Press, 1950) and J. B. Pritchard, ed., *The Ancient Near East in Pictures ANEP* (Princeton University Press, 1954). These stand as two of the greatest contributions to this monumental effort to understand the environment out of which the Bible emerged. This collection of epics, myths, laws, and history capture a wide range of human experiences in the Ancient Near East during the first and second millennium.
7 A full overview of the vocabulary is in Davidson *Flame of Yahweh*, 7–12
8 Deborah Sawyer *God, Gender, and the Bible* (London: Routledge, 2002), 29
9 See M. H. Pope 'Fertility Cults', *The Interpreter's Dictionary of the Bible* (Nashville:

Abingdon, 1981), 265

10 See Davidson *Flame of Yahweh*, 18

11 Gerhard von Rad, *Genesis* (Philadelphia: Westminster, 1972), 14

12 Eugene Maly 'Genesis' in Raymond Fitzmyer et al ed. *The Jerome Biblical Commentary* Vol 1 (London: Geoffrey Chapman, 1974), 11

13 cf. F Brown, S.R. Driver, and C.A. Briggs, *Hebrew and English Lexicon of the Old Testament* (Oxford: Clarendon, 1952), 142

14 Davidson, *Flame of Yahweh*, 19

15 Ibid., 29

16 See Raymond Collins 'The Bible and Sexuality' *Biblical Theology Bulletin* 7 (1977), 153

17 Davidson, *Flame of Yahweh*, 42

18 Ibid.

19 Ibid., 44

20 Cf. Hvidberg, F.F, 'The Canaanite Background to Genesis 1–3' VT 10 (1960), 285–294

21 On etiological Legends, see Richard Soulen *Handbook of Biblical Criticism* (London: Lutterworth, 1977),.95–96

22 John Hayes *Introduction to the Bible* (Philadelphia: Westminster, 1981), 147

23 See for example Daniel Boyarin, "Are There Any Jews in the History of Sexuality?," *JHSex* 5 (1995): 348–53,

24 Louis William Countryman, *Dirt, Greed, and Sex : Sexual Ethics in the New Testament and Their Implications for Today*. (Philadelphia: Fortress Press, 1988), 31–32

25 Moshe Greenberg, *Ezekiel 1–20 : A New Translation with Introduction and Commentary*, 1st ed. (Garden City, N.Y.: Doubleday, 1983), 289

26 Robert A. J. Gagnon, *The Bible and Homosexual Practice : Texts and Hermeneutics*. (Nashville: Abingdon Press, 2001), 85

27 Michael Carden, *Sodomy : A History of a Christian Biblical Myth*, 1st ed. (London; Oakville, Conn.: Equinox Pub., 2004)

28 As Listed by Richard B. Hays, "Awaiting the Redemption of Our Bodies: The Witness of Scripture Concerning Homosexuality," in *Homosexuality in the Church: Both Sides of the Debate*, ed. Jeffrey S. Siker. (Louisville, Ky.: Westminster/J. Knox Press, 1994), 3–17, 5. Hays himself does not support this contentinon.

29 Phyllis A. Bird, "The Bible in Christian Ethical Deliberation Concerning Homosexuality: Old Testament Contributions.," in D. L. Balch ed. *Homosexuality, Science, and the "Plain Sense" of Scripture*. (Grand Rapids: Eerdmans., 2000), 142–76, 147

30 George R. Edwards, *Gay/Lesbian Liberation : A Biblical Perspective*. (New York: Pilgrim Press, 1984), 46.

31 Derrick Sherwin Bailey, *Homosexuality and the Western Christian Tradition*. (London, New York,: Longmans Green, 1955), 54–55

32 See for example Martti Nissinen, *Homoeroticism in the Biblical World : A Historical Perspective*. (Minneapolis, Minn.: Fortress Press, 1998), 46

33 Gordon J. Wenham, *Genesis 16–50, Word Biblical Commentary ; Vol.2*. (Dallas, Tex.: Word Books, 1994).

34 See for example the essential agreement between Gagnon, *The Bible and Homosexual Practice*, 76 and Carden, *Sodomy: A History of a Christian Biblical Myth*, 20–21.

35 See the list in Gagnon, *The Bible and Homosexual Practice*, 75.

36 The exception to this is Susan Niditch, "The 'Sodomite' Theme in Judges 19–20: Family, Community, and Social Disintegration," *Catholic Biblical Quarterly* 44 (1982): 375–78, who argues that Judges fits its context better than Genesis 19 and must be seen as the earlier account.

37 If Judges 19 is not dependent on Genesis 19, then it is simply interesting to note the similarity of the two accounts and to recognize that these narratives represent something that is abhorrent (whether it be homosexuality or abuse of hospitality) to the authors of the text.

38 See discussion in Stuart Lasine, "Guest and Host in Judges 19: Lot's Hospitality in an Inverted World," *JSOT* 29 (1984): 37–59,

39 Gagnon, *The Bible and Homosexual Practice*, 95

40 For example: Michael Carden 'Genesis' in Deryn Gest et al ed. The Queer Bible Commentary (London: SCM, 2006), 37

41 Ibid., 366. Gerhard von Rad 'The Joseph Narrative and Ancient Wisdom' in *The Problem of the Hexateuch and Other Essays* (Edinburgh: Oliver & Boyd,1966), 292–300. Donald Redford, *A Study of the Biblical Story of Joseph* VTS 90 (Leiden:Brill,1970)

42 John Holder 'The Issue of Race: A Search for a Biblical Perspective' JRT 49 (1992 – 93), 44– 59

43 Frank Spina *The Faith of the Outsider* (Grand Rapids: Eerdmans, 2005), 181,

44 Ibid., 130–1

45 Possibly the most extensive of such arguments is Tom Horner, *Jonathan Loved David : Homosexuality in Biblical Times*, 1st ed. (Philadelphia: Westminster Press, 1978)

46 Nissinen, *Homoeroticism in the Biblical World*, 55.

47 Davidson *Flame of Yahweh*, 165–7

48 James Jones 'Making Space for Truth and Grace' in Kenneth Stevenson ed. *A Fallible Church – Lambeth Essays* (London: DLT, 2008), 57

49 David Gunn *The Story of David* (Sheffield: JSOT, 1982)

50 Ibid., 97 –98

51 Joseph Blenkinsopp *The Pentateuch* (New York: Doubleday, 1992). Norman Whybray *Introduction to the Pentateuch* (Grand Rapids: Eerdmans, 1995)

52 Erhard Gerstenberger, *Leviticus : A Commentary*, 1st American ed., *The Old Testament Library*. (Louisville, Ky.: Westminister John Knox Press), 1996

53 Mary Douglas, *Purity and Danger: An Analysis of Concepts of Pollution and Taboo*. (Harmondworth,: Penguin, 1970), 54.

54 Nissinen, *Homoeroticism in the Biblical World*, 38.

55 John Boswell, *Christianity, Social Tolerance, and Homosexuality : Gay People in Western Europe from the Beginning of the Christian Era to the Fourteenth Century*. (Chicago ; London: University of Chicago Press, 1980), 100–1

56 Gagnon, *The Bible and Homosexual Practice*, 130–31.

57 Jacob Milgrom, *Leviticus : A Book of Ritual and Ethics*, Continental Commentaries. (Minneapolis, MN: Fortress Press, 2004), 196

58 See further discussion on the relevant passages below.

59 Countryman, *Dirt, Greed, and Sex : Sexual Ethics in the New Testament and Their Implications for Today*. 26–28.

60 Douglas, *Purity and Danger*.

61 Gagnon, *The Bible and Homosexual Practice* 120.

62 John Holder 'Religion and Theology a Journey into the Experiential' JRT

63 Helmer Ringgren *Israelite Religion* (London: SPCK, 1966), 158ff

64 Gerhard von Rad *Old Testament Theology Vol.I* (New York: Harper and Row, 1962), 28

65 Gerhard von Rad *Old Testament Theology Vol.II* (New York: Harper and Row, 1965), 228

66 Keith Carley *Ezekiel Among the Prophets* (London: SCM, 1975), 49

67 W. McKane *Proverbs* (London: SCM, 1980), 336–341

68 H. H. Rowley 'The Interpretation of the Song of Songs'in Rowley ed. *The Servant of the Lord and Other Essays on the Old Testament*. (London: Lutterworth Press, 1952) 187–234

69 Roland Murphy 'Canticles of Canticles' in Raymond Fitzmyer et al ed. *The Jerome Biblical Commentary* Vol 1 (London: Geoffrey Chapman, 1974), 506

70 On the interpretations of the work see: Brevard Childs *Introduction to the old Testament as Scripture* (London: SCM, 1979), 571–573. Werner Schmidt *Introduction to the Old Testament* (London: SCM, 1984), 311ff

71 Murphy 'Canticle of Canticles', 508

72 On the issue of race as at work here and in other areas of the Bible see, Holder 'The Issue of Race'

PART 3:
SEXUALITY IN THE NEW TESTAMENT

Paula Gooder

Introduction

When we move into the New Testament, we can see a continuation of many of the themes of sexuality found in the Old Testament. Perhaps the most important innovation within the New Testament is that although some key figures are married,[1] some of the most prominent characters (John the Baptist, Jesus and Paul) appear to be celibate, at least by implication since their wives are never mentioned. Although there are some who would argue that New Testament silence on the subject assumes that they were married rather than the reverse,[2] the majority of scholars believe that all three, John the Baptist, Jesus and Paul, remained unmarried.

In fact the argument often put forward in favour of their married status – that it would be so unusual for someone of this period to remain unmarried that their married status should be assumed – is questionable. There were some significant exceptions to the rule that everyone was married in the first century. For example at least some of the Essenes were celibate,[3] as were the Therapeutae.[4] Perhaps even more remarkable is the fact that Philo and Josephus report this celibacy with approval. Philo says that it is 'an enviable system' and Josephus that it 'deserves our admiration'. Far from being a horrific distortion of the norm, both Philo and Josephus considered celibacy something to be admired if not followed personally.

Within the New Testament, we can find seeds of a shift towards an approval of celibacy. The characters of John the Baptist, Jesus and Paul can only be regarded as celibate by silent implication but this strand is one which grew in importance in the post-New Testament period and affected attitudes towards sexuality in the early Church.

1. Sexuality in the Gospels

The Birth Narratives

The narrative of the New Testament opens, in the Gospels of Matthew and Luke, with a portrayal of the birth of Jesus. The significance of these accounts for our current study is that despite the fact that God in Jesus becomes fully human, he does so outside of a human sexual act. The process by which Jesus is conceived of the Holy Spirit remains a mystery. Matthew's Gospel states simply that Mary was found 'having in the womb from the Holy Spirit' (Matthew 1.18). Luke's description of the event is not much more illuminating than Matthew's, in that Mary is informed by Gabriel that she will 'conceive in her womb' (Luke 1.31), and when she asks how this can be because she is a virgin, Gabriel replies that 'the Holy Spirit will come upon you and the power of the Most High will overshadow you'. The language employed here suggests that the conception may be comparable with the baptism of

Jesus or with the transfiguration, and is reminiscent of the descriptions of God's presence descending to the tabernacle during the wilderness wanderings. The vague references in both accounts, however, stress the fact that the conception of Jesus takes place by a means unnamed and possibly inexpressible.

Popular interest in the veracity of the assertion of the virginal conception in these accounts has distracted interest away from the unusual nature of the description of the conception of Jesus without a sexual act. Within both Ancient Near Eastern and Graeco-Roman tradition, there was widespread belief in the idea of someone being born from a human mother and divine father, though in these instances the most common form of conception was through a sexual act.[5] There were versions, however, of myths in which divine impregnation took place without sexual union and with a virgin.[6] An important difference between the New Testament accounts and these mythological narratives is the amount of information they contain. The Gospel accounts are sparse in the extreme and consequently distinguish themselves from their much more elaborate mythological counterparts; even in accounts of supposedly virginal conceptions the imagery of golden showers or being entered by light had an implication of divine sexuality. The reason for the oblique references in both Matthew and Luke's Gospels to the virginal conception is that they were attempting to emphasize that the conception and birth narratives that they portrayed were far from the complex, sexual images contained in so many other contemporary texts.

Jesus' Attitudes to Adultery, Divorce and Remarriage

Jesus' teaching on divorce and remarriage not only occurs in all three Gospels and twice in Matthew,[7] but is also cited by Paul in 1 Corinthians 7.10–11 as being from the Lord ('not I but the Lord'). The importance of discussion about divorce in the first-century context can be seen in the fact that John the Baptist's imprisonment and subsequent beheading were due to the fact that John had criticized the marriage of Herod Antipas to his brother Philip's divorced wife (this Philip is not to be confused with Philip, the tetrach of Ituraea and Trachonitis mentioned in Luke 3.1, who was married to Herodias' daughter Salome but was probably Antipas' half-brother). The sin in this instance was two-fold: first, Herod had married a divorced woman and second, he had uncovered the nakedness of his brother's wife, contrary to the command of Leviticus 18.16.

Jesus' statements about adultery, however, are not restricted to divorce. In the Sermon on the Mount, before he turns to divorce he raises the question of other forms of adultery. For Jesus the kingdom's requirements of morality are much higher and more stringent than Jewish legal requirements. Consequently, against a background that forbids the act of adultery (Exodus 20.14 and Deuteronomy 5.18), Jesus forbids inner thoughts about adultery. The reason for this becomes clear in Matthew 19.9 (paralleled in Mark 10.11–12) which contains an extended discussion about divorce. Despite slight differences in account, the significance of the discussion about divorce in Matthew 19 and Mark 10 remains the same. Jesus has in mind in these passages a creation ideal, which he sees fulfilled once more in the kingdom. This ideal can be seen in the quoted conflation of Genesis 1.26 and 2.24, when Jesus says that 'from the beginning' God created them 'male and female' and said: 'For this reason a man shall leave his father and mother and be joined to his wife, and the two shall become one flesh.' The logic at work in this quotation is that God created man and woman as a male and female expression of himself and that this is why they are driven to leave home and form a new male and female unit. The joining together of men and women in marriage is a creation imperative; the command that allows divorce was provided because of hardness of heart (Matthew 19.8). The values of the kingdom require a return to the creation ordinance, rather than staying with what was provided due to hardness of heart.

One of the important differences between the Gospels is Matthew's addition of two phrases into the discussion of divorce in 19.1–12. If we compare the question asked by the Pharisees in Mark 10.2 with that asked in Matthew 19.3, we notice that in the former they simply ask, 'Is it lawful for a husband to divorce his wife?', but in Matthew, 'Is it lawful for a man to divorce his wife *for any cause?*' Jesus' reply also differs: in Mark his reply is '(w)hoever divorces his wife and marries another commits adultery against her', whereas in Matthew it is 'whoever divorces his wife, *except for unchastity*, and marries another commits adultery'. This addition of *except for unchastity* can also be found in the Matthew 5.32 discussion of divorce. There is much discussion in scholarship about whether Matthew has *changed* the original meaning of Jesus' saying by inserting these two phrases or whether he has *clarified* it.

As is often the case the discussion here finds its roots in hermeneutics. One of the important areas of discussion is whether the 'Matthean additions' help us to understand the cultural background against which to read this discussion or whether Jesus' prohibition of remarriage after divorce stands regardless of the discussion in Judaism of the time.

Scholars such as Craig Keener and David Instone-Brewer[8] understand Jesus' discussion against the background of the discussion between Rabbis Hillel and Shammai about the grounds upon which someone could divorce. Rabbi Shammai said that divorce was only possible if a man found indecency in his wife, whereas Hillel allowed it if she spoilt the dinner. This discussion centred upon a first-century interpretation of Deuteronomy 24.1: 'When a man, after marrying a woman and having relations with her, is later displeased with her because he finds in her *something indecent . . .*'. Hillel and his followers interpreted the verse as containing two grounds, 'any matter' and 'indecency';[9] whereas Shammai understood it only to include indecency. If this is seen to be the background to the Pharisees' question then they are inviting Jesus to join in the discussion with Hillel and Shammai about how to interpret this verse. In this context Jesus is understood to be agreeing with Shammai in his conclusion and allowing divorce in the case of indecency. It should also be noted that Instone-Brewer argues that this debate is so embedded in first-century culture that it is implicit in Mark and Luke where it is not stated.

Other interpretations of the passage such as those by Gordon Wenham and William Heth understand this discussion not against the background of the first-century context but against the background of the Old Testament allowing of divorce, and would identify three periods for differing views on divorce.[10]

1   Pre-Mosaic tradition in which divorce was forbidden
2   Mosaic tradition in which divorce was allowed
3   Kingdom tradition which returned to the pre-Mosaic stance.

Thus these passages are understood to be opposed to divorce and remarriage.

Whatever one's conclusion upon this debate the significance of the divorce discussions is that they emphasize the importance of marriage and the maintenance of marriage within Jesus' kingdom values

Marriage in Heaven

This question is picked up slightly differently in Mark 12.18–27 (and parallels Matthew 22.23–33 and Luke 20.27–40) in a discussion about marriage 'in the resurrection'. The question from the Sadducees is set up as a means to trip Jesus up, since the case presented by the Sadducees (of a woman who has married seven brothers and then dies herself), while possible, is highly unlikely and seems to be presented as an argument against resurrection taking place at all. The practice of Levirate marriage to which they refer (called *yibbum* in Hebrew) is condemned in Talmudic tradition but seems to have been acceptable still in the first century, though to what extent it was actually practised is less clear.

The answer Jesus gives to this question stands as an intriguing counterpoint to his answer on divorce, which pointed to the joining of man and woman as an essential part of creation. One might expect that in the resurrection, humanity would be in a state similar to that in the Garden of Eden when male and female were created to be one, but his answer in this instance gives a different perspective. In the resurrection there will be no marrying or being given in marriage (i.e. neither for men nor women) but people will be like the angels (Matthew 22.30 and Mark 12.25) or equal to the angels (Luke 20.36). Scholars are not agreed about whether being like the angels refers to the fact that angels do not marry,[11] or that they do not die.[12] In fact it is most likely that both of these are meant, in that post-resurrection humanity will become more like heavenly beings on the new earth: worshipping eternally before God, free from pain and fear, not marrying and immortal.

One of the questions that this raises is whether it reveals anything about Jesus' understanding of marriage. Some argue that marriage will no longer take place because it will no longer be necessary, as all humanity will be immortal, procreation is unnecessary and marriage is redundant,[13] while others view it more in terms of exclusivity of relationship. The depth of relationship that takes place in marriage is now available to all human relationships, rendering marriage unnecessary.[14]

Women Caught in Adultery

Another place in which to explore Jesus' attitude to sexuality is in the passage which speaks of women of what we might call ill repute, in other words women who were prostitutes or who had been caught in the act of adultery. It is traditional to list these as Mary Magdalene, the Samaritan woman in John 4 and the woman caught in adultery in John 7.53—8.11.[15] The problem here is that Christian tradition has loaded sexual sin onto some of these passages in a way that is not really supported by the text. It is now widely accepted that Mary Magdalene was neither a prostitute or a woman caught in adultery, or more accurately that this is not something that can be deduced from the text.

Mary Magdalene is cited in biblical tradition as a follower and benefactor of Jesus and the disciples (Luke 8.3), someone from whom demons had been cast out (Luke 8.2) and one of the group of women who went to Jesus' tomb after his burial (Matthew 27.56, 61; 28.1; Mark 15.40, 47; 16.1, 9; Luke 24.10; John 19.25, 20.1, 18). A conflation of her character with the woman from the city who was a sinner (Luke 7.36–50) and in some instances also with Mary of Bethany took place in subsequent Christian tradition. It is also worth noting that there is little in the text to suggest that the woman referred to as from the city and a sinner in Luke 7.36–50 was either a prostitute or an adulteress. The text simply does not say what the sin was and it may not be referring to sexual sin but to another act that led to social exclusion.

Likewise the widespread belief that the Samaritan woman had sinned in some way is predicated on the assumption that she had control over her marital status and was responsible for her own divorce (if she was divorced and not widowed since the text does not say). It was not possible for women to instigate divorce within Jewish culture at the time, added to which neither she nor Jesus makes any comment about her sexual status apart from the fact that she had had five husbands and was not married to the current one. This is not indicated as being sinful, and it is quite possible that the undercurrent of the conversation is hurt and vulnerability rather than sin.

Whether or not we include these characters under the rubric of sexual sin affects our reading of how Jesus responds to it. For example, if the Samaritan woman had committed a sexual sin Jesus responded surprisingly by not even mentioning it, let alone condemning it. In the case of Luke's woman of the city and the woman caught in adultery (John 7.53—8.11), Jesus' response is similar. In Luke 7.36ff., he forgives her sin and then commands that she does not sin again; and in John 7.53—8.11 he refuses to condemn her and then also commands that she does not sin again. In both situations the sin is acknowledged for what it is but is not condemned – as this might have led to death – but this lack of condemnation is coupled with the command that the woman does not sin again.

The intriguing question is whether the woman of the city has already received such treatment from Jesus, since her anointing of Jesus' feet is said to arise from the great love that she has for him because much has been forgiven her. If this is the case why then does Jesus forgive her again? One common option is that her love is proleptic: it anticipates the forgiveness that she will receive. Another option is that this is in fact the second time she has been forgiven, in the pattern of Jesus' command to multiple forgiveness (Matthew 18.21–22), and therefore gives an indication of how we should react to sin, i.e. with lack of condemnation followed by an exhortation to sin no more.

2. Sexuality in Acts

Notes on Porneia

Although the book of Acts does not refer very much to sexuality, one important reference is worthy of our attention here. The 'Apostolic decree' in Acts, sent by the assembly in Jerusalem to the Gentile Christians, requested various things: that they should abstain from things polluted by idols, from fornication, from things strangled and from blood (Acts 15.20, 29, and 21.25).

The crucial word, for our purposes, is clearly fornication, which translates the Greek word *porneia*. The question that arises is what did James mean when he used the word in this context? At a simple level, it is clear that James was asking the Gentiles to live by the same sexual moral code as the Jews and that this included faithfulness of relationship in marriage. Against the backdrop of the attitude towards sexuality within the Bible the decree seems to have been asking the Gentiles to treat sex as a gift of God.

The question that has exercised scholars most in this area is the extent of the meaning of the word *porneia*. Part of the problem is that this is such an all-encompassing word for anything that happens outside of a monogamous faithful relationship that it is hard to tie down precisely what it means, and in a sense this will have been the purpose of choosing it to highlight the fact that the Gentiles are being requested to worship God faithfully, to be faithful in relationship and to avoid murder (although these final two requests might actually have more to do with dietary regulations than with a general command to preserve life).

In his book on unity in the Early Church, Achtemeier set out the range of different meanings attributed to *porneia*, which includes fornication, incest, prostitution, homosexuality or marriage to an idolater.[16] The potential broad range of the word causes people to attempt to understand the background that stands behind its usage here, which might enable us to narrow its meaning a little.

The two most common Old Testament backgrounds proposed for the Apostolic decree are rabbinic 'Noahic' laws and laws for sojourners living in the land in Leviticus 17—18. In the Talmud, seven Noahic laws are cited. These are prohibitions against idolatry, adultery, the shedding of blood, the profanation of God's name, robbery, injustice, and eating the flesh of a living animal.[17] Their significance is that as Noah is the father of both Gentiles and Jews it is reasonable to assume that they could apply to Gentiles as well as Jews. The problem with this as a possible background is that it takes no account of the four prohibitions that are not mentioned in the Apostolic decree and that the Babylonian Talmud was written hundreds of years after the Apostolic decree.[18] Another possible background for this decree is Leviticus 17—18 which, roughly speaking contains the same prohibitions as the Apostolic decree, as well as many more.[19] The question here is, given the number of prohibitions not mentioned in the Apostolic decree, whether a range of those mentioned in Leviticus 17—18 can be deemed to be included under the rubric of *porneia*. Those who believe that this is indeed the case see *porneia* as referring to the full range of sexual prohibitions mentioned in the two chapters, including homosexuality.[20]

3. Sexuality Within the Pauline Tradition

Paul's own attitude to sexuality is much more negative than can be found elsewhere in the Bible. The majority of his discussions about sexuality focus upon occasions where things have gone wrong and need correction. The one place (1 Corinthians 7) where he talks about marriage and where he might have been positive about sexuality, we encounter at best a lukewarm and at worst a deep hesitation about the joining of men and women. This needs to be understood in terms of Paul's vision of spreading the gospel as widely as possible as swiftly as possible. Those with family ties were then as now much more restricted in what they could do. Nevertheless, Paul's apparent negativity towards sexuality in general has had a great impact on subsequent Christian attitudes to sexuality.

1 Corinthians 5—7

The most concentrated of Paul's discussions about sexuality can be found in 1 Corinthians 5—7 where he addresses a number of issues within the Corinthian community. It is important to recognize that, although chapters 5—7 all contain material relevant to an exploration of sexuality, Paul's attitude to the matters contained within it differs from passage to passage. Chapter 5 contains condemnation of an act so terrible that Paul can barely contain his outrage; chapter 6.1–11 contains condemnation of those who look after their own interests at the expense of others and 6.12–20 moves on to a more general discussion of what liberty in Christ does and does not entail. Chapter 7 is of a different quality entirely and contains Paul's answers to the Corinthians' queries about marriage, separation and divorce.

Against Acceptance of Porneia

The issue that makes Paul explode with fury in 1 Corinthians 5 is that the Corinthians remain complacent when there is a case of blatant *porneia* in their midst. Unlike the Apostolic decree in Acts 15, Paul goes on to define what the *porneia* is in this instance: someone having a relationship with his step-mother. The reason for Paul's outrage is that under the rubric of sexual immorality this form is of such a kind that even the Gentiles do not tolerate it: Thiselton notes that the sexually explicit Roman poet Catullus was horrified at someone having a relationship with his step-mother.[21] It is important to recognize, however, that Paul's anger is two-headed. As well as his fury at this act of extreme immorality, he is also angry with the Corinthian community for their complacent attitude in condoning it.

One of the challenging elements of this passage is Paul's verdict on what should happen to the offender in this case: 'you are to hand this man over to Satan for the destruction of the flesh, so that his spirit may be saved in the day of the Lord' (1 Corinthians 5.3). There is a widespread divergence of opinion upon what is meant by this. A large number of scholars conclude that this means that the man is handed over either to die generally,[22] or to be executed by civil authorities.[23] As Thiselton astutely points out, however, this widespread view does not account for the salvation hoped for by Paul in the second half of the verse and that Paul's real hope is that the man will have a change of heart and return to right living within the community for his own salvation.[24] Most commentators before the twentieth century believed that this had in fact taken place and that the offender to whom the community must reaffirm their love in 2 Corinthians 2.3–11 was in fact the same offender as is found in this passage. Many modern scholars, however, reject this identification in favour of another offender who has verbally abused Paul.[25] Whether or not this offender is the one rehabilitated in 2 Corinthians 2.3–11, Paul's point remains: those who commit such acts of *porneia* must be excluded from the community in the hope that they will change their practice and thus achieve salvation. Paul's ultimate hope here is that the offender can be reintegrated into salvation and the corporate body of Christ.

Against Serving One's Own Interests

Paul next turns his attention to those who only seek their own gain. In this particular context his wrath is caused by those whose desire to get their own way so drives them that they will go to court rather than allow the matter to be heard satisfactorily within their own community. Thiselton points out that the crucial matter here is that, although Roman criminal courts were renowned for their justice, civil courts were run on the expectation that something would be given to the judge for a favourable verdict.[26] It is likely, therefore, that this is why some of the Corinthian community were resorting to civil law suits because they could then be more certain of a favourable verdict. Paul's condemnation, then, is of those whose concern to get their own way overrides the welfare of others within their Christian community.

It is in this context that Paul draws in a range of other 'sins' which are to be evaluated as of the same type as this grasping attitude. This passage should be read in the light of the preceding chapter, 1 Corinthians 5. It is of course not the committing of sin that means that one cannot inherit the kingdom of God; Paul acknowledges all too readily in Romans 7 that being in Christ does not immediately alter one's behaviour for the better. The point is not whether someone sins, but whether they persist in sinning and are allowed to do so by their community. The examples Paul has given so far, of the man living with his stepmother and the members of the community who like to go to court to solve disputes, are examples of persistence in behaviour. The additional examples he now gives are of a similar kind. These people, like the others he has just mentioned, are so concerned with their own welfare that they ignore the welfare of the community as a whole.

The list that Paul moves on to is traditionally called a 'vice list' by scholars as it sets out the limits of behaviour acceptable within the body of Christ. Vice lists are widespread within the Graeco-Roman world and acted as the counterpart to virtue lists: those which laid out the characteristics for which one should strive. Paul contains both virtue and vice lists in his writings and uses them, like their Graeco-Roman counterparts, as a means of encouraging the kind of behaviour one might expect within the body of Christ. Although there is disagreement about which passages within the New Testament should be counted as part of the virtue and vice lists,[27] scholars are widely agreed that these lists played an influential role in shaping behaviour within early Christian communities.

This particular vice list in 1 Corinthians 6.9–10 contains a variety of vices apparently grouped together:

- fornicators, idolaters, adulterers, male prostitutes, sodomites;
- thieves, the greedy, drunkards, revilers, robbers.

One of the interesting features of this list is that the generic term *porneia* (fornicators) is used alongside the much more specific vices of adultery etc., which raises the question of whether it had a more specific meaning for Paul that could be used alongside the others. Although much attention is paid to two of these words (male prostitutes and sodomites) it is important to recognize that Paul draws a firm boundary around any kind of behaviour that disrupts and undermines the life of the community.

Notes on Malakoi *and* Arsenokites

As mentioned above, the words that have been the focus for most discussion on this verse are the ones translated male prostitutes (*malakoi)* and sodomites (*arsenokoites*). These words have been variously translated by English translations, something which indicates that it is not easy to come to a clear translation of them. The first word *malakoi* literally means 'soft' and is used to mean 'soft clothing' in Matthew 11.8. *Arsenokoites* does not appear to have been used before the writings of Paul, though many scholars believe it to signify someone who sleeps with (*koites*) men (*arseno*).

The word *malakoi* is understood by a large number of New Testament scholars to mean 'soft' and therefore effeminate, and thus to mean the passive partner in a homosexual relationship.[28] Other scholars, however, understand this word more as referring to 'call boys', that is, younger boys within Greek society who acted as male prostitutes.[29] Others still understand the word and *arsenokoites* that follows it entirely in terms of pederasty.[30] Dale Martin makes the word even broader and interprets 'soft' here as someone who enjoys decadent living.[31]

The word *arsenokoites* is equally disputed. The question is how to understand the meaning of a word that has no discernible use outside Paul's inclusion of it in two lists (here and in 1 Timothy 1.10). The point is whether Paul's word here translates the equally inelegant Hebrew phrase from Leviticus 18.22, 'you shall not lie a man (as) the lying of a woman', though as Thiselton points out, the question is not whether Paul can be shown to be translating the word exactly but whether he is viewing the subject in the same way.[32] Again there is a broad range of opinion. As with the first word, a large number of scholars are agreed that *arsenokoites* refers to the active partner in a homosexual relationship and is properly translated 'sodomites'.[33] Others disagree. Again Scroggs understands the word to refer to a man who keeps a 'call boy' as a 'mistress',[34] and in similar vein Martin understands it to refer to men who seek to exploit other people by means of sex. One important element of his theory is that in both the New Testament vice lists and other subsequent ones, like the *Acts of John*, these words are placed between sexual and economic misdemeanours, which might suggest that this word is to be understood economically as well as sexually.[35]

Marriage and Divorce

Paul moves from a section in which he demonstrates clear, boldly argued opinions into one in which he demonstrates much stronger nuance and reflection. This is almost certainly because 1 Corinthians 7 is written in response to certain questions to Paul and not as a result of a misdemeanour that needs correction. In his commentary on 1 and 2 Corinthians, Witherington provides a helpful backdrop for understanding Paul's discussion of this issue. He notes that Roman marriages were normally arranged for financial reasons and did not require a ceremony in order to be enacted. All that was necessary was the intent to marry, likewise divorce could be achieved by saying '*tuas res tibi habeto*' (take your things and go).[36] Consequently most pleasure took place outside of marriage, encouraged by the many religions which featured temple prostitution. He also notes how important it is to understand Paul's comments here in terms of this view of the imminent end of the world. His concern to complete his task before the end times occurred made most other things fade into the background.

Many scholars today would argue that 1 Corinthians 7.1, '(i)t is well for a man not to touch a woman,' must be understood as something that the Corinthians have said to Paul in a letter to which he is responding.[37] Once this is understood the following discussion (7.2–7) makes much more sense, because Paul then modifies this statement considerably, saying that those who are married must act properly as married people and give themselves to each other entirely. The rest of the chapter is best summed up with the words 'stay as you are'. If you are a widow or widower don't marry (7.7–9), if you are married remain so (7.10–11), even if you are married to a non-Christian try to stay married (7.12–16). This applies to social status as well as married status (7.17–24). If you are unmarried Paul's advice is to stay that way because of the looming crisis that is to come (7.25–38).[38]

Paul's absorption in his task of proclaiming the gospel and fear for what was looming in the future mean that 1 Corinthians 7 presents a cautious attitude to sexuality which veers towards the negative. Paul does not appear to support the view of sex as a gift, instead it is for him something which gets in the way of the much more important task of proclaiming the gospel to the ends of the earth.

The Wrath of God and Human Wickedness – Romans 1.18–32

Another significant passage for understanding Paul's attitude to sexuality comes at the beginning of Romans. Here Paul begins by setting out the terrible situation which he perceives pagan attitudes to have brought about. This is largely directed at the Gentiles though from time to time it is clear that he includes the Jews in so much as they have behaved like pagans.[39] The whole passage opens with a statement about God's wrath being revealed against ungodliness which will lead in 1.24 to God giving them up. This sets up Paul's argument for the rest of the chapter in which he describes what they have done to call forth God's wrath and then what the consequences of this behaviour are.

The steps of Paul's argument here are as follows. God has revealed himself through creation (Romans 1.19–21) but despite this humanity chose not to worship him and instead exchanged proper worship of God for the worship of lumps of wood

(Romans 1.22–3). In other words humanity chose idolatry over the proper worship of God. As a result God 'gave them up'. N. T. Wright notes that this phrase has echoes of Psalm 81.12 ('So I gave them over to their stubborn hearts, to follow their own counsels') and God's reaction there to the Israelites' determination to worship idols. This reveals that although the surface meaning of this text is a criticism of Gentiles, it is in reality a criticism of all idolatry regardless of who is practising it. The significant feature of this verse is that God gave them up to what they desired – in other words they were simply allowed to do what they wanted but then had to live with the consequences.

The consequences are that they were 'given up' to follow the degrading passions that they wished to follow. Numerous scholars point out that the sexual acts are not the things that call forth God's wrath; they are the result of the wrath that God already has sent upon the earth for idolatry.[40] These acts are evidence that God's wrath is already at work in the world.[41] The major result of this is being driven by passion and sexual perversion, in other words the God-given gift of sexuality becomes a curse and a punishment rather than the gift that it was intended to be. Paul continues this theme in verse 28 by pointing out the further results of idolatry: because people did not see fit to keep God in mind God gave them up (the third time this phrase is used here to emphasis the point)[42] to an unfit mind. There is a deliberate play on words going on here in the Greek between 'not seeing fit' and having an 'unfit' mind. Again the consequences are entirely self-imposed. Paul ends this passage with a rhetorical flourish and a list of all the vices which come naturally from worshipping the creature rather than the creator. It is interesting to note that Paul has moved on from sexuality at this point and instead gives a vice list of general wicked deeds from 'unrighteousness' at the start to 'ruthlessness' at the end.

Romans 1.26–27

There is wide-reaching disagreement about the interpretation of Romans 1.26–27 and it is impossible to include all possible interpretations of the verses here, but a few key discussions will be explored below. Many scholars interpret these verses as a straightforward reference to homosexuality (including lesbianism). For example, N. T. Wright notes in his commentary that homosexual practice was included here by Paul not only because Jews regarded homosexual practice as a classic example of pagan vice but because it also corresponds to what humans have done in exchanging the truth of God for a lie.[43] There are others, however, who consider the references in this passage to refer to matters other than homosexual practice. It is important to recognize here, as elsewhere, that the majority scholarly view is that these verses refer to homosexual practice but that there are those that disagree with the majority. The reference to the different possible views below is not intended to imply that they are of more weight than the majority view.

One of the areas of discussion considers what is meant by the phrase 'contrary to nature'. For example, James Allison points out that St Augustine and Clement of Alexandria did not understand this passage to be a reference to lesbianism but to women who have anal intercourse with men, thus he argues that lesbianism is not necessarily the obvious meaning of the text.[44] The crucial issue that lies beneath this, then, is a belief in complementarity and that the purpose of sex is procreation. Anything other than this is 'contrary' to nature. The importance of complementarity is also stressed by those who believe that this text is talking about lesbianism, as the same point holds.[45]

Frederickson offers yet another understanding of what is going on here. Reading the text against a Greek philosophical background, he argues that the phrase 'natural use' (translated 'natural intercourse' in the NRSV) refers not to same-sex relations but to passion. The Greek aversion to passion, he maintains, drives Paul's usage here and it is this that is, for him, contrary to nature.[46]

Another argument about Romans 1.26–27 concerns whether Paul believed it to be sinful or not. For example, Countryman draws on Jewish understandings of purity and impurity to argue that Paul's mention of same-sex relations represents 'dirty aspects of Gentile culture' but that these are not in the same league as the sinful vices listed in Romans 1.29–31.[47]

Another significant area of discussion is about whether Paul's criticism is of homosexual behaviour or of the kind of sexual practice that went on in Gentile temple worship. Here a direct link is made between idolatry and the practice that Paul criticizes here. Thus the argument goes that it is homosexual practice in the context of idolatry that is so condemned by Paul here, not homosexuality *per se*. Martin goes on to argue that it is wrong to read the fall into the text and instead Paul is here referring to a Jewish belief that civilization was declining as a direct result of idolatry.[48]

There are many other discussions of this passage as well but these give something of a flavour of the type of debate that takes place about 1.26–27.

Romans 2.1

The passage ends with a reminder that applauding such actions in others is as bad as doing them oneself. It is important to remember, however, that chapter 2.1 follows on immediately from the end of this passage with the word 'therefore', showing that it is dependent on what has come before. Given the tone of chapter 1, it is somewhat surprising to read Paul saying here that 'you have no excuse, whoever you are, when you judge others; for in passing judgement on another you condemn yourself, because you, the judge, are doing the very same things'. It is likely that the reference here is not just to 1.32 (there seems little evidence that the Jews applauded wicked behaviour) but to the whole of 1.18–32.[49] The tendency to idolatry and to worship the creature rather than the creator is so great in all people, that people should not judge lest they end up judging themselves. J. D. G. Dunn also suggests that the act of judgement of another could itself be understood to be placing oneself (a creature) in the role of creator.[50]

There is disagreement among scholars about the import of Romans 2.1. There are some scholars who argue that this is a crucial move in Paul's argument and exists to 'set a trap for anyone who read his words with feelings of moral superiority or religious bigotry'.[51] In other words, scholars who hold this view would argue that judging others when in danger of sliding into the same sins as are listed in 1.29–31 is as great a crime as the sexual acts referred to in 1.26–27. Others, however, argue that this is to misunderstand the passage and that the fact that 'Paul was seeking to establish that all/any sin equally rendered people culpable to God's judgement does not mean that all sins were equally egregious for Paul'.[52]

The Pastoral Epistles

The Pastoral epistles contain a vice list very similar in content to 1 Corinthians 6.9 as well as an exhortation of expected behaviour on the part of bishops, deacons and elders.

Another Vice List

1 Timothy 1.10 contains a vice list similar in many ways to the one in 1 Corinthians 6.9. It is notable for the fact that it also uses the word *arsenokoites*, like the 1 Corinthians passage, but does not here include *malakoi*.[53] It is also notable because the order in which the sins are set out mimics quite closely the order of the second part of the Decalogue, so much so that it appears to be a reflection and expansion on what it might mean in the context of the community to which the letter is being written.[54] If this is true, then 1 Timothy 1.10 can be seen as a practical interpretation of how the ethics of the Ten Commandments are to be enacted within the community or communities of the recipients.

Bishops and Deacons

It is interesting to note that the advice offered for the conduct of bishops (1 Timothy 3.2), deacons (1 Timothy 3.12) and elders (Titus 1.6) is the same as regards matters of sexuality: they should be the man/husband of one woman/wife.[55] Knight surveys the possible options for what this might mean:

1 that they should be married (i.e. only married men could be considered)
2 that they should have only one wife for their entire life (i.e. if their wife died they should not remarry)
3 that they should not be polygamous
4 that they should be faithful.[56]

He does not include the possibility that it refers to remarriage after divorce and forbids those in leadership from doing this. He is probably correct in doing so because, since 1 Corinthians 7 so explicitly states that those in Christ ought not to remarry, it is unlikely that this would be in doubt for leaders of the Christian community. Likewise few hold to the view that marriage is an essential pre-requisite for leadership within the church: Paul's own position – though not as a bishop, deacon or elder – would suggest that this is unlikely. In the same way, the command in 1 Corinthians 7.39 that a widow should be 'free to marry anyone she wishes, only in the Lord' makes the second option equally improbable.

The question of polygamy, however, is certainly in view in this statement, since there is evidence that Jews of the New Testament period continued to practise polygamy and that this practice continued into the late fourth century, when Theodosius enacted a special law against polygamy among the Jews. The question is not so much whether this command prohibited polygamy but whether it *only* prohibited polygamy and not other forms of infidelity as well. In fact, it seems most likely that this is a command against all forms of marital infidelity, including polygamy but not only including it.

4. Sexuality in the Rest of the New Testament

2 Peter 2.7

The reference in 2 Peter 2.7 is worthy of only a short note. The verse refers directly to the story of Lot in Sodom and Gomorrah and states that despite Lot's being worn down by the indecency/sensuality/ licentiousness of the lawless, God rescued him. It is clear here that the author of 2 Peter is referring back to the tradition in Genesis 13—19 which makes repeated reference to the wickedness of the city. The crucial question, differently answered by different scholars, is whether the indecency/sensuality/ licentiousness of the lawless refers to their general behaviour or to the particular narrative of Genesis 19, which some take to be a description and condemnation of homosexual desire.

Jude 7

The book of Jude is worthy of a brief mention as it refers to Sodom and Gomorrah's punishment by eternal fire because of 'sexual immorality and going after other flesh'. The question is what these two phrases mean in this context. The first phrase, 'sexual immorality', translates the Greek word *ekporneusasai* which simply means 'fornication'; the second phrase again literally means 'other (*heteras*) flesh'. The crucial question is whether these two phrases refer to the same thing or two different things.

Robert Gagnon opts to interpret these two phrases as unconnected.[57] Consequently he views the first (sexual immorality) as ambiguous but probably relating to homosexual acts because of the reference to Sodom and Gomorrah and its linkage with homosexual practice. This is supported by scholars such as Kelly who note that Sodom was proverbially associated with homosexuality.[58] He further argues that, since the Genesis 19.1–11 passage does not appear to recognize that the men knew that the visitors were angels, a better interpretation of these two phrases is that they are linked but not the same thing. Thus because of their pursuit of homosexual practice they unwittingly put themselves in the way of desiring sex with the 'other flesh' of angels.

Another interpretation of these phrases is that they are a single unit and not two linked but separate phrases. Thus Richard Bauckham proposes that this verse should be translated 'which practised immorality in the same way as the angels and hankered after strange flesh'.[59] Thus his argument is that the fornication of the angels was that they desired sex with humans (see Genesis 6.1–4) and that occupants of Sodom and Gomorrah sinned in the same way by desiring angelic flesh, and hence sex with angels.

Revelation

Themes of sexuality are also present in the book of Revelation.

Not Defiled by Women

The increasing value placed on celibacy that we observed in the New Testament appears to reach its highest form ever in Revelation 14.4: '(i)t is these who have not defiled themselves with women, for they are virgins'. There are a variety of views held on the significance of this verse. Some argue that it is an appeal to the virtues of celibacy, and indeed this interpretation has shaped much of the churches' thinking about the nature of celibacy over the past 2000 years. Others argue that it refers not to celibacy but to those who have remained faithful within marriage to a single wife, thus those who have refrained from sexual immorality. Others still think that it is a figurative description of those who have not worshipped the beast and have remained faithful to God.[60] If this passage is indeed an exaltation of celibacy, then we can see that this attitude towards relationships has already begun to develop within the Christian communities; if it is not, then it presents a much more familiar support of fidelity and condemnation of adultery.

The Bride of Christ

In marked contrast to apparent aversion to the married state found in Revelation 14.4, one of the major images of the future redemption of the world is of Christ preparing to marry his bride (Revelation19.7, 21.2 and 9 and 22.17). This union between Christ and the new Jerusalem will encompass the union between Christ and all those who will 'have the right to the tree of life and may enter the city by the gates.' It is important to recognize that, contrary to popular interpretation, the marriage in Revelation is not between Christ and the church but between Christ and the New Jerusalem. Those who have the right will be welcomed through the gates of the city and caught up in the marital joy of Christ and his bride. The identification of the bride with the church has happened via Ephesians 5.25–33, which speaks of Christ's love for the church in giving his life up for her being like the love of a husband for his wife. This has subsequently been transferred onto the bride image of Revelation and the assumption made that the wife in Ephesians is the bride of Revelation.

Summary and Conclusions

This survey of New Testament attitudes to relationships and sexuality has been brief in the extreme. As a result there has been space only for those passages which talk explicitly about relationships, a wider picture of the New Testament attitude to sexuality would have emerged if there had been time to explore, for example, attitudes to the body and the spirit/soul.

From what we have been able to explore, however, we can see that the New Testament writers uphold marriage and oppose anything that undermines it. *Porneia* in all its forms is widely condemned as undermining of married relationships. It is, however, possible to see Paul's lukewarm attitude to marriage in 1 Corinthians 7, the apparent celibacy of John the Baptist, Jesus and Paul and the possible reference to celibacy in Revelation 14.4 as the seed out of which the honouring of celibacy in later Christian tradition grew, though this is not the only interpretation of this evidence.

Alongside a description of New Testament attitudes towards sexuality, has been the aim to present a range of scholarly interpretations of these passages. The results are somewhat dizzying. The scope of possible opinions on sexuality in the New Testament is broad and appears to be getting broader all the time. A purpose of the process of mutual listening is to acknowledge the breadth of the views that can be held by scholars who engage with the Bible seriously and thoughtfully and to become aware of ways of interpreting the text that differ from our own.

This section has been concerned with attitudes to sexuality in general within the New Testament. These attitudes have been included in order to frame the central concern of this whole volume: homosexuality. New Testament attitudes to homosexuality and homosexual practice remain an area of dispute among New Testament scholars but, although views on the subject differ widely, most scholarship can be seen to fall into one of three categories.

1   By far the majority view is the view that the New Testament condemns homosexual practice.
2   Another group of scholars accept that the New Testament is opposed to homosexual practice but would argue that this is due to cultural attitudes that no longer hold sway. These scholars would point to the gap between first- and twenty-first-century culture as the reason for not condemning homosexual practice today.
3. Yet another group of scholars would deny that the New Testament opposes homosexual practice on the grounds that the texts use words that are hard to translate or that they are referring to pederasty or temple prostitution and not to homosexual practice between mutually loving partners.

The purpose of this section has not been to evaluate the different positions but to present them and to acknowledge their existence. This is only one step in the ongoing process of mutual listening and acts as a resource to facilitate further discussions on the subject.

Notes to Part 3

1   For example Simon Peter who is said to have a mother-in-law (Luke 4.38).
2   E.g. William E. Phipps, *Was Jesus Married? The Distortion of Sexuality in the Christian Tradition*, 1st edn (New York: Harper & Row), 1970.
3   See Philo, *Hypothetica* 11.14–17; Josephus, *Jewish War* 2.8.2 and *Antiquities* 18.1.5.
4   This tradition is not entirely new in the first century, Jeremiah 16.1–4 reports of the command to Jeremiah to remain single on the grounds that disaster is coming for offspring of those to whom he prophesies. It is also highly likely that Banus, the prophet who wandered in the wilderness (Josephus, *Life* 2.11) was celibate.
5   Examples of this include Sargon of Akkad who is reported to have been born to a peasant mother and mountain God father, or Heracles (Hercules) who was said to have been born

from the union of Zeus and Alcmene, the wife of a Theban general.

6 Perseus, for example, is said to have been conceived by a virgin when Zeus took the form of a shower of gold and, in some versions, Mithras when god entered his mother as a shaft of light (though others have him being born from a rock).

7 Matthew 5.32 and 19.9; Mark 10.11–12 and Luke 16.18.

8 See, for example, David Instone-Brewer, *Divorce and Remarriage in the Bible: The Social and Literary Context* (Grand Rapids: Eerdmans, 2002) and Craig S. Keener, *And Marries Another: Divorce and Remarriage in the Teaching of the New Testament* (Peabody: Hendrickson, 1991).

9 This arises from the use of the Hebrew here *ervat davar* and Hillel understood *davar* in this verse to mean any matter.

10 William A. Heth and Gordon J. Wenham, *Jesus and Divorce: The Problem with the Evangelical Consensus* (Nashville: T. Nelson, 1985); Gordon J. Wenham et al., *Remarriage after Divorce in Today's Church: 3 Views* (Grand Rapids: Zondervan, 2006).

11 Joseph A. Fitzmyer, *The Gospel According to Luke: Introduction, Translation and Notes*, 1st edn (Garden City: Doubleday, 1981), 1305.

12 John Nolland, *Luke 18.35–24.53, Word Biblical Commentary, Vol. 35c* (Dallas: Word Books, 1993).

13 W. D. Davies and Dale C. Allison, *A Critical and Exegetical Commentary on the Gospel According to Saint Matthew, Vol. 3, The International Critical Commentary* (Edinburgh: T & T Clark, 1997), 227.

14 Maurice Wiles, 'Studies in Texts: Luke 20.34–36', *Theology 50* (1957), 500–2.

15 It is worth noting, although it is not directly relevant here, that some, though not all scholars, think that this is more Lukan in style than Johannine and may have been misplaced into John's gospel.

16 Paul J. Achtemeier, *The Quest for Unity in the New Testament Church: A Study in Paul and Acts* (Philadelphia: Fortress Press, 1987), 84.

17 Babylonian Sanhedrin 56a 'Our Rabbis taught: seven precepts were the sons of Noah commanded: social laws; to refrain from blasphemy, idolatry; adultery; bloodshed; robbery; and eating flesh cut from a living animal'.

18 J. T. Sanders, however, has proposed that we find in Acts 15 a very early version of the Noahic laws: Jack T. Sanders, *The Jews in Luke-Acts*, 1st Fortress Press edn (Philadelphia: Fortress Press, 1987), 120–1.

19 See Leviticus 17.2–9; 17.10; 17.13–15; 18.6–26.

20 Robert Gagnon, *The Bible and Homosexual Practice: Texts and Hermeneutics* (Nashville: Abingdon Press, 2001), 435–6.

21 Anthony C. Thiselton, *The First Epistle to the Corinthians: A Commentary on the Greek Text, The New International Greek Testament Commentary* (Grand Rapids: Eerdmans, 2000), 385–6.

22 Hans Conzelmann, *1 Corinthians: A Commentary on the First Epistle to the Corinthians, Hermeneia: A Critical and Historical Commentary on the Bible* (Philadelphia: Fortress Press, 1975), 97.

23 J. D. M. Derrett, '"Handing over to Satan": An Explanation of 1 Corinthians 5.1–7', *Revue Internatioanle des Droits de L'Antiquite* 26 (1979), 11–30.

24 Thiselton, *The First Epistle to the Corinthians*, 399.

25 V. P. Furnish, *Ii Corinthians, The Anchor Bible* (New York: Doubleday, 1984), 164.

26 Anthony C. Thiselton, *1 Corinthians: A Shorter Exegetical and Pastoral Commentary* (Grand Rapids: Eerdmans, 2006), 89.

27 Possibly the most extensive list was provided by G. Mussies, 'Catalgoues of Sins and Virtues Personfied', in *Studies in Gnosticism and Hellenistic Religions*, ed. R. van den Broek and M. J. Vermaseren (Leiden: E. J. Brill, 1981), 315–35, who identified the following passages as part of these lists. *Virtue Lists:* 2 Corinthians 6.6–7a; Galatians 5.22–23; Ephesians 4.2–3, 32–5.2; 5.9; Philippians 4.8; Colossians 3.12; 1 Timothy 3.2–4, 8–10, 11–12; 4.12; 6.11, 18; 2 Timothy 2.22–25; 3.10; Titus 1.8; 2.2–10; Hebrews 7.26; 1 Peter 3.8; 2 Peter 1.5–7; (1 Corinthians 13.4–7). *Vice Lists:* Matthew 15.19; Mark 7.21–22; Romans 1.29–31; 13.13; 1 Corinthians 5.10–11; 6.9–10; 2 Corinthians

12.20–21; Galatians 5.19–21; Ephesians 4.31; 5.3–5; Colossians 3.5–8; 1 Timothy 1.9–10; 6.4–5; 2 Timothy 3.2–4; Titus 1.7; 3.3; 1 Peter 2.1; 4.3, 15; Revelation 9.21; 21.8; 22.15.

28 See, for example, C. K. Barrett, *A Commentary on the First Epistle to the Corinthians*, *Black's New Testament Commentaries* (London: A & C Black, 1968), 140; this position is also supported by Gagnon, *The Bible and Homosexual Practice*, 306–12.

29 Robin Scroggs, *The New Testament and Homosexuality: Contextual Background for Contemporary Debate* (Philadelphia: Fortress Press, 1983), 85–122.

30 Ben Witherington, *Conflict and Community in Corinth: A Socio-Rhetorical Commentary on 1 and 2 Corinthians*, Grand Rapids: Eerdmans, 1995), 166.

31 Dale B. Martin, 'Arsenokoitês and Malakos: Meanings and Consequences', in *Sex and the Single Savior: Gender and Sexuality in Biblical Interpretation* (Louisville: Westminster John Knox, 2006), 37–50, 43ff.

32 Thiselton, *The First Epistle to the Corinthians*, 450.

33 See, for example, David F Wright, 'Homosexuals or Prostitutes? The Meaning of [Arsenokoitai] (1 Corinthians 6.9, 1 Timothy 1.10)', *Vigiliae Christianae* 38 (1984), 125–53; and James B. DeYoung, *Homosexuality: Contemporary Claims Examined in Light of the Bible and Other Ancient Literature and Law* (Grand Rapids: Kregel Publications, 2000).

34 Scroggs, *The New Testament and Homosexuality: Contextual Background for Contemporary Debate*, 108.

35 Martin, 'Arsenokoitês and Malakos: Meanings and Consequences'.

36 Witherington, *Conflict and Community*, 170–81.

37 See, for example, Antoinette Clark Wire, *The Corinthian Women Prophets: A Reconstruction through Paul's Rhetoric* (Minneapolis: Fortress Press, 1990), 87.

38 Drawn from Witherington, *Conflict and Community*, 173.

39 See discussion in N. T. Wright, 'The Letter to the Romans', in *The New Interpreter's Bible* (Nashville: Abingdon Press, 1994), 395–770, 428–34.

40 See, for example, Ernst Kasemann, *Commentary on Romans* (Grand Rapids: Eerdmans, 1980), 44.

41 See the discussion in Richard B. Hays, *The Moral Vision of the New Testament: Community, Cross, New Creation: A Contemporary Introduction to New Testament Ethics*, 1st edn (San Francisco: Harper, 1996), 385.

42 Gagnon correctly points out that these three usages are not temporal but an emphasis of the same act of giving over, Gagnon, *The Bible and Homosexual Practice*, 252.

43 Wright, 'The Letter to the Romans'.

44 James Allison, *Undergoing God. Dispatches from the Scene of a Break-In* (London: Continuum, 2006), 124–5.

45 See, for example, Richard B. Hays, 'Relations Natural and Unnatural: A Response to John Boswell's Exegesis of Romans 1', *Journal of Religious Ethics* 14 (1986), 184–215.

46 David E. Fredrickson, 'Natural and Unnatural Use in Romans 1.24–27: Paul and the Philosophic Critique of Eros', in *Homosexuality, Science and the 'Plain Sense' of Scripture*, ed. D. L. Balch (Grand Rapids: Eerdmans, 2000), 197–241.

47 Louis William Countryman, *Dirt, Greed and Sex: Sexual Ethics in the New Testament and Their Implications for Today* (Philadelphia: Fortress Press, 1988), 104–23.

48 Dale Martin, 'Heterosexism and the Interpretation of Romans 1.18–32', in *Sex and the Single Saviour*, 51–64.

49 See, for example, J. A. Ziesler, *Paul's Letter to the Romans*, *Tpi New Testament Commentaries* (London: Valley Forge: SCM; Trinity Press International, 1989), 81.

50 James D. G. Dunn, *Romans 1–8*, *Word Biblical Commentary*, Vol. 38a (Dallas: Word Books, 1988).

51 Martti Nissinen, *Homoeroticism in the Biblical World: A Historical Perspective* (Minneapolis: Fortress Press, 1998), 112.

52 Gagnon, *The Bible and Homosexual Practice*, 284.

53 See discussion above on these words.

54 See the discussion in George W. Knight, *The Pastoral Epistles: A Commentary on the*

Greek Text (Grand Rapids: Eerdmans, 1992), 83–4.

55 The Greek word for 'men' can also mean 'husband', as the word for 'woman' can also mean 'wife'.

56 Knight, *The Pastoral Epistles*, 157.

57 Gagnon, *The Bible and Homosexual Practice*, 87–8.

58 Kelly, commentary on Jude 261.

59 Bauckham, *Jude*, 54.

60 For a full discussion on the options, see David Edward Aune, *Revelation 6–16*, *Word Biblical Commentary*, Vol. 52b (Nashville: Thomas Nelson, 1998).

Chapter 4

The Witness of Tradition

Jaci Maraschin, Samson Fan and Phil Groves

Introduction

As the previous chapter explained, Anglicans have always combined their belief in the authority of Scripture with a respect for tradition. They have, however, also always understood themselves as both Catholic and Reformed and so accepted the need for even well-established traditions to be open to challenge and development. Our discussions on sexuality need therefore to be set in the context of both honouring the church's tradition and recognizing the possibility that this tradition may be in error in some ways. What does this mean in relation to our thinking about sexuality? Professor Oliver O'Donovan, explaining the claim in the St Andrew's Day Statement that the Church 'assists all its members to a life of faithful witness in chastity and holiness, recognizing two forms or vocations in which that life can be lived: marriage and singleness (Genesis 2.24; Matthew 19.4–6; 1 Corinthians 7 passim)', writes (italics added):

> As it stands, the claim that there are two and only two such forms, though well supported, as the authors think, from Scripture, is not directly a biblical one but claims the authority of unbroken church tradition. If that tradition were shown to be essentially defective (i.e. without the supposed support of Scripture) or (less implausibly) to be more accommodating than has been thought (e.g. including homosexual unions as a valid variant of marriage), then, of course, there would be no general difficulty. But that supposes a radical development in the church's understanding of the tradition. The Statement does not rule such a development out a priori; in principle, *no Anglican who believed, as Anglicans are supposed to believe, in the corrigibility of tradition could rule it out a priori.*[1]

The chapter that follows aims to provide tools to help you think about the nature of tradition and how we should evaluate proposed changes to our traditions. Because this is its aim, little of what follows is directly on the issue of homosexuality or the generally negative understanding of homosexuality found in Christian tradition.

The work is a joint contribution from **Jaci Maraschin** (who brings a wealth of experience as a Brazilian liturgist who has contributed to the Anglican Communion over many years especially as part of the Anglican team on the Anglican–Roman Catholic International Commission) and **Samson Fan** (a young Chinese scholar who brought both enthusiasm and order to the thinking). Their work was facilitated by Phil Groves, as much by asking the questions and editing the responses. The fact that English was not the first language of either Samson or Jaci presented new ways of looking at things.

After a brief context-setting Jaci and Samson introduce the crucial distinction between tradition (the transmission through time of the apostolic faith) and traditions (usages or habits giving expression to tradition and open to change). Drawing on Hooker and other theologians, they then help us think through the relationship between tradition and both Scripture (picking up some of the themes in the first section of chapter three) and reason. Contemporary gay consciousness is then described as a new challenge facing the church which has led some Christians to call for the blessing of same-sex unions. This call to change our traditions needs to be tested not only to see whether it is compatible with Scripture but also how it relates to the tradition of the Church. To help in that testing more detailed analysis is then offered of four areas where there have been recent calls to change our traditions in the Communion – in relation to marriage, polygamy, divorce and remarriage and the ordination of women. The developments in these areas are sketched and it is seen that calls to change have been heeded but also resisted and rejected in the recent past. In each area, questions are suggested to help you consider what can be learned from these issues and how they might help us as we consider calls to change certain traditions in relation to homosexuality. The final section reminds us that as Anglicans we are simply part of the one, holy, catholic, apostolic church and introduces thinking about tradition and authority that has arisen out of work between Anglicans and Roman Catholics on ARCIC.

In the rich diversity of human life, encounter with the living Tradition produces a variety of expressions of the Gospel. Where diverse expressions are faithful to the Word revealed in Jesus Christ and transmitted by the apostolic community, the churches in which they are found are truly in communion. Indeed, this diversity of traditions is the practical manifestation of catholicity and confirms rather than contradicts the vigour of Tradition. As God has created diversity among humans, so the Church's fidelity and identity require not uniformity of expression and formulation at all levels in all situations, but rather catholic diversity within the unity of communion. (ARCIC, *The Gift of Authority*, Paragraph 27)

1. Context

In 2002 the synod of the Diocese of New Westminster passed a resolution authorizing the use of rites of blessing for same-sex unions and this was endorsed by the Bishop. Although at the time of writing New Westminster remains the only diocese in the Anglican Communion that has taken this step, there are numerous groups asking for a similar development in many of the churches of the Communion.

In societies where gay unions are accepted and celebrated – either as marriages or as civil partnerships – the Church is facing questions from ordinary people and from the media as to why it is not prepared to bless such partnerships.

In other societies – especially in ones where homosexuality is illegal or regarded by the culture as shameful – the possibility that the Anglican Communion could accept homosexuality has forced mission leaders to constantly face questions in a way that hinders their mission and compromises the life of their church. One example is from Egypt:

The Episcopal Church in Egypt, being part of the Anglican Communion, is seen to adopt the same teaching of the Church as in America and Canada. We spend a lot of time explaining that we disapprove of these decisions and we hold the traditional teaching of the Anglican Communion as expressed in the Resolution 1.10 of Lambeth Conference 1998. Some believe us, others do not . . . *All this hinders our daily mission and work.* (Bishop Mouneer Anis, Primate of Jerusalem and the Middle East)[2]

Within these societies people cannot conceive how such a question can even be considered by a church. For many in the Communion to bless such unions is no less than the blessing of sin.

It would be wrong to assume that the differences of opinion in the Communion were purely cultural. There are cultural aspects and they will be considered in the next chapter; however, the differences are often expressed as being over faithfulness or otherwise to apostolic tradition. Some claim that to reject the blessing of same-sex unions is to 'defend the faith once delivered to the saints' and to do otherwise is to break from the tradition of the Church. Others disagree, they argue that to remain faithful to 'the faith once delivered to the saints' is to express the gospel of love and develop traditions to express that gospel in the blessing of same sex unions.

This chapter aims to enable you to consider how Anglicans have handled tradition and traditions in other contexts. We begin by attempting to define the difference between tradition and traditions. This distinction is not perfect and we are aware of limitations, but we believe it is a helpful tool to enable discussion.

2. Tradition and Traditions

We offer here an introduction to the way Anglicans have looked at tradition in relation to Scripture and reason. This is complex because the one word often carries two distinct meanings. We will try to distinguish between them by referring to 'tradition' and 'traditions'.

Tradition is understood as the transmission from generation to generation of the original belief held by the primitive ecclesial community. It is well exemplified in Jude 3: 'I find it necessary to write and appeal to you to contend for the faith that was once for all delivered to the saints.' The 'faith once for all delivered to the saints' has been interpreted as the gospel of Jesus Christ, the gift of God's salvation to humankind. When taken in this sense, it is a living experience of the resurrection of Jesus in the life of his Church. This is a kind of truth beyond all understanding but, nevertheless, set to be lived as *koinonia* (communion).

The process of the transmission of 'the faith once for all delivered to the saints' becomes part of tradition. Tradition itself means 'handing on' and so it presupposes senders and receivers, and between the sender and the receiver there is communication, and where there is communication there is interpretation. To guard against unwarranted changes the aim of the Church is to seek to be faithful to the tradition as 'delivered to the saints'.

Guided by the Holy Spirit, believer and believing community seek to discern the mind of Christ amidst the changing circumstances of their own histories. Fidelity to the Gospel, obedience to the mind of Christ, openness to the Holy Spirit – these remain the source and strength of the community. (Life in Christ, ARCIC II, 6.33)

Traditions are understood **as** the temporal expression of tradition, also described as usages or habits. This is how it is described in the 39 Articles:

Of the Traditions of the Church

It is not necessary that Traditions and Ceremonies be in all places one, or utterly like; for at all times they have been divers, and may be changed according to the diversity of countries, times, and men's manners, so that nothing be ordained against God's Word. Whosoever, through his private judgement, willingly and purposely, doth openly break the Traditions and Ceremonies of the Church, which be not repugnant to the Word of God, and be ordained and approved by common authority, ought to be rebuked openly, (that others may fear to do the like,) as he that offendeth against the common order of the Church, and hurteth the authority of the Magistrate, and woundeth the consciences of the weak brethren.

Every particular or national Church hath authority to ordain, change, and abolish, Ceremonies or Rites of the Church ordained only by man's authority, so that all things be done to edifying. (Article 34)

Traditions are open to change, indeed Article 34 supposes that traditions have to change in different countries, times and cultural contexts so that nothing should be done against God's Word.

Cardinal Newman agreed that the Church had to change to remain the same:

[A great idea] in time enters upon strange territory; points of controversy alter their bearing; parties rise and fall around it; dangers and hopes appear in new relations; and the old principles appear in new forms. It changes with them in order to remain the same. In a higher world it is otherwise, but here below to live is to change, and to be perfect is to have changed often.[3]

One example of such a 'great idea' might be Galileo's proposal that the earth circles the sun. In Galileo's time a literal reading of the Scriptures – such as Psalm 93.1 – led the Church to consider that such an idea was blasphemous, a denial of the biblical witness and against essential core doctrine.[4] Once the scientific discovery had been explained and accepted in society the Church changed the way it interpreted Scripture, stressing the poetic nature of the psalms and opposing literal interpretations, but continuing to assert the majesty of the creator God in a wonderfully created world.

Questions

For many the blessing of same-sex unions is a departure from tradition. It is against the 'faith once delivered to the saints'. For others the emergence of publicly recognized, exclusive, lifelong unions of fidelity and care is a contemporary 'great idea' which the Church must adopt by developing its traditions in order to be faithful to 'the faith once delivered to the saints' in a new cultural context.

- In advising against 'the legitimizing or blessing of same-sex unions' were the bishops of the 1998 Lambeth Conference rejecting a proposed change to the faith?
- Or were the bishops advising against the development of a ceremony or rite of the Church which is a genuine expression of the gospel of love and justice which is central to 'the faith once delivered to the saints'?

You may already have an answer to these questions, but we hope we can enable you to better understand your own answer and to consider the answers those who disagree with you might give.

We now consider the relationships between tradition, Scripture and reason and draw upon the foundational Anglican thinker Richard Hooker.

3. Tradition and Scripture

The Reformation debates centred on the alternative claims for the priority of Scripture over tradition or for tradition over Scripture. Those who supported the reformers' proposition of *sola scriptura* argued that the Scriptures were given directly from God's revelation without the mediation of the Church, and so scriptures should have absolute priority. Extreme Calvinism argued against there being any place for tradition in the forming of theology and rejected anything which was not expressly endorsed by Scripture.

The Catholic Church argued that God gave his only Son Jesus Christ and in him became flesh and, consequently, human, 'for us and for our salvation'. This deposit of faith was delivered to the saints and maintained through apostolic succession. The Council of Trent decreed, '(the Synod) following the examples of the orthodox Fathers, receives and venerates with an equal affection of piety, and reverence, all the books both of the Old and of the New Testament – seeing that one God is the author of both – as also the said traditions, as well those appertaining to faith as to morals, as having been dictated, either by Christ's own word of mouth, or by the Holy Ghost, and preserved in the Catholic Church by a continuous succession' (Council of Trent, Decree Concerning the Canonical Scriptures, 1546). Thus the Scriptures are a very significant part of the deposit of faith, but not understandable outside the tradition of the Church. It was within the context of the Sacred Tradition that the Bible emerged and the Sacred Tradition determines how the Bible is to be interpreted.

Hooker sought to define an Anglican perspective on the debate:

There are two opinions concerning the sufficiency of Holy Scripture, which are entirely opposed to each other, and both wrong. The Roman Church teaches that Scripture is insufficient and if traditions are not added then it does not contain all the truth God has revealed and these truths are required for all people for their salvation. Others rightly condemn this opinion, but they support another dangerous extreme. They argue that Scripture not only contains all that is necessary, but all truth completely and that any additional understandings are not only unnecessary but the opposite of the gospel, unlawful and sinful. They say that anything said of

God or to do with God which is not expressly in the Scripture – even though it seems to be reverent and good – is hurtful. Just as overblown praises given to humans often gets in the way of them receiving proper compliments for good things they have done; we must be careful not to make Scripture out to be more than it is, because if we do we may end up defending things not present in it and cause those wonders which it does contain to be less valued. (Richard Hooker, *Of the Laws of Ecclesiastical Polity*, The Second Book, 7, modernized version by Philip Secor)[5]

Hooker rejects the Catholic proposition which maintained Scripture was insufficient in itself and required further revelation. He also rejected the extreme Calvinist position that Scripture was not only sufficient but complete, so that anything not expressly mentioned was to be seen as evil, including, for example, printed prayer books and vestments. If, he argued, you said all truth was in Scripture, you would have to find all knowledge within it and defend what Scripture said about geography or history, rather than focusing on the glorious truths held within concerning the salvation of all.

Hooker asserted that Scripture was sufficient, but that the Church should endorse traditions compatible with Scripture. Hooker placed great store in reason, not in contrast with Scripture and tradition but alongside them.

4. Tradition and Reason

Scripture indeed teaches us things which nature does not, things which our reason by itself could not reach into. Yet we believe those things taught by Scripture because we know by reason that Scripture is the word of God . . . We must have, therefore, some former knowledge, some presuppositions, which gives us assurance in our hearts. (Richard Hooker, *Of the Laws of Ecclesiastical Polity*, The Third Book, 12 and 13, modernized version by Philip Secor)[6]

Faith is the basis from which we follow Christ. Baptism candidates are not asked if they can prove the existence of God or to give a logical account of salvation in Christ, but if they believe. And they answer, 'Yes, I do, I believe.' The Creeds begin with: 'I believe . . . ' or 'We believe . . . ' not 'We have proved . . . ' Faith is the human answer to the gospel. But the New Testament asks us to give reason for the hope that is in us (1 Peter 3.15). The Second Letter of Peter stresses the importance of knowledge:

His divine power has given us everything needed for life and godliness, through the knowledge of him who called us by his own glory and goodness . . . You must make every effort to support your faith with goodness, and goodness with knowledge, and knowledge with self-control, and self-control with endurance, and endurance with godliness, and godliness with mutual affection, and mutual affection with love. (2 Peter 1.1, 5–7)

The relation between faith and reason is not a simple one. The failure of the Catholic Church to accept the scientific findings of Galileo was shameful, something recognized by Pope John Paul II in 1992. The response of some in the Church of England to Darwin's theories of evolution was equally dismissive. However others, including evangelicals, welcomed his theories, and most modern commentators on Genesis have found their understanding enriched by being released from attempting to use the Bible as a science handbook, a purpose, they contend, for which it was never intended.

The Lambeth Conference of 1978 recognized 'the need for deep and dispassionate study of the question of homosexuality, which would take seriously both the teaching of Scripture and the results of scientific and medical research'.[7] Such a scientific and medical study is presented in the final chapter of this book. Science is asked more complex questions now than in the time of Galileo – his hypothesis was simply and unquestionably right; the science of human diversity is more complex and the results provisional. Even if this were not the case, however, the scientific context never determines theology, but constitutes part of the context within which we listen to God.

Our purpose here is to understand the particular relation of reason to Scripture and tradition. Human beings were created by God in his 'image and likeness' . . . 'from the dust of the ground' (Genesis 1.26—2.7). The result of this act of God was a 'spiritual body', which means a unity of chemical and biological elements with distinct features which have been called 'soul', 'spirit', 'mind' or 'reason'. The rational dimension is responsible for the human capacity for discernment throughout life, permitting choices, decisions, commitments and actions. We are not mere robots, but thinking persons able to create intelligent relationships with our fellow creatures and with God.

The Scriptures teach us that as the result of sin we have all been deprived of the original blessing of creation and fallen into corruption. This is why human reason becomes subject to error. One of the aims of salvation was and is the redemption of reason. The Logos (reason), as the Greeks liked to call the eternal Second Person of the Trinity, 'became flesh' in order to reveal that real life (or saved life) was not only rational life, but 'incarnate reason'. The Scriptures, then, were written with the purpose of witnessing to this truth, at the same time pointing to the mystery of divine life as a 'secret and hidden' mystery (cf. 1 Corinthians 2.7).

The 'faith once for all delivered to the saints' was, certainly, delivered to 'rational' saints. Jesus endorsed the command to love God with all our minds as well as our hearts, souls and strength (Luke 10.27). Paul delivered carefully thought out and rational responses to the churches to which he wrote his letters. The revelation of God was given to his rational creatures. This is why through the long history of theology (reasoning about God) wise Christian writers tried time and again to understand the mystery of faith. Anselm described theology as 'faith seeking understanding'.[8] To understand the Scriptures we need to use our rationality.

Hooker believed that God had inspired holy writers to include in the Scriptures the truth (as logical form), which transcended our rational capacities for understanding. In this he was in line with patristic and medieval theologians such as Origen:

We have spoken briefly about the inspiration of the divine Scriptures. We must now tackle the question of how they should be read and understood, since many mistakes have been caused by the failure of the multitude to discover the right way to approach the sacred writings. (Origen, *De principiis*, IV, 2,1)

Hooker argued against those who dismissed reason on the grounds that it was dangerous because it was unbiblical. He argued that they used reason itself to dismiss reason,
whereas he quoted Paul who asked those who heard him to judge his words for themselves (1 Corinthians 10.15), in other words to use reason. His conclusion was:

> There is nothing in the nature of reason to preclude its use, rather the same Spirit,
> which has revealed the things that God has set down in his law, may also be
> thought to aid and direct us in finding out by the light of reason what laws are
> advisable to be made for the guiding of his Church alongside those that are in
> Scripture. (Hooker, *Of the Laws of Ecclesiastical Polity*, Third Book, X, 18, mod-
> ernized version by Philip Secor)[9]

From the beginning, God gave created humanity the gift and instrument of reason,
under the guidance of the Holy Spirit, in order to recognize his word in the Bible and
to lead us into all truth. This opens up the possibility of doctrinal and theological
development as well as of hermeneutical and exegetical advances. At the same time
we have to recognize, humbly, the possibility of wrong reasoning caused by our
fallen human condition. This calls all theologians, interpreters and preachers to
humility and to openness of heart.

> Reason is more, and not less, rational when it takes for its proper theme the truth
> of God, when it seeks to unite the truth which we find in the gospel in one synthe-
> sis with the many truths with which life in the world is continually confronting us.
> There are no truths but truth, and the many truths will not finally coalesce into
> one truth until the last day, until that consummation in which the meaning of
> everything will be laid bare. (J. V. Langmead Casserley, *Graceful Reason*, p. 162)

Reason is not a simple single category. The Fathers relied on Platonism for the formulation of the early Christian Creeds. Augustine regarded Neo-Platonism as just
common sense and Aquinas looked to Aristotle as a basis for his theology. Against
the rationalism of Descartes, Pascal proposed the 'reason of the heart' which technical reason did not know. European philosophical categories are questioned by some
non-Western Christians, for example in Archbishop Tutu's promotion of the African
concept of Ubuntu, stressing the communality of all humans.

Scripture cannot even be read without the engagement of our reason. The Church
cannot exist without the development of traditions, but it ceases to have identity as
the community of God if Scripture and tradition are ignored as we seek to hold to
the faith given to those who encountered the living, crucified and risen Christ
through direct contact and the mediation of the Holy Spirit.

5. Tradition, Scriptures and Reason, and the Legitimacy of Blessing Gay Unions

The Archbishop of Canterbury has said that the 1998 Lambeth Conference Resolution 1.10 is the present 'mind of the Church'. If it is to remain as such we need to be
clear as to why this is so. If we are to change, we need to be clear as to how any
change is in line with the tradition of the Church.

Some readers will ask: How can anyone seriously argue for such a radical change in faith that is so clearly wrong?

Some will ask: How can we not change in a world where we see how good gay partnerships are?

In the previous chapter it was argued that for any change to be Anglican it would have to be compatible with Scripture. Anglican theology accepts that this does not demand that such changes in traditions be explicit in Scripture but that traditions are compatible with Scripture and in accordance with the deposit of faith, the tradition of the Church, the essential gospel.

Some will question why we need to do this at all. It is important to recognize that the desire to question the traditions does not stem from a desire to destroy the Church, but because a significant number of Anglicans are proposing that the emergence of the open acceptance of gay and lesbian relationships in many societies around the world presents a new context within which the gospel is preached.

Oliver O'Donovan argues against the presumption that we should accept the blessing of same-sex unions, but he contends that the contemporary gay consciousness is what Newman called a 'great idea'. Not that it is a good idea, but that it is a significant innovation, right or wrong. O'Donovan states:

> The world has never seen a phenomenon like the contemporary gay consciousness. There have been various patterns of homosexuality in various cultures, but none with the constellation of features and the persistent self-assertion that this one presents.[10]

This would suggest that the phenomenon is something which cannot be ignored as we remain faithful to the Bible and tradition. We may be challenged to change our traditions, but the blessing of gay partnerships will not be the only possible response; other options will be to consider how we proclaim the transforming power of Christ and how we enable our churches to become communities of friendship for all, including those who are open and honest about their attraction to people of the same gender.[11]

6. Changing and Reaffirming Traditions

To assist us in thinking about the realities of reaffirming or changing traditions we will consider four examples both of how we have changed traditions in the Anglican Communion and how we have rejected changes to the traditions in the past. In the first, marriage, there has been Anglican consensus for change in our traditions. In the second, polygamy, there has been consensus that there should be no change. In the final two, divorce and remarriage and the ordination of women, there have been change in some parts of the Communion but not in others.

Example 1. Marriage

The development of the understanding of sexuality in the Bible is looked at in detail in the previous chapter. Here we look at developments in the traditions of marriage in the Anglican Communion beginning with the *Book of Common Prayer*.

Marriage in the Book of Common Prayer

In Chapter 3 we saw that the paradigm of Eden was a relationship between Adam and Eve that was both for companionship and for procreation. We saw that sex was a blessing from God and seen as good. The Church of England began with a break with the traditions of the medieval Church by allowing the marriage of bishops, priests and deacons. Article 32 'Of the Marriage of Priests' states:

> Bishops, Priests and Deacons are not commanded by God's Law, either to vow the estate of single life, or to abstain from marriage: therefore it is lawful for them, and for all other Christian men, to marry at their own discretion, as they shall judge the same to serve better to godliness. (Article 32)

This was a decisive break with Catholic order. There was little biblical precedent both for celibacy – Jesus was single and it could be argued that all the apostles, including Paul, were single – and for married leaders; 1 Corinthians 9.5 speaks of married apostles, and the pastoral epistles indicated that leaders could be married. The decision to allow priests to decide if they wished to marry was not based upon Scripture alone but it was a reasonable decision compatible with Scripture.

When it came to the understanding of marriage itself *The Book of Common Prayer* was in line with the tradition of the medieval Church. For Thomas Aquinas marriage was for the purpose of begetting and rearing children with the additional purpose of the prevention of fornication. Duns Scotus added the need of a contract to legitimize 'the mutual giving of the bodies for carnal copulation'. Aquinas believed that the sexual act was unworthy of humanity because it deprived people of reason. It was only legitimized and excused in marriage because of the blessings which it brought in procreation.

The *Book of Common Prayer* did not call marriage a sacrament, and introduced an element of mutuality, but still retained the medieval theological traditions. The purposes of marriage were set out in three clauses:

> First, It was ordained for the procreation of children, to be brought up in the fear and nurture of the Lord, and to the praise of his holy Name.
>
> Secondly, It was ordained for a remedy against sin, and to avoid fornication; that such persons as have not the gift of continency might marry, and keep themselves undefiled members of Christ's body.
>
> Thirdly, It was ordained for the mutual society, help, and comfort, that the one ought to have of the other, both in prosperity and adversity. (1662 *Book of Common Prayer*)

Martin Bucer, a Protestant reformer, criticized this order of the purposes of marriage. For him, as well as some other Protestants, the order was wrong. Companionship for help and comfort should come first, procreation and regulation of sexual activity were secondary. Gillian Varcoe says that 'Cranmer's liturgy puts the regulation of sex in an entirely negative way that owes more to Augustine of Hippo than to Scripture or to emerging Reformation theologies of the vocation to the married state.' For her: 'The service reflects a history of Christian suspicion of the body and of sexual expression, and a concomitant elevation of celibacy as more holy than marriage.'[12]

Modern Revisions to Marriage Services

Revisions of the marriage service in the Anglican Communion were inspired by many factors. After Vatican II the liturgical movement influenced many churches around the world. The Anglican churches in their different cultural settings perceived the need of a new language in order to communicate what they meant by marriage, but revisions soon went beyond linguistic changes.

The Church of Australia published its first *Book of Common Prayer* in 1978 after a long process of experimentation and reflection. The new book stated the purposes of marriage in two different forms. The first form followed the 1662 rite in describing the purpose of marriage as being for the procreation of children, for living a chaste and holy life and for mutual companionship, help and comfort. However, the second form was markedly different. It first described the purpose of marriage as being 'for the well being of mankind, and for the proper expression of natural instincts and affections with which he has endowed us'. This was followed by the commendation of companionship and for the 'establishment of a new family' where children can be born and nurtured. In addition, the rubric allowed a prayer for the blessing of the couple by the gift of children to be omitted when appropriate. It meant a change in the long tradition that affirmed that the chief purpose of marriage was procreation.

In England the 1928 revision of the Prayer Book had seen marriage as primarily for 'the increase of mankind according to the will of God', but the 1980 *Alternative Service Book* (ASB) followed the Australian changes. The ASB was markedly more positive about marriage than the BCP. It said: 'The Scriptures teach us that marriage is a gift of God in creation and a means of his grace', which defines marriage as a sacramental act through which God is made known. The purposes of marriage were listed as love, mutual comfort and help and 'that they may have children'.

In 2000 the Church of England replaced the ASB with *Common Worship* and further developments were adopted. *Common Worship* says:

> Marriage is a gift of God in creation
> through which husband and wife may know the grace of God.
> It is given that as man and woman grow together in love and trust,
> they shall be united with one another in heart, body and mind,
> as Christ is united with his bride, the Church.
>
> The gift of marriage brings husband and wife together
> in the delight and tenderness of sexual union
> and joyful commitment to the end of their lives.
>
> It is given as the foundation of family life
> in which children are [born and] nurtured
> and in which each member of the family, in good times and in bad,
> may find strength, companionship and comfort,
> and grow to maturity in love.
> (Marriage Service, *Common Worship*, Church of England, 2000)

The change from the BCP to *Common Worship* is marked. Marriage is regarded as a way to 'know the grace of God' and its primary purpose is that the married couple should be united with one another. The 'delight' of sexual union is to bring the couple together into joyful commitment. Marriage is given as a basis of family life in which children are nurtured and all may grow to maturity. The blessing of procreation is significant, but it is recognized that it might not be part of the family's future and therefore not the primary purpose of marriage. Perhaps this reflects the social trend where a huge majority of couples coming to be married in the Church of England already live together and many already have children, either from their mutual relationship, or from previous relationships, married or unmarried. It also reflects English society's acceptance of couples who choose not to have children and use contraception as well as those who know they are unable to have children. The service says that marriage 'enriches society and strengthens community' and so is a vital part of human life.

There has been a relative level of harmony over the development of the traditions of marriage liturgies across the Communion. While African Anglican prayer books, such as those from Nigeria, Kenya or Southern Africa, continue to emphasize the significance of the birth of children within marriage, just as in England and Australia, they emphasize that companionship is a significant function of marriage. For example, the Church of Nigeria (Anglican Communion) adopted the form of words of the ASB of the Church of England except they emphasized the priority of companionship by adding the words 'primarily', 'also' and 'lastly' to the relevant clauses:

> Marriage is given primarily that husband and wife may comfort and help each other, living faithfully together in need and in plenty, in sorrow and in joy.
>
> It is also given, that with delight and tenderness, they may know each other in love, and through the joy of their bodily union, may strengthen the union of their hearts and lives.
>
> Lastly, it is given that they may have children and be blessed in caring for them and bringing them up in accordance with God's will, to his praise and glory. (*The Book of Common Prayer*, Church of Nigeria (Anglican Communion), 1996)

Questions

- Marriage traditions have changed over time and in different cultures. Have these changes reflected Scripture or have they been influenced by cultures?
- Read the marriage service in your own church. How does it hold together Scripture, tradition and reason in the context of your nation at this time?

A Gay Reflection on the Changes

The revisions to Anglican prayer books have placed an emphasis on the mutuality of marriage and its significance for both the man and the woman in experiencing the grace of God. The God-given need for companionship is met in the God-blessed union in marriage. The delight of sexual union is primarily for the building up of the married relationship. Procreation is a blessing but is not a vital purpose of marriage, although marriage is vital for the nurture of children and is valuable in the community.

Some gay people reflect that:

- Many gay and lesbian people desire to experience the grace of God through faithful monogamous partnerships blessed by God.
- Such relationships will be strengthened through physical expression of love between partners.
- Gay partnerships are a gift as they enrich society and strengthen community.

Does the gay reflection above affect your attitude to the changes in marriage traditions?

Example 2. Polygamy

The Church has consistently affirmed monogamy as the expression of the will of God for married people. We have seen that monogamy was the paradigm of the garden of Eden, but it is also clear that polygamy was part of the culture of Ancient Israel. It was usually a response to childlessness in the first marriage, a sign of economic status or a means of forming alliances with other families. There is no Old Testament law which proscribes it, but it is regulated in Deuteronomy 21.15–17 to prevent a breakdown in social cohesion. Opposition to polygamy is in the Pastorals, but it could be argued that the Bible is more positive about polygamy than homosexuality. Certainly it is no more negative.

During the great missionary expansion of the Church monogamy was a discipline demanded of evangelized peoples. Western missionaries challenged the social structures of peoples in America, Asia and Africa and monogamy was seen as an essential aspect of Christianity. Chinese cultural norms adopted Western monogamy (even where Christianity itself was not accepted) and indigenous North American cultures were forced into conformity. In some, but not all, African cultures polygamy has continued to be a normal aspect of life, practised among those who follow their Traditional Religion, Muslims, and also those who would call themselves 'Christians', but who are often regarded as nominal believers. In most denominations polygamists are barred from ordination and often from communion.

Even in African cultures which practised polygamy it was not always regarded as an ideal. Many families were reluctant to allow a daughter to marry a polygamous man. Polygamous marriage was often a practical response of care for a widow rather than something thought of as a positive good. As in Ancient Israel, the main reasons for polygamy were a response to the childlessness of a first marriage, the need for labour or a method to cement political alliances.

The second meeting of the Anglican Consultative Council in Dublin, Ireland, in 1973 considered polygamy and monogamy. They took as a foundational document *Christian Marriage in Africa* by Adrian Hastings – a book commissioned by the Archbishops of Cape Town, Central Africa, Kenya, Tanzania and Uganda – which offered four approaches:

a   Polygamy is simply a sin, comparable with adultery.
b   Polygamy is an inferior form of marriage, not sinful where it is the custom but always unacceptable for Christians.
c   Polygamy is a form of marriage less satisfactory than monogamy and one which cannot do justice to the full spirit of Christian marriage, but in certain circumstances individual Christians can still put up with it, as they put up with slavery, dictatorial government, and much else.
d   Polygamy is one form of marriage, monogamy another. Each has its advantages and disadvantages: they are appropriate to different types of society. It is not the task of the Church to make any absolute judgement between them (ACC-3, page 36).

The Council adopted option (c) and recommended that 'in the case of the conversion of a pagan polygamist, he should be received into the Church with his believing wives and children' so long as that was the will of the local Christian community and in 'a context where the Church's teaching on monogamy is strictly recognized'. From the start churches found the combination of offering the full love of God and maintaining the challenge to obedience a hard task. They found that some would wait to be baptized until they were satisfied with the number of women they had married. Others declared they had one wife but maintained a separate local wife. Others 'lapsed', married a further wife, and sought to return to the community following public confession, but still married to the additional wife.

In the 1980s Archbishop David Gitari of Kenya gained wider awareness of the debate and at the 1988 Lambeth Conference proposed a similar approach to that of ACC-3. His intention was to offer pastoral accommodation in difficult circumstances but he was seen by some to be allowing room for a rekindling of polygamy in modern Kenya. Modern Kenyan society places great strains on the practice of monogamy. Edith Njoki Njiiri observed three strong forces which are influencing men to take up polygamy in the modern world. These may well be replicated across Africa. First, the strong emphasis on childbearing encourages men who were childless in their first marriage to seek a second wife. Their families press them to do so and a reduced status could affect their chances of promotion in work and within society. Second, urbanization leads men to seek work in the city, but they often leave their wife in the village. In the city they frequently take another wife and move between the two. Third, an early marriage to an uneducated wife can become difficult for a man who is now gaining education and better employment. He may marry a wife suitable to the circles in which he is now mixing.

Njiiri regarded modern moves to accept polygamous men as a threat to the gospel and especially as a continuing form of oppression of women by men. While she accepted the pastoral concern for the whole family of new converts who were polygamous prior to hearing the gospel, she questioned the motives of her Archbishop and others in promoting liberality on such a matter.

The Church of Uganda states its position similarly in these terms:

Perhaps the most degrading form of gender inequality was the African tradition of polygamy and divorce at will, which left many women neglected or even destitute. The biblical teaching of marriage between one man and one woman in a loving, lifelong relationship liberated not only women, but also the institution of marriage and family. (Church of Uganda Position Paper on Homosexuality, 2005)

Anglican churches across Africa struggle with how to pastorally respond to men and women seeking to convert and who are living in polygamous relationships, but they have become firmer in their support for monogamy. They were happy with the definition of Christian marriage as being between 'a man and a woman' in Resolution 1.10 of the 1998 Lambeth Conference.

Questions

- Archbishop Gitari was proposing changes to allow a pastoral response to people in ploygamous societies; was he right to do so?
- Did he have the right answer?
- How would we know?

An African Reflection on Polygamy and Homosexuality

Polygamy was part of the life of the nation of Israel. In many cultures it was not easy to give up polygamy and it is still difficult to encourage some cultural groups to embrace monogamy. However, churches, notably the Church of Uganda and the Church of Nigeria (Anglican Communion), have remained true to the biblical witness and the tradition of the Church in encouraging monogamy. Some pastoral accommodation has been made in some situations, but there are many congregations where communion will be denied those who have chosen polygamous marriages.

Many Christians who have rejected polygamy reflect that:

- The biblical arguments for the acceptance of homosexuality are similar to those for the acceptance of polygamy.
- Despite cultural demands, both are contrary to biblical witness and the tradition of the Church.
- Accepting gay unions will lead to dysfunction in the community, just as accepting polygamy leads to an immoral society.
- Pastoral care needs to be offered to gay people, but not the blessing of sinful relationships.

Does the African experience of polygamy change the way in which you understand the issues of homosexuality?

Example 3. Divorce and Remarriage

We have looked at changes in the traditions of the Church on marriage – changes that have received a high level of consensus across the Communion. We have considered the reaffirmation of a tradition of the Church in support of monogamy. We now consider an example where there is divergence in the Communion, divorce and remarriage.

The vision of marriage as fruitful, life-long, full of the grace of God, is not always sustained in the realities of life. Its very goodness, when corrupted by human frailty, self-centredness and sin, gives rise to pain, despair and tragedy, not only for the couple immediately involved in marital difficulty or breakdown, but also for their children, the wider family and the social order. (ARCIC, *Life in Christ,* #63)

The paradigm of Eden was of a relationship which had no end. Jesus was asked about divorce and referred to the Old Testament Law. Deuteronomy 24.1–4 did not proscribe divorce but set limitations on its practice (see also Leviticus 22.13 and Numbers 30.9). However, divorce is condemned in Malachi 2.10–16 and it is regarded by Jesus as a sign of imperfection, not what God intended from the beginning (Mark 10.1–12). Jesus implies an acceptance that divorce happens in our fallen world, but did not seem to allow remarriage. Whether the blessing of remarriage is compatible with Scripture is a subject on which Anglicans disagree.

The Lambeth Conference of 1908 recognized, with alarm, the breakdown of family life and increase of divorce. The bishops had pastoral concern for men and women who were the innocent parties of divorce following their spouse's adultery, but they refused to bless remarriage in any circumstance.

When an innocent person has, by means of a court of law, divorced a spouse for adultery, and desires to enter into another contract of marriage, it is undesirable that such a contract should receive the blessing of the Church. (Lambeth Conference 1908, Resolution 40)

The Lambeth Conferences of 1930 and 1948 strengthened the Church's opposition to divorce. The 1908 conference clearly instructed the churches to ensure that remarried divorcees could receive Holy Communion, but in 1958 it was recognized that there were differing views across the provinces of the Communion.

The 1958 Lambeth Conference was the last one to pass resolutions directly on divorce. The previous Lambeth Conference had strongly condemned the liberalization of divorce laws in Great Britain and the United States and the 1958 Conference suggested Christian couples contemplating divorce should seek to forgive each other and be reconciled in their marriage.

Since then individual churches of the Communion have developed differing traditions. Some allow priests, who wish to do so, to bless the remarriage of a divorced person or even to offer a full rite of marriage. Others refuse communion to divorced people. Some provinces ordain men and women who have been divorced and remarried or who are married to men or women who have been divorced. For other churches this is not considered a possibility: divorce is a bar to ordination and even to communion. Different Anglican provinces deal with the matter according to their cultural, social and theological experiences. But, so far, this matter has not been a divisive one.

Questions

Some Anglicans believe that the plain reading of Scripture is compatible with the prohibition of remarriage after divorce in any circumstances while others believe that the teaching of Jesus is compatible with the remarriage of divorced people. These decisions have been left to individual provinces and to the conscience of individual priests. There is a diversity of pastoral responses in the Communion.

- What is the practice in your church? Do you agree with it?
- How do you remain in communion with those who disagree with you?
- Is it possible for our Church to tolerate in the same way a diversity of traditions with regard to the blessing of same-sex unions?
- In churches where it is permissible to bless the remarriage of divorced people, priests are encouraged to do as they believe and are not forced to participate in such blessings. If churches of the Communion were to bless same-sex unions, would such a clause be enough to hold unity?

Reflections on Divorce, Remarriage and Homosexuality

- Some gay Christians find that Churches are ready to go against the tradition of the Church and bless, and even remarry, divorced straight people even though this is against Scripture, but they are not prepared to do the same for gay couples. They wonder why this should be.
- Some argue that a better hermeneutical approach shows that Jesus approved of remarriage.
- Some believe that the remarriage of a divorced person should not take place in church and the rule should apply to gay unions.

Has reflecting on divorce and remarriage changed the way you understand the blessings of gay unions?

Example 4. The Ordination of Women

Ordination

So far we have concentrated on the claims to legitimacy or otherwise of the blessing of same-sex unions. The bishops of the 1998 Lambeth Conference also resolved that they could not advise the ordination of men and women in same-sex unions. This remains the 'mind of the Communion', but again the Church exists in cultures where people are questioning if this should continue to be the advice. In seeking to enable a dialogue we will consider the example of the ordination of women. Once more as an analogy we will seek both similarities and differences between the two.

The ordination of women and the ordination of gay and lesbian people in part-nered relationships are analogous – in that they are both changes in tradition – but they are not the same. Gay Christians have always been ordained, but they have either publicly remained celibate or have been married. Women were more obviously excluded from ordination. The grounds offered for exclusion are about life choices (the choice to have a partner), not sexuality itself. It is important to be absolutely clear that support for one does not demand support for the other. Some are opposed to the ordination of women, but are at least ambivalent about the ordination of gay men. Others are in favour of the ordination of women, but absolutely opposed to the ordination of homosexual clergy. It is not argued here that there is a fundamental link between the two.

The Windsor Report considered the process which led to the acceptance of the ordination of women as a reality in some provinces of the Communion as an example for any process towards any acceptance of the blessing of gay unions and the ordination of priests in such unions. It is important to remember that during the 1970s and 1980s divisions over first the ordination of women in some dioceses and then the consecration of women bishops in New Zealand, the USA and Canada threatened to divide the Anglican Communion.

Ordination and Scripture

The New Testament mentions some norms for the ministry. Ministers should be humble (Mark 10.43–45), take care of the Church as overseers (Mark 20.28), be an example in speech and conduct, in love, in faith and in purity, in reading the Scrip-tures to the public and exhorting and teaching (1 Timothy 4.12–16). The First Letter of Peter puts it in a beautiful way:

> Now, as an elder myself and a witness of the sufferings of Christ, as well as one who shares in the glory to be revealed, I exhort the elders among you to tend the flock of God that is in your charge, exercising the oversight, not under compulsion but will-ingly, as God would have you do it – not for sordid gain but eagerly. Do not lord it over those in your charge, but be examples to the flock . . . in the same way, you who are younger must accept the authority of the elders. And all of you must clothe your-selves with humility in your dealings with one another. (1 Peter 5.1–5)

Anglican Ordination

The Anglican Church from its foundation accepted the significance of due process in the ordination of deacons, priests and bishops. Article 23 declares that: 'it is not lawful for any man to take upon him the office of public preaching, or ministering the Sacraments in the Congregation, before he be lawfully called, and sent to execute the same.' It is true that the Anglican Communion recognizes the priesthood of all believers in virtue of their baptism but, nevertheless, it has reserved some pastoral and sacramental actions to the ordained ministry.

The earliest Anglican Ordinal links this to the Scriptures:

It is evident unto all men, diligently reading holy scripture, and ancient authors, that from the Apostles' time there hath been these orders of Ministers in Christ's Church; Bishops, Priests, and Deacons: which offices were evermore had in such reverent estimation, that no man by his own private authority might presume to execute any of them, except he were first, called, tried, examined, and known to have such qualities as were requisite for the same; and also, by public prayer, with imposition of hands, approved, and admitted thereunto. And therefore, to the intent these orders should be continued, and reverently used, and esteemed, in this Church of England, it is requisite that no man (not being at this present Bishop, Priest, nor Deacon) shall execute any of them, except he be called, tried, examined, and admitted, according to the form hereafter following. (Preface to the First Anglican Ordinal, 1550)

The Anglican Communion believes that the orders of Bishops, Priests and Deacons were developed from the experience of the life of the community of Jesus. This does not necessarily imply a direct and explicit action by Jesus in the course of his earthly life. A distinction needs to be drawn between what Jesus is recorded as saying and doing, and his implicit intentions which may not have received explicit formulation till after the resurrection, either in words of the risen Lord himself or through his Holy Spirit instructing the primitive community. 'All this I have spoken while still with you. But the Counsellor, the Holy Spirit, whom the Father will send in my name, will teach you all things and will remind you of everything I have said to you' (John 14.25–26). (ARCIC I, *Clarifications on Eucharist and Ministry*, 9)

Women in the Anglican Priesthood

The Revd Florence Lee Tim-Oi was ordained as the first woman priest in the Anglican Communion in 1944. She was asked to work amongst the Chinese congregations in Japanese-occupied territories during the Second World War, a task impossible for men. However, at the 1948 Lambeth Conference the bishops refused to sanction the ordination of any further women priests. To preserve the unity of the whole Anglican Communion and to prevent the increase of the conflict between the Bishop of Hong Kong and the Archbishops of Canterbury and York, Lee Tim-Oi resigned her post, but did not renounce her ordination, continuing with her pastoral work in China.

Lee Tim-Oi's continued presence and witness set a precedent and in 1971 a new Bishop of Macau and Hong Kong followed his predecessor's example and, after consultation with the ACC, ordained two more women to the priesthood. The churches in the USA, Canada and New Zealand followed soon after. At the 1978 Lambeth Conference there was a real feeling that the ordination of women to the priesthood could split the Church and requests were made for the process to slow down, but most of the provinces of the Communion have now followed suit. However, a sizeable minority – 11 of the 38 – have not done so, but this has not split the Communion as feared.

Among the primary objections to the ordination of women was that the Scriptures taught that women could not be leaders and preachers in the Church. However, some saw in the Scriptures a basis for another tradition which included women in leadership. However, the tradition of the Church was firm and singular. It was argued that women were not among the apostles and had never been priests in any of the major denominations at any point in history. Objectors agreed with the Vatican Congregation for the Doctrine of the Faith which issued a statement in 1995 affirming that 'the Church has not power to ordain women to the priesthood' and many left the Anglican Church over what they saw as a Church-dividing issue.

The objections to the change in the tradition were strong once more at the 1988 Lambeth Conference and at the time it seemed as if the Communion might not survive. The fear was of the consecration of women bishops as bishops were ministers of the whole Communion and not local ministers. The consecration of three women bishops soon after the conference was the context for a commission headed by Archbishop Eames who was asked to consider how the highest level of communion could be maintained. Questions were raised as to who had the authority to enact such a change in practice and theology. Bishops represent the whole Church in a way priests do not, so some who had remaained in the Church to that point saw the consecration of women bishops as a Church-dividing event.

This is not the place to enter into the details of the issues surrounding women's ordination, but to consider how these questions were handled. The Windsor Report argues that the process was well ordered and consultative,[13] but this ignores the fact that both in the USA and in Uganda 'irregular' ordinations were followed by provincial assent. Authority was taken by individual bishops, retired bishops in the USA and the active Bishop Festo Kivengere in Uganda, to ordain women who were only later fully accepted.

The 1978 Lambeth Conference decided that each province, while mindful of the maintenance of the whole communion, had the autonomy to decide for itself if it was willing to develop traditions in its own context:

> The Conference also recognizes:
> (a) the autonomy of each of its member Churches, acknowledging the legal right of each Church to make its own decision about the appropriateness of admitting women to Holy Orders. (1978 Lambeth Conference, Resolution 21)

We come back to where we started, Newman's image of the river. For some the 'great idea' that women and men could be equally suitable as priests and bishops confirmed that the Church could change its traditions in order to proclaim unchanged 'faith once delivered to the saints'. For others the rock was not a 'great idea' but an obstacle, which diverted the Church from a true path into a way of secularism and schism. The act of ordaining women was one of denial of the 'faith once delivered to the saints'. Practical solutions have been sought to maintain as much communion as possible, but this has involved for some the refusal to receive communion at the same table as other Anglicans. In England the divisions are formalized with the consecration of Provincial Episcopal Visitors (commonly known as flying bishops) who, with the full agreement of diocesan bishops, serve congregations who cannot in good faith accept the ministry of women priests.

Questions

The ordination of women to the priesthood was a significant development in tradition which some regard as incompatible with Scripture and alien to the 'faith once delivered to the saints'. Others believe it to be compatible with Scripture and the only option in their culture in order to defend the 'faith once delivered to the saints'.

- Do you think that it was right for individual provinces to have autonomy to decide to ordain women as priests and bishops?
- Once a majority had made that decision is it right for others in the Communion to continue to oppose women's ordination?
- If you are in the majority in your province on women's ordination, how have you maintained communion with the minority?
- If you are in a minority, has the majority enabled you to flourish in the gospel?
- How have differences affected your relationship with Anglicans elsewhere?

The open ordination of gay and lesbian people in partnered relationships would be a significant development in the tradition of the Church analogous to, but not the same as, the ordination of women. The ordination of women was about the created order and the place of gender in leadership and salvation. All agree that women and men are equally good, but some argue for gender-specific roles on theological, not ethical, grounds. To ordain men and women in same-sex partnerships is to endorse as moral behaviour that has traditionally been condemned as immoral. For some the ordination of a partnered gay man or lesbian is the blessing of immorality.

- Do individual provinces have the autonomy to decide to ordain partnered gay clergy?
- What kind of provision would be appropriate for those who dissent?

7. Authority in the Church

During Jesus' earthly ministry 'the crowds were astounded at his teaching, for he taught them as one having authority, and not as their scribes' (Matthew 7.28–29). After his resurrection, Jesus met the eleven at the mountain in Galilee and said: 'All authority in heaven and on earth has been given to me' (Matthew 28.18). In the first case 'the crowds' recognized his authority. In the second, before his ascension, he was conscious of his authority.

Article 20 expresses the authority of the national church to decree 'Rites or Ceremonies' and to settle disputes of faith, provided they are in accordance with the Scriptures.

The Church has power to decree Rites or Ceremonies, and authority in Controversies of Faith: and yet it is not lawful for the Church to ordain any thing that is contrary to God's Word written, neither may it so expound one place of Scripture, that it be repugnant to another. Wherefore, although the Church be a witness and a keeper of Holy Writ, yet, as it ought not to decree any thing against the same, so besides the same ought it not to enforce any thing to be believed for necessity of Salvation. (Article of Religion 20)

In the Anglican Church in Canada the debate was entered into over whether the blessing of same-sex unions was doctrine, core doctrine, or about a ceremony. The Canadian General Synod of 2007 agreed that it was doctrine but not core doctrine (a doctrine held in the Creeds) and so the Church had authority to decide to bless or not to bless. The 2007 General Synod decided that they would not authorize the blessing of same-sex unions, but that they had the authority to do so if they considered it compatible with Scripture.

7.1 ARCIC II and Authority

The Anglican Roman Catholic International Commission studied Authority and presented the following to the Communion and to the Vatican:

> The exercise of authority can be oppressive and destructive. It may, indeed, often be so in human societies and even in churches when they uncritically adopt certain patterns of authority. The exercise of authority in the ministry of Jesus shows a different way. It is in conformity with the mind and example of Christ that the Church is called to exercise authority . . . for the exercise of this authority the Church is endowed by the Holy Spirit with a variety of gifts and ministries. (ARCIC II, *The Gift of Authority*, #5).

Authority signifies a power to act and reach final decisions, which, if necessary, can be delegated to others. It also denotes witness and credibility. In the case of Jesus, it derives from the Father and is transmitted by the power of the Holy Spirit. In the history of the Church, authority relates to Scripture, tradition and reason.

(a) Tradition, which is a dynamic process, receives its authority from the saving events it transmits. 'It is far more than the transmission of true propositions concerning salvation. A minimalist understanding of Tradition that would limit it to a storehouse of doctrine and ecclesial decisions is insufficient . . . In the economy (*oikonomia*) of God's love for humanity, the Word who became flesh and dwelt among us is at the centre of what was transmitted from the beginning and what will be transmitted until the end' (ARCIC, *The Gift of Authority*, #15). The authority of tradition is tested by the gospel and is received by the Church when assembled in ecumenical councils. In this way it can be said that the authority of tradition testifies also to the tradition of authority.

(b) The Protestant Reformation stressed the authority of Scripture. 'The formation of the canon of the Scriptures was an integral part of the process of tradition. The Church's recognition of these Scriptures as canonical, after a long period of critical discernment, was at the same time an act of *obedience* and of authority (ARCIC, *The Gift of Authority*, #22). This means that the authority of Scripture is only received within the Church under the guidance of the Holy Spirit.

(c) The authority of reason expresses itself through the *magisterium* of the Church helped by tradition and Scripture. 'The Church must continue faithful so that the Christ who comes in glory will recognize in the Church the community he founded: it must continue to be free to receive the apostolic Tradition in new ways according to the situations by which it is confronted. The Church has the responsibility to hand on the whole apostolic Tradition, even though there may be parts which it finds hard to integrate in its life and worship. It may be that what was of great significance for an earlier generation will again be important in the future, though its importance is not clear in the present' (ARCIC, *The Gift of Authority*, #24).

8. Conclusion

The relationship between the tradition of the Church, which is a link to the reality of the saving life, death and resurrection of Jesus Christ in the power of the Holy Spirit and which binds us to the Father, and the ever-evolving traditions of churches is complex. We have seen examples of positive changes and developments and we have seen examples of dangerous innovations. The gift of discernment is rooted in respect for traditions, the authority of the Bible and our God-given ability to think as we live out the gospel in ever-changing contexts. We hope this chapter will enable you to appreciate the complexity and grant you clarity.

Collect for Advent 2 – *Book of Common Prayer*

Blessed Lord,
who caused all holy Scriptures
to be written for our learning:
grant us so to hear them, read, mark, learn,
and inwardly digest them,
that we may embrace
and ever hold fast the blessed hope
of everlasting life,
which you have given us
in our Saviour Jesus Christ;
who lives and reigns
with you and the Holy Spirit,
one God,
for ever and ever.
Amen.

Notes

1 O'Donovan, Reading the St Andrew's Day Statement online at http://www.fulcrum-anglican.org.uk/page.cfm?ID=63

2 From *A True Hearing* (Anglican Mainstream, 2005), 72.

3 John Henry Newman, *On the Process of Development in Ideas*.

4 'The world is firmly established, it cannot be moved' (Psalm 93.1); see also 1 Chronicles 16.30, Psalm 96.10, Psalm 104.5 and Ecclesiastes 1.5.

5 Original text: Two opinions therefore there are concerning sufficiency of Holy Scripture, each extremely opposite unto the other, and both repugnant unto truth. The schools of Rome teach Scripture to be so insufficient, as if, except traditions were added, it did not contain all

revealed and supernatural truth, which absolutely is necessary for the children of men in this life to know that they may in the next be saved. Others justly condemning this opinion grow likewise unto a dangerous extremity, as if Scripture did not only contain all things in that kind necessary, but all things simply, and in such sort that to do anything according to any other law were not only unnecessary but even opposite unto salvation, unlawful and sinful. Whatsoever is spoken of God or things appertaining to God otherwise than as the truth is; though it seem an honour, it is an injury. And as incredible praises given unto men do often abate and impair the credit of their deserved commendation; so we must likewise take great heed, lest in attributing unto Scripture more than it can have, the incredibility of that to cause even those things which indeed it has most abundantly to be less reverently esteemed.

6 Original text: Scripture indeed teacheth things above nature, things which our reason by itself could not reach unto. Yet, those things also we believe, knowing by reason that the Scripture is the word of God . . . There must be therefore some former knowledge presupposed which doth herein assure the hearts of all believers.

7 Lambeth Conference 1978, Resolution 10.3; Lambeth Conference 1988, Resolution 64.1.

8 *fides quaerens intellectum*.

9 Original text: In the nature of reason itself there is no impediment, but that the selfsame Spirit, which revealeth the things that God has set down in his law, may also be thought to aid and direct men in finding out by the light of reason what laws are expedient to be made for the guiding of his Church, over and besides them that are in Scripture.

10 Oliver O'Donovan, 'Good News for Gay Christians', available online at <www.fulcrum-anglican.org.uk/news/2007/20070108odonovan7.cfm?doc=179>.

11 For how such a response might look see: The Zacchaeus Fellowship, *Transformed by an Encounter with Christ* (Cambridge, Ontario: The Zacchaeus Fellowship, 2006).

12 In C. Hefling and C. Shattuck (eds), *The Oxford Guide to The Book of Common Prayer: A Worldwide Survey,* p. 510.

13 The Windsor Report, Para. 12–21.

Chapter 5

Homosexualities and Culture

Terry Brown, Victor Atta-Baffoe and Phil Groves

Additional material from Griphus Gakuru and John Kevern

Introduction

This is a key chapter in the book. It concludes section two by examining culture as an aspect of the third traditional component of the Anglican way – reason. It also acts as a transition from this section's more conceptual and theological material to the focus on listening and dialogue in the following third section where we encounter more directly human beings in their cultural settings. The Virginia Report presented to Lambeth 1998 spoke of 'reason' as 'simply the human being's capacity to symbolize, and so to order, share and communicate experience' or 'what can be called "the mind of a particular culture", with its characteristic ways of seeing things, asking about them, and explaining them'. It then said, 'If tradition is the mind that Christians share as believers and members of the Church, reason is the mind they share as participants in a particular culture'.[1] The interplay with Scripture and tradition was then described in the following terms:

> Anglicanism sees reason in the sense of the 'mind' of the culture in which the Church lives and the Gospel is proclaimed, as a legitimate and necessary instrument for the interpretation of God's message in the Scriptures. Sometimes Scriptures affirm the new insights of a particular age or culture, sometimes they challenge or contradict those insights. The Word of God is addressed to the Church as it is part of this world. The Gospel borne by the Scriptures must be heard and interpreted in the language that bears the 'mind' and distils the experience of the world. Tradition and reason are therefore in the Anglican way two distinct contexts in which Scriptures speak and out of which they are interpreted.[2]

What the Virginia Report goes on to say has particular bearing on our discussions on sexuality: how we understand ourselves as sexual beings, and the fact that the relationship between sexuality and society varies enormously across cultures. It is therefore vital that in considering sexuality we recall that:

> The experience of the Church as it is lived in different places has something to contribute to the discernment of the mind of Christ for the Church. No one culture, no one period of history has a monopoly of insight into the truth of the

Gospel. It is essential for the fullest apprehension of truth that context is in dialogue with context. Sometimes the lived experience of a particular community enables Christian truth to be perceived afresh for the whole community. At other times a desire for change or restatement of the faith in one place provokes a crisis within the whole Church.[3]

We hope in the few brief pages of this chapter to enable you to think more clearly about your own culture, others' cultures and the relationship of Christ and mission to those cultures. In order to try to understand how Christians have sought to relate their faith to their culture the chapter begins with H. Richard Niebuhr's five types of relationship: Christ against culture; Christ transforming culture; Christ above culture; Christ and culture in paradox; and Christ of culture. Four case studies from across the Communion then illustrate how reality is much more complex than these ideal types, and seek to help you consider your own attitudes. An alternative type, called Culture in Christ, is explored by a Ugandan contributor from his experience of biblical Christianity and martyrdom.

After noting that the Bible is also a culturally located document, a brief introduction is offered as to how insights about our various cultures today – and the culture of the Bible – can be gained from the discipline of anthropology. The final two sections begin to relate this more directly to the areas of current disagreement and tension in our Communion life. In order to encourage and enable mutual listening brief and limited examinations are offered of both European and African cultural assumptions. You are encouraged to use these to think about your own cultural assumptions and understand better those who come from a different culture. The last section warns against simply thinking about 'homosexuality'. It argues that it is necessary to realise that the diversity of cultures leads to a diversity of homosexualities in and across those cultures. This raises the question of whether we need to take more care to explore fully our different experiences and understandings of the phenomenon to which we are seeking to develop a biblical, pastoral Christian response. Here again, the real work is left to you the reader, as you are encouraged to engage with your own preconceptions as we proclaim that Christ is one, the Lord and saviour of all, in the diversity of human cultures.

The writing of this chapter has involved many people both mentioned and unnamed within the text in order to draw on the diverse cultures of the Communion. We value the advice they have all given. The main authors are **Terry Brown**, a bishop from Melanesia, and **Victor Atta-Baffoe**, a theologian from Ghana, each of whom brings a wealth of intercultural experience; but many people have contributed to this chapter.

CULTURE AND CHRIST – AN INTRODUCTION

1. Culture

Culture should be regarded as the set of distinctive spiritual, material, intellectual and emotional features of society or a social group, and that it encompasses, in addition to art and literature, lifestyles, ways of living together, value systems, traditions and beliefs. (UNESCO Universal Declaration on Cultural Diversity)

Culture is the complete way of life, or the complete experience, of a group of people, both as a community and as individuals, within their personal, local and global environments.

Culture and Christianity

Question: Is culture ultimately of deep significance for Christian faith and practice?

The answer we give to this question will affect our theological response to liturgy, church practice and ethics as we seek to follow Christ in a real world.

Broadly speaking, two answers have been given to this question:

The first is a strong NO: Christianity is essentially and ultimately a divine revelation, through the divine and human person of Jesus Christ and Holy Scripture, not dependent upon or shaped by human cultures – 'the faith once delivered to the saints'. In this view, Christian faith and the Church are often arrayed against human cultures where they are sinful and in need of conversion. 'Culture' and 'experience' are not fundamental theological categories.

The second is a strong YES: Christianity – still essentially and ultimately a divine revelation through the divine and human person of Jesus Christ and Holy Scripture – is *mediated through* a great variety of human cultures, from the beginning of creation, through the narratives of the Old Testament, through the life of Jesus Christ in first-century Palestine, through the expansion of Christianity to the Graeco-Roman world of St Paul, through two millennia of missionary expansion of Christianity to thousands of different cultures in almost every corner of the world today – 'the faith once delivered to the saints' – both shaping and shaped by the cultures that contain it. In this view, just as sound does not travel through a vacuum, Christian revelation is not possible without the human cultures (including languages and symbols), which are part of God's creation, through which it is transmitted. 'Culture' and 'experience' become serious theological categories, to be dealt with alongside revelation, and, indeed, intimate to it.

Most of us move between these two poles in how we live and proclaim the gospel.

Models of Christ and Culture

Many years ago H. Richard Niebuhr, an American church historian, in his book *Christ and Culture* put forward five models of how historically the Church has related with culture.[4] The work remains a classic and is still a good starting-point for thought on this issue, despite its limitations.

Niebuhr's Five Models

(1) Christ against Culture

In this view, 'culture' is primarily sinful, and Christian conversion consists of rescuing Christians from the impure culture to the new life of the redeemed and pure community, the church. Monasticism, the Anabaptist movement, Puritanism, elements of the missionary movement and certain revival movements all partake of this model.

Separation is the theme.

(2) Christ transforming Culture

In this view, the church still maintains a critical stance towards culture, but also recognizes that it is an essential part of it. The church's role is to transform the sinful parts of culture (for example, violence, slavery, greed and sexual immorality) to bring them into conformity with God's revelation in Jesus Christ. Christian social justice movements, Christian involvement in education and elements of the missionary movement partake of this model.

Transformation is the theme.

(3) Christ above Culture

In this view, while elements of the culture may be highly valued and developed (for example, literature, music, art, social relationships), Christian revelation, as divine and uncreated, occupies a spiritual realm above culture, a world unto itself, accessed by faith rather than culture. The medieval theology of Thomas Aquinas and the 'Neo-orthodoxy' of Karl Barth are examples of this model.

The hierarchical superiority of revelation over culture is the theme.

(4) Christ and Culture in Paradox

In this view, while both Christian revelation and culture are highly valued and deeply inter-related, they are ultimately in a situation of paradox, two parallel worlds that must be lived independently. Niebuhr cites Martin Luther's theology of church and state as an example of this model. Perhaps the life of a Christian who is a member of the military would be a more contemporary example – he or she is required to be equally loyal to both the authority of Christ and the authority of the state – which can lead to crises of conscience.

Paradox or puzzlement is the theme.

(5) Christ of Culture

In this view, a particular Christianity so identifies with its culture that it becomes a part of it, such that there is no distinction between the Christian community (including its understanding of Christian revelation) and culture; thus, Christianity can offer no challenge to the culture whatsoever, even where it is deeply flawed. Niebuhr cites nineteenth-century German 'culture Christianity' (a frequent name for this model) which reshaped Christianity in its own image and made way for the accommodation of large parts of the German church to Nazism in World War II.

The identity of Christ in culture is the theme.

Models (1) and (5) are the extremes – full separation and full accommodation – with the intermediate categories (2), (3) and (4), examples of attempting to bring Christ and culture together in various ways and proportions. However, it is perhaps best not to see these models as points along a line or continuum, but rather points along a circle in which the extremes (1) and (5) come together as neighbours, sometimes blurring into one another.

All the models (and many others may be added, for example, **Christ alongside culture**, a Paraclete or Advocate model, particularly in cross-cultural and post-colonial settings) occur in Scripture and many Christians move in and out of all the models, depending on the situation and issues.[5]

Case Studies

Case Study 1 – The Church of Uganda

The Church of Uganda Position Paper on Scripture, Authority, and Human Sexuality May 2005 places that Church's stand in the context of the historic development of the Church in the nation.[6] The model of Christ transforming culture is the dominant model in the Church of Uganda and one which the Church seeks to share with the rest of the Communion. This is made clear in the paper:

The Heritage of Holy Scriptures in the Church of Uganda

The story of the Church of Uganda is one of obedience to the preaching and teaching of the gospel, according to the Bible. When the early missionaries announced the gospel of Jesus Christ to our fore fathers and mothers, they responded to the word of salvation. They acknowledged that Jesus is Lord and Saviour and for that reason gladly obeyed His word in Scripture. The transforming effect of the Bible on Ugandans generated so much conviction and confidence that even ordinary believers were martyred in the defence of the message of salvation through Jesus Christ that it brought. The adherents of the East African Revival, that broke out in the late 1920s and early 1930s (a movement that has shaped the ethos of our Church), were simple people who learned to take God at His Word. For the Church in Uganda, to compromise God's call of obedience to the Scriptures would be the undoing of more than 125 years of Christianity through which African customs, belief, life, and society have been transformed for the better. For instance:

- Most traditional African societies were solely based on oral culture, which limited the ability to share ideas beyond the clan or ethnic group. For many centuries most of the African languages were un-written. The Bible was the first book in African vernacular. Thus African languages have been enriched and recorded.

- For many of our tribes, revenge was an esteemed virtue. If a family had been violated, the first instinct was to gather the clan or ethnic group, arm them, and seek revenge on the family, clan, or ethnic group of the offender. As the Bible came with the authority of Christ, it revealed a God that is greater than the evil spirits and the kingdom of darkness that controlled so many people's lives. In this realm of relationships, the Bible has had a profoundly transforming effect with the teaching of Jesus on forgiveness.

- Traditional Ugandan society was driven by family loyalties with little basis for loving those beyond your blood ties. Strife and mutual exploitation were rampant. The Bible brought the teaching of Jesus to love your neighbour and even your enemy. And, while there are remains of this old culture, the Bible gives a moral and spiritual basis for transforming culture. At the same time, the Bible affirms certain esteemed values of our culture like community life and hospitality – we have found our home in Scripture.

- Some traditional African societies believed, for example, that if women ate chicken they would grow a beard. So, women were often denied access to nutritious food and other social benefits on the basis of superstitions. When the Bible came alive during the East African Revival, the Holy Spirit convicted men of sins of oppression and began the progressive empowerment of women that is continuing today.

- Perhaps the most degrading form of gender inequality was the African tradition of polygamy and divorce at will, which left many women neglected or even destitute. The biblical teaching of marriage between one man and one woman in a loving, lifelong relationship liberated not only women, but also the institution of marriage and family.

- Traditional African objects of worship, which were limited to families and clans, had established a system where no central beliefs could be held or shared beyond the ethnic setting. Ancestral spirits, natural phenomena like earthquakes, lakes, and mountains, could not satisfy the African's quest for the living God. The Bible's revelation of Father as Creator of all things, the Son as redeemer, and the Holy Spirit as the life-giving Spirit of God brought hope for deliverance from the fatalism that resulted from worshipping created things rather than the Creator.

- The Bible has also been a transforming agent in modern/contemporary African societies. The growth of the Church in Africa is a contemporary phenomenon. Most African societies are more cosmopolitan in nature and relate a lot more. The churches have been at the forefront of transforming society. The Bible message, through church leaders, has significantly contributed to the ongoing transformation of politics. Even Archbishop Janani Luwum was martyred for calling our political leaders to biblical accountability.

- It is the Church's commitment to the Authority of Scripture and the biblical values of abstinence before marriage and faithfulness within marriage that enabled the Church in Uganda to provide leadership in formulating a national response to the HIV/AIDS that has finally brought down the infection rates making Uganda the success story it has become in the fight against the HIV/AIDS pandemic.

- Contemporary Ugandan society has been transformed through Scripture's teaching and we no longer live only in our ethnic enclaves and there are inter-marriages. The gospel has caused us to form a new tribe from every language, nation, tribe, and tongue.

For us in the Church of Uganda, the Bible is the cherished source of authority that is central to the faith, practice, and mission of our Christians. It is an absolute treasure that no one can take away. For ministers, the Bible is the basis for ministry: preaching, teaching, Christian nurture, pastoral care and counselling. If you take away the Bible from our bishops and clergy, they have nothing to offer the world. For all God's people, obedience to this Bible is the source of confidence, abundant life, and joy.

As a Church we are committed to the contextual issues relating to our mission which include (without being limited to) widespread dehumanizing poverty, HIV / AIDS, malaria, conflicts, Islam and secularism. We strongly believe that the procla-mation of the Good News of the gospel of the risen Lord and Saviour (Jesus Christ) is an answer to these issues confronting us as a Church in Mission today.

We also believe that the Church of Uganda has a mission to the Anglican Com-munion to share the treasure of the Scriptures and to call other parts of the Com-munion to recognize and to submit to the Authority of Scripture as the place of transformation into abundant life.

Accordingly, we believe that the Anglican Communion would then have a gift to offer the world. Repentance and obedience to Scripture is not judgement; rather, it is the gateway to the redemption of marriage and family and the transformation of society.

The Church of Uganda will continue to challenge the rise of the acceptance of homo-sexuality by calling individuals and societies to transformation in Christ:

We believe that God is calling the Church of Uganda to seek continual transfor-mation from the Word of God written, in preaching repentance and faith in Christ and develop ministries of pastoral care that don't ostracize, shun, or reject those tempted by homosexual desire. We acknowledge that God is calling us to come alongside those who give in to the temptation of homosexual desire and show them the power of the Word of God to bring joy, peace, and satisfaction to their life through repentance and obedience to God's Word.

The Church of Uganda clearly identifies with the model of **Christ transforming culture** as a basis for its mission in Uganda and in the Anglican Communion.

Case Study 2 – The Experience of the Indigenous Peoples of North America.[7]

The dominant attitude of the missionaries towards the Indigenous nations of North America was that their cultures were primarily sinful – there are records of a few missionaries whose experience was very different, but it is also clear that they were quickly dealt with or removed. This attitude lived out led to the systematic destruction of these cultures, including the banning of the use of indigenous language, music and dance. Sending children to residential schools by force destroyed family structures and left a virtual spiritual, mental, and physical moonscape of loss.

The missionaries may have seen themselves as agents of **Christ transforming culture**, but it was clear that their intention was to replace the culture with a 'Christian culture' – their European culture. Thus, the missionaries were using two models: to the Indigenous peoples they saw **Christ against culture**, but they saw the **Christ of culture** expressed in their own European traditions. They believed that 'civilization is not present if the institutions of Western culture are not available' and assumed the superiority of 'civilization'.[8] The results were disastrous and the peoples suffer to this day. At best, missionaries were complicit in intentional plans for the virtual annihilation of Indigenous people in North America; at times they were actively part of the process.

In recent years the Episcopal Church and the Anglican Church of Canada have seen the need to repent. The pain and injury served to Indigenous people by the church continues to be heard and the recent progress of Indigenous people's rights were partially successful in aiding in the church's partial hearing. Indigenous peoples have survived the attempts to remove their culture from them. For example, the materialism and scientism of Europeans have been rejected by Indigenous peoples:

> The cosmology of the West, still prevalent in many contemporary 'mission' efforts, was an unchallenged partner of the colonizing churches. It is significant that after 500 years of systematic proselytism the rejection of this aspect of the West is one of the defining characteristics of indigenous spiritual identity and renewal. This is true even among aboriginal Christians, as the Canadian developments demonstrate.[9]

The complex social structures of the Indigenous peoples in living in harmony with one another and with the natural world has compared favourably with European models of power and domination. Western ideas of ownership and control have led the world to the point of ecological disaster. Indigenous people consider such ideas blasphemous, absurd and destructive.

Bishop Mark MacDonald is the first National Indigenous Bishop who ministers both in Canada and the USA. In trying to describe the results of conversations directly observed in Indigenous communities in over 18 different North American dioceses he says:

> The Niebuhr categories do not speak to the sophistication and dynamic complexity I hear emerging in Native communities regarding the role of 'Christ and Culture' in the Indigenous context. First, there is an emerging sense of the dynamic presence of the Christ, as the living Word of God, in pre-colonization culture, and as saving presence in the triumph of life over death in Indigenous communities during colonization, including its present phase. Second, as Asian theologians have pointed to the need to discuss Creation History, as opposed to just Salvation History – meaning the Christ's work is directed at all Creation and not just humanity – the elders underline that Christ's work is towards all Creation.[10]

Indigenous Anglicans have considered the conflicts over human sexuality, but as a secondary matter – something that has effect and impact, but not something that is decided definitively in Indigenous communities – a sub-topic for them of more pressing concerns over marriage. Bishop Mark identifies some emerging themes:

First, the elders feel that this is for them to decide, using Scripture, their stories and traditions, and their experience as a guide (Scripture being pre-eminent for most if not all). Second, they express some surprise at the difficulty that many other cultures seem to have trouble accepting into their churches diversity in general, and gay and lesbian people, in particular. Third, with almost no exceptions, the elders say that marriage is the issue for them, not the acceptability of homosexual behaviour. It is not at all self-evident in their communities that marriage, as understood by them, is an equivalent, in any form, with the relationships of homosexual persons. This appears due to the fact that they do not look at marriage as a social contract, blessed by the church. For many, it is the embodiment of their cosmology – male-female being one of the chief ways that they look at the universe. This was seen long before this discussion in the widespread refusal to honour divorce in many Northern Indigenous communities. I hear with amazing regularity, 'What does all of this mean about marriage? We don't worry much about the other things.'[11]

Martin Brokenleg introduces us to the differing concepts of gender in his Lakota people. He says they identify three genders, with some Indigenous peoples having more.[12] Gender is not assumed to be identical to sex in Indigenous communities and some male children choose to live as women, characterized by choosing to speak the language in a female idiom, or 'to be a man who speaks as a woman' or in Lakota *wi'i'nkte*.[13] Donald Whipple Fox comments:

Wi'i'nkte does not line up as easily with the English terms of gay, lesbian, bisexual, transgendered, or intersexed. *Wi'i'nkte* would cover all of them and probably more. However, in thinking of what it personally means to me to be *wi'i'nkte*, it involves bringing balance to creation.[14]

People of this alternate gender are sometimes spoken of in English as Two Spirit people. Gender roles in indigenous understanding can have many variations – male, female, male/females and female/males. Male female/males and male /females – Two Spirit identities – are known by particular names in the language of the people. For some the spirit of a woman resided in the body of a man and the spirit of a man in the body of a woman. It is remembered that these two spirited people were respected for who they were, took part in religious ceremonies and brought peace. A Two Spirit is both male and female – the vessel can be either male or female in some traditions and their roles are varied. It would be a modern European imposition to describe such people as gay or lesbian. The Indigenous challenge to European cultural values comes from the requirement for an acknowledgement that human life is not easily defined and labelled and that respect should be given to people to be who they are. There is a general understanding that every part of God's creation should be treated with respect as it holds the essence of the Creator and disrespecting any part of creation is disrespecting our Creator.

Bishop Mark comments:

> Although many in the urban communities are comfortable with discussion of two-spirited people, it does not have as much traction in other areas, which is not to say it is rejected. The People of the Land appear to be still making up their minds. At this point, I would say, that when it is, it seems that it will be different from either of the primary views that are expressed on these issues in the public forum.

The Indigenous response transcends Niebuhr's categories.

Case Study 3 – South Africa

As a child Nelson Mandela identified the axiom of the missionaries he encountered as: 'To be Christian was to be civilized and to be civilized was to be Christian'.[15] Just as in North America many of the missionaries in Southern Africa adopted – in reference to African cultures – **Christ against culture** and – in respect to European cultures – **Christ in culture**.[16] The height of the expression of this belief was a theological system called apartheid, which they supported by direct appeal to the Bible, especially Romans 13.1–7.

This was countered in the Kairos Document of 1985 that challenged the apartheid reading of the Bible.[17] The so-called biblical order of white domination and state rule was countered by an understanding of God on the side of the oppressed, setting the prisoners free and a call for justice and reconciliation. The theologians who drew it up saw it as an attempt to develop, out of their perplexing situation, an alternative biblical and theological model that would lead to forms of activity that would make a real difference to the future of their country. They argued that 'reconciliation' was not enough, and claimed that: 'There can be no real peace without justice and repentance'. They criticized 'Church Theology' because it separated the spiritual from the political; it was otherworldly. They understood that the Bible was about engaging with the world and transforming their society. First they saw that the church itself had to be transformed from offering pastoral support to challenging and working for the replacement of the government of the day. The model adopted was one of **Christ transforming culture**.

The Church in Southern Africa has also followed the model of **Christ transforming culture** in challenging the patriarchal structures of traditional South African society. This was seen as being in accord with Jesus' attitude to women in the Bible. This goes beyond the ordination of women within the church but asks critical questions about gender roles within the society and how those inform the continued development towards a free society. The society can only be free once women are free.

The South African Church has had a diversity of voices on the blessing of same-sex unions. For some, such as Desmond Tutu, the full acceptance of gay relationships has been seen as a continuation of the struggle against oppression and against apartheid. He writes:

> It is not acceptable for us to discriminate against our brothers and sisters on the basis of sexual orientation just as it was not acceptable for discrimination to exist on the basis of skin colour under Apartheid. We cannot pick and choose where justice is concerned . . . God is looking then for a society in which there are no outsiders; in which all are within and treated with respect and dignity.[18]

Tutu argues for an understanding of **Christ transforming culture** so all are included in society. He is aware that many Christians and churches disagree with him on the full inclusion of gay and lesbian people both in South Africa and around the world, but the model he uses of Christ and culture is one many do share.

Case Study 4 – The Church of England

The Church of England is a diverse Church and all of Niebuhr's models are to some extent reflected in its life. Many churches embrace the culture of the nation, while others deny the culture or seek to transform it. It is not possible to say which model is dominant within the Church. However, in relation to its response to homosexuality, the official response has embraced the model of **Christ and culture in paradox**. This is not to deny all the other models working alongside this response and they are represented below.

As an established Church, part of the state, the Church of England has a unique relationship to the culture of England. In the 1950s and 1960s the Church made a distinction between its moral opposition to homosexuality and its support for the decriminalization of homosexual acts. A study guide commended by the bishops to the Church sets out that this continues to be the official position:

> The combination of beliefs that we find in the case of Archbishop Ramsey – a belief that homosexual activity between consenting adults should not result in criminal prosecution combined with a belief that the Church could not rightly bless homosexual relationships – remains the official position of the Church of England.[19]

In the context of some calls for a loosening of traditional teaching, the 1987 General Synod passed a strong motion which affirmed that the only proper context for sexual activity was within a permanent marriage relationship. The bishops issued pastoral guidelines in 1991 which argued for respect to be shown to lay members who believed God was calling them into faithful same-sex relationships while maintaining that such options should not be available to clergy. The growing acceptance of such relationships in the culture led many to believe that the Church could not oppose those seeking to live in such relationships, but neither could it bless them. A paradox developed in the tacit support for a growing acceptance of gay rights in English culture and the separate restatement of traditional church morality.

In 2005 the bishops of the Church of England issued a pastoral statement addressing the implications of the Civil Partnership Act, which was passed in December of that year.[20] The Church maintained its moral stance by refusing to sanction church blessings of such partnerships, but it co-operated with the government in the framing of the legislation and supported provisions for inheritance rights for gay couples.[21] The pastoral statement carefully balances the commitment to traditional teaching with an acceptance that within the culture gay and lesbian couples were to be fully accepted. There is no compromise on the Church's teaching on marriage between a man and a woman as the only appropriate context for sexual activity, but no challenge to the wider society to conform to this teaching – **Christ and culture in paradox**.

Tensions have arisen in the Church of England and these have been partly in respect to differences over understandings of the relationship between Christ and culture and these were visible in the debate on the bishops' pastoral statement in civil partnerships in the February 2007 General Synod.[22] Some continue to call for the Church to embrace the secular culture as offering new revelation to the Church – a **Christ in culture** view. They propose change in the church to reflect change in culture. Others embrace a **Christ above culture** perspective in seeking to define for the culture the limits of Christian same-sex relationships from a church perspective. Some either reject the culture and name it as sinful – **a Christ against culture** response – or seek to model alternative life styles for those who have unwanted same-sex attraction – a **Christ transforming culture** response. The latter have called for biblical witness to the nation and are uncomfortable with the official Church of England response to the secular acceptance of civil partnerships for same-sex couples. Of course the situation is more complex as some ask for the Church to take a lead in transforming culture by blessing gay and lesbian couples, and so the differing attitudes to culture are only part of the diversity of approaches to human sexuality in the Church of England.

Reflection on Christ and Culture

The case studies illustrate how Niebuhr's categories need handling with care, but they can enable us to understand how our Church is operating. It is interesting to reflect that the model of **Christ transforming culture** is maintained by both Desmond Tutu – who argues for the acceptance of the blessing of same-sex unions – and the Church of Uganda which vigorously opposes such a change.

It is also interesting how similar the responses of Nelson Mandela and Mark Mac-Donald are to the attitude of the missionaries. When a group declares itself against a culture or cultural practice – embracing **Christ against culture** – it often closes in upon itself and develops a culture of its own, which it sometimes identifies as its 'Christian culture'. But this very identification of faith and culture then becomes Niebuhr's model of full integration and accommodation embracing the **Christ in culture** model, in which the flaws of the particular faith and culture reinforce themselves into a new kind of inflexible 'culture Christianity'.

The Anglican Way, at various times and places, has exemplified all these models. Puritan, Evangelical and Catholic movements have sought at various times to separate themselves from what they have seen as the culture of the age, whether into conventicles, prayer groups, monastic communities or renewal movements. Anglicans of all theological persuasions have participated in movements to renew and transform society, for example, in the anti-slavery movement or movements to relieve the poor. The various powers Anglicans have found themselves under (Church, Crown, Parliament, military, religious society) have sometimes made for paradox and contradiction. Pietism, whether Evangelical, Catholic or charismatic, has sought a spirituality that has put God first and human culture second. And the Establishment of the Church of England, the influence of the European Enlightenment, the close association of the missionary movement with colonialism (both political and economic), and inculturation in the Global South have meant that accommodation has been part of the Anglican tradition. All the models have both positive and negative potential. The gift of the Spirit is to use them appropriately.

Questions

- Which model has been the dominant model or models in your Church?
- Which model or combination of models do you find attractive?
- What are the strengths and weaknesses of that model?
- Which model or combination of models do you react negatively to?
- What are the weaknesses of those models?
- Can you see any strengths in them, either in your context or in other contexts?

2. Christ, Culture and Martyrdom: A Ugandan Reflection

Griphus Gakuru

Introduction

The Ugandan Church has played a significant part in the growth of the Church in East and Central Africa and around the world. The Church of Uganda looks to the Martyrs as the foundation of the church and around the Anglican Communion they are treated with great respect. Griphus Gakuru offers us a reflection on the Martyrs to inspire us. He then gives a consideration of a theological model which he describes as **Culture in Christ** from his perspective as a Ugandan.

The Uganda Martyrs 1885–1887 – Commemorated 3 June

The Uganda Martyrs were mainly young men, numbering thirty or so, both Anglican and Catholic. Known as Bagalagala (pages) in King Mwanga's palace, they were drawn from among different clans to undergo training for future political leadership. They were to be well grounded in and be prepared to defend the Kingdom of Buganda and their way of life. King Mwanga was an absolute despot. One of the aspects of training the young men received was in acknowledging the power of the king over them. The king, also called Ssabasajja (Husband of men), often demonstrated his power by performing homosexual acts on the trainees. In relation to the king they would remain permanently in a submissive position like a wife. Modern notions of the rights of wives were unknown; to this day it is a serious insult to an African man to be called 'woman'.

On becoming Christians the pages discovered that in Christ all are equal; that degrading treatment is evil and unacceptable – whoever commits it – and must be resisted; that God's word prohibits homosexual acts; that the highest duty of man is that rendered to God in worship and listening to his word. This led the pages to resist the king's absolute authority, absconding from palace duty, and committing the ultimate act of disobedience in refusing to have sex with him. To the martyrs a decision had to be made on individual level, whether to retain their cultural aspect of power relations or to accept the Christ in whom all are equal before God. They decided to filter out this cultural aspect, accepting to die. They were burnt alive singing praises to God. It has to be emphasized that the martyrs were not Euro-peanized, neither was there a programme of Europeanization. On the contrary, the emphasis was on growing a native African church that worshipped and served God in its own context and culture in Christ. The martyrdom of the pages was the beginning of a thoroughgoing persecution that saw all missionaries out of Uganda. Even Alexander McKay, the engineer CMS missionary whom the king had always needed, had to flee to an island in Lake Victoria.

But if the king thought that by killing the Christians he had extinguished Christianity, he was mistaken. More and more people began to be inquisitive about the faith that could give such power to an individual as to resist the king and sing praises while they are literally burning. As a result Christianity spread like a wild fire, and soon it is the Christians who were to protect the same king from being deposed by his Muslim officials. Whereas in 1890 there were about 200 Christians, by 1908 the number had risen to 63,000. Martyrdom was thus the real birth of the Ugandan Church.

Culture in Christ

A helpful theological model that worked for the early Church can be more accurately described as **Culture in Christ**. This model, emphasized by St Paul in a trans-cultural context, was characterized not by Christ transforming culture, but Christ dissolving both culture and identity, to the extent that, for example, St Paul could say: 'For me to live is Christ, to die is gain' (Philippians 1.21). Christ's dissolving culture emphasizes four things:

First, that there is a good degree of continuity of most aspects of one's culture in Christ. Every culture is preparation for the Gospel. A person's Christian expression will have an inextricable cultural flavour to it. The aspects and elements of culture that are 'soluble in Christ' under particular circumstances are those that do not conflict with Christ and his way. Those aspects of culture that are not compatible with Christ will not dissolve in Christ and are thus to be filtered out to leave behind a clear Christian life lived out in that particular cultural context. This filtering out of aspects of culture may sometimes be comparable to one's own death. Martyrdom at different levels is thus a key characteristic of culture in Christ (see John 12.25). The words of the Archbishop of Canterbury are pertinent here:

> Christianity was always a religion of conversion: and that means it has always proposed to human beings that what has been taken for granted about their identity, their possibilities and their relationships isn't necessarily fixed or final. Conversion is choosing to be different; it is a step out of the culture you once belonged in . . . What this involved in practice was, for many of the earliest generations, martyrdom – the ultimate countercultural statement . . . Martyrdom claimed that there was a hidden reality, deeper and more lasting than the culture that currently prevailed . . .[23]

It should be added that those who did not lose their lives physically became living martyrs or confessors and this is the category into which the vast majority fell. A more recent example of this model in Europe was the German Confessing Church of the Hitler years. Dietrich Bonhoeffer and his fellow Christians who escaped prison were equally martyrs.

Second, the Culture in Christ model and its corollary of martyrdom is strongly individual based. A person makes their own decision, makes up their own mind, to follow Jesus. Joy and peace, which are highly individualized categories, are categories that the Ugandan Church, which is built on the blood of indigenous martyrs, expresses again and again. It is the martyrdom aspect that also causes the Ugandan Church to find difficulty in comprehending the voices that insist that homosexual acts cannot be overcome through repentance and conversion to Christ. The question posed constantly is, what is the cost of discipleship? Is anything too important to lose in the face of Christ? Are there circumstances whereby the 'I' of personal identity will not bend into the 'C' that surrenders to Christ?

The Culture in Christ model with its emphasis on a personal decision to surrender one's culture and identity to Christ will be opposed to the approach of forced conversion such as that witnessed in North America with its attendant Christ in culture model. Forced conversion is bound to result into a church whose faith is not organic and where Christians are not at ease with what they received, regarding it not as their own. With Culture in Christ we see a faith not in resistance to what was received, but one in joy and peace.

Third, Culture in Christ, with its individual based nature, enables a person to cross cultures, motivated by the love of Christ. In Uganda one of the strongest forces of intertribal cohesion has been the East African Revival. Men and women from all tribes in fellowship call each other brother and sister, meaning that they now belong to the same new tribe of Christ. Cultural distinctions remain but they are overlooked, with the confidence that Christ is all in all. The highest rate of intermarriages in Uganda is among revivalist Christians who have made a personal decision to follow Jesus and see other cultures not as a threat to theirs but as complementary in Christ.

In the early Church it is the Culture in Christ model that facilitated the spread of Christianity from among the Jews to the Gentile world, and among the gentiles from one nation to another. When Peter rejected the non-kosher food that was lowered from heaven, a voice from heaven reprimanded him, saying that he should not call unclean that which God has made clean. Culture in Christ enables the person to take Christ wherever they go and like St Paul, become 'all things to all people', in order that they might save some (1 Corinthians 9.22). A person whose model is Culture in Christ will accept other cultures, knowing that the Spirit will sift out those aspects that will not dissolve, but still leave her or him with sufficient ground both to listen and to communicate relevantly to those she or he encounters.

Fourth, Christ dissolving culture implies that no culture is to be taken as *the* culture, to live by. The problem with the transformation model is that it suggests the possibility of a culture that we can strive to attain and, when we have attained it, become complacent, presumptuous and judgemental. This certainly was the case in the Ugandan Church. The first surge of the East African Revival produced a transformed culture, this was then endorsed as the Christian culture. The transformed culture extended to issues like hairstyle, dress, food, drink, entertainment and which books were permitted to be read. Whereas that new transformed culture seemed to work in the early years, it gradually became problematic, resulting in a schism in the late 1960s between the *Bazukufu* (those that are awake) and the *Bebafu* (those that are asleep when they are supposed to be awake). The former were those who clung to the early transformed culture, and the latter were the rising post-independence middle class and those who aspired to be like them. They embraced more aspects of a western lifestyle unless they were clearly inconsistent with a biblical Christian life. In my early years as a born-again Christian at university, I was torn apart between these two groups and felt confused as a result. I had to make up my mind by searching the Scriptures (see Acts 17.11), eventually settling down in the *Bebafu*.

I am not sure I like this label – *Bebafu* – it is a label imposed upon me. It is a sign of the problem with the Christ transforming culture model in practice. The *Bazukufu* are uncritical of their transformed culture and are at times unwilling to accept that there are as many Christ/culture solutions as there are cultures. In the world of chemistry, a solution of common salt is not the same as that of sugar, yet they are both useful in daily life. No salt or sugar contaminated with sand, however fine the sand may be, will be any use unless the sand is filtered out. And the filters of such insoluble cultural aspects should be the Spirit of Christ, the Scriptures, the context of soluble culture, a consideration of the concerns of the wider church, and a consideration of the personal circumstances of an individual. We should insist, as the vast majority of Anglicans do, that the written word of God is the venue, the event and the act that filters out aspects of culture that are insoluble. It is absolutely essential, in this writer's opinion, that claims of post-biblical revelation to justify new behaviour trends, or claims that the Bible is antiquated and unable to speak to us today are inconsistent with received truth, and merely result in endless philosophical arguments.

The cross-cultural aspect of Culture in Christ could be useful in our cross-cultural church. It would help us to seek to understand the varieties of Christian expression and why some aspects of behaviour are common practice in some cultures whereas in others those very aspects would be seen as immoral.

For example, think of two men walking hand in hand in your capital city. In Kampala it would be a common sight: it is a delight for two men to be holding hands and there is no implication that they are homosexual – it is a normal part of friendship. In London it would be remarkable if the two were not gay men, probably conscious of an open display of affection. In Europe African Christians are unlikely to do as they would in Kampala: I would be reluctant to hold the hand of my friend in Oxford Street. In Africa I encourage my European brothers to hold hands with me and rejoice in our friendship. In Europe the act would be as sand, insoluble; in Africa the cultural expression is not only acceptable but good.

An African reading the story of David and Jonathan in the books of Samuel will understand it as friendship, whereas a European Christian will suspect homosexuality. A European Anglican man visiting Africa should be comfortable to hold hands with his African brother. They remain European, but an aspect of cultural behaviour that was insoluble in one culture is now soluble in another. As long as they are in Africa, they are both European and African in Christ.

We now return to the question of the role of culture and identity in the expression of faith. It is the view of the writer that culture should be allowed to play a significant role in the way every part of the Anglican Communion lives out the gospel. But that culture should be soluble in Christ, whereby the solubility is determined not intellectually or philosophically, but primarily though not exclusively by Christ as revealed in the Scriptures. It should be a culture that is open to change both temporal and geographical, and one that is marked by a personal commitment to Christ and by martyrdom in the cause of love and freedom.

3. The Bible and Cultures

An introduction to some hermeneutical methods is presented in Chapter 2 of this book. One hermeneutical method that has emerged over the last 30 years is the social-scientific critical method. In the 1980s scholars such as Bruce Malina argued that the sociological assumptions of the writers of the New Testament were completely different to those of his own North American culture. He argued that a sociological and anthropological study of the cultures of peoples living around the Mediterranean Sea would enable a better understanding of the texts.[24] He proposed a model-based approach favoured by social scientists and formed a model of cultural attitudes to shame and honour, which he applied to passages from the New Testament.

Critics have argued that Malina made too much of the foreigner approach and did not recognize the differences between the cultures of time of the Roman Empire and of today in the Eastern Mediterranean lands. However, social sciences have been utilized by a growing number of scholars in order to understand the Bible as we have it.[25] For example, Richard Burridge has pointed out the similarities between Roman biographies and the gospels. It used to be common to hear that 'the gospels are not biographies', but we now know that they are not *modern* biographies.[26] Such a realization has a great effect on how we read them as they were intended to be read.[27]

The same sociological tools used to understand cultural diversity in today's world enable a better understanding the writers of the gospels and the letters. We cannot assume that all cultures are like ours and it would also be wrong to assume that the cultures of the lands of the New Testament were all the same. Letters were written to Jewish and gentile communities and some of these were rural and traditional while others cosmopolitan and dynamic. The hermeneutical debates on human sexuality have asked questions about the cultural assumptions of differing cultures about homosexuality and the meanings of words at the time of the writing of the texts, not what they were before or became afterwards. The question asked is whether there is such a thing as homosexuality that is not culturally defined.

We therefore return to the question of Christian faith and the social sciences, especially anthropology.

4. Anthropology

The eighteenth- and nineteenth-century missionary movement played an important role in the rise of the social sciences of ethnology and anthropology. Reflecting Niebuhr's models above, missionaries ranged from those who strongly rejected the cultures in which they found themselves, to those who were impelled to study and understand them. Even missionaries who began with a negative view of the culture they were seeking to evangelize often shifted to a more positive view, as they began to 'get inside' new cultures and appreciate their complexity and rationale. Most parts of the Anglican world can produce an Anglican missionary who detailed the culture in which he or she worked. In Melanesia, Robert Codrington, Charles Fox and Walter Ivens come to mind. In Uganda John V. Taylor is well known worldwide. From the work of early missionary-ethnologists modern anthropology emerged: a social science that attempts, without prejudice, to understand a whole culture, in all of its complexity and interactions.

However, both missiology and anthropology have moved far beyond the subject-object model of action, whereby the 'other' (whether individual or culture) becomes the 'object' of evangelism or scientific study by an external agent possessing the criteria of truth (whether a missionary or anthropologist). Local churches have emerged in very many different and complex cultural settings (far removed, sometimes, from their original evangelizers, or from the New Testament world) able to articulate their own Christianities and, indeed, evangelize in their own way. Likewise, 'foreign' cultures have produced their own articulate social scientists, who can 'do' anthropology and other social sciences 'from within'. Western European/North American hegemony is finished in this respect, in terms of giving ultimate definitions of what is right for or true of 'the other'.

Despite this caveat, from which much can be learned, both Christian mission and secular anthropology (as the study of cultures, including Christian cultures) continue to flourish. Both have shifted from a Newtonian subject-object model to a model more participatory and holistic, often with a bias towards the historically powerless such as women, the poor, the enslaved, children, the subaltern and the outcast. This bias towards the powerless is not really new for Anglicans. George Herbert wrote of the situation of the poorest and most miserable of his parishioners in seventeenth-century England, 'evident miseries have a naturall priviledge, and exemption from all law.'[28]

While anthropology has had its practitioners holding *a priori* assumptions about culture (for example, advocates of structuralism), for the most part contemporary anthropology is highly experiential, attempting to discover, articulate and make alive what makes cultures, including individuals within them, work, in all their complexity and on-going development. Typically, an anthropologist today – who is as likely to be a woman as a man and an African, Asian or Pacific Islander as a European – looks at a culture as: an interaction and synthesis of the traditional culture in all its complexity; external political and cultural influences such as westernization or modernity, external religious forces either adopted or rejected; and economic life both local and global. Emphasis is likely to be quite local, but also global; dynamic rather than static.

Thus, anthropology has moved away from the study of 'primitive' peoples to a study of any human culture or subculture – including contemporary European cultures, practices and institutions which once saw themselves as normative and so not available to study. Even Christianity and churches (whether Global North or Global South) are subject to anthropological scrutiny. The overall aim of contemporary anthropology is understanding and articulating the world's great cultural complexity, both local and global.

While an anthropologist will adopt a 'value free' stance for methodological purposes (to allow the other's view to be fully and accurately heard), she or he certainly has personal values which may be reflected in the choice of area of study and there may well be the assumption that some good will come out of the study. Positive outcomes might be considered to be the strengthening of a traditional culture in the face of westernization, helping people better to synthesize the traditional culture and modernity, sharing the positive aspects of the culture with the rest of the world, seeking alternative models of behaviour to one's own culture's, reduction of violence and other destructive behaviour within the culture, or the anthropologist's own personal growth.

For an anthropologist to present sympathetically and accurately a culture that has many ethnically problematic aspects to it (for example, violence against women, sexual exploitation, and gross inequalities) does not mean that the anthropologist subscribes to those values. There is often confusion about 'cultural relativism'. A good anthropologist adopts cultural realism for heuristic reasons such as the desire to discover truth, rather than for the belief that all cultures and all religious are equally good and true.

Anthropology and Christianity

Early missionary ethnologists studied foreign cultures to enable their evangelization; they frequently found that their study of these cultures led to a greater appreciation of non-white peoples, sometimes destroying contemporary European stereotypes about them. They questioned ridiculous ideas such as 'primitive consciousness', 'animal-like existence', and the 'simplicity' and limited communicability of 'primitive languages'. Some Europeans questioned the capacity of 'native' peoples to be vessels of Christianity or even their existence as human 'persons', and missionary ethnologists challenged those prejudices. Missionaries and early mission churches had to change and adapt to social structures and practices very different from those they were familiar with. Ethnological and anthropological study became a tool for a better quality of Christianity, more suitable to the local context.

The use that Christians today make of anthropological or cultural studies (or of any social science for that matter) will depend very much on the theological significance which that Christian places on culture and which models they embrace. However, no matter where one is in Niebuhr's typology, culture cannot be ignored. To deny the importance of culture is rather like denying the importance of oxygen just because we cannot see it.

Following Niebuhr and the history of Christian missions, one can again draw up a variety of models of the relations of Christian mission with culture for today, again going from opposition to accommodation. The models are not mutually exclusive:

(1) Knowing a culture to reject and destroy it.

Much of the nineteenth-century missionary movement was essentially hostile to the cultures it sought to evangelize, destroying traditional cultural practices, languages and religions. This approach remains today, whether on the 'right' (fundamentalist Christians burning idols) or the 'left' (Christian feminists seeking to destroy patriarchal cultures). Certainly in some situations, destruction of sinful cultural practices is appropriate.

(2) Knowing a culture to evangelize it from within.

This approach is much more sympathetic to the non-Christian culture (whether an un-evangelized group of the Global South or the secularism of the Global North) and seeks to appreciate its positive aspects, perhaps as *preparatio evangelica* (preparation for the Gospel). It is out of this tradition that ethnology emerged.

(3) Knowing a culture to promote mutual understanding and better cross-cultural relationships.

In many parts of the world today, for example, in much of the Muslim world, evangelism is simply not possible. However, for its own survival if nothing else, the church can enter into relations of friendship and mutual understanding with the cultures and religions that surround it. These relations are simply an expression of Christian love.

(4) Knowing a culture to learn from and appreciate it.

This view sees all human cultures as part of God's creation, all human beings (despite their flaws and wrong beliefs) as created in God's image, all works of art, music and literature a reflection of God's glory and all truthful speculation a reflection of Jesus Christ the Truth. This is the approach of Christian humanism and it remains attractive in a time of narrowing human sympathies.

(5) Knowing a culture to adopt it.

While not impossible for a Christian, this approach is fraught with many dangers and difficulties, from the sheer impossibility of dropping all one's cultural presuppositions and totally adopting those of another, to rejection by both the old and new cultures. Whether Christianity still has any cutting edge in such a situation is an open question.

For any cross-cultural understanding, listening is crucial. Perhaps the above range can be re-phrased as moving from virtually no listening involving the rejecting of a culture on the basis of only a very little exposure to it, or so much listening that it results in the loss of one's self in the reality of another.

Questions

- Which of the above approaches to culture do you find most attractive?
- Do you find you can hold more than one approach?
- How aware are you of your own cultural assumptions and how they might be different from others?
- Can you view another culture without judging it?
- Are you aware of the diversity of cultures and subcultures within your setting?
- Do you believe the church needs to understand its cultural setting as it practises theology and ministry?

5. Diversity of Cultures

The Anglican Communion as we know it found its first definitive expression in the document entitled *Mutual Responsibility and Interdependence* [MRI] *in the Body of Christ*, presented to the Anglican Congress of 1963 held in Toronto, Canada. In the 1950s Stephen Baynes (the first Executive Officer of the Anglican Communion) critiqued Englishness as one of the then defining marks of Anglicans all over the world. Anglican churches in Bombay, Zanzibar and Nova Scotia looked English, the language of Anglican worship was English and the hymns were from English hymnals. He argued against 'cultural confessionalism' and saw the principles of mutual responsibility and interdependence – based in provincial autonomy and mutuality – as a way to hold together a growing communion that could embrace diverse cultural expressions.

Much of the debate over human sexuality has focused on the proper limits of such diversity. Archbishop Akinola of Nigeria sums it up in this way:

> In the last five years we have had this endless controversy in the Anglican Communion. To the world this is about homosexuality. To us it is just a symptom of the real problem. Homosexuality is not peculiar to Anglicans but Anglicans have the courage to discuss it openly. The issue is that there are members of our Anglican family who are not paying attention to scripture, but are giving prominence to modern culture. They are bringing new principles to interpret scripture. The word of God has precedence over any culture.

We aim to offer contrasting worldviews and how they challenge one another and to enable you to consider the significance of Archbishop Akinola's observation.

The European Worldview

European cultural assumptions are shared by those who live in Europe and by those of European origin living throughout the world, though not necessarily uncritically. Some dominant themes are universal human rights, freedom of choice, democracy and the right to privacy. These assumptions underpin western European democracies and international institutions such as the United Nations.[29] They originate in the Enlightenment philosophy of the autonomous individual which emerged out of the break-up of corporate medieval European Catholic culture, the rediscovery of classical philosophy and the rise of science, further developed in the Reformation with its affirmation of the importance of the individual in matters of faith and decision-making, as well as the need for political tolerance and harmony in the face of centuries of bloody political and religious conflict. Indeed certain of these cultural assumptions are reflected in the Anglican Reformation and its later development. They were also spread to the Global South through colonialism and decolonization and are reflected, for example, in the Westminster and American-style democracies around the world. These assumptions are still ingrained, and continue to develop in European thinking and political institutions such as the European Union and reflect some of the modern 'liberal' values of which Archbishop Akinola is critical. In broad terms, mindful that they do not apply in their entirety to all persons and all groups (some indeed resist them), here are four strong themes of the western European worldview:

Human Rights

The assumption that all human beings are born equal with the rights to be happy and to control their lives is considered to be self-evident. The denial of such rights is seen as oppression. William Wilberforce and those who sought to end the slave trade established that slaves were human. They ran campaigns that posed the question 'Am I not a man and a brother?' and 'Am I not a woman and a sister?' The right to freedom has been extended over the last 200 years and human rights have been the basis for all kinds of freedoms. Church groups on this basis challenged the use of child labour and struggled for the right of education for all. Successive barriers to human freedom have been fought against in the name of human rights, especially racism and sexism. The Universal Declaration of Human Rights is a fundamental pillar of the United Nations and leads to calls as diverse as clean water for all, a living wage and no discrimination on the basis of gender, ethnicity, sexual orientation or age.

Freedom to Choose

European culture values the freedom to choose as an absolute good. It is regarded as diminishing and inhuman to have choices made for you. Growing to maturity is about gaining choice and control of your own life; good living in old age is about retaining independence and choice. Capitalism is the expression of this goodness, as the choices of the community will shape the dynamics of society. The experimentation with a controlled economy through communism is regarded as a failure and confidence is placed in 'markets' to solve human problems through the availability of choice. Education and financial independence are vital to being able to choose and so are seen as good.

Democracy

The expression of choice in the public domain is democracy. The right to self-determination has emerged over the last 500 years as an ultimate good. Archbishop Cranmer believed in the right of a monarch to rule and this is expressed in the Book of Common Prayer. The excesses of Queen Mary crushed his faith in the monarchy and in England all such notions were limited following the Civil War. In France they were destroyed by the excesses of monarchy prior to the French Revolution. Claims by the British state to control their overseas colonies were first rejected in the American War of Independence. They were finally destroyed by the breaking up of the British Empire, first in India and then across the world as the winds of change swept across Africa in the 1950s and 1960s.

Westminster-style democracy combines the requirement for strong government with the right of the people to determine their own lives by a system that is adversarial with the winner taking all power. Opposition is encouraged in thought but not in violent action as the losing party hopes to take power at the following election. Dissenting acts are allowed when to do otherwise would be an affront to human rights. Those who were complicit in the Holocaust were not allowed to plead that they were only obeying orders.

The Distinction between Public and Private

There is a growing consensus that the purpose of the state is to provide freedom of choice by ensuring that one person's freedom does not restrict that of another. It is recognized that total freedom for all is not possible, and the question arises as to the limits of public interference to as to enable private liberty. A good example has been recent legislation in many countries on smoking in public buildings. The human rights of the smoker are contrasted with the human rights of those who share those spaces and are in danger of contracting cancer. In many countries specific smoking areas were proposed, but rejected, as workers had to service those areas. It would not be possible to discriminate against non-smokers in employment terms. The state offers personal freedom through the defining of public space. Individuals are free to smoke at home as they have liberty to choose for themselves. Thus the guiding principle is that freedom is unlimited provided it does not harm any other person.

Reflections on the Expression of European Cultural Values in the USA

In the USA these values have been assumed to be 'self-evident' from the foundation of the nation.[30] However, these rights have not been available to all. People of African descent, indigenous peoples and women were excluded from these rights in the USA and each has had to fight for justice and freedom. The Civil Rights movement was a religious and political movement characterized by the Revd Martin Luther King Jr and the struggle for justice is seen by many as a mission imperative, not in conflict with the good news of Jesus for it is the good news.

We offer you a page from the blog of the Bishop of California. Bishop Marc introduces Jasper who brings together many of these western European cultural values with Christian faith. In the terms of the Ugandan theological reflector above, this might even be seen as an example of 'Culture in Christ', as personal, cultural and faith values all come together in a single witness.[31]

Jasper is a high school student and member of Our Saviour, Mill Valley, where I heard him eloquently participate along the line of the post below regarding the heart of the Episcopal Church and our place in the Anglican Communion. I was deeply moved by what he had to say, and by his commitment.

'Every year at Advent we hear the story of John the Baptist, crying out in the wilderness that something great is coming. We hear also of how crazy he was, how so few people listened, but we know now that he was right. Something wonderful was indeed coming. That something was a someone, Jesus of Nazareth, who would go on to preach a message of love and equality, echoing John's call to lower every mountain and fill in every valley. We call ourselves Christians because we dedicate ourselves to loving and serving all that God has blessed.

'Today, we are that voice in the wilderness, crying out for the earth to be made flat so that every human being may walk on equal ground. We are shunned by 'mainstream' Anglicans, cast out by the community that was supposed to be our home. We are told that the split is our doing, that we are to blame for this schism.

And in fact, we are. It was our decision to consecrate a gay bishop, to elect a female presiding bishop, and to insist that it is our right to do these things. But let's be proud of that. Any communion that would not allow us to recognize the equality of God's children is not a communion we should be a part of.

'We see in the stories of Jesus' ministries to the prisoners, the lepers and the outcasts of society in his day a message that no one is below the love of God. We are all God's children, and we know that what we do unto the least of the people of God, we do unto God. Every time that we allow an injustice to be perpetrated against a gay man or a lesbian woman, the marginalized of today's world, we allow the attacker to harm our beloved God, and in our negligence we are guilty. It is not enough to stand on the sidelines, and hope that someday things will be better. We must make our stand for those that society considers 'outcasts' if we are to be worthy of the Kingdom of Heaven.

'It is not easy to take a stand on so divisive an issue. In our fractured world, I would much rather advocate unity and reconciliation. Only one glance at the newspapers is enough to remind me that this world is defined by East vs. West, Shia vs. Sunni, red vs. blue. I do not want to support splitting the world yet another way. But this is not a division on ethnic, religious or political differences. This is liberty vs. inequality. This is right vs. wrong, and there can be no reconciliation with wrong.

'This is not just a struggle for members of the gay and lesbian community. I am not gay, but I owe it to my family members and friends who are gays and lesbians to take a stand. I owe it to the individuals who fought and sacrificed for the Goldberg family during the dark years of Nazism. I owe it to all who have taken stands in the past. I owe it to Jesus himself, who gave everything for each and every one of us.

'The wilderness is never an easy place to be, but let us not despair as the Anglican Communion leaves us. Someday, those who understand the absolute equality of human life will be more numerous than the stars. In the meantime, it is up to us to proclaim the bold message of Jesus, Lincoln, Martin Luther King Jr., and Harvey Milk, even if it seems that no one is listening. The Anglican Communion divided will not stand, but the 'fierce urgency of now' demands us to stand up. We cannot compromise with what we know is wrong. Forget your fears, disregard the prevailing opinions, remember Christ and join us on the journey to the Mountaintop.'

This short statement, written by a young person full of passion for the Gospel, demonstrates the cultural assumptions through which the Bible is interpreted by many Anglican Christians in the USA. The first thing to notice is that this Gospel is grounded in the Bible with reference to the story of salvation announced by John the Baptist and lived out by Jesus. This calls us into loving service and the struggle for justice in the world – two of the five marks of Mission of the Anglican Communion. However, he continues by asserting that it is the 'right' of The Episcopal Church [TEC] to elect who they will as bishop in the Church with the Anglican Communion seen as infringing those rights. He sees mission as being grounded in the call to love all, but it also references previous struggles for liberation in the history of the cultural development of the USA. Jasper is of Jewish origins and reflects on the Holocaust experience when Jews were targeted and murdered in huge numbers, and along with them those labelled 'homosexual'. He also references the struggle for civil rights, naming Lincoln and King with the gay rights activist Harvey Milk (all of whom were martyred for their beliefs) and calling us to journey to the Mountaintop to see the promised land, a reference to King's famous speech recalling Moses in the wilderness.

Within this framework the just solution is self-evident and any delay in the implementation of justice is a denial of justice and thus runs contrary to the Gospel. Decisions can legitimately be made through a democratic process and if such a vote goes against the stand for justice then a solution is to break away and form a group which will democratically decide in favour of justice for lesbian, gay, bisexual and transgendered people. The nature of democracy in its European form is for a winner takes all approach based upon a Westminster model, which gives clarity to political decision-making.

Some internal critics of the justice agenda within TEC share the same cultural assumptions and base their arguments on those foundations. Their fundamental criticisms are that such theological innovation ignores all mention of salvation, of repentance and denies biblical authority. But they often argue within the bounds of common cultural understandings.

Discrimination against people because of their race, gender or sexuality is condemned, but standards of behaviour are affirmed. The distinction between identity and behaviour is significant in loving all people, even though all are sinners, but condemning sinful behaviour and not blessing it. This approach is sometimes known as welcoming, but not affirming. Significant to this approach is the condemnation of *all* sexual activity outside of marriage, heterosexual or homosexual so that it is clear that all people are treated with equality and their human rights preserved. In this context Bishop Howe of Central Florida argues:

> The origins of homosexual orientation are complex and still under intense debate. Lifelong celibacy is an arduous calling to self-denial, and the admonition to appropriate God's power and grace to change one's sexual orientation is certainly a challenge of faith. Homosexuals often find it hard not to resent such a demand being made of them by heterosexuals who are at least potentially free to express and enjoy their sexuality within the marriage relationship. Discussion of all these matters needs to take place within a context of mutual respect, mutual repentance and the sharing of burdens – in short, within the Christian community as it is called to function by its Lord. Heterosexual persons must not speak to or about homosexuals from a position of self-righteousness or superiority. But for the grace of God in Christ, none of us can stand.[32]

Such a stance is deliberately intended to oppose homophobia (the irrational fear of homosexuality) but understands justice as being an offering of choice to all people to live within the traditional teaching of the church or to decide to reject the way of Christ. The offering of choice as a good is located in a different place. The individual has the choice to be in the church and live by the rules or to live outside the church, but not the choice to live in the church and choose to live in a same-sex relationship. Fear is expressed that the right to choose to seek assistance from therapy and prayer ministry for those with unwanted same-sex attraction will be limited by the forced closing of such programs through political pressure. The right to choose such therapy is defended as a human right.

Democracy is also affirmed by those who oppose same-sex unions. David Lumsdaine in *A True Hearing* makes the point that: 'North America as a whole has strongly rejected the legitimacy of same-sex marriage, in state after state, often by margins of 2 or 3 to 1.'[33] Writers in *A True Hearing* criticize those who undermined democratically passed resolutions of general conventions of TEC by ordaining partnered gay and lesbian priests. The Resolution 1.10 of the 1998 Lambeth Conference has status not only because it is compatible with Scripture, but also because it was democratically passed by an overwhelming majority of bishops.

The USA is admired around the world as a beacon of freedom. Its cultural assumptions have allowed freedom of religion and worship; and have led to an end to slavery and to the liberation of women in society. But European enlightenment cultural assumptions are not self evident to all. Indeed, within The Episcopal Church there have always been those critical of its tendency towards excessive individualism, congregationalism, and liberalism, arguing that the Church's Catholic ecclesiology requires more respect for and unity with the whole body of Christ, both within the Episcopal Church and beyond. But at the same time, solidarity for justice has also extended beyond its borders, for example, in the fight against apartheid, poverty and unjust political regimes. The Episcopal Church has frequently been critical of its government's and transnational corporations' roles on the global stage and it is unfair to equate those activities with the views of The Episcopal Church.

Some within The Episcopal Church are questioning the common cultural basis of both sides in what has been an acrimonious dispute, and seeking to learn from other cultural experiences. They see that one side engages in detailed analysis of specific biblical texts while ignoring wider biblical concerns and the other side fails to engage in serious theology. For example, John Kevern claims that the 'liberal' side sit light to doctrine and deploy a discourse that seems to me unbiblical and problematic from a Christian point of view. He considers the key is to challenge the cultural assumptions that underpin both sides in the North American debate.

Kevern argues that there is parochialism in modern American Episcopalians who assume that what happens in their local church is normative, which sometimes expresses itself in an unconscious liberal imperialism. The predominant discourse is rights based with both sides seeking to cast themselves as oppressed in order to claim rights. Justice issues are refracted by the American stories of slavery and civil rights. He notes:

Most interlocutors in my classes (or elsewhere) seem to have no idea that they speak from a very particular philosophical background (the British Enlightenment, taken to the extreme). They simply regard their views as 'self-evident'. Which is why it is doubtful that any progress can be made unless we can get behind the limitations of this pervasive Enlightenment anthropology.

He argues that what is absent for many people in the pews is a sense of a whole, let alone a duty toward the whole. They really do not see the implications of, say 1 Corinthians. The 'whole' is for most the parish they are in or their diocese and for some the province, but not the Communion. In recent controversies a common reaction to the perception of being 'told what to do' is to reject the Archbishop of Canterbury and all other Instruments of Communion as foreign authorities and assert

'We fought a revolution to be free'. The inclination to 'cut off', as an expression of the frontier individualism – which is held in great respect – can be a reason to escape the hard work of engagement, especially with those who are in disagreement with you. The assertions of 'justice deferred is justice denied' and commitment to 'the faith once delivered to the saints' are statements designed to win all in a democratic process which produces winners and losers. Change on both sides happens incrementally and through living with the other as Wilberforce and Lincoln understood.

He argues that the way forward is for TEC to engage with the whole as we have never engaged before, for a genuine worldwide listening process to take place and in which no one 'cuts off'. Jesus Christ the saviour of the whole world calls us to nothing less. The second requirement is to engage in serious theological exploration of the human person made in the image of the Triune God, which takes the Bible seriously and gives due respect for tradition and reason, without privileging 'experience' but not diminishing the other.

Some African Reflections on European Cultural Assumptions

While Americans and Western Europeans are able to ignore the cultural assumptions of others, though at their own peril, Africans and other indigenous peoples live within two or more cultural contexts every day. The dominating and pervasive Western European cultural values run through the history of slavery and colonization. The influence of multinational companies and of Non Governmental Organizations (NGOs) founded on Western liberal values is growing all the time. For Africans the values they encounter in these institutions are not self-evident; indeed they frequently run contrary to African ways of thinking and behaving.

Human Rights

It is wrong to think that African culture objects to human rights. However, the way that human rights are being implemented feels to many like a new colonial imposition. Multinational corporations and NGOs demand that their local employees sign documents against discrimination on the grounds of gender, ethnicity and sexuality. It is not that these are objected to but that they are imposed from outside. When organizers demanded the right to have a Gay Pride march through the streets of Accra, the capital of Ghana, they did so without consultation. Questions were asked as to whether this was the best way to engage the community. African culture does not deny individual rights, but it felt like a Western agenda being imposed on Ghanaian culture. Without discussion conventions are being imposed rather than being adopted and owned by the people.

African culture speaks of the ethic of responsibility as well as freedom. For an African it is hard to conceive of a happy and fulfilling life not lived in community. Human rights are only expressed within community rights. African philosophy is frequently expressed by proverbs, proverbs concerning the significance of community outnumber proverbs on any other subject. One Ghanaian proverb is:

A forest from the outside is one, but when you get closer each tree stands in its own place.

This proverb expresses the individuality expressed in the corporate. Such concepts have been most articulately communicated to Western minds by the expression of *Ubuntu* in the thought of Desmond Tutu. An individual can find his humanity provided she or he is related to the wider family. For an African the carrying of a family name is valuable as you carry responsibility for the family and this cannot be ignored in the search for individual fulfilment.

Freedom

The African experience of the European search for freedom has been the enslaving of people, colonialism, dependency, and most recently the awareness that European industrial utilization of natural resources has led to climate change. European freedoms have come at a cost and this has been paid by Africans and other indigenous peoples. The call for reparations are complex in the extreme, but there is a feeling that white Europeans – whether they live in the USA, Australia or in Europe – need to realize that the cost continues to be borne by those who suffer extreme weather causing drought and floods in the context of structural economic disparity.

Freedom to choose is not seen as an ultimate good. This can be witnessed in African attitudes to marriage. There is an acknowledgement that marriages arranged without consulting the couple are unacceptable, especially when it focuses on an economic arrangement and the exchange of teenage girls. However, to marry against the wishes of parents is also an extreme that has serious consequences for the couple and the community. Consensus is important, and while agreement can be difficult, it needs to be sought so the children of the marriage have identity. In African cultures you do not marry an individual – you marry a family. The families come together and are united by the union of two people and such bonds underlie the harmonious life of a community. Divorce is complex and needs negotiation with both families, not just between the individuals, because marriage is not a contract, it is a covenant to ensure stability within the whole community.

Democracy

Democracy was not invented by the Greeks and brought to African peoples by British colonialism. It existed in the communities of Africa before explorer and missionary arrived. Most communities were consensual in their structures, based not on majority rule, but on seeking a common mind. Many communities were nomadic, and a decision to move to new land was a matter of life and death; and so the wisdom of all is required to make the right choice and the co-operative action of all to implement it. A Ghanaian proverb says:

Let us go and ask the old woman.

The meaning is that all are to be consulted, and while the eldership of most tribes was predominantly male, the whole community had to participate in the process. African culture reflects a respect for elders – they have been through issues before – and prayer and contemplation. Quick decisions are for simple questions, but difficult questions require more time. Another proverb:

Go and consult your pillow.

European visitors often remark on African concepts of time. The time something happens is when it happens, not always by a prearranged schedule. Decisions are made when they are right to be made and a decision made too early, or one made by a majority and imposed on the minority, leaves problems for a community in division and ongoing antagonism.

What was introduced to Africa was not democracy, but the Westminster style of divisive and combative democracy with winner takes all concepts and majority decisions. Mkunga Mtingele argues that the colonial authorities introduced the concept of chiefdom into communities that had previously run on consent, and that this continues to be mirrored in the Anglican episcopacy.

Public and Private

The right to do as one likes so long as it does not hurt anyone else is incomprehensible to the African mind. There is a responsibility on every individual to build up the common life. Merely not hurting another is a sin of omission because you are limiting your contribution in the life of all. Traditional African life was communal life, each relying on one another. It is impossible for an individual to survive for long alone; the task of fetching water, preparing food, caring for cattle and goats and of planting and harvesting required allocation of roles and commitment to the whole. The distinction between public and private is false, especially in a small compound where there are no secrets.

The Prominence of Marriage and Procreation in African Cultures

African social systems focus on the birth and nurture of children as a vital expression of the regeneration of the community. Marriage and other forms of legal sexual unions are meant to ensure procreation and the preservation of life. The responsibility of all is to marry and have children. Therefore, singleness and childless marriage are an affront to the common good. The happiness of the elderly is dependent upon the care they receive from their children. The hope of every African is to be dependent upon their children in old age. The desire to retire to Florida or Bournemouth, far from family, cannot be comprehended; and so another proverb is:

If you think you are doing well you had better take care of your father and mother.

In this context homosexuality is seen as unAfrican in that it is a deviation from the goals of community life in the continuation of the life of the community. Africans will often question how European life will continue if gay marriages are allowed. They cannot conceive how the gay person will be cared for in old age. So, while homosexual behaviour is well known in Africa, homosexual identity is a deviation from the purpose of the family and is seen as a threat to community.

The Diversity of African Responses to the Communion Debate on Homosexuality

The initial reaction of the majority of African Christians has been to reject the blessing of a behaviour which is seen as sinful both in African culture and in the Bible, and to reject an identity which is a threat to marriage and the continuation of the community. As such the natural response is to support those who are standing for traditional morality and to insist that sexual activity is only properly engaged in a marriage between a man and a woman. If the listening process is a series of angry demands for the 'human rights' of those who seem to bring disruption into the community, there is little chance of a sympathetic hearing.

However, there is significant unease felt by many at the breaking up of the Communion. The realization that the fragmentation of the Anglican Communion will mean a break in relationships with some who are respected and loved and have been long considered part of the family in Christ is not taken lightly. For some this has been expressed in clear calls for repentance as a path to reconciliation. African Christianity, especially that connected to revival, has emphasized the disconnection with the sinner until open confession, frequently in church within a main service, is received.

Other voices have desired a different process. It is recognized that Africa has changed and there is no return to the past. While some live in rural compounds with extended families crossing generations living together, many now live in cities, in small apartments. Links to family and home are typically stronger than in European families, but they are not as intimate as they were. The requirement of hands to assist in the harvest has been replaced by the requirement to limit the number of mouths to feed from a salary. Christian values have been seen to challenge traditional values with the development of inter-ethnic marriage and the valuing of women in society. In this context there are those who believe they need to learn from 'the experience of homosexual persons', but this does not imply any encouragement for same-sex blessings or the acceptance of ordained partnered gay or lesbian clergy.

If conversations are possible then they cannot be based upon the demands for individual human rights; instead the good of the community that allows the flourishing of all will be central. As such ethical considerations will be primary. Discussions, which Westerners would see as intrusions into a private world, are vital for open understanding. Theologically the framework of salvation and a respect for the authority of Scripture are basic to any discussion. Most important is an openness to be prepared to change. Africans are familiar with strong and even angry dialogue that results in changes of thought and action, but they expect all to be prepared to change. Any attitude which is understood as a claim that educated and developed American or English people are instructing backward Africans is totally unacceptable. Listening can only happen if those who call for the blessing of same-sex unions are prepared to have their minds changed as well in the formation of a consensus and are not heard to be simply demanding that Africans 'progress'.

Most significantly, it cannot be expected that any such dialogue should lead to a quick decision. The process of being prepared to change works both ways, and new insights and developments are possible as God leads us to a new future. The demand for justice now is one that sits uneasily in contexts where injustice is seen every day in poverty and oppression. The desire for justice burns strongly in every African as they search for development and status, but all are aware that it will come in God's time and not to a prescribed timetable.

Questions

- What are the cultural values that underpin the way you read Scripture?
- Do you identify with European cultural values, African cultural values or are your cultural values different?
- What have you learnt from other cultural perceptions?
- How could your cultural perceptions challenge those of your brothers and sisters elsewhere?

---

6. Diversity of Homosexualities

Global anthropological study over the last century and a half (not to mention historical studies of different cultures going back millennia) have made it clear that there have always been in all cultures of the world human behaviour that can be termed very broadly 'homosexual'. That is, some expression of overt sexual activity involving another person of the same sex has always been known of. However, this activity is so diverse in its motivation, meaning, practice, intensity, social support (or lack of it), self-description, degree of secrecy and relation to other social relationships, that it is more accurate to speak and write of 'homosexualities' rather than 'homosexuality'.[34]

This use of the plural follows a movement in all the social sciences to speak of cultures, ideologies and even religions in the plural – for example, Indigenous peoples, Melanesian cultures, socialisms, Marxisms, democracies, feminisms, contextual theologies, Pentecostalisms and even Anglicanisms (or 'Anglican Ways'). Such an approach does not deny common features within a given group sharing the same name but uses the plural to recognize the great diversity that exists within the sometimes haphazardly applied single name. Again, this affirmation of diversity, complexity and plurality is empirical and experiential, based on observed reality, not a post-modern ontological affirmation that there is no common ground from which one can address this diversity. As Christianity is as much local as global, Christians should be in sympathy and support to describe these many diverse and local truths.

Another point of using the plural 'homosexualities' is to make it clear that one simply cannot take one's own assumptions about sexuality and homosexuality into cultural or sub-cultural settings other than one's own and assume and apply them in the new situation. Indeed, cross-cultural experience will make it clear that even the basic question of whether a practice or activity is 'sexual' or 'homosexual' is culturally determined. In some cultures a public kiss is not sexual, in others it is intensely sexual; in some cultures two men holding hands and caressing one another is not sexual, in others it is; in some cultures, stepping over someone's extended legs is sexual, in most cultures it is not; in some cultures a welcome hug of a stranger's genitals is not sexual, in other cultures it is sexual assault.

Here are descriptions of just a few homosexualities existing in global cultures. They are not mutually exclusive.

Examples of Homosexualities

(1) A homosexuality that has no or little relationship to sexual desire. For whatever reason, a cultural group has decided that certain homosexual activities are needed for personal growth and maturity, or for full inclusion in the group. The homosexual practices go on for what is perceived as the common good. People may derive sexual pleasure from the activity, but that is secondary or perhaps not even of importance.

(2) A homosexuality in which a group, whether male or female, takes on the social (and often sexual) role of the opposite sex – whether women as warriors or men as cooks.

(3) A homosexuality in a culture in which the number of sexes and/or genders is expanded beyond two (male and female) to a third gender and/or sex. This person may be thought to have special spiritual powers.

(4) A homosexuality of a person who is physically inter-sexual – for whom any possible sexual relationship by definition has a homosexual element.

(5) A homosexuality of a person who is convinced he or she was born into a body of the wrong sex, who feels that a sex-change operation is the only answer to their identity.

(6) A homosexuality that is transient, apparently a part of human development, eventually dropped in favour of heterosexuality.

(7) A homosexuality that is manifested in one or more intimate, adult, same-sex friendships of many aspects and much depth, sometimes (perhaps not often) expressed in overt sexual terms. The friendship(s) may last over many years but may also cease.

(8) A homosexuality rooted in a large number of people of the same sex living together and having little contact with the opposite sex (prisons, boarding schools, theological colleges, religious communities, plantations, mines), or where contact with those of the opposite gender is impossible, so that homosexual relationships are all that are available.

(9) A homosexuality of transient and anonymous homosexual encounters, in public toilets and parks.

(10) A homosexuality that is coercive, exploitative, non-consensual and ultimately violent.

(11) A homosexuality based at least partly on economic interests – giving pleasure to the rich tourist, expatriate or local person for the sake of gifts and money.

(12) A homosexuality coming out of both deep mutual friendship and deep-seated same-sex sexual desire, that seeks to combine deep permanent friendship and exclusive sexual intimacy, perhaps aspiring to the model of Christian marriage – a permanent, faithful and stable partnership.

(13) A homosexuality that recognizes its same-sex attraction but channels it into a single non-sexual friendship or many non-sexual friendships and maintains celibacy.

(14) A homosexuality that finds no outlet with another person and is expressed in a life of masturbatory fantasy, perhaps aided by pornography or by making friends with those one finds sexually attractive.

(15) A homosexuality that exists, recognized or unrecognized, within Christian marriage – perhaps happy, perhaps unhappy – which may result either in divorce or a decision to stay within the marriage.

(16) A homosexuality that has defined its own identity and ideology – 'gay', 'queer', 'lesbian', 'bisexual' etc.

(17) A homosexuality that sees itself has having been transformed into heterosexuality or asexuality – 'ex-gay', 'post-gay', 'ex-lesbian' etc.

(18) A homosexuality in which a person enjoys sexual relations with persons of both the same and opposite sexes, and tries to work out a situation in which this is possible.

(19) A homosexuality in which a person is attracted to people of both the same and opposite sexes, but lives in faithful commitment to one person.

(20) A homosexuality in which those engaged in it do not regard themselves as 'homosexual' because while engaged in a genital act with a member of the same sex their sexual fantasies are heterosexual.

The above are just a few examples of 'homosexualities' in the plural. As can be seen they are very different from one another. They come from around the world. None is definitive and an individual may identify with more than one. They are all activities of real human beings with real human lives, not theoretical examples. These human beings are fully a part of the human family. Many are baptized and communicant Christians, indeed, Anglicans. We may approve, we may disapprove, but they are there, waiting for us to enter into relationship with them, even if we do not know it, we are already in relationship with them.

If one uses the Pauline scriptural model of **Culture in Christ** pointed out above, the question arises whether any of these homosexualities as aspects of culture can be taken into Christ and redeemed, or whether all, without exception, must be excluded. Some, obviously, must be excluded – for example, the kind of homosexuality exhibited in the story of the Ugandan Martyrs. No one can condone such abuse, which was as violent as it was sexual.

However, if a gay or lesbian couple (perhaps united in a civil partnership or legal marriage, perhaps together for many years, perhaps with children, biological or adopted – (Section 12) – but who have had no church relationship for a long time – want to come back to the church as active Christians, to become part of an Anglican parish and to provide Christian education for their children – what does the church do? This is a very real question for many Anglican congregations and clergy in many parts of the world today. Does one refuse them, saying that they are not welcome until they break their relationship or perhaps pledge themselves to celibacy? Or does one accept them as participating in an emerging new Christian lifestyle, which for them also means faithfulness – to the community, the world and to each other – even unto martyrdom.

This list of homosexualities and the African experience described above also raise the major issue of homosexuality as identity and/or behaviour. For some cultures, such as most African cultures, full-scale homosexual identity is a greater problem than isolated homosexual behaviour, since homosexual identity is seen as threatening to community and family life. Indeed, some homosexual behaviour may go on but without homosexual identity. For other cultures, typically North American, homosexual behaviour without open and public homosexual identity is seen as a problem, regarded as dishonest and hypocritical. And to this must be added the theological point, enunciated throughout this volume, that for Christians, our primary identity is in Christ, in whom there is neither Greek nor Jew, male nor female, slave nor free and (many would add) gay nor straight. The next chapter will address this fundamental issue of identity.

Questions

- What different kinds of homosexualities have you had direct experience of personally, in your family, in your culture, in other cultures?
- Which in the above list do you believe cannot be incorporated into the Christian Way?
- Which in the above list do you believe might be incorporated into the Christian Way?
- Which in the above list might be morally neutral and therefore not a threat to the Christian Way?

7. Conclusion

This chapter presents the complexity of being a global Church in the face of complex cultural (in the broadest sense) diversity. Initially the Anglican expression of Christianity was linked to a single cultural expression – that of the developing independent nation state of England. Over the last two centuries the Communion has been forced to face the diversity of cultures within which Anglicanism is expressed and to seek to work with the variety of models of the encounter of Christ and Culture.

If the Anglican Communion is to continue in its global expression the conversation between cultural expressions will need to continue. As Andrew Walls has written:

> The church must be diverse because humanity is diverse; it must be one because Christ is one. Christ is human, and open to humanity in all its diversity; the fulness of his humanity takes in all its diverse cultural forms. The Ephesian letter is not about cultural homogeneity; cultural diversity had already been built into the church by the decision not to enforce the Torah. It is a celebration of the union of irreconcilable entities, the breaking down of the wall of partition, brought about by Christ's death (Ephesians 2.13–18). Believers from the different communities are different bricks being used for the construction of a single building – a temple where the One God would live. (Ephesians 2.19–22)[35]

Any assumption of cultural superiority is likely to be false, for all cultures have gifts of great value as we seek to be one in Christ. What is needed is the gift to suspend one's own cultural assumptions to enter sympathetically into the cultural assumptions of another.

The task of 'listening to the experience of homosexual persons' is rooted in the desire to love and cherish all people, to offer and receive the good news of Jesus Christ in mission, to learn from the experiences of others different from ourselves, and to offer pastoral care for all. Inevitably the engagement with people who live out a huge range of homosexualities will be a cross-cultural experience for all concerned and in which all are forced, if they take the exercise seriously, to modify their views.

When early anthropologists first went to the 'field' (a term shared with missionaries!), they did not generally go to colonial officials, traders, missionaries or other intermediate persons for information, rather they went directly to the cultures and persons they wished to understand and relate with. They lived with them, listened to them, interacted with them, loved them and even hated them. This participatory, incarnational approach they shared with, and perhaps even learned from, the best of the missionaries. Listening was direct, without an intermediary.

To take culture and experience on this issue seriously is to enter into direct and personal relationship with the homosexualities (that is, the homosexual people) on one's doorstep. We need to engage with those in our family, our church and community members and beyond, through thoughtful conversation, friendship and study. We are also able to listen as homosexual Christians from all corners of the globe are writing of their diverse experiences. Whether local or global experience, what is needed is patient mutual listening and understanding, then moving to theological reflection and action.

The process of listening to and reflecting on the experiences of real people, for whom the Gospel is experienced in very difficult cultural terms, in the light of Scripture and the insights of the social sciences, is the traditional Anglican theological approach, for example, in generations of Lambeth Conferences. It was how the 1988 Lambeth Conference dealt compassionately with the issue of polygamy. The aim is to come to some conclusion that continues to affirm the authority and truth of Christian revelation in Scripture but recognizes the cultural realities and offers a loving pastoral response, really addressing the issue raised.

A Christian theologian mindful of, listening to and relating with the world's homosexualities (through real people) may conclude that there are positive things to be learned about love, friendship, intimacy, sharing, faithfulness, personhood, commitment, playfulness, joy and the surprising grace of God. There is much to be learned also about sin and failure.

Likewise, homosexual Christians (including contributors to this chapter) should not underplay the sinfulness of some homosexualities and, indeed, our own potential to fall into sin. We also need to listen to one another and seek unity in Christ to proclaim the good news to all.

In an age of closing doors of mutual understanding in so many areas (interfaith sympathy and understanding, friendship and solidarity across huge economic and social gaps, the just sharing of global resources, the relation of women, men and families, the health of the planet, ideological reconciliation) careful listening and a more culturally self-critical but open approach is needed in so many relationships. One still hopes that the Anglican Communion can model this listening and self-critical but open approach as it deals with the difficult ethical issue of homosexuality. If the Communion can do so with this issue, others will follow more easily.

There is always the danger that we as Christians, appropriately committed to dissolving our own Cultures into Christ, become isolated from other Christians in other cultures and remain unaware of their particular concerns and needs. Here deeper cultural self-awareness and deeper awareness of the cultures of others is an enormous asset. Here the empathetic approach of early missionaries and contemporary anthropologists can be a good model. Reflection upon the various models of Christ and Culture (historic and emerging) also help us to move forward in a way in which Christ and the Holy Spirit genuinely rule our lives and relationships, both local and global. This chapter has sought to encourage listening across great gaps of culture and personal experience in the area of homosexuality; but that listening must extend even more broadly, both within the church and without, where all too often separation and fragmentation are preferred to maintaining unity within the Body of Christ and within the family of all God's created humanity.

Notes

1 The Virginia Report 3.8–11.
2 Ibid., 3.10.
3 Ibid., 3.11.
4 H. Richard Niebuhr, *Christ and Culture* (New York: Harper, 1951).
5 For a good critique of the limitation of Niebuhr's models in post-colonial Christian contexts and a suggested alternate model, see Ray Whitehead, 'Christ and Cultural Imperialism' in Christopher Lind and Terry Brown, eds., *Justice as Mission: An Agenda for the Church* (Burlington, Ontario: Trinity Press, 1985), 24–34.
6 'The Church of Uganda Position Paper on Scripture, Authority, and Human Sexuality May 2005' in *A True Hearing* (Anglican Mainstream and the Church of England Evangelical Council, 2005), 91-7. Available online: http://www.anglicancommunion.org/listening/world/docs/doc6.cfm.
7 I am very grateful for the assistance of Bishop Mark MacDonald, Debbie Royals and Donald Whipple Fox in preparing this example.

8   Mark MacDonald's essay 'The Gospel Comes to North America' available online: http://www.globalsouthanglican.org/index.php/comments/the_gospel_comes_to_north_america_bishop_mark_macdonald/

9   Mark MacDonald, 'Aboriginal Christianity/Ecological Christianity: A Church of and for Turtle Island' available online: http://www.anglican.ca/im/2007-09-06_mm.htm.

10 This quote was from an email to the editor. See MacDonald: 'The Gospel Comes to North America'.

11 These points are made in more Western idioms than they are expressed within the Indigenous communities and so are only an approximation of the concerns.

12 Martin Brokenleg, 'Lakota Hca' in Terry Brown, ed. *Other Voices, Other Worlds*, 5–14.

13 Ibid., 9.

14 From an email to the editor.

15 Nelson Mandela, *Long Walk to Freedom* (London: Abacus, 1994), 14.

16 Not all followed these precepts. The role of some agents of the London Missionary Society puts them outside this categorization.

17 'The Kairos Document' 1985 available online: http://www.bethel.edu/~letnie/AfricanChristianity/SAKairos.html.

18 Desmond Tutu 'Foreword', in Duncan Dormor and Jeremy Morris, ed. *An Acceptable Sacrifice? Homosexuality and the Church* (London: SPCK, 2007), ix.

19 *Some Issues in Human Sexuality* (London: Church House Publishing, 2003), 25–6.

20 'Civil Partnerships- A pastoral statement from the House of Bishops of the Church of England' Available online: http://www.cofe.anglican.org/news/pr5605.html.

21 Ibid., paragraph 14.

22 ' General Synod – Summary of Business Conducted on Wednesday 28th February pm' Available online: http://www.cofe.anglican.org/news/gspm2802.html.

23 Rowan Williams, 'Archbishop of Canterbury's Liverpool lecture – Europe, Faith and Culture' Available online: Europehttp://www.anglicancommunion.org/acns/news.cfm/2008/1/28/ACNS%204362.

24 Bruce Malina, *The New Testament World – Insights from Cultural Anthropology* (London: SCM, 1983).

25 John Elliot, *Social-Scientific Criticism of the New Testament* (London: SPCK, 1995). See also David Horrell. *The Social Ethos of the Corinthian Correspondence: Interests and Ideology from 1 Corinthians to 1 Clement – Studies of the New Testament and Its World* (Edinburgh: T & T Clark, 1996), 9-59, David Horrell, ed. *Social-Scientific Approaches to New Testament Interpretation* (Edinburgh: T & T Clark, 1996).

26 Richard Burridge, *What are the Gospels? A Comparison with Graeco-Roman Biography* SNTS MS 70 (Cambridge: CUP, 1992).

27 Richard Burridge, *Imitating Jesus: an Inclusive Approach to New Testament Ethics* (Grand Rapids: Eerdmans, 2007).

28 George Herbert (1593-1633) *A Priest to the Temple*, Chapter 12.

29 See Rowan Williams, 'Archbishop of Canterbury's Liverpool lecture – Europe, Faith and Culture' Available online: Europehttp://www.anglicancommunion.org/acns/news.cfm/2008/1/28/ACNS%204362.

30 'We hold these truths to be self-evident, that all men are created equal, that they are endowed by their Creator with certain unalienable Rights, that among these are Life, Liberty and the pursuit of Happiness.' Declaration of Independence 1776.

31 Guest Blogger Jasper Goldberg; 19 December 2007 http://bishopmarc.vox.com/library/post/guest-blogger.html. *A True Hearing* (Oxford: Anglican Mainstream, 2005), 55. At the time of publication Canada had passed laws enabling gay marriage, but the point is that democracy is still of fundamental significance.

32 John W. Howe *SEX: Should We Change the Rules?* Available online: http://www.ldolphin.org/howe/howe.shtml#anchor7414071.

33 *A True Hearing* (Oxford: Anglican Mainstream, 2005), p. 55. At the time of publication

Canada had passed laws enabling gay marriage, but the point is that democracy is still of fundamental significance.

34 The word 'homosexuality' itself dates only to the end of the nineteenth century, when social scientists invented a word to name, describe and group these practices.

35 Andrew Walls, 'The Ephesian Moment – At a Crossroads in Christian History' in *The Cross-Cultural Process in Christian History* (Maryknoll, New York: Orbis, 2002), 78.

Chapter 6

Sexuality and Identity

Janet Trisk and Sue Burns

Introduction

Among the most important questions we ask about ourselves and others are, 'Who am I? Who are you?' Central to all listening is learning to understand someone in their own terms rather than simply assuming we know who they are. That is particularly important because for some people the questions about sexuality currently being discussed in the Communion are far from purely abstract or academic. They are questions which they feel touch on their personal identity at a deep level.

The bishops at Lambeth recognized this and spoke about sexuality and Christian identity in the sub-group report on Human Sexuality which Resolution 1.10 commends. That report quoted the following words from the St Andrew's Day Statement:[1]

> There can be no description of human reality, in general or in particular, outside the reality in Christ. We must be on guard, therefore, against constructing any other ground for our identities than the redeemed humanity given us in him. Those who understand themselves as homosexuals, no more and no less than those who do not, are liable to false understandings based on personal or family histories, emotional dispositions, social settings, and solidarities formed by common experiences or ambitions. Our sexual affections can no more define who we are than can our class, race or nationality. At the deepest ontological level, therefore, there is no such thing as 'a' homosexual or 'a' heterosexual; there are human beings, male and female, called to redeemed humanity in Christ, endowed with a complex variety of emotional potentialities and threatened by a complex variety of forms of alienation.[2]

Although this chapter includes further theological reflection upon identity – especially on how we understand our identity in Adam and in Christ – this is not the focus here. What follows is focused instead on 'listening to the experience of homosexual persons' as they consider with us issues of sexuality and identity. It is therefore an invitation to deepen our understanding and no particular views on the relationship between sexuality and identity are specifically endorsed.

Our guides here are **Sue Burns** from Aotearoa, New Zealand and Polynesia and **Janet Trisk** from Southern Africa. In contrast to all the other chapters, however, it is not their voices which predominate. Sue and Janet spent many hours meeting with Christians in order to hear their testimonies. They met people who consider themselves identified by the bishops of the 1998 Lambeth Conference by the term 'homo-sexual persons'. As noted in the introduction, this includes a wide range of people who self-identify under various names – gay, lesbian, ex-gay, bisexual, transgender and post-gay. Each person's story is unique and there are therefore a variety of perspectives to be found in what follows. Sue and Janet found that most of those they spoke with did not relate to the St Andrew's Day Statement on identity. They therefore concluded that, rather than focusing on that statement here, they would offer us a record of what they heard, with some additional commentary in order to allow each reader to consider the testimony with them.

Sue and Janet engaged in a program of listening to enable these voices to be heard both by their own personal listening and by engaging with emailed testimonies from around the world.

As they introduce the testimonies they also encourage us to stop and to reflect and to pray. They also ask questions of us as readers about our own stories and about how we are reacting to what we read. This chapter is, therefore, quite different in style from the three previous more academic chapters. For many it may make difficult and uncomfortable reading. We are asked to listen deeply and to wrestle with deep personal questions such as 'Who am I?', 'Why is naming their identity so difficult for some people?', 'Who are we in Christ?', 'What are gay and lesbian people telling us about ourselves as a church?'. The hope is that it will encourage you, if it is possible in your own context, to get to know other Christians whose personal experience gives them particular insights into questions of sexuality and identity.

Sexuality and Identity

Human identity is profoundly complex, and there are multiple answers to the question: 'Who are you?' It may be that we ourselves are not sure of how to answer our own question: 'Who am I?'

We may have found that our understanding of who we are has changed with age, with circumstances, with deepening self-understanding, with learning from others. In this chapter the authors invite you to notice your own responses to this question or speak with others.

Exploring identity is further complicated if we answer other people's questions for them.

The authors are inviting us to listen in a way which begins by recognizing that when we first meet a person there is much we do not understand. Understanding grows in the process of listening to people speaking for themselves. We think it important that we do not begin by answering the question 'Who are you?' for others. This can lead to an impression that we assume we know more about other people than they know about themselves. The very idea of a listening process grows out of this: we cannot fully know who someone is unless we have listened to them answer their own questions about their identity.

Listening

This chapter begins with an invitation to listen. It contains the voices of people we have met and of a few who have spoken in response to the listening process. It is as if they have invited us as guests in their lives. If it is possible read their voices out loud; the words may have much greater impact on you. When you have listened to each voice we ask you to pray for the person.

When you reflect on what these people have to say to you please

- imagine that they are sitting in the same room as you
- speak as if they are listening to you just as you have listened to them.

You will hear the voices of gay and lesbian people. Some of these people live in the Global South and have often not been listened to. There are voices from different ethnic groups, from those who have experienced colonization by dominant cultural groups. When you listen you will hear a range of theological understandings and life choices. The voices of those who describe themselves as 'gay' in the past and 'restored' in the present are here. We attempted to meet with as wide a group of people as we could but inevitably the group is not comprehensive. We represent snapshots taken at particular locations at this particular time. Each extract comes from a longer narrative; some people appear more than once in the chapter. As readers you may like to follow them through in the text.

It has been said that we approach the biblical text by listening in reverent expectancy. Similarly, we approach other human selves with the same reverent expectancy, 'considering their unique personal identity and personal history with care and with attentive respect, or what the New Testament writers call agape, creative regard for the Other; it is a love prompted by will and not by "like-mindedness".'[3]

This is the manner in which we, the authors, are hoping to engage with you, the readers. We acknowledge and respect your relationship with God, your understanding of faith and the life experiences which you bring to this conversation. We anticipate that some things we say will not be understood and might offend. Nevertheless, within a commitment to listening with agape, we invite you to grow with us in this task of listening together.

Bartimaeus reminds us of the need to have a context in which we can talk about sexuality and identity.

I came from a Christian home; I was the youngest of eleven. My father was a church minister; we lived in a village. I was the minister's kid and expected to be good. Things happened to me. There was pressure from the community to live a good Christian life, to be a good example. I couldn't share with anyone. We don't talk about sex in our culture. It is taboo. I was so confused.

Questions

In your experience, where have you been able to talk about yourself?

Have you had times when you have been unable to speak about something which has been important to you? What was the effect of that on you?

Bartimaeus talks about what made it impossible for him to speak about sex. What are the similarities or differences with your situation?

Who am I?

Who is the human subject? How can we speak of identity? Do we have choices in regard to who and what we are? Is there some continuity between who I am today and who I was yesterday? Is there some unchanging core to me? Am I different when I am alone or with others?

Exercise (you may choose to do this alone or with another person)

1 When you describe yourself to a person who has a similar role to you (i.e. a priest, teacher, a minister's spouse, bishop, journalist, etc.) what do you tell them about yourself? What do you not tell them about yourself? What do you not need to tell them about yourself?
2 When you describe yourself to someone new at a meal, what do you tell them about yourself? What do you not tell them about yourself? What do you not need to tell them about yourself?
3 When you meet a friend you haven't seen for some time, what do you tell them about yourself? What do you not tell them about yourself? What do you not need to tell them about yourself?
4 What similarities and differences have you observed in the way you speak about yourself in different contexts?

Now listen to Simon

On an individual level I am somewhat fragmented: a third culture person, a celibate homosexual, an evangelical Christian, and a post-modern Westerner . . . but I am not post-modern in one key feature; I believe in authority, because God has made us to live under authority. Many post-moderns have abandoned authority, particularly the authority of the institutional church. I respect the authority God puts above us even when at times I am in disagreement.

Simon has described himself to you. How would you describe yourself to him?

Matthew describes himself:

My commitment to Jesus was made at a time in my life when I did not know which way to turn. I did not want to live a gay life and did not know how I would ever find a partner who I could love and share my life with. At the same time, I did not know how I could possibly manage to live a straight life. The early days of my commitment to Jesus were spent mostly in deep private prayer, begging to be changed.

Given the choice, I imagine very few people would ever choose to be gay. When church leaders refer to the gay issue, many fail to understand this point at all. They refer to 'gay tendencies', 'homosexual acts', 'sexual preference' and 'gay lifestyles'. I don't 'tend' to be gay, I don't occasionally perform homosexual acts, I don't prefer to be gay, and I certainly don't choose a gay lifestyle. All of these terms indicate some level of choice, but what many people don't seem to understand is that being gay is who I am, just as being heterosexual is who they are.

Matthew has spoken of his identity as something which is not about choice. He sees it as a fundamental part of his human nature.

What do you notice as you listen to people speak of their identity?

One of the ways we understand identity is to listen to the voices within ourselves, including the Holy Spirit, as we listen to the voices of others. As you hear the next stories, note down:

- The things which surprised you;
- The things which angered or delighted you;
- The parts which interested you, about which you would like to hear more.

Kiki: 'I had to start keeping secrets about my sexual life. When it finally came out in the open everyone around me made me feel so odd with what I really am.'

Isaac: 'A homosexual orientation is as profound and all-embracing as a heterosexual one. What you find attractive, stories that move you, romantic feelings and inclinations, songs and poetry, you name it, they all operate on same-attraction. So to regard the shape of one's genitalia as of greater significance than one's whole inner climate as a person, if I can put it like that, seems to be absolutely crass.'

Titus: 'No matter in which culture one is, people automatically make assumptions about people they are meeting for the first time. When I am meeting people for the first time I am an outsider looking in. I can't be as much "me" as heterosexual people can be. Because I don't know how these new people will respond to me. It's such a relief to be at events when everyone is gay, or I know everyone. There is always an element of distrust. I have to work hard on that so it doesn't seep into other areas of my life. Learning to hide becomes second nature and this is how I survive. Safety is a big factor. It's not the same as being black in white racist society because one's blackness is evident from the outset.'

Matthew: 'From my earliest memory of sexual thought, I have always been attracted to other men, and I have no idea why. My mother was never overbearing, my family life was "normal", I was never classically effeminate, I did not play with dolls, I played rugby at school, and yet as far as I can remember I have always been gay. I mention this, not to promote the theory of "gay genes" or that of being "born gay", but to stress the fact that being gay has never been a choice for me. It is not something that I have a preference for, or anything that I decided to do.'

Persis: 'I am more and more storying my identity as gay male. Queer is a surprise, as I am surprised by my identity. I was surprised to discover I was gay; it's never been a problem to me. I live my gay life as openly as possible, it is not a problem . . . I resist "being gay" now. "Gay" is an identity, identity is about struggling and separating into pigeon holes, stereotypes. Queer theory is talking about difference. Queer is not about sex, it is not about prescription and not about who [you have sex with]. I make tea in a queer way, that's what fascinated me . . . I always knew

I had physical attraction to men. I chose to be gay. As far as gay identity goes, there are as many reasons people are gay as there are gays in a room . . . Sexuality is constructed not genetic, there is a story of discovery of sexuality and therefore identity. Some see it as genetic, they always knew they were different from the womb, for others it dawned on them later and it was a choice.'

Naming identity is difficult for some

In most cultures it is unacceptable to describe oneself as homosexual. The conflict felt by many gay and lesbian people between what they understand to be their 'true selves' and what society demands of them can be immense. Imagine having to pretend to be someone other than who you are. Here are the voices of some who experience their own gay identity as struggle, conflict, violence:

Joanna: 'Lesbian women in [my society] can't talk about it because of the gendered society. The State and the culture enforce Christianity so that we can't even picture lesbian women there.'

Simon: 'In my last term at college I commenced a relationship with a woman. She tried to understand my sexuality, and she accepted that it would be difficult for me to change. We had two years together. It gave me a taste of the world of heterosexual couples with social events, and family settings that I did not experience as a single guy. Many people wanted the relationship to succeed, especially relatives. But that added to the pressure that I felt. Many times I asked God, "What is the right thing to do? Should I try to go straight, to embrace the relationship fully and get married? Or should I end it? If so, should I end it sooner rather than later so as to let her get on with her life?' Eventually I decided not to prolong it . . .." When I look back at that relationship, I feel it illustrates the pain and confusion that people with a same sex orientation can feel. There is pain in every direction. Whether you try to go straight or you try to be a celibate homosexual, life is difficult. There are no easy answers. In my own life it is a case of learning to trust God and to be content with where I am, who I am and what God is doing in my life. It doesn't help to yearn for a different life; better to be content with what I have.'

Matthew, whom we have already met, similarly became engaged and finally broke off the engagement without explaining to his fiancée why he was doing so.

Jonathan married in response to society's expectations. He says: 'The question is which way to jump? An answer is to jump the way of male organs and let that make the decision. It's the decision which is expected, how society is built: the man with business life who the church demands to stay there . . . Married for life and no alternative . . . But within me was something different pulling constantly so that the chosen side was not . . . me. There was something within me, something different making me a liar. My life with God and everything it represented was false. The decision to lead a gay lifestyle was a choice to move over the other side. I sacrificed comfort [and lived with] the thought that God was not going to accept me. But I knew that [it was that understanding] of God which was too small to accept me.'

James: 'By the time my son was born, I had, largely through my wife's influence, found a new kind of spirituality . . . we met three other couples, each on the periphery of the church, each for their own reasons. We would meet each week at church time in one or other's houses and have an alternative worship experience. This small group became really strong, though I never felt free to mention my sexual orientation. I know that it was discussed in my absence and that there was a range of acceptance levels right from total acceptance to abhorrence.'

This conflict between the true self and the demands of society have led some gay and lesbian people to attempt suicide.

Please follow the same pattern of reading, pausing and reflecting

Joanna: 'Lesbian women are raped by family members to remind them what their place is or kicked out of the house. This results in many young gay people on the streets.'

Matthew: 'For all of my teenage years, I tried desperately to deny the fact that I was gay. All of my friends were straight, I had girlfriends, I did all of the things that straight teenagers were supposed to do. I did all this in the desperate hope that I would become straight. The last thing in the world that I wanted was to be gay. I felt totally worthless. I remember thinking that even people who committed murders were better than I was because at least they were straight. I tried to commit suicide one night when my best friend went to bed with his girlfriend at a party. I hated myself so much for wishing it was me that he took to bed that I thought the only solution was for me to be dead. Thankfully, those times are in the past and I reflect on them now only to highlight the fact that being gay was for me the furthest thing away from a choice.'

Bartimaeus: 'In the city I was confused. I lived a homosexual life. I tried men. I was not content, I tried to get answers. It was big. I was trying to find my identity and answer my questions. I turned to violence on the streets. If I talk with people and they called me poofter I punched them. My homosexual life was a secret. I had a relationship with this Muslim guy for over a year. I was still searching and asking the questions. Was I supposed to be a born a woman? Sometimes I feel like a woman, sometimes a man. It was all secret. I was sick in heart, sick in heart . . . I had tried to commit suicide; I got a rope, I was drinking and sniffing. So I was skinny. I put the rope round my neck and jumped and then a fear grabbed me, I swung my legs to reach the seat and I untied the rope. It was the prayers of those saints which saved me. I collected all the suicide letters and burned them.'

Rufus:

'One particular evening I went out with some of the Italians for dinner. Days later a young man traced me out and demanded 1 million naira. He allegedly accused one of the Italian experts of groping him, which to the best of my knowledge was not true. He went further to accuse me of planning the whole incident. He threatened to do bodily harm to my person if I didn't let him have his blackmail fee from the Italian.

'I didn't take the threat as seriously as I ought to have until this young man along with several other men attacked me on New Year's Eve, beating me almost unconscious, taking my phone, camera and money. The injuries I sustained during the beating have left me with physical and emotional scars for life.

'I decided to get really involved in church activities on campus thinking it would be a safe place to hide. Was I wrong?! I was welcomed with the preaching of my early years that homosexuality is a sin all over again! I felt like I was between the devil and the deep blue sea, the depression now sets in again. This time I tried to commit suicide by taking an overdose of sleeping pills. If not for the timely intervention of my room mate who discovered me and took me to the campus clinic where I recovered. I probably would have died.'

Exercise

What we have done so far in this section is introduce you to cameos of people's stories which contain elements of their understanding of their human identity. The risk in doing this is that you hear only what we, the authors, want to say rather than the unique voices of those who have spoken to us or who have allowed their stories to be told.

Before you move on to the discussion on Christian identity, prayerfully read *either* Akan's story *or* Simon's story at the end of this chapter in the Resources section.

Christian Identity: Who am I in Christ?

'If anyone is in Christ they are a new creation, the old has passed away, the new has come!' (2 Corinthians 5.17).

'As many of you as were baptized into Christ have put on Christ. There is neither Jew nor Greek, there is neither slave nor free, there is neither male or female; for you are all one in Christ Jesus' (Galatians 3.26–28).

'Just as the body is one and has many members, and all the members of the body, though many are one body, so it is with Christ. For by one Spirit we were baptized into one body – Jews or Greeks, slaves or free – and were made to drink of the one Spirit' (1 Corinthians 12.12–13).

Let us listen again to some of the people we have already met speak about how they understand their identity in Christ as gay and lesbian people.

Paul: 'My primary identity is as a Christian and not as a gay person but I am forced the other way round because I am not so welcome any more.'

Isaac: 'Being in Christ means to share in the life of the Blessed Trinity, even if I do so very unconsciously – at least in this world. And the fact that God and I are compatible in this way shows that I am made in his image, and that I shall grow and change from glory to glory in him and with him throughout eternity. It also means that God dwells in me even now, and that I am called to manifest him in the world.'

Phillip: 'Belonging to the church was where I discovered who I was. Belonging to other groups tells me who I am. In the Church our identity is found through baptism, being in Christ is the basic and every individual brings a whole host of their own identities to this. I bring all which makes me who I am.'

Rufus: 'I am at a point in my life where I can proudly say I am a gay Christian who is worthy of God's love. No approval desired or required of anybody except my Master, Lord and Saviour, Jesus Christ who died on the cross of Calvary to redeem my soul.'

Persis: 'The whole of creation is reconciled in Christ, every atom, molecule is charged. The church is merely the community response, it is true of all people, even the stuff we can't connect with. It is held in the love of God somehow, all sexuality, every struggle of sexual beings.'

Bartimaeus: 'My identity is in Christ. He does not see heterosexual or gay. At the heart there is no such thing as heterosexual or lesbian. We are created male and female. The Bible is the living testimony. I see myself as a human being created by God, a man, with some feminine parts we all have but that does not mean homosexual . . .'

Some of the voices you have just heard speak about Christian identity as an individual identity; others locate it in the church. This raises questions for us about the corporate and communal character of identity. We do not define ourselves simply as individuals, either in the case of human identity (belonging to the human family) or of Christian identity (belonging to the Christian family). Because some parts of the church are perceived as unwelcoming to gay and lesbian people belonging to the church can also be a conflicted experience for them.

Kiki: 'Actually the church became the last place I wanted to go here with the members of the Christ family making me feel unwanted.'

Luke: 'If you come out within an ordinary church setting there is an issue whether you are actually a Christian, which is a pretty big thing. Suddenly your Christian faith is questioned.'

Paul: 'In the church 200 years ago this was not called an issue because there was a huge space but now there is less space. So there is reason to live a cautious life. It is a tension when you are "out", there are stressors for the church and once you [leave the church] . . . you are out of the way.'

Rufus: 'My whole life, what I desired the most was to be worthy of God's love, but how could this come to be when all I hear from the only place I go for refuge (the church) is total condemnation?'

David: 'I firmly believe in the Christian principle of life after death and the imminent return of our Lord Jesus Christ. I also believe in the work of the Holy Spirit in the life of the believer. For some reason I am also gay – but that does not negate my faith. I mentioned my lack of hope in the church – but I have a hope in a future in God and Christ. In our faith we have the resources to cope with whatever 'befalls' us. In my case being gay and disabled . . . It is very sad that the churches seek to 'gay bash' – and I have experienced that many times. It seems that the church sets itself up as judge and jury, rather than emphasizing our Lord's message to "Come unto me".'

Anna: 'At [our church we] learnt to look at the Scriptures in more depth. We were hungry and we have learned and grown. [The ministers] have helped us to find a more contextual understanding of key passages which have been hurled at people calling them abomination, rejected and perverts. The desperate fear says, "Does God love me?", "Am I going to hell?" To get me out of that deep dark box under-standing of faith, to see it as part of my personhood. How did I define myself and face God who supposedly hates people because they feel what I feel?'

In a time of silence, please pray for the church, the body of Christ, when we have failed to be what we claim to be.

Having listened to these descriptions of painful rejection, please think about times when the church has fulfilled the vocation to be inclusive and hospitable.

Does Christian identity involve change?

What it means to be 'in Christ' is not universally agreed. Some Christians believe that being a Christian involves healing from homosexual identity which is described as 'sexual brokenness':

Bartimaeus: 'I went to Living Waters and God released me . . . My older brother [who had abused me when I was a child], I went to him and embraced him. When he saw me coming he knew I was going to talk with him about it. I embraced him and affirmed him. He said: "How do you do it?" I said, "Jesus." I affirmed him even though he ruined my life. I said, "I love you and respect you."

'Through Living Waters the Lord restored all the things I missed in my child-hood.

'Some people say to me, "Does homosexual thought cross your mind?" Yes, when the thought crosses my mind it is temptation. I call on the power of God, you cannot go past that. I know where I stand in Christ . . . It was a testimony to what God can do . . . My identity is in Christ.'

Simon faithfully sought change. Let us listen to him.

Simon:

'I think Exodus[4] does a great job with gays who are willing and able to change. I believe in the power of God to change lives and I followed all the steps – the prayers, dealing with my parents, forgiveness – but I did not change to being het-erosexual. I know that some do change, and even get married, but many retain the same-sex orientation. I believed God could have changed me, but he didn't. It left me realizing I had to work with what I had.'

Some people have had the need to change imposed on them:

> **Nathaniel:** '[I was] told that they loved me but it was clear it was wrong and that I needed to get rid of the evil. [They had] a prayer group and they brought in another pastor for an exorcism. This was traumatizing.'

> **Matthew:** 'I spoke to a church pastor. I was put through an exorcism. The process was horrific and very damaging. I was not cured.'

Christian understanding of human identity

We have heard the experiences of a number of people of what it means to them to be Christian and gay or lesbian. Now we need to ask how Christianity understands what it means to be human. There are, of course, many theological possibilities in answering the question, for example humanity as covenant partners with God. Perhaps the most significant understanding of what it means to be human is the idea of humanity as being in some sense 'the image of God'. What, however, does this mean?

Theologies of liberation, in particular, have reminded us that too often the image of God has been seen to be the image of those who are dominant in church and society – what one writer has referred to as free, heterosexual (and we might add 'white') men.[5] This is simply creating God in our own image. Who or what then is the image of God? Answers to the question have usually fallen into two broad categories. The first gives priority to the stories in Genesis 2 and 3 of the creation and 'fall' and uses Adam as the archetype of what it means to be human. The second approach gives priority to humanity as redeemed in Christ, and views Jesus as the archetype.

Adam as archetype

The classic exposition of the first category (Adam as archetype) was articulated in western Christianity by Augustine. In Augustine's early writing against the Manicheans he followed Origen in seeing human beings as created first as a male and female unity. The 'image of God' was constituted by the interior intellect. Later he changed his ideas and wrote that male and female differentiation was created from the beginning and that gender hierarchy – the female subordinate to the first created male – was part of the original design. He believed that both men and women have intellects but the woman represents the inferior, subordinate part of humanity:

> . . . the woman together with her own husband is the image of God, so that the whole substance may be one image, but when she is referred to separately in her quality as helpmeet, which regards the woman alone, then she is not the image of God, but as regards the male alone, he is the image of God as fully and completely as when the woman too is joined with him in one. (Augustine, *De Trinitate* 7.7.10)

Responding to Pelagius from the account of creation in Genesis 2 and 3 Augustine taught that:

- Adam was the pinnacle of creation, created for relationship with God, blessed with righteousness and perfection, but who fell from this state, thus bringing sin into the heart of human existence.
- Gender hierarchy was part of God's original creation (Adam first then Eve).
- Adam and Eve would not have died if there had not been the first sin.
- Adam was not deceived by Eve, but because he was kind, he went along with her so that she wouldn't be punished alone.
- Through the 'fall' the *Imago Dei* was lost and henceforth all humans were marked from birth with original sin.

This anthropology came to dominate both modern Catholic and Reformed theology – to the extent that other ideas have by and large been lost. However, the teachings of some of the pre-Augustinian theologians may be usefully distinguished from Augustine's views. For example:

- Irenaeus taught that although the triune God created humanity in the divine image, human beings are not the true image of God. The true image is the Son. Furthermore the image is not something 'in' humanity, but the direction in which we are to grow. For Irenaeus, Adam and Eve were not created perfect, but created so that they could grow into what God called them to be, namely perfect relationship with God (Irenaeus, *Epideixis*).
- Clement of Alexandria distinguished between the divine image and likeness: all human beings are created in the image of God and are called to grow into the likeness of God by cultivating rational control over passions of the body (Clement, *Stromata* 2, 23 and 3, 16).
- Gregory of Nyssa understood the term 'image of God' in Genesis 1.27 to refer to the purely spiritual being, a reflection of the divine Logos, lacking mortal body and gender. However, God anticipated that this intellectual being would choose disobedience and so gender duality was added by God in anticipation of the fall. Only through virginity could a person begin to restore the self to its original nature and grow into the likeness of God (Gregory of Nyssa, *On the Making of Man*, 387–427).

Jesus as archetype

Jesus as the image of God offers us a different starting point. Christianity affirms that Jesus is the revelation of God and therefore the perfect *Imago Dei*. (See for example Colossians 1.15 and 2 Corinthians 4.4). Paul contrasts the old Adam and Jesus as the 'new' Adam (see Romans 5.12–21). The point he is making is that humanity no longer uses Adam as its point of reference, but Jesus. Being 'in Christ' is what it means to be human, rather than trying (and failing) to obey the law of Moses. This idea was expressed by Karl Barth when he noted that being Christian is what it means to be fully human.[6]

Starting to understand our identity in Christ (rather than in Adam) has some very important consequences:

1 We also proclaim Jesus as God, part of the Trinity (or as Moltmann[7] would say, community), if we base our anthropology on Jesus we also recognize that to be human and in the image of God means to be in community as the Trinity is community.

2 The historical Jesus gives us a model for what it means to be the image of God – caring, healing, proclaiming, challenging injustice. In other words being the *Imago Dei* is not a set of ontological categories but implies a Christ-like way of life. Leonardo Boff particularly explores this understanding.[8]

3 As Augustine pointed out, the 'body of Christ' refers not just to the historical Jesus of Nazareth but also the gathered Christian community, the church. What this suggests for an anthropology based on Jesus is that we discover who we are (our identity) in the church – a community of differently gifted people who are called to be bread, light and hope for the world.

What are gay and lesbian people saying to the church?

It is a myth of Western thought that we are individuals separated from one another: consider a mother and child. Where does the self end and the other begin? Consciously and unconsciously we become part of one another. In Southern Africa there is an expression which translated is 'I am because we are.'

At its best, this is what the Anglican Church is like, where we make room for differences and we hold on to one another despite differences.

Through this chapter you have listened to the voices of some gay and lesbian people. You may have appreciated some of the things you heard; you may have been offended by others. The question which remains is, How can we share our common identity as the Body of Christ, in order to bring his hope and love to the world together? In other words, how can we be 'the Church' and fulfil the mission of the Church? Some of the people you have met have some suggestions.

Modisa: 'In our search for a church I went to several churches and phoned several ministers to explain that my partner and I are gay and we wanted to come back to church. Finally I spoke to the priest, who invited me to come and talk to him. I told him our whole story and his only response was "Come and see if you like us."

'The church has a wonderful choir. Music is very important to me. The minister also made a conscious effort to welcome us. He would meet us at the church door and showed us we were welcome. His actions made me feel like I was in a warm bath. The congregation accepted us because the minister did. He didn't preach or talk about gay issues, but just by his actions he showed we were welcome.'

Simon: 'I am looking for different patterns of friendship which include some degree of intimacy. These friendships are difficult to find, whether with straight guys or with other Christian homosexuals.

'I hope that I will be content with what God has given me; to be thankful, and to go on taking opportunities to serve God and people. To build friendships; to give to others the best that I can give. I am not counting on relationships or intimacy because I know that's too much to expect or even hope for. I don't expect anything from anyone.

'[I hope that the church] would live out what the Bible teaches; that it would become a transforming force by spreading the good news of God's grace and faithfulness. In regard to homosexual people I hope that the church will be challenged to accept and care; to love the sinner and not the sin. Many churches seem unwelcoming to un-churched people. People walk in and walk out and fail to connect. It's especially true for homosexuals.'

Matthew and Nathaniel: 'We believe in Jesus as Saviour and live life with Jesus as part of it and that the Bible is for [our]guidance. I [Matthew] wake up in the morning and pray about the things [I] have to do.

'[We believe] God wants life in relationships, in committed relationships [but] we are not offered the option of steady committed relationship. We would like the church to offer these relationships. [Our relationship] is not about sex but about sharing the fullness of life.'

Lydia: '[I think] we are all equal in the eyes of God, unified in our mission. I want to have a deep sense that I am equal to any person sitting next to me. [This would be shown by having] equal status within church statutes.

'We can't have a civil union at St A's . . . In a sense talking about things makes us equal members. Equal in church and equal in relationship to God but I know they are words and not reality.

'[I hope that] there will be a more honest discussion within the Anglican Church so that some of these myths and misunderstandings about gay people can be dispelled. That there will be recognition that we basically want the same as others and do not have strange spiritual beliefs and that we can actually learn from one another.

'[I hope that] there will be an understanding of diversity, overcoming obstacles, persevering through, finding solutions to problems. Gay Christians have all got stories of survival against the odds, these stories are so powerful. Gay people have enormous skills, intuition, empathy, deep compassion and understanding of suffering.'

Persis: 'When Gene was elected it meant so much to me. My sadness about the church is that I have no place to stand. There is no safe place for gays. I want a bishop to say it. We need to find a place to belong. There are so few in the church and that is why Gene Robinson moves me.'

Paul: 'I don't just want to be in a gay world, so I hope that the spaces in the Christian community will be for as wide a spectrum as possible. I hope that there will continue to be genuine listening. That everyone will do some listening so that we can become more authentic as the Christian Church.'

Some of our reflections

1   The Anglican Communion is diverse in a range of ways. These narratives have shown us that identity requires generous relationships in which to grow, and that identity in Christ has diverse expressions. Can you think about ways in

which your diocese has embraced various expressions of difference and expressed diversity?

2 'Therefore, as God's chosen people, holy and dearly loved, clothe yourselves with compassion, kindness, humility, gentleness and patience. Bear with each other and forgive whatever grievances you may have against one another. Forgive all these as the Lord forgave you. And over all these virtues put on love which binds them together in perfect unity' (Colossians 3.12–14). Paul's exhortation reminds us to attend to our own lives in the same way as we attend to the life of another. Paul provides us with a description of the clothing in which to meet people in a pastoral setting. Clothing which is woven in patience, compassion, kindness and gentleness and which is a visible expression of our fundamental identity in Christ. We are icons of Jesus.

3 Throughout this chapter we have worked with an understanding that identities are both created and constructed. Therefore we respond, in a framework which recognizes that people grow into their potential in multiple social relationships and settings one of which, for those in Christ, is the Church. The Church is the principal setting we are addressing here because of our roles within it. Our multiple contexts, including different cultures, will shape appropriate pastoral responses. This will mean that where identity is produced collectively pastoral responses will be created accordingly rather than imposing a western response to the individual. We are cautioned to be careful in applying ideas across geographical and theological locations. Responses to gay and lesbian people may be part of wider conversations on self-determination for indigenous people.

4 In many cultures, non-Western and Western, sharing food is central to building community and shaping the identity of participants. Meals demonstrate hospitality and inclusion. Drawing on our identity in Christ we share the Eucharistic feast to re-member ourselves in this identity. In the liturgy of Aotearoa, New Zealand and Polynesia, we say:

> E te whanau, we are the body of Christ,
> By one Spirit we were baptized into one body,
> Keep the unity of the Spirit in the bond of peace.
> Amen. We are bound by the love of Christ.

An Invitation to Prayer

As we close our time with you, we would like to gather with you and the people in whose lives we have been guests. We have been helped to formulate the prayers through the words of some of the people to whom we have listened.

We pray to the Father in the power of the Spirit and in union with Christ.

With thanksgiving we name Matthew; Nathaniel; Simon; Persis; Phillip; Isaac; Kiki; Lydia; Anna; Titus; Bartimaeus; Aaron; Johannes; Isaiah; James; Jonathan; Paul; Zac; Joshua; One; Modisa; Joanna; Luke; David; Hemi; Ara; Akan; Rufus.

Through listening with agape to people in the text and in conversation we have experienced many responses. With thanksgiving we name our responses.

Pause.

We give you thanks for these and all your gifts. We re-present gay and lesbian people through these phrases and pray with them
'We don't talk about sex in our culture. It is taboo and I was confused.'
May we create communities where children and people who are most vulnerable find fullness of life.

'I can say in all honesty that I have had an extremely difficult life and the only thing which has made this possible is God himself.'
May we each know our dependence on you.

'I have been to the bottom of the trough and I am not afraid of anyone's questions.'
May we bear one another's burdens and so fulfil the law of Christ.

'I am tired of being an issue not a person.'
May we remember that we and all your people are created for your good purpose.

Holy and eternal God,
In you we live and move and have our being.
In all our cares and occupations,
Guide and govern us by your Spirit,
That we may both remember and reveal your presence;
through our Saviour Jesus Christ.
Amen.

Hear what the Spirit is saying to the Church.

Thanks be to God.

Resources

1. The Formation of Identity

Scholars across a number of disciplines, for example theology, psychology, anthropology, political studies, sociology, feminist theory and linguistics, are paying attention to human identity and how identity may be understood. The questions they face are complex. For example: Is there a clear, authentic set of characteristics that may be used to establish identity, whether the identity is sexual, national, racial or ethnic? Or is identity a fluid, changing, contextually bound concept? We may consider the example of what it means to be 'black'. It is often assumed that this is an enduring trans-historical and trans-cultural description. Yet as the recent history of South Africa reveals, 'black' is by no means a settled category, at times meaning anyone who is not white, at others excluding people of Asian descent and people of mixed-race descent. Indeed even the description 'person' may be seen to be culturally and contextually shaped. Slaves, women and children, for example, were not 'persons' in many Near and Middle Eastern cultures in biblical times. Conversely, in some countries for legal purposes a company may be said to be a person.

Another set of questions revolves around the place of our embodiedness in the understanding of our identity. Has identity to do with physical attributes such as sex, size, shape, skin colour? Is identity affected or even defined by physical disability? Or has identity nothing to do with these 'surface' attributes and rather with the capacity to reason? If physical attributes contribute to identity, what part do they play? Are these physical attributes themselves social or cultural constructs? For example, Madan Sarup[9] contends that 'race' (which he always writes in inverted commas to indicate that the term is problematic) is not a biological or scientifically verifiable fact. James Cone of course recognizes this when he describes Jesus as black.[10]

Discussions around identity are underpinned by a tension between essentialist and non-essentialist or constructionist perspectives. The term 'essentialist' is generally employed when the categories of race, class, sex, sexual orientation, and so on are seen to be innate. Against this view of there being some 'essential' nature of, for example, race or sex, is the constructionist view, which posits that these categories are social and cultural constructs. It should be noted that the terms 'essentialist' and 'constructionist' when applied to identity are not unproblematic. Too often they have been set in opposition to one another, whereas a number of writers point out that more appropriately the two positions should be seen as two ends of a continuum. Likewise even constructionists often rely upon 'essential' terms such as 'woman' or 'history' or 'culture' for their arguments.

Whatever approach one takes to the question of identity, one inevitably comes to the realization that identity is somehow related to another – whether the other be mother, history, language, institution, person, text or God. Identity is relational. Identity is relational even (and some would argue, particularly) when relationship is denied or ignored. As John Caputo has it:

> . . . identity is not the self identity of a thing . . . but implies a difference within identity. That is the identity of a culture is a way of being different from itself; a culture is different from itself . . . the person is different from itself. Once you take into account this inner and outer difference, then you pay attention to the other and you understand that fighting for your own identity is not exclusive of another identity [but] is open to another identity.[11]

In many societies and cultures this goes without saying. Most of the cultures of Southern Africa, for example, understand that identity is not individual but communal – 'I am because we are.'

Identity is multiple and proliferating and the self is a self- (or selves-)-in-process. We need also to remind ourselves that differentiation takes place not only within the self and between ourselves and others, but between others too. In other words just as 'I' am not singular in my identity, the other is not a generalizable other. There are often many 'others' – for example 'woman' as the other to man is not a generalizable other.

Thus it has been said that Woman is a 'name' . . . that makes woman appear to be the same kind of unitary subject as was the male subject of philosophical and political discourse and that works to suppress all other differences (race, class, sexual choice). It uses the frame of gender to create a false identity (Benjamin 1995:11).

Sexual orientation is no different. It is too easy to categorize (and does violence to) 'the gay man', 'the lesbian experience' or whatever other category of identification we choose to use as a label.

2. Two stories

(These are the stories which are referred to in the exercise earlier in this chapter.)

Akan's story

'I am Akan, a group leader in Changing Attitude Nigeria (CAN). CAN is a pressure group within the Church of Nigeria (Anglican Communion), a group which seeks for the protection and rights of gay, lesbian, bisexual and transgendered people at large.

'I am from Nkanu Local Government Area of Enugu state, Nigeria. I was born into a family of six of which I am the third child. I have four brothers and a sister. Though I was born into a family who belonged with the Assemblies of God family I later became a member of the Anglican family here in Jos.

'Both my parents are still alive and they both know about my sexuality. They have refused to say anything about it to me apart from my mum, who always in her prayer makes mention of it and always rebuke that spirit in our house saying it's an evil spirit, but never has she said it to me.

'Right from my younger age I have noticed that I have feelings for the same sex as myself. When I see men I fall for them more easily than a female. So I will say that I was born with it, it is an inborn thing. I never made myself that way, but I grew up to find myself this way. I know very well that God made me this way. One thing I know I did when I knew what I was – I never condemned myself. I have always loved the way I am and nobody can tell me anything that will make me change my mind. It is something that I feel in me and I love myself. I have seen occasions when people insult gay people and I begin to ask myself why? I ask different questions like, AM I NOT HUMAN like them? Most especially questions are asked in a place like Nigeria where it is seen as a taboo, but that has not given me any reason to deny myself.

'The Bible has said so many things about gay people which I am not here to talk about, because if God so loved me and made me this way, then the best thing for me is to love myself and serve God who has made me this way.

'As I can recall very well, in the year 2003, I went with some of my friends to a party in Port Harcourt where I was arrested with some others and we spent two good weeks in the police cell. Then it was a hard time for me, because my father got to know about it but as I have said before, he never said anything to me. If not for God's intervention and some people who stood by us then, it would have been a different story. I was there in person and I can tell how it feels like when your society does not accept you and you have a lot to offer to your society. You just feel like an outcast. But I have always drawn courage from people like Mr Mac-Iyalla who have been bold to come out from the closet.

'Now after that incident in Port Harcourt, my father told me to leave my home base town of Warri and go back to school for my direct entry which I was not ready to do then. He also told me not to make gay friends again, which I know I can't do without.

'But back in Jos I got the invitation to attend the first meeting of CAN in Abuja, from 25 to 27 November 2005. For the first time in my life I noticed gay Christians coming together to form a group. I never imagined it happening in my life and it made me feel relieved. I asked myself this question, How can Christians who are gays come together to form a group? For the first time I found myself being accepted and also that I can work for God and still be myself.

'With that spirit I came back to Jos and opened the CAN chapter of Jos group which has been growing in numbers. But there was a shock waiting for me, because I forgot I was still in Nigeria and people here have a different view of it. The meeting was always held in my room and each Sunday my room was full with gay people having our meetings, not knowing that people around have been watching and also reported the issue to my landlord who told me to leave his house. That was a trying moment for me. I wrote to the group then and I was assisted in some ways, only for me again to find out that I have also been reported to my church in which I am a member of the choir and I was also told to leave the choir.

'Then I asked myself again, does God really hate me that much? I never gave up, I joined the Anglican family but in a more careful way to also protect myself. I left the compound and moved to another place where I am now, but our meetings are no longer held in my house but in a member's house who feels comfortable with it, and it has been moving fine.

'One thing about life is that people will never stop talking about you until you die. I hear a lot about me and I take it as a way of making people know who I am and also come to accept me.

'There is one thing I always encourage myself with, that was when I saw Rev Colin and Rev Rufus at our last meeting in Togo and also Mr Mac. When I saw them I got courage from them to keep up the good work. It is not easy to be gay in Nigeria and accept yourself, but with God on our side we, the CAN leaders and members shall get to our destination.

'I must not fail to say here that the Jos group of CAN is growing at a rate we have never imagined. God is helping us and we look forward to a day when we shall live as others in our country Nigeria.'

Simon's story

'I was raised as a missionary kid with a strong Christian heritage. It was devastating to realize at fourteen that homosexuality was my sexual preference. I was saying in my prayers, "How can this be? How can God use me or love me the way he would someone who is straight? How can I live with this?"

'My life was complicated further by being a third culture person. (When you are brought up in a different culture and you are not from your parents' culture which you return to, it is like having a third culture of your own.) For me the teenage years were painful. I was an outcast because of my different background and worldview. And I felt I would be doubly outcast if I owned up to being gay. So I did not talk about it, not to friends, who were few, or parents or pastors.

'After leaving home I moved a number of times over eight or nine years. I was a student, then unemployed, then working, then unemployed again. I did voluntary work for a charity and for my church in Auckland. I was designated the role of dealing with people who walked in off the street. There were many in an inner-city church.

'I met a transsexual. He came to church to find out what it was all about; he was motivated by having a boyfriend who was being counselled by the pastor. Interaction with this person challenged me to look at life on "the other side of the tracks".

'Around then I was impacted by the verse in 2 Corinthians 12: "God's power is made perfect in weakness". Paul was talking about his thorn in the flesh. We don't know what his was but I knew mine. God's power was demonstrated in Paul's weakness and I realized that God could use mine; my sexual orientation to be a bridge into the lives of others with that orientation. If God could use me it would be the Holy Spirit's work, not mine. But to do that work I needed to be open about myself.

'I went into the gay scene with a mission. I went to "K Road", to meet with trans-sexuals and was invited into their homes. I was introduced to gay bars and night clubs. I made friends and learned about the gay scene – how to relate in the gay culture. I learnt that in the gay culture, touch is crucial. It is integral to communication. People need more than words. Gays, in general, experience intimacy deprivation . . .

'During this time the pastor challenged me to do the Exodus programme. He wanted me to have more support and to explore personal issues. I went through the whole course and found it helpful in a number of ways. It gave me insight into the homosexual condition; how it develops. It helped me to work through these issues with my parents. It emphasized the power of God to heal hurts and remove guilt.

'I went to Bible College for three years. I was still at the early stages of talking openly. I concentrated on my studies and only related on a shallow level with fellow students. I was always aware that I needed to be careful about who I opened up to.

'I made a few friends, mainly female friends. (It is often easier for homosexual males to open up to females. I think this is because there is not so much concern about whether or not they like you.)

'In my third year I was elected student leader. I gave a devotion in which I explained how I could relate to the woman in Luke 7.36–50, because I am a sinner saved by God's grace in spite of my sexual orientation. It was a significant moment for me and for some of the people listening. Some thanked me later; others did not know what to say. Some were critical. They were critical of me for not being clearly against homosexuality. You have to expect a spectrum of responses from any audience, so it was not surprising.'

Notes

1 *The Official Report of the Lambeth Conference 1998* (Pennsylvania: Morehouse, 1998), 94–5.

2 'The St Andrew's Day Statement' available online: http://www.ceec.info/library/positional/St%20Andrew's%20Day%20Statement.rtf.

3 Anthony Thiselton, *Interpreting God and the Postmodern Self: On Meaning, Manipulation and Promise* (Grand Rapids: Eerdmans, 1997), 51.

4 Exodus International is an organization that serves many countries. See http://www.exodus-international.org/.

5 Steve de Gruchy, 'Human Being in Christ: resources for an inclusive anthropology' in

P. Germond and S. de Gruchy (eds), *Aliens in the Household of God: homosexuality and Christian Faith in South Africa* (CApe Town: David Philip, 1997), 233.

6   Karl Barth, *Church Dogmatics Vol. III* (Edinburgh: T&T Clark, 1956).
7   Jürgen Moltmann, *The Trinity and the Kingdom of God* (London: SCM Press, 1981).
8   Leonardo Boff, *Safe on the Edge: Religion and Marginalized Existence* (San Francisco: Harper and Row).
9   Madan Sarup 1996, page 171.
10   James Cone, *A Black Theology of Liberation* (Philadelphia: J.B. Lippincott, 1970).
11   John Caputo 1997 13.

Chapter 7

Christian Spirituality and Sexuality

Joseph Galgalo and Debbie Royals

Introduction

One way of describing what we are engaged in as a Communion and in using the resources of this book is the task of spiritual discernment. Among the claims being made by some Anglicans is that they have experienced the Spirit of God at work in the lives and relationships of people in same-sex unions. The Episcopal Church, when asked in the Windsor Report to explain 'how a person living in a same-gender union may be considered eligible to lead a flock of Christ', claimed that 'Christian congregations have sought to celebrate and bless same-sex unions because these exclusive, life-long, unions of fidelity and care for each other have been experienced as holy.'[1] This chapter seeks to explore claims such as these by considering questions relating to spirituality and sexuality.

More than with any other chapter in the book this chapter consciously brought together two people whose understanding and experience of same-sex relationships was quite different and asked them to get to know and listen to each other. **Debbie Royals** wholeheartedly owns the statement quoted above from *To Set Our Hope On Christ*. Her spirituality is informed by living a life of commitment to Christ as an indigenous person who is in a covenanted relationship with her female partner. **Joseph Galgalo**, in contrast, finds it difficult to comprehend as Christian any claim that a same-sex union can be holy. He brings to this conversation a depth of spirituality which emerges from his evangelical heritage in the Church of Kenya and from his understanding of the Christian heritage through his insightful academic study of the Church Fathers. What they have in common is a desire to hear each other and the clarity, personal relationship with Christ and academic ability that enables them to respond to each other.

Joseph and **Debbie** came together for a week to listen to one another, work together, travel together, read the Scripture together and pray with and for one another. This was one of the most uncertain of all the partnerships established in the creation of these resources. There was no guarantee that they would find any common ground. They were specifically asked not to seek a compromise. In contrast to most of the other chapters no joint statement was expected. The goal was to clarify both the differences between them and those things they hold in common. During the week they met with members of the Iona Community – a dispersed Christian ecumenical community working for peace and social justice, rebuilding of community and the renewal of worship – who were able to talk about their experiences of the spiritual life as lesbian and gay people within their inclusive community of prayer and action. **Joseph** and **Debbie** asked hard questions of those they met and of one another. They did so, however, in a spirit of mutual respect and without trying to diminish or victimize the other.

This chapter is written in the form of a conversation which follows the flow of the dialogue of the final day. It covers a wide range of crucial questions – their understandings of spirituality and sexuality and the relationship between them, the nature of gender identity (Debbie identifies as a Two Spirit person) and how sexuality and spirituality relate to personhood, various expressions of spirituality and sexuality in different relationship patterns and in different cultures, and finally how these themes relate to such important theological concerns as creation, holiness, the example of Jesus and covenant. As with the earlier chapters, this can only provide an introduction to these major themes. For that conversation both Phil Groves and Adrian Chatfield were privileged to be present. They heard the conversation and occasionally asked questions but the conversation was between **Debbie** and **Joseph**. Common ground was found, but differences are not papered over or hidden. In what follows **Joseph** and **Debbie** speak for themselves. But this conversation is not over. No resolution was reached but both trust in Jesus Christ who is to reconcile all things (Colossians 1.19–20).

As you read, listen carefully to what they are saying to each other and consider how you would have joined in the conversation if you were present. Then see if you can find ways in which you can enter similar conversations and dialogue with other Christians who view things quite differently from you. Both **Debbie** and **Joseph** learnt more about their own spiritual journey from the encounter. We hope that as you share in some of that encounter and pray as you read their conversation and the Scriptures to which they refer that your own relationship with Christ will also be enriched and enlivened.

Christian Spirituality and Sexuality

A conversation between a Kenyan Evangelical Anglican minister and a Native American woman who is a priest and in a committed relationship with a woman.

Spirituality

Joseph:

Spirituality describes the principles and disciplines that guide our life in God, through Christ with the Holy Spirit, in starting, maintaining and enriching our personal and corporate relationship with God in Christ. This can be expressed in different ways but commonly in worship, life of prayer, proclamation, *koinonia* and mission. As 1 John 1.1–4 puts it, it is a declaration of what was received, experienced and witnessed as the 'word of life' and living life in reality of this received truth. Spirituality is a journey into truth, the acquiescence towards God where harmony of the personhood as the totality of bodily and spiritual reality is achieved in communion with God. It embodies beliefs and practices such as religious experiences, worship, and confession of faith, which necessarily incorporates, informs and shapes our ethics, morality and doctrines. This is a 'typical' Christian traditional understanding of spirituality.

Debbie:

Yes, I agree this is a Western Christian view of spirituality but I would like to add one point. Spiritual reality is achieved in communion with God and each other. God set before us, in creation, the invitation to be with God and with each other.

Let me first say that I cannot and do not speak for all Native Americans or all Indigenous people. I can only offer what I have come to understand through my culture and faith about the subject we address here. For me spirituality includes relationship with God the Creator though and with all of creation. It is a way of life inseparable from any part of creation and directly linking life and living to our Creator. The living 'word' is inherent in creation and is experienced as learning, knowledge, understanding and unity in diversity. The beliefs and practices expressed in prayer, song, and dance – through and with the body – fortify what God has already made perfect while living in the ambiguity that presents opportunities for learning, knowing and understanding – the true essence of life. The spirituality of Indigenous thought perceives all things with essence and therefore spiritual, all things in relationship to the other and therefore spiritual, and all things of God and therefore good.

We also realize that within creation there are things that are not of God but of man. The essence of God in what is good is obvious. It can also be obvious where God is not present. The more subtle places call for us to be discerning and open allowing that we might seek to know or understand those things that we may not have previously known or understood and therefore becoming closer to God and creation.

Joseph:

'Good' may be the proper due of God's creation, but in reality we know that there is a lot that is evil and anything but good in the fallen world in which find ourselves. We therefore maintain – all things are not necessarily spiritual, but that spirituality is realized in positive response to God's invitation to be in relationship with him, a relationship which informs, defines, shapes and forms the basis of our relationship with the rest of creation. Two assumptions underlying this understanding are that human being is essentially oriented towards the spiritual, and, secondly, that God is the centre of that orientation. This raises for us a question, which will be part of the focus of this paper: does this assumption imply that sexuality, which primarily may focus on the sensual and is person-oriented much more than God-oriented, is opposed to spirituality? If, as we said, sexuality integrates bodily and spiritual dimensions of existence we submit that there is a connection between spirituality and sexuality – exploration of this connection will provide us with the other part of the focus of our discussion.

Debbie:

God created all things good. A relationship with God is expressed through our relationship to God and our relationship with others. Spirituality and sexuality are inseparable, in that our sexuality or the expression of our identity as understood in our sexuality, is part of that creation and therefore also good. This is why the words of John are so important:

> We declare to you what was from the beginning, what we have heard, what we have seen with our eyes, what we have looked at and touched with our hands, concerning the word of life. This life was revealed, and we have seen it and testify to it, and declare to you the eternal life that was with the Father and was revealed to us. We declare to you what we have seen and heard so that you also may have fellowship with us; and truly our fellowship is with the Father and with his Son Jesus Christ. We are writing these things so that our joy may be complete.
>
> This is the message we have heard from him and proclaim to you, that God is light and in him there is no darkness at all. If we say that we have fellowship with him while we are walking in darkness, we lie and do not do what is true; but if we walk in the light as he himself is in the light, we have fellowship with one another, and the blood of Jesus his Son cleanses us from all sin. If we say that we have no sin, we deceive ourselves, and the truth is not in us. If we confess our sins, he who is faithful and just will forgive us our sins and cleanse us from all unrighteousness. If we say that we have not sinned, we make him a liar, and his word is not in us. (1 John 1.1–10)

Spirituality is expressed in many forms. In the liturgical sense, spirituality finds its expression in community through, for example, common prayer and singing. An individual piety is put aside in preference for corporate prayer. This is also true in many Indigenous cultures where ceremonies include extended family members, clan members and entire communities. But it must be said that the corporate expression of spirituality is not more important, does not carry more weight than that of the individual, but rather that the expression of one's spirituality in union with another is in itself a rewarding and binding experience in the face of God. Take for example the Scripture passages that refer to the teaching of the Lord's Prayer.

> He was praying in a certain place, and after he had finished, one of his disciples said to him, 'Lord, teach us to pray, as John taught his disciples'. He said to them,
>
> > 'When you pray, say:
> > Father, hallowed be your name.
> > Your kingdom come.
> > Give us each day our daily bread.
> > And forgive us our sins,
> > for we ourselves forgive everyone indebted to us.
> > And do not bring us to the time of trial. (Luke 11.1–4)

Spirituality is also lived out in the mission of the church particularly as it applies to our call to serve God through others. For The Episcopal Church, as an example, the emphasis of our theology is based on the Baptismal Covenant. The Baptismal Covenant becomes the definition of mission – focusing on justice and peace, the dignity of every person and our willingness to reach beyond the barriers we have created to separate us from each other whether by race, class, sex, or any other wall. It is these central values that draw us together in all our diversity.

Sexuality

Joseph:

Let us continue with this discussion on one assumption that sex (as in being male or female) is the key word in sexuality. Sexuality, therefore, primarily involves sexual differentiation as male or female. It broadly encompasses expressions of gender identity, attitude to self and others, perceptions of maleness and femaleness and a whole range of physical, emotional and cognitive expressions of self.

Four key concepts stand out in this understanding of sexuality – sex (as in male, female), gender identity, perceptions, and expression of self in light of how we and others perceive our sexual identity. This is an important indicator that sexuality has both personal and social dimension with values, norms, expectations and boundaries or limitations. It has physiological, psychological, cultural and philosophical components as well as linguistic components with regard to terms or grammar that constitutes sexuality-talk or perception.

This may include attraction, desire, intimacy, love, trust, jealousy, procreation, commitment, friendship, companionship, worth as well as risks that may go with any of this. Potentially any of this could be expressed negatively as in resentment, mistrust, hate, fear, abuse, loneliness, and all sorts of destructive outcomes of any of this emotions or actions. The goodness of sexuality is expressed primarily in relationship with self and others, and like any other relationship carries the potential for danger. Also, human being is a totality of body and spirit, and since the physical and spiritual dimensions constitute the totality of who we are, sexuality then, being integral to our human nature, transcends bodily existence and integrates a spiritual dimension.

Debbie:

Sex is a biological term based on anatomy – genes, hormones. Its connection to God and creation are inherent in each being as a reflection of God's image and blessed as in Psalm 139. Gender is a social, cultural, psychological term with imposed and constructed roles related to identity.

Sexuality combines the biological and social perspectives. The balance between the two honours and empowers a dynamic, not static, understanding of the co-creative powers of God. Identity takes into account the individual's experience of cultural expressions. All cultures construct sex/gender systems and do not always divide them neatly into male/female. Attraction, desire, intimacy, love, companionship, friendship and commitment are innate descriptions of levels of expressing relationship with God through and with another person.

Some of the most detrimental expressions of being out of relationship with God are oppression, hate, discrimination, exclusion and all levels of racism – denials of the great command to love one another as God loves us. To understand sexuality in theological terms we must take into account a person's awareness of his or her own body. We can begin to do this only after we have peeled away the layers of discrimination and prejudice that prevent us from seeing the person. Being 'gay' is more than sexual expression. In broad terms, being 'gay' is an expression of sexuality that cuts across gender barriers arriving at sexual identity and a person's experience of God and creation.

Joseph:

We are, first and foremost, human beings made in the image of God, and secondly male, female, gay or straight. On the basis of 'being in the image of God,' I acknowledge that we all deserve to be treated with the dignity befitting one made in the image of God, and on this basis alone, accepted, loved and valued. We are not in dispute over questions of justice here. If I may ask, however, must sex be part of the package for me to be truly seen to accept and love another human being? I find it hard to accept the nuance that one must express the acceptance and love of God for the other through indiscriminate sexual relationships or expressions.

Debbie:

Certainly, all relationships do not include sexual intimacy or expression. However, it is impossible to separate out individual sexuality from the person. Sexuality should not be indiscriminate, but it is essential to being and, when expressed intentionally with love and commitment, God is present in the union.

Gender Identity

Debbie:

Gender identity is a crucial consideration for the conversation about spirituality and sexuality. Gender identity does not have a universal understanding. Western cultural norms have often been understood to be universal and so the diverse understandings have rarely been considered in their fullness.

Cultures construct the sex/gender systems from their understanding of their relationships with God and with one another. The individual's experience of these cultural expressions is found in identity. Understanding that gender is dynamic and not static can account for an experience of God and creation that does not judge the abundant nature of God.[2]

Anthropological approaches to gender identity enable us to challenge our own perceptions of sex, gender and sexuality. Broad cultural patterns illuminate the meaning of gender diversity – understandings of gender diversity illuminate aspects of sex/gender systems.

In some Indigenous cultures roles are assigned by observing young prepubescent children: seeing how they play and speak and whom they identify with. Different genders play differing roles in the community; they speak differently, dress differently and have different occupations and ceremonial roles. One example might be that females take on female roles, speaking 'longer', more poetically and men 'shorter', more practically. Men hunt and women tend and nurture. Some of those who are physically boys speak 'longer' and tend and nurture, some women speak 'shorter' and hunt.

Cultures vary in the extent in which gender diversity has sacred or spiritual associations or ritual powers. For example, some Native (North) American cultures understand a multi-gendered system valuing gender diversity – male, female, male females, female males and non-specific genders and a balance of male and female known to some as 'Two Spirit'. The term 'Two Spirit' might suggest a narrow two-gender perspective to some but, more importantly, it links the spiritual nature of identity and relationship.

My own personal experience of my culture and myself might serve as a good example. As a child born fully human and in a female body, it was apparent to my community from very early on that I was equally comfortable in the roles traditionally understood to be those of women or men. Whether I was dressing, playing or leading, the roles I expressed were both male and female. Outside the safety net of family and community my identity was limited by those whose understanding comes from what my physical features suggested – I am a woman. In my early pubescent years, it became clear that it was more natural to express my sexuality with another woman than with a man. But, I married a man and gave birth to two very wonderful boys who I enjoyed raising very much. When my husband left the relationship, I was blessed with an opportunity to reconnect my identity and my understanding of my identity with my Native community and The Episcopal Church.

As I have matured, I have experienced the power of oppression particularly in the area of sexuality. I understand how limited the boundaries can be when we permit the dominant society to assert its own understanding over other less dominant cultures highly misunderstood. I have grown to understand that my Indigenous community celebrates my identity spiritually and with that spirituality comes responsibility – to live with integrity honouring our culture and traditions and the wisdom that has been passed down to us by our ancestors. I understand better now that by living in this way I am living in balance and harmony with creation and therefore in closer relationship to God.

I express myself in what many people understand as male and female roles. As a priest in The Episcopal Church these nuances are less visible in this context. But in an urban environment where many Indigenous people struggle to understand what it means to be 'Native' the influence of the early missionaries is apparent – heterosexual relationships are the 'norm'. Alongside (not in contrast) is an intentional reclaiming of 'nativeness' sometimes demonstrated by the strength of traditionally matriarchal societies or an emerging sense that sexuality, roles and identity are being considered in their complexities.

The Two Spirit person is one example of complex roles and identities found in many Native (North) American communities. Being Two-Spirit is as much about spirituality as it is about sexuality. The ambiguity of these roles and identities poses a challenge for understanding them in the context of predominant cultures who identify sexuality as only male or female and spirituality as a relationship with God defined through religion.

Sister José Hobday, Seneca, Iroquois and Seminole and a Franciscan nun describes her understanding in this way.

> I cannot understand the hang-up in white culture and Church towards the homosexual. In our native tradition we don't even have a word for homosexual. And it is well known among us that often the homosexual was the most spiritual member of a tribe, who played powerful roles as counsellors to some of our most important chiefs.[3]

Indigenous cultures also hold up hospitality – loving God and loving neighbour – as a value that defines all relationships. Indigenous cosmology (systems of religious beliefs and a way of seeing the world where transformation and ambiguity are recurring themes) is mostly counter-cultural to the surrounding Westernized mentalities which define knowledge through scientific proofs. But Indigenous cultures are comfortable with more ambiguity – a person is both masculine and feminine, possess qualities of both. Individuals are free to transcend the sex/gender assignments at birth into the gender which is manifested by the transformational diversity that can also appear ambiguous.

Joseph:

Sexually ambiguous cases definitely abound in our societies today. This has caused a lot of confusion as to precise definitions of gender identities. Some people deliberately blur the distinctions between the sexes through sexual ambiguity or bisexuality in behaviour or dress, but this does not, however, eliminate the fact that human beings are normally gender-specific and that gender identity is about quality of being male or female and the distinctions of persons according to their sex kind. If I may quote Edith Humphrey on this,

> From the creation narratives we learn that our human sexual differences are key to our identity. Genesis 1.27 stresses both diversity and unity: 'So God created Adam in his image, in the image of God he created him, male and female he created them.' Again in Genesis 2 and 3, God is said to have created Adam and Eve with equal dignity, in a complementary but asymmetrical relationship. This relationship is presented as part of the initial and perfect will of God. 'It is not good for the man to be alone . . .' [He is then paired with a woman]. Sexual distinctions are thus part of God's good . . . creation.[4]

Gender identity is therefore based on God's original design. Maleness and femaleness are basic to our natural (as in creation) gender identities, and it is this differentiation which becomes definitive for sexual relationships as explicitly evident in God's design. The world in its present state is a far cry from the original 'goodness'. Sexuality and gender identity, like any other aspect of creation now are deeply affected by deprivation, limitations, corruption, sickness, oppression, greed, selfishness, and loss of direction, purpose and true meaning. In a fallen world confusion and complexities abound. There may be categories, to give an example, of persons who may not fit into one or the other of the two categories of God's original design. It is possible that one may be born with both male and female organs, or possesses what Debbie called 'Two Spirit' even though physically they may be recognized as either male or female. With every respect to such individuals, I believe that such is not the norm but an incongruity possible to occur in a fallen world. Such occurrences often are seen in all examples of deformities and inconsistencies, whether scientifically explicable or not. It is not part of God's original design but a reality of the diminution of the original 'goodness'.

Within most African traditional societies, gender identity was based on sexual distinctions as in male or female sex. As in the Hebrew Bible, this was understood as divinely given boundaries. The birth of any child is received with joy and celebrations. It is an important rite of passage and the beginning of a long socialization process that is intricately entwined with the child's identity as either male or female. As family, relatives, friends and neighbours gather to anxiously await the safe delivery of one who entered into labour, the very first announcement is usually of the sex of the child. The first question from any person who was not near to hear the announcement is, 'Is it a boy or a girl?' Anything else other than one or the other of these two categories is regarded as a curse that must be got rid of. Children born with severe deformities or sex differentiation that is inconsistent with the 'normal' or 'natural' categories are never 'received' in the usual celebratory way. My guess is that not many beside the midwives may have the opportunity to see such a newborn. We can only guess what happens to them.

Because of the influence of Christianity most parents would now bring up any child and baptize them. Even today, however, there are clear preferences for a boy child to a girl child and for an able-bodied child over a child which exhibits physical differences from the norm. A child who may not fit the norm may suffer rejection. This is one of those cultural practices, beliefs, that the gospel must correct. It, however, gives us insight into the traditional gender understanding. Let me be clear we must accept every child for who they are and rejoice in the gift of God to us. .

I guess such 'inconsistencies' may be addressed if we appreciate there are cases in which we may have to separate sex and spirituality. My point is, can't one be asexual and spiritual? Must sex be a definitive element in our spirituality?

Debbie:

The ambiguities I have addressed are not related to the individual's identity but rather to the general perceptions and understandings of the diversity of sexual identities by others. I am neither confused nor making a deliberate attempt to blur distinctions when I describe myself as a female who identifies as both male and female (as defined by society) and my obvious femaleness is not a definitive indication that I would 'naturally' be in a relationship with a man.

> To be gay is much more than just practising sex with someone of the same gender . . . It is, in broader terms, an expression of sexuality that cuts across and breaks gender barriers (how they are formed, their prescriptions and hierarchy). To be gay is, consequently, to feel alienated in many ways within a dominant hetero-patriarchal system that dictates the thoughts and practices of the prevailing socio-political and economical order.[5]

Sexuality, Spirituality and Personhood

Joseph:

The subject of spirituality and sexuality are each in its own unique way so intertwined with personhood. The desire for a meaningful, affirming and true sexual expression is perhaps only matched by the aspiration for spiritual meaning and satisfaction. Spirituality and sexuality are both about positive living, positive use of life synergies, and about personhood in relation to life lived before God, with God, self and others. Both are about the search for meaning of what it is to be a human person. It is an intimate longing for fulfilment and the search for fullness of being. Sexual or spiritual expression is therefore deeply in resonance with that which constitutes being a human person both as individualized reality and as integrated identity. Perceptions of personhood are, however, always contextually determined.

Nothing in our contexts shapes our perceptions and attitudes toward sexuality as culture and religion. Cultural norms and religious teachings or faith convictions often are the firm foundations upon which sexual ethics are built. Despite the close connection between the two, culture and religion have generally tended to confine sexual expressions to privatized and tightly controlled quarters of life in the fear that uninhibited sexual expressions and diversities may be detrimental to spirituality or more specifically spiritual growth. If God created human persons as sexual and spiritual, where does the tendency to suppress sexuality in order to boost spirituality come from?

Debbie:

Relationship with God preceded a relationship with another. The relationship between sexuality and spirituality is found in the transcendent experience of God, and knowing and experiencing God within and through another person in a way that we cannot experience God alone. God gave us sexuality as a means for procreation and companionship, and spirituality and sexuality together create God's perfection. Sex is a unifying experience, requiring total surrender to the mystery that comes from that experience, and it is in that mystery that we know God. The absence of procreation does not diminish the sacredness of sexuality especially when we consider the ongoing sexual relationship of couples who have been together beyond their reproductive years and are yet sexually active. We must also consider that many couples who are unable to reproduce together often find adoption to be an equally reflective experience of 'procreation'.

For some religions, sex is a thing to be controlled. The way I understand this need for control suggests to me that the power of God is present in the act and therefore must be approached with the same reverence that one approaches God. I might also suggest that fear of that power presents an opportunity to interpret the mind of God, make unequivocal statements about how God 'feels' about sex and develop standards to reflect the fear.

Augustine never overcame his disgust with and fear of sex as is apparent in this statement, 'Nothing so casts down the manly mind from its [rational, spiritual] heights as the fondling of women, and those bodily contacts which belong to the married state.' Aquinas paraphrased Augustine when he said 'because marriage is designed for procreation, a man who loves his wife too passionately is an adulterer.' He warned husbands that a wife's touches give her dominion over her husband's body and drag him to a 'slavery more bitter than any other'.[6] Our Christian roots have been greatly influenced by these theologians and their thought. Their attitude towards sex and sexuality have influenced Churches worldwide and may suggest why the Song of Songs does not appear in the mainstream readings in the church. Instead the book is sometimes viewed as an allegory for the church's love of God, suggesting the fear of the intense poetic expressions of love found in the book.

As the book stands it is an appropriate celebration of the *eros* that leads to and finds its consummation in romantic love. The Song of Songs affirms that *eros* is a valued aspect of the human nature God created. The Song of Songs demonstrates the spiritual connection to God through another in an equally reverent sexual relationship free from domination, coercion or force. This is sacred ground and we must approach it with caution and vigilance in preventing our own needs, fears, or agendas to interfere with a relationship with God or another. Erotic sexuality in this context is not a permissive, promiscuous, 'anything goes' value system but in fact it is a very demanding, mature system of morality.

Expressions of Spirituality and Sexuality

Friendship/Companionship

Debbie:

There are ample examples of friendship/companionship found in the Bible. In fact, in the Old Testament, the central characters of Abraham and Moses might be described as God's friends. In the New Testament Jesus built his ministry around friends such as the twelve disciples and women such as Mary and Martha and Mary Magdalene.

Peter Atkinson writes about Christian friendship in his book *Friendship and the Body of Christ*. He writes about the recovery and importance of deep covenanted friendships between people of the same and opposite sex.[7] He refers to another author, Alan Bray, who explored the intimate friendships of 'brotherhood' (*adelphopoiesis*) in medieval times. Some of these were blessed in the church with liturgical forms remarkably similar to the marriage ceremony. He also writes about the tomb monuments in ecclesiastical settings where two men or two women are buried together. These examples of friendship speak about an essential need for companionship – someone who will visit you when you are sick, someone who will accompany you shopping or running errands, someone who knows you well enough that they could offer empathy and understanding for and with you as we journey in our daily lives.

The passionate intimacy expressed by David for Jonathan and the deep loving affection expressed by Jesus about the disciple who he loved and was lying close to his breast at the table provide us with examples of relationships of friendship/companionship. They are identified with as the kind of companionship/friendship relationships desired by those who describe themselves as 'gay' or 'lesbian'.

The question is whether this companionship love/agape love has any erotic content. Some may see the relationship between David and Jonathan as deeply entwined in erotic love even if it is not expressed. The relationship between Jesus and the apostle he loved is sometimes identified in the same context. But what may be most important is that the 'feelings' were present and yet not condemned.

Joseph:

Sex undeniably has spiritual dimension to it, and no wonder many see it as a 'sacred act' and approach it with utmost reverence befitting of a 'holy act'. Indeed there is 'an almost sacramental element in sexual intercourse, within the mystery of a "one flesh" marriage relationship, that is, between a man and a woman, created in the image of God.'[8] Spirituality, on the other hand, does not have to have sex in it for it to be complete. God created us as sexual beings but He does not require of us to necessarily express our sexuality in order for our spiritual relationship with him to be complete or acceptable. You do not need to know someone sexually for you to know God. Every individual, male or female, is made in the image of God and depending on the measure of God's grace and revelation given to each, they can know God. It is not that all loving relationships have to include sex for us to please God. A father and a daughter, mother or son can live in loving relationship without it having to turn sexual. We can enjoy the fullness of our sexual being even when we cannot or may not enjoy sex. Our sexuality, regardless of how we understand it is complete even when it does not involve sex.

Many have postulated the idea that Jonathan and David were homosexual on account of seeing a homoerotic sub-text in the story of 1 Samuel 18.1–3:

> Now it came about when he had finished speaking to Saul, that the soul of Jonathan was knit to the soul of David, and Jonathan loved him as himself. Saul took him that day and did not let him return to his father's house. Then Jonathan made a covenant with David because he loved him as himself.

I can understand that anyone reading this text through the lens of a gay person may see here the homosexual love of one man for another. But in a context, like that of David and Jonathan where same-sex relationships is far from the accepted norm, the language only employs the analogy of the power of erotic love to express the deep brotherly love between David and Jonathan. While David goes on to mourn that his love (agape, LXX) for Jonathan 'was more wonderful than that of women', this does not mean it was sexual love (*eros*) cf. 2 Samuel 1.26. There are obvious cultural reasons why such interpretation is inadmissible. People read into the text meanings which otherwise are alien to the context when they resolutely believe that what they are looking for in a given text is really there objectively. The 'romantic' reading of this text, and the insinuation that Jesus may have been gay, is inconsistent with contextual norm and out of step with the general spirit of the Hebrew Scriptures. Given the historical or contextual realities of the Israel of David and Jonathan's time (or Jesus' time, for that matter) and the general thrust of the Hebrew Scriptures regarding homosexual relationships, the text is about anything but same-sex romance.

Love and Committed Relationships

Debbie:

Loving and committed relationships hold grace in common. In marriage, this grace is the coming together of two in one flesh, while in friendship it might be said that they express the grace of two in one soul. The expression of one's sexuality within a loving and committed bond evokes an experience of God in the way the two people relate to God, each other and the world.

Loving and committed relationships are not always inclusive of sexual interactions. Nor is sexuality necessary to love another person or to be committed to them. Sharing mutual love and commitment is not simply a gift of grace but a grace that is shared, visible and complemented by others. Being loved is something we experience by grace and the fact that we can love another is grace – the real miracle is that the love of two people coincides – the true gift of grace and a very real example of the *mystery* that is God.

Genuine love is delicate, complicated, vulnerable, infinite and has a variety of expressions. It is that part which makes us 'inferior only to the angels' (Psalm 8.5).

Joseph:

Indeed, 'loving and committed relationships are not always' about sex. Most loving relationships indeed should and must have nothing to do with getting sexually intimate. We definitely have a problem when a culture becomes so obsessed with sex that every form of physical contact is almost always seen as sexual. It is a sign of a sexually obsessed culture that John 13.23 is regarded as a sexual overture. The King James Version was happy to translate the verse: 'Now there was leaning on Jesus' bosom one of his disciples, whom Jesus loved' in a non-sexualized society, but in today's world the New International Version reads: 'One of them, the disciple whom Jesus loved, was reclining next to him.' The change is not in meaning, but because of the sexualization of society.

In my Kenyan culture, Christians would often conclude a prayer meeting with the words of the grace while standing and holding hands. In formal worship, most churches would always have a time for sharing of peace which is expressed by 'kiss of peace' but only between people of same sex. It is also common greetings that people of same sex will often not only shake hands but also give each other a very generous hearty hug. These acts of physical contact are not remotely sexual in tone, intention or otherwise but are a genuine expression of friendship and love. Jesus was a friend to all – men and women, sick and healthy included. He often was a very physical person touching those with whom he comes into contact. Aren't we rather trivializing issues if we read sex into all his encounters?

Celibacy

Debbie:

The imposition of the practice of celibacy as a way to demand sexual abstinence of all those who do not fit the heterosexual mould reduces the question to sexual intercourse. It does not recognize the complexity of humanity and sexuality. The concept of celibacy results in a theology which denies the incarnational embodiment of a person called to celibate life.

Celibacy is a path chosen by those individuals who are not called to the experience of God through and within a relationship with another person. Celibacy has long been a part of the Christian tradition. The tradition of celibacy precedes the message of freedom, autonomy, and communities of co-equal disciples preached by Jesus. Celibacy is a nurturing ground for solitude and communion with God.

As sexual beings, all our relationships have a sexual dimension. We relate through our bodies and we relate through gender. Meeting someone who we see as a life partner enhances our psychological and emotional health, creates balance in our life and energizes our call to be whole.

Celibacy is a chosen life or a call to live as a sexual being in a way that precludes committed sexual relationships, which are genitally active. The reasons individuals choose celibacy differ from person to person. Some wish to make a single-minded commitment to the person of God – not to be single but in relationship with God. At times this includes individuals that want to give themselves totally to one thing like scholarship, missionary work, art, or music with few opportunities to meet a potential partner, let alone someone who is compatible with this life choice. Some choose to be celibate as a part of their call to priesthood, as in the Roman Catholic tradition, or religious orders. Other persons who have suffered traumatic experiences that prevent them from feeling safe enough to encounter another in an intimate relationship also find themselves in celibate lifestyles.

There are varied reasons for singleness and celibacy. Within each context is the element of choice and it is just as critical for singleness and celibacy as it is for marriage. Any sense that celibacy is imposed, required, unwelcome or circumstantial adds negativity to this life choice.

Celibacy is a gift and a call that precedes the Christian rules of celibacy for religious orders. As a gift and a call celibacy is a charism or gift from God that symbolizes the consecrated wholeness of the relationship between an individual and God. The gift or call to celibacy may or may not involve a sacrificial element but, whichever it is, the choice is that of the individual. It is this freedom that reflects the creative nature of God and holds it up as authentic and an ideal of love. In highly patriarchal societies where marriage is upheld as the norm, celibates struggle to affirm the uniqueness, the sense of completeness and the need for integrity of the individual.

While the church recognizes and honours celibacy in religious orders and as a recognized call it also underscores the restrictive nature of mandatory celibacy in other cases. It is as sexual beings that celibacy is embraced and lived out as a symbol of wholeness in God. It is for this reason primarily that the church must reassess its perception of celibacy and surrender ownership of this gift, finding new language to redefine its meaning and value.

Celibacy may be the right path for some but not for all, and only the individual can discern the true and authentic gift of celibacy.

Joseph:

The way of the cross is every Christian's vocation, epitomized by Jesus' call, 'pick up your cross and follow me', which among other things mean denying oneself in pursuance of the will of God, even when such may not be the will of the believer. This model, as embracing and inclusive as it is, is also uncomfortably demanding. The circle inclusively draws in all while at the same time remaining nothing else but a circle with clear boundaries. This comes with a highly demanding covenantal relationship where all within the circle of covenantal love are to give their all or nothing. The price is the demand to live according to some 'ground rules'. These apply to all who willingly join the all-inclusive circle, even if we cannot make sense of them.

They apply whether or not we accept them and whether or not we are *able* to fulfil them. If we do anything, including sexual acts, which depart from the relevant ground rule, then it puts us into a collision path with spirituality. Everything remains holy and spiritually edifying only if enjoyed within the circle and in accordance with whatever particular rule applies to it. If a gay person finds it hard to choose celibacy or abstinence – the choice is clear – it is either to choose obedience to the word of God (even when we may not fully understand why such prohibition is given in the first place) or submit to the desires of the flesh. If a straight person finds it hard to remain faithful to their husband or wife, thinking what harm does it do to have a second sexual relationship, the choice is clear, either to choose obedience to the word of God or submit to the desires of the flesh.

I guess the question could be similar for the case of a widow or a widower who may not find a suitable marriage partner but finds the option of abstinence difficult to choose. I guess, you would not recommend it is OK to take whatever opportunities for casual sexual relationships that may come by as long as such makes the person happy – would you?

Debbie:

Sexual relationships outside of committed and loving relationships are really not the issue as I understand it. There are loving and committed relationships between heterosexual as well as homosexual persons. Within the context of these relationships is the experience of holiness and a strengthened spiritual bond between the couple and God. I would not put any couple in a loving, covenanted and committed relationship into the category of sex for the purpose of pleasure. I would not question their ability to be in union with God through the other person whether they are persons of the same or opposite sex. I understand that as the conversation progresses, but you seem to be clear that God only blesses heterosexual couples who are married and there is no indication that God also blesses men and women who are bound by commitment and monogamy in same-sex partnerships. And I think you are placing homosexual couples into a category of unfaithful heterosexual persons which, of course, they are not if they are living within the same moral and ethical standards of faithful relationships. 'Stepping out' breaks the bond of commitment whether you are heterosexual or homosexual.

Culture, Religion vis-à-vis Sexuality and Spirituality

Joseph:

The Hebrew Scripture depicts human beings as created not only as rational, spiritual and moral creatures but also as sexual beings. Both of the Genesis creation narratives introduce human beings as sexual beings created in the 'image of God' (Genesis 1.1—2.4) consisting of both male and female (1.27). Sexuality, alongside the rest of creation is declared 'very good' (1.31). Genesis also indicates that sexual union is primarily for the purpose of procreation, that is, to 'be fruitful and multiply' as well as for the purpose of companionship, that is, 'it is not good for Adam, and for that matter Eve, to be alone.' The Genesis narratives also set clear boundaries within which sexual relations could be expressed. This is set as monogamous and hetero-sexual. There is no hint that sexual relations between male and female expressed within this set boundaries is detrimental to the spirituality of the parties involved. Strict regulations and purity laws with regard to sexuality are dealt with in Leviticus.

The Levitical laws govern every issue of importance to the well-being of Israel. Every matter considered significant, ranging from foreign affairs to family relations, was brought under strict regulation of these laws. Sexuality was regarded as impor-tant among issues that demanded human response to the divine promise as seen by the number of references to it. Issues such as protection of the land and the proper conduct in matters of sexual relations have a prominent place in the laws. With regard to sexual conduct there are prohibitions against incest, adultery and many other sexual relations regarded as illegitimate. Because the Hebrew Scripture sees sexuality in relation to intimacy and community, it logically limits genital sexual expression to the context of marriage. This is regarded as godly and legitimate. In the light of present-day anthropological studies it makes sense to conclude that such laws are not simply irrational fears of ancient minds expressed in the strange language of purity, uncleanness and taboos, but served practical functions in defeat-ing chaos and promoting social order. They preserved the harmonious existence and well-being of the entire creation.

The New Testament takes over and applies much of the Old Testament's sexual value system. The influence from Greco-Roman world on the early church, however, shows a departure from this heritage in one important sense. From the second century onwards there appeared views that tend to suppress the erotic even within marriage in an effort to promote spirituality. Enjoyment of sexual pleasure was seen as spiritually degrading and desires of the flesh as a hindrance to a state of spiritual blessedness. Practices such as sexual asceticism, celibacy, single life came to be promoted as of great religious value. An attempt at reinterpreting and spiritualizing biblical references to eroticism or sexual pleasure is also commonplace among the very early Fathers. Jerome, for example, interprets the Song of Songs as a metaphor for the mortification of the flesh in desire to be one with God. With reference to the same book, Origen, who castrated himself to become a eunuch for the kingdom of heaven, warned Christians: 'Everyone who is not yet rid of the vexations of flesh and blood and has not ceased to feel the passion of his bodily nature should refrain com-pletely from reading this book.'

Most of the Fathers from this period taught that sexual intercourse was shameful and spiritually degrading and should be reserved only for the purpose of pro-creation. Sexuality is God-given and therefore good; yet seen as a venue for sin and temptation and in this sense not only inferior to the spirit but also an 'enemy'. The teaching that flowed from this dualism of the spirit and the body is that sensual desires be subjected to the spirit and that the only good desire is the desire for God. Auxiliary to this view is that women were inferior to men. Women were seen as sensual and worldly whereas men represented the rational and spiritual. This gave rise to the commonplace belief that women were dangerous; a stumbling block to men's spiritual progress. Such beliefs underlie the ascetic practices of many early church movements such as the Montanists, the Novatians and the Encratites ('abstainers' – known to teach abstinence even within marriage).

Expressing the fears of sex and temptations that come through women, Augustine

(354–430 CE), wrote: 'Nothing so casts down the manly mind from its [rational, spiritual] heights as the fondling of women, and those bodily contacts which belong to the married state.'[9] Thomas Aquinas (1225–74) taught, 'Because marriage is designed for procreation, a man who loves his wife too passionately is an adulterer.'[10] Peter Lombard (1100–64) taught that the Holy Spirit leaves the room when a married couple has sex, even if they do it without the intention to gratify the desires of the flesh.[11] This negative view of sex and sexuality cannot be justified from the Bible unless by way of twisted, strained or prejudiced interpretations. The negative views of the Fathers are a reflection of their context influenced greatly by neo-Platonic and Stoic philosophies. Their influence on Christian sexual ethics, values and equality of sexes, however, has been very significant; whether it has been helpful is a matter of debate.

Most traditional cultures, such as my own African culture, have a more positive view of sex and sexuality. They too, however, have tightly defined and socially determined gender roles, sexual perceptions, identity and relations. They are a lot more similar, in this sense, to views generally expressed in the Hebrew Bible, which forms the basis of Jesus' sexual ethics and morality as presented in the New Testament. The African traditional culture highly values human sexuality. In this tradition, sexual asceticism, celibacy, and the single life have no spiritual value. Sexual intercourse establishes a marriage and procreation is a religious duty. Sexual pleasure and enjoyment is valued, although it is incidental to the act of procreation and strictly confined within the marriage context. Sexual intimacy is about reproduction and inconceivable apart from marriage and procreation. Productivity in sexual matters is measured in successfully begetting children. Childlessness will necessitate alternative form of marriages such as polygamy, Leviratical marriage or a close relative helping out with a brother or a cousin who is unable to get children with his wife. These are all done within clearly defined limits, rights, obligations and socially sanctioned moral and ethical framework of sexuality and sexual relations.

In the traditional setting the only acceptable form of sexual relations is heterosexual sex, strictly practised within the marriage context only. This means sexual expressions are genital and context specific. It is within this prescribed context that sexual intercourse serves one specific purpose – to establish a marriage, a rite of passage without which the individual is seen as an incomplete person. This makes marriage a religious duty and blessing. It is a meritorious, charitable and humanitarian act, not as an end itself, but as a means of procreation. Anything else contravenes the norm and is deemed as culturally inappropriate. Homosexual acts are then necessarily considered a taboo, which if contravened carry the danger of spiritual pollution. This has relevance in ways it disrupts established social order, structures of thought and corrupting of relations and thereby affecting natural order of things. Traditional culture, therefore, limits sex to heterosexuality and disapproves other sexual expressions. Several religious models are used to uphold and reinforce this teaching.

Debbie:

Scripture presents humans created in the image of God. They were gifted one to the other for procreation and companionship – both equally important but not dependent on the other for sanctification. I have not been able to locate any passages in

Scripture that definitively describe the 'clear boundaries within which sexual relations can be expressed', but I am clear that the Jewish laws of purity are apparent in Leviticus. However, for clarity in this document, I am not comfortable making definitive statements that select particular passages to demonstrate what is or is not acceptable behaviour in Christian life – accepting one passage and not another defeats the integrity of my own understanding. I am also clear that biblical exegesis provides ample evidence of the cultural influence of the writers within the text. In addition, I am reluctant to make assumptions based on my own logic on the one hand but feel confident in presenting the ideas that may lead to more discussion in this area.

I appreciate these insights into African traditions and wonder how they compare in their more indigenous practices to the pre-colonized/missionary traditions. I cannot help but be surprised that African culture does not share the diversity of sexual identities found in other parts of the world. But I have in previous sections of this document presented another cultural perspective on gender identity and roles.

Since we have been deprived of the feminist theological voice until recently, and because our Christian faith is based on justice I would agree that those cultures whose view of the 'female' role as solely for the purpose of carrying forward cultural identity and more specifically valuing then only male heirs is an injustice that suggests that women are only valuable for their wombs and that their personhood is inferior to ability to reproduce.

Creation

Joseph:

The traditional model of creation holds that sex differentiation of same species defines and determines the basic order of nature. This particularly recognizes that human beings are created similar (as humans) yet different (as male and female). The similarity provides the basis for limiting sexual relations to members of the same species and that the difference between the same species regulates and marks internal boundaries. The internal boundaries are often about appropriate sexual practices or forbidden sexual acts such as incest, cross-generational sex, cross-gender sex, and among some traditional cultures boundaries within endogamous or exogamous clans. At the primary level, this model sees God as creating a category of existence that is both similar and different from his divinity. The similarity is the basis of the relationship between God and creation evident in the authenticity and validity of a real *analogia entis* between God and creation. It is in the difference that the meaning and purpose of sex is shown and the logic of such design becomes obvious. Whereas God creates through the power of the Spirit, the human being procreates through the power of sex. The underlying principle is, therefore, that sex must enhance the good of creation and as a divine gift conform to divine precept. This explains why it should be heterosexual, morally acceptable and dignified in honouring every aspect of God's creation.

The creation model also tries to shape human relationship on the basis of God's character and the nature of his relationship with his creation. God is compassion and love. Human beings have elements of this compassion and love because God is in us and we are in God. So our basic, natural way of being is a reflection of God. Our relationship with God is an internal connection, is from the gifts that God has shared with us. In the same way, we need to connect with others and God has given us the faculties in order to do this, including our sexuality and physicality. We are to use these gifts in ways that advance fullness of being in all their social and personal aspects. The model presupposes that God has prescribed for us a particular way to live, which if his creatures depart from that, such act negates in some sense the fullness of being.

Debbie:

Yes, as we have already talked about, there is a direct relationship between sexuality and spirituality. Enhancing the good of creation is a divine gift that takes many forms. I do not agree that the only product that demonstrates that creation has been enhanced is that of a child created in the union of a heterosexual couple. There are many children in this world who were conceived by forced sexual intercourse and violence – the children certainly are the gift but the act that created them is not an act that I would describe as 'enhancing creation'. I think the problem with this statement is that it implies that children are the only outcome of sex that would enhance the good of creation. I think we both understand sexual relationships between non-fertile couples who adopt children or couples whose lives are enriched by their sexual encounters with each other long into old age are also enhancing the good of creation.

My experience is also that the sexual encounter of a loving committed couple (even those of the same sex) does bring about or enhance the good of creation in the sharing of their love with each other and those around them. Sex is a response to and a reflection of the divine gift known by many couples with varying gender identities.

God is compassion, love and humans have elements of that as God is in us and we are in God. Psalm 139 describes the intimacy of relationship with God assuring us that God has been and continues to be an active player in creation. We are foundationally made in the image of God and given gifts of the Spirit to share with others. Our relationship with God can be known through our internal spiritual life or it can be revealed to us through our interconnectedness with all of creation. How we connect includes our sexuality and physicality with friends and family and others – through greetings, touching, kissing, etc. Our physical beings touch and connect in many ways.

Holiness

Joseph:

Holiness is living within the miracle of creation in perfect balance, so that I am no more or less than what God made me and that my relationship to God must inform and shape similar relationships that I have with all that God created, including the plants, animals and stars. To be more than what I have been created to be would be to take on a higher role than that which is intended for me. Less than what God created me to be would mean not honouring God who made me and all that was made. Holiness in this sense means harmony between creator and creation, and honouring all that and taking one's rightful place within it. Being in relationship with God as the source of our knowledge of what is holy or unholy is primary to the understanding of holiness. Holiness is at the same time a state of being and a process of participation in the being of God, who is holy, holiness being an attribute of God. Central to the concept of holiness, therefore, is harmony, relationship and unity between creation and creation on one hand, and creation and the creator on the other hand. Many cultural religions subscribe to this understanding of holiness. African traditional religion, for example, cannot perceive holiness apart from being in relationship.

An African view of life and of the entire cosmic reality within which a person finds oneself is best summed up in this basic African philosophy: 'because I relate therefore I am'.[12] This underscores the African understanding of the unique oneness of reality. As Pierre Erny rightly observes, 'The African cosmos is like a spider web: its least element cannot be touched without making the whole vibrate. Everything is connected, interdependent.'[13] The reality of existence is in its interconnectedness conceived as a kind of 'vitalism' or life-force which pervades the whole of nature making inconceivable the idea of the existence of one part of nature in total independence of the other. The 'oneness' is basically maintained through a rhythmic liturgy of life that demands holiness or ritual cleanness in every aspect of life. Purity or holiness is paramount to the harmonious existence of the whole community including family, relatives and clan within which the individual finds identity, belonging and the fullness of being or completeness as a person.

From the perspective of the individual, the process of belonging is regulated and maintained by their compliance with societal norms and values meant to nurture common life. The individual upholds certain standards and lives within certain internal boundaries that govern interpersonal relationships. 'Proper rituals and relationships that reinforce their connection with the "tribe" (community) renew the recognition of the universal life force that flows within and through the person as a whole. On a very concrete level this is reflected in the considerable social orientation of African people.'[14] Sex is wholesome, ritually pure, godly and of spiritual value if it affirms common life and respects set boundaries of relationships. Harmony is broken and the holy is defiled if the set boundaries, values and norms are contravened. Absence or deficiency of holiness is outwardly manifested in broken, illicit or 'unnatural' relationships that challenges and negatively impacts the nurture of common life and general well-being. This cultural understanding of holiness is opposed to depersonalized sexuality on one hand, and on the other, a strictly individualized spirituality that rejects the wider context of relationships, which properly must extend beyond the individual to society and the entire creation.

Traditional Christian understanding generally depicts holiness as living life in conformity with the will of God. Obedience (or disobedience for that matter) is central to this understanding. The doctrine of the Fall provides the backdrop to the belief that there has been a gulf between humanity and God ever since humanity disobeyed God at the beginning of creation. Whether the Fall is a historical reality or not, evidently it is a present reality, where humanity lives in 'fallenness' at all levels of existence, including separation between God and his creation and conflict within creation itself. The price and consequences of separation and conflict includes brokenness, incompleteness, separation, pain and suffering in creation. God's intention is to gather all things back to himself and redeem all things from the chaos into which it has fallen. This is a process, which among other things requires human co-operation with the Spirit of God. It is within this context that the believer takes seriously the scriptural call to holiness. In here, it is sufficiently made clear that human sexuality like everything else has its proper place of holiness if it has to remain pleasing to God. That place, according to the scriptural testimony, is a monogamous marriage between a man and a woman. This is God's design for holiness and spirituality within which sexuality finds its proper place.

Debbie:

Holiness is living within the miracle of creation in perfect balance, so that I am no more or less than what God made me, and my relationship to God is the same relationship that I have with all that God created, including the plants, animals and stars. To be more than what I have been created would be to take on a higher role than that which is intended for me. To be less would be not honouring all that God made me and all that was made to be. There is a Native American wisdom that resonates with something that Joseph said in his response above.

Web of Life

by Chief Seattle

Teach your children what we have taught our children – that the Earth is our Mother. Whatever befalls the Earth befalls the sons and daughters of the Earth. If men spit upon the ground, they spit upon themselves. This we know.

The Earth does not belong to us, we belong to the Earth. This we know. All things are connected like the blood that unites one family. All things are connected.

Whatever befalls the Earth befalls the sons and daughters of the Earth. We did not weave the web of life; We are merely a strand in it. Whatever we do to the Web, We do to ourselves.

Holiness is also living in community and relationship as God intended. Since the beginning of time there has been relationship – the elements of the earth with each other, humanity with the earth and the earth with humanity, all living things – and their relationship to God. Scripture provides many examples of falling out of relationship and through the life of our Elder Brother Jesus (God incarnate) we also have examples of how to redeem ourselves from those separations. The causes of the separation are what I have learned keep us from being in relationship with God and are therefore the things that must be brought back into balance with God and creation. Holiness then is right relationship or 'walking in balance'. The right and the wrong dualistic views of the Western world cannot be compared to this more inclusive ambiguous view of worldly things.

Holiness is mostly interpreted in a community rather than through individual perceptions that can easily be weighted. Our emphasis as Christian in the Episcopal/Anglican traditions is of course not on the fall, the cross or atonement but rather within the context of Jesus' death and resurrection inviting us into a new life free of 'sinfulness'. This along with the waters of baptism bring all things into new creation. Within this context both this Indigenous and Christian perspective come into balance with each other as we journey together not as a stumbling block to another but in support of a living community of faith.

Life and Example of Jesus

Joseph:

Jesus' life is a reminder to us of what God intended for us from the beginning, providing us with an opportunity to understand what may have been misunderstood in the time before Jesus' birth, and his life and resurrection are symbolic of God's complete care and love, no holds barred. Jesus offers a foil to misused or misunderstood law, by questioning its interpretation and application. Jesus' life gave us examples of justice and peace and love and compassion that are challenging us to live as people of God. Jesus did not condemn the Samaritan woman but allowed her into relationship, knowing full well what she had done. That holds much power. The example of Jesus telling stories without giving us clear answers, but giving us sufficient information to help us respond responsibly is an incredible gift. This model provides us with an incarnational basis of human relationships – a meeting of the other as and at where they are. This model should not be construed to mean that 'anything goes' in the name of love and justice. Jesus never intended that. His model was – meet, embrace and recommend a way of life that fruitfully leads to the fullness of life that God desires for the whole of creation. The recommendation often comes in commands – 'go and sin no more,' 'go and show yourself to the priest,' 'your faith has made you well,' etc. even in the greatest commandment he gives, the love of God comes first, which entails total surrender to God's will and thereby informs the second commandment, namely, the love of neighbour.

Could we push the argument for 'anything goes' a little bit further? Jesus challenges people's sense of values and judgments and ethics by radically reinterpreting them. But by no means does Jesus give ethics as a way to God. He outlines ethics as challenge. But there is THE way to God, which is Jesus, the whole truth and the whole life, and says that this work is not complete, but the Holy Spirit will lead us into the fullness of the truth. It is a model that lays a foundation, but leaving us with great 'openness' to building on the foundation as the Spirit may lead. We must then, however, take cognizance of the fact that Jesus redefines what good relationship is. In doing this, he distinctively begins with inclusiveness but then leads to the paradox of only staying in if you 'do my Father's will'.

Debbie:

Within the life of Jesus there are many examples of teaching through parables. My elders used 'parables' to teach about God and the world. The key to parables is as Joseph mentioned above. There is never a definitive ending. Our Elders just like Jesus were confident that God had already gifted us with everything that we need to be able to understand what is required to live in right relationship with God and the world. I also think that the parables of the New Testament are what make the Bible a 'living' document that has survived for centuries and is still held up as a way to know and understand what it means to be a Christian. Parables cannot mean to us today exactly what they have meant to our ancestors as they have read them because our knowledge of the world has changed just as our relationship with the world changes. For example, there is a more global knowledge of the world today.

Jesus reminded us over and over in his life that every person and every thing has value – in other words, God created us in God's image and we are, therefore, innately good and sacred beings. Jesus admonished those who would use laws, class, food, sex, race or any other difference to separate ourselves from each other. I believe that Jesus served as a model for justice and peace and redeemed all those who might have considered themselves 'unworthy' in the context and culture of the time. Jesus charged us to do the same. I understand this as unity only through diversity and diversity necessary to unity. The holistic way of viewing God's own Son, his purpose and his life is to understand that by putting law before unity rather than seeing laws as a means to build unity. Inclusiveness is challenged when we consider that every law has the potential to leave someone out. But, if laws are designed as a reflection of loving God and loving ourselves and our neighbour in the same way, laws most likely would be different than those we saw in the Old Testament that divided the chosen from the 'other' and led us to the sin of racism and exclusion.

The most incredible message was delivered not only through the cross, and Jesus submitting to God's will but it came from the redemptive acts throughout his life as sealed by the resurrection. Jesus reminded us of God's unconditional love and encouraged us to do the same. This model did not give us permission to do whatever we wanted but the guidelines as set in the ten commandments of the Old Testament and the two great commandments of the New Testament act as a guideline for discerning right relationship and right action.

A Covenant Model

Joseph:

Sex is basically sacred and spiritually value laden because it typically takes the form of a covenant. Sex without a covenantal basis is comparable to a domestic dog gone wild with no lead, hence capable of every dangerous element of destruction. Sex within moral boundaries is a religious act; a man and woman unite as one flesh, a covenant of God. Paul expresses that a union of man and woman is comparable to the union of Christ and His Church, implying that sex outside of marriage does violence to this image of Christ and His Church. When sex is knocked out of the picture or the equation with regard to relationship between human and God, it breaks the connection that God intends to bind sex, love and covenant making. The logic to this is that peace, justice, honour and dignity can only be given in matters of sex and sexual morality if done in the context and in light of the covenant we have with God. Genuine confession to another of our failure to love one another as we ought can only truly arise from our genuine confession to God of our failure to love God as we ought and keep his covenant. A covenant relationship with God is based on joyful loving obedience towards God. When we obey God's covenantal boundaries, which in all wisdom are intended for the good of humanity and all of God's creation, sex becomes a beautiful spiritual act. Accepted and understood within God's covenant of love there is something transcendent about sexual union. This is all good except for the complexity that arises within God's covenant boundaries when it comes to sex. Christian Tradition, as we noted, places godly sexual union within the covenant of a monogamous marriage between a man and a woman. Where does this leave faithful, sexual and spiritual beings who are capable of fulfilling sexual relations only with members of their sex?

God calls us body and spirit and endows us with gifts of the Spirit for service that blesses self and others. The calling with which God calls us is to newness of life, and must bear fruit. This can mean different things for different people. Whereas some are called to a life of marriage and service, some may be called to a life of celibacy and service. Since God's design is that of monogamous marriage between man and a woman, those incapable of this are then called into celibacy. This is not simply cultural but natural in keeping with the design of creation. This design refutes that love that flows between two people who are partnered can be expressed only through sexual relations. Whereas such love could be an overarching commitment of service to God and being a living example of the gospel message, sex does not have to be factored here. Adultery or unfaithfulness could afford a parallel here. Such sexual relations may be mutual, loving, and even admirable but such does not take away the offence of a sexual relationship outside the covenantal box of God's love. For those incapable of the covenant of marriage, the covenant of celibate life is the ideal. Sex 'outside the box', therefore, is deleterious to the human spirit.

This traditional Christian teaching may not be acceptable to many modern-day believers but also a great majority of traditional cultures. The African tradition, for example, has a high respect for marriage and in contrast to Western innovation of celibacy. Respect is given to those who are married, which is linked to the continuation of the family. Independence comes when you get married, and a sense of wholeness. You are incomplete until you are married.

The relationship between sexuality and spirituality is the transcendent experience of God, and knowing and experiencing God within and through a monogamous partnership in a way that we cannot experience God alone. God gave us sexuality as a means for procreation and companionship, and sex and spirituality together create God's perfection. It is unifying, requiring total surrender to the mystery that comes from that experience, and it is in that mystery that we know God. The absence of procreation doesn't diminish the value: it is both, not one or the other. However sex is not required for spiritual wholeness. Sexuality is not of itself a means of knowing God. Singleness is not a deprived state, in which God is less well known. We can know God in the silence of our own ascetic isolation. This however has its limitations, because you can in this way only know God in a subjective way, whereas the involvement of another person pushes you outside your comfort zone and into the mystery of what and who God can be.

Debbie:

The primary covenant relationship is our Covenant with God as created beings in a world created by Him. Our Covenant with God can be reflected in many ways, some of which we have talked about particularly as expressions of our spirituality through our sexuality. Covenants are also understood in expressions of friendship and those who are called to a life of celibacy.

The covenant of marriage reflects a sacred bond between two persons called to live in a monogamous life together. Their covenant with each other is also a covenant with God because it is through their sexual and spiritually deepening connections that they are able to know God and be connected to God. Persons of the same sex who have entered into a monogamous and committed relationship with each other also have the potential to experience God in God's fullness through their relationship to and with each other – and that includes sexual expressions. This is an example of a covenanted relationship whether or not it is recognized, celebrated or blessed in liturgical forms within the Church.

Our life with God calls us to be fruitful. Jesus said that it is by their fruit that his followers would be known (Matthew 7.20), not by their adherence to the rules. Paul lists the fruit of the Spirit as love, joy peace, patience, kindness, faithfulness, gentleness and self-control, and points out that against such things there is no law. Many who know persons who are in faithful, monogamous and partnered lives will testify that these gifts are present individually and together. While some single persons find fulfilment alone, this is not true for others who are called into relationship with another.

The fruits of the Spirit can manifest themselves in many ways often presenting us with the challenge to recognize the face of God in another. But the most powerful experience of God is found in the unexpected. Many heterosexual couples have brought me closer to God and so have many same-sex couples. Two women in a covenanted partnership brought a transforming power to a once divided, conservative congregation. Their love for each other is infectious. You can't help but be affected by their love for each other and everyone around them. It reminds me of those times when a child laughs from deep inside making it impossible not to laugh along.

The covenant relationship of love is not limited to bearing only children as fruit. In fact, there are many heterosexual couples who are unable to produce children together, but if they are called to a life of parenting there are many possibilities for that to be made real for them. Others are called to lives without children. With all the abandoned children in the world it is also amazing that many same-sex couples are able to live out their calls to parenthood by adopting.

What is clear is that our Covenant with God as Christians challenges us to defend the persecuted and disenfranchized. When Jesus gave us the two great commandments we were given a new measure for all relationships. Our Covenant with God as Christians presents us a challenge for justice and love, defending the poor and speaking up for those whose voices are being drowned out by power and control.

Our Covenant with God is complex coming to us through and with the transcendent experiences of God in our Spiritual lives and in our total identity as sexual beings.

The covenant that God makes with us as humanity varies in detail but always is initiated by God, driven by his grace and love to be in communion with humanity, intended for the good of humanity, so it comes with a blessing, but also has demands on the part of humanity. There are specific requirements in the old covenant which are clarified and made more inclusive in the new. The new dispensation sets the criteria by which the old is understood, giving guides and interpretations – continuity, non-contradiction – providing us with greater clarity.

The Episcopal Church liturgy of baptism includes a Baptismal Covenant intended to represent the transformational experience of conversion, being marked as Christ's own for ever. Within the context of the Baptismal Covenant are the following promises: to attend regular Christian worship, resist evil, repentant for sin, live a Christian life modelling Gospel values, seek and serve Christ in our neighbours, striving for peace and justice among all people and respect the dignity of every human being. In this very complex discussion, the Baptismal Covenant may serve as a lens for understanding our relationship with God – our spirituality. As sexual beings created in God's image our identity – however we understand ourselves – serves as the vessel for expressing our spirituality. In the process, our spirituality is expressed in community and in some cases, when we are gifted with the grace of being in a loving and committed relationship we know God through and with that person – our partners on the journey.

Concluding Remarks

Debbie:

As a Native American woman (Pascua Yaqui from Tucson, Arizona) and a priest in the Episcopal Church I seek to live with integrity serving Christ in every person. I have experienced the transformational love of our elder brother Jesus Christ and am committed to continued prayer and daily study of Scripture – I depend on them. My brother in Christ, Joseph, has been a companion on this path to understanding God. I realize that he struggled with my identity as a Two Spirit in a committed, loving relationship with another woman, but he recognized my commitment and faith in God. We agree on so much. We both understand sexuality and spirituality to be linked together. We both detest the trivialization of sex. We object to the way Western society described sex as dirty and evil and we object equally vehemently to the way modern Western society turns everything into being about sex. I rejoice that African men greet each other with physical touch in church and outside without a hint of eroticism and that African women do the same. However, I believe that the gender roles God has made are more wonderfully complex than purely male and female. I believe that the fruit of the Holy Spirit is on many faithful, committed partnerships between people of the same sex and that they are bringing new life in their shared experience of God to us. I believe that the witness of Jesus and Paul in the Bible calls us to seek evidence of holiness in fruitfulness and strive for justice and harmony in all creation.

Joseph:

This has been such a humbling experience. It is no simple task seeking wisdom and God's grace in a difficult situation that calls for wise and honest choice of words to say to a dear friend whose lifestyle conflicts with my belief system. Whose discernment and appropriation of the words of life are irreconcilably opposed to my understanding of the same. I come out of this more convinced than ever before that the basic contention between people on the different divide of this debate is fundamentally about the authority and sufficiency of Scripture. It is about what we cherish most in our lives – our values, happiness, life choices, etc. vis-à-vis the place and relevance of Scripture. There are many biblical injunctions that I may never understand the logic of their demand but am willing to go beyond reason and by faith sincerely pray: 'Lord, your will be done, not mine.'

Notes

1 *To Set Our Hope on Christ* (New York: The Episcopal Church, 2005), paragraph 2.0.
2 Nanda, Serena *Gender Diversity: Crosscultural Variations* (Illinois: Waveland Press, 2000), 11-26.
3 Sister José Hobday was a faculty member at the University of Creation Spirituality in Oakland, CA.
4 Edith Humphrey in *The Homosexuality Debate: Faith Seeking Understanding*, Catherine Hamilton, ed. (Toronto: ABC Publications, 2003), 41.
5 Mario Ribas in Terry Brown, ed., *Other Voices, Other Worlds* (London: DLT, 2006), 222.
6 *Summa Theologica* II/II g.54 a.8.
7 Peter Atkinson, *Friendship and the Body of Christ* (London: SPCK, 2004).
8 David Peterson, ed., *Holiness and Sexuality: Homosexuality in Biblical Context*, (London: Paternoster, 2004),129.
9 Quoted by Aquinas in *Summa* II/II q.151 a.3 ad 2.
10 *Summa Theologica* II/II g.54 a.8.
11 Raymond Lawrence, *Poisoning of Eros* (New York: Augustine Moore Press, 1989), 30.
12 John S. Mbiti, *African Religions and Philosophy* (Garden City, New York: Doubleday, 1970), 1.
13 Pierre Erny, *Childhood and Cosmos: The Social Psychology of the Black African Child* (New York: New Perspectives, 1973), iv.
14 Na'im Akbar, 'Rhythmic Patterns in African Personality'. Available on line at: http//www.africawithin.com/akbar/rhythm.htm.

Chapter 8

The Witness of Science

David de Pomerai and Glynn Harrison

Introduction

The earlier sections of this book have set the scene in terms of mission and listening, introduced the resources found in the authorities of Scripture, tradition and reason, and introduced the voices of homosexual persons reflecting on identity and a dialogue on spirituality and sexuality between two Anglicans of quite different views. This final section returns to a much more technical and academic style. It does so by looking to the work of two Anglican scientists which helps us understand what biology – particularly genetics – and psychology can tell us about homosexuality.

This book is likely to be read by people with a theological background and may be challenging for those who do not have an understanding of science. You may also want to read the contents with a Christian you know who is a scientist, perhaps a doctor or a science teacher.

Both **David de Pomerai** and **Glynn Harrison** are working scientists in British universities. They bring their skills to enable us to consider the research which has taken place over recent years in their own fields. As noted in the introduction, Lambeth Conferences and other Instruments have repeatedly requested study of scientific evidence but this has rarely been done in Anglican documents on sexuality. As a result scientific claims are sometimes made by advocates of different theological positions that are difficult to assess. To help in this task, this chapter reviews the literature and its bearing on Christian discussion. **David** focuses on the possible biological causes of homosexuality in the hope that the scientific research may help answer such questions as to whether or not homosexuality is biologically fixed. **Glynn** examines the question of whether those who do not wish to experience same sex attraction can experience significant change in their sexual feelings and desires, as claimed by some Christians. Although they are experts in the their respective fields – David is a biologist, specifically a geneticist, while Glynn is a professor of psychiatry, specializing in schizophrenia – neither of them were personally involved in any of the research they report here.

What follows is often highly technical and quite complex. However, as all truth is God's truth, it is vital that Christians thinking about sexuality be as well informed as they can be about the findings of different scientific studies. It is important to acknowledge, nevertheless, that both David and Glynn are clear that the science they present is not conclusive. Furthermore, even if it were conclusive science, as faithful Anglicans, they do not believe it is for science to have the last and determinative word on how we should then live as Christians or order ourselves as churches. That fact is why this is only one of eight chapters in this book and it is important that its findings are related to the other chapters, particularly those in section two of the book exploring Scripture, tradition and reason.

One of the features of scientific investigation – in contrast to the immediately preceding chapters – is that it seeks to be dispassionate, neutral, objective and impersonal. Some of the language in this chapter may therefore seem to you to be clinical and even dehumanizing. Glynn and David recognize this and it is another of the reasons they believe that, although science has a place, its place is limited and needs to be put alongside the more personal stories found elsewhere in this book.

While some readers will have a good knowledge of science, many will not. The book is designed for those who are more competent in theology than science. David and Glynn therefore begin their sections with an overview of their papers, summarising their main sections and findings. If you do not have a scientific background you may wish simply to read these and then follow up in more detail any sections that particularly interest you. As in all the chapters, the conclusions they reach are their own but we believe their work represents a major contribution to this often neglected aspect of the discussion among Christians and hope it will help you deepen your understanding of the mystery of human sexuality.

PART 1:
BIOLOGICAL MECHANISMS IN HOMOSEXUALITY:
A CRITICAL REVIEW

David de Pomerai

Executive Summary

Is homosexuality innate or learned, biologically fixed or changeable and open to choice? Science has provided a variety of possible biological explanations for homosexuality, although the current evidence is far from conclusive, and environmental or psychosocial explanations are clearly also important. The paragraphs below summarize each of the main sections of the full review.

(1) **Prologue.** This sets out the terms, definitions and methodology of this review, drawing key distinctions between exclusive homosexuality (HS), bisexuality (BS) and same-sex attraction (SSA). The basic elements of the peer-review process used in science are outlined, justifying greater trust in the scientific literature than in the unsupported opinions and comments to be found on the internet and in the popular media.

(2) **A brief primer on DNA and genetics.** Essential basic concepts in developmental biology and genetics are described, including the principles of inheritance from parent to offspring, the distinction between identical and non-identical twins, the fundamentals of copying DNA during cell division, and the concept of the gene as a section of DNA specifying the production of one or more proteins, whose effects are

seen as a heritable trait. DNA changes termed mutations result in altered protein products that can sometimes cause disease. In some cases, carriers with only one copy of a mutated gene are at an advantage compared to people with two normal copies, whereas those with two mutated copies suffer from severe disease.

(3) **Sex, gender, hormones and sexuality in humans.** Gender in humans is determined at two levels – one genetic, the other hormonal. Abnormalities and imbalances in either or both of these can result in intersexes who are neither fully male nor fully female. The Kinsey scale describing human sexual orientation (from exclusively HS to wholly heterosexual) is discussed, as are some of its limitations (e.g. in regard to BS).

(4) **The Nature/Nurture debate and the importance of twin studies in the HS debate.** Human characteristics are determined partly by our genes (Nature – i.e. heritable traits) and partly by our environment, culture and upbringing (Nurture). Most complex behaviours are influenced by both Nature and Nurture. Studies of twins can shed some light on this question, because identical twins carry exactly the same set of genes, whereas non-identical twins are no more closely related than ordinary siblings (sharing only half of each other's genes). Twin studies suggest that there must be *some* genetic contribution to homosexuality (since identical twins are more similar for HS than non-identical twins), but that the environment is also important. Genes may influence female HS to a greater extent than male HS. The limitations and confounding factors affecting twin studies are also noted.

(5) **'Genes for' homosexuality.** There have been several searches for gene variants (alleles) that might contribute to HS, but media reports of so-called 'gay genes' have been greatly exaggerated. For one particular subtype of male HS (apparently inherited through the mother), there are now four candidate alleles that might be involved. At most, these studies identify local variations in the DNA of homosexuals (compared to heterosexual controls), but there is no proof that these represent variant genes, nor any clear link to HS. So far, none of these alleles shows the tight statistical association required to prove such a link.

(6) **Hormonal influences on HS.** Many masculine characteristics are determined by male sex hormones (androgens). It has been suggested that female HS may be linked to unusually high androgen exposure in the womb, and male HS to unusually low androgen exposure. Although the evidence is rather weak and confusing, there does seem to be a stronger link for female HS. Even so, only a minority of women exposed to high androgen levels in the womb will subsequently develop HS. Although prenatal exposure to androgens in the womb has a marked effect on the length-ratio of the second to fourth fingers (2D:4D ratio) in men versus women, this ratio does not shows any clear relationship to HS.

(7) **HS and the brain: neuroanatomy and pheromone responses.** Suggested differences in brain structure between homosexuals and heterosexuals remain unproven and controversial. However, brain responses to sexual stimuli (including possible sexual attractants known as pheromones) show clear differences between these

groups. Heterosexuals respond only to pheromones of the opposite sex, whereas homosexuals respond to those of the same sex. It is unclear whether such brain responses are fixed (hard-wired) or remain open to change.

(8) **Fraternal birth order and male HS.** For males only, there is a marked increase in the prevalence of HS among younger brothers, rising by roughly one third for each older brother in the family. There is no apparent effect of older sisters, nor any similar birth-order effect for female HS, unless the definition is broadened out to include SSA. Suggestions that this fraternal birth order (FBO) effect might result, e.g., from childhood abuse by older brothers are undermined by the fact that the FBO effect relates only to the number of full older brothers, and is unaffected by adopted older brothers. One suggested biological explanation is that the mother may become progressively immunized against male-specific proteins with each successive male pregnancy, and that the antibodies raised against these proteins might predispose the male foetus to later HS. Although this model lacks direct support, there is at least a well-known precedent involving the Rhesus factor.

(9) **What evolutionary rationales might account for HS?** Exclusive HS seems to present an evolutionary paradox, since presumably such individuals rarely if ever have children. How then is it possible for variant genes (alleles) promoting HS to become widespread in the human population? Various suggestions have been advanced. Although homosexuals may have few children, their empathic and nurturing qualities may promote cohesion among family or clan groups, whereas aggressively heterosexual males may be disruptive. This kin selection idea finds little direct support, but other group selection models remain plausible. It is possible that men carrying one copy of an HS-promoting allele may be at a reproductive advantage, e.g. because females find empathic and nurturing qualities attractive among men. Alternatively, the reproductive benefits of such HS-promoting alleles may be more apparent among female relatives of homosexual men, and there is some evidence that such women may have more children than average. As yet there is no clear evidence favouring any one model over the others.

(10) **Conclusions.** The available data suggest multiple redundant or overlapping biological mechanisms that could cause, or predispose towards, homosexuality. There may well be differences in causation between male and female HS, and also between HS, BS and SSA.

1. Prologue

This review asks whether homosexuality might sometimes arise from innate biological causes that cannot be chosen. The theological and pastoral implications of this are left for others to explore. I bring to this study some 30 years of academic teaching and research in genetics, bioethics and animal development. I am also an ordained Anglican priest and a member of the Society of Ordained Scientists (SOSc). My aim here is to review the recent scientific literature addressing the core questions as fully and impartially as possible.

Asking scientists for absolute certainty misses the whole point of doing science, which is to strive for ever-closer approximations to reality by testing predictions from current hypotheses and refining those hypotheses in the light of the results obtained. Science is always in a state of flux, with received wisdom being constantly challenged by new findings and alternative hypotheses or interpretations. Science offers provisional rather than definitive answers. Even so, science is much more than a social construct agreed by its practitioners, as reflected in our everyday experience that science does actually work in the real world: drugs help to cure people, aeroplanes fly, and most of us make use of computers or telecommunications devices.

Much of the material reviewed below has no direct experimental basis, because experimentation on human subjects (perhaps especially in the area of sexual orientation) is unethical. Many of the proposed biological mechanisms are therefore based on associations or correlations, which do not provide any *proof* for a causal link. There is a famous statistical correlation – extending over many years – between the annual birth-rate in Sweden and the annual migration of storks over that country. Despite impressive statistical credentials, it would clearly be absurd to suggest a causal link here! This example should hang like a warning sword of Damocles over all the correlations reviewed below; the possibility remains that some of them may result from mere statistical flukes. Nevertheless, it is implausible to suggest that they can *all* be dismissed so lightly; many of them are likely to reflect direct or indirect causal links. This caveat should not be construed as a get-out clause by those who refuse to countenance the possibility that HS might be innate rather than chosen. It is also worth pointing out in passing that recall bias poses real problems in studies using retrospective questionnaires about past behaviour or influences.

Before beginning to address the science, it is necessary to clarify the terminology to be used in this review. Homosexuality (HS) is used here to describe sexual attraction *exclusively* to members of the same sex (whether male–male or female–female); however, this need not necessarily imply overt sexual activity, which is a matter of choice. Bisexuality (BS) denotes sexual attraction to members of *both* sexes, where choice must obviously affect a person's behaviour. Finally, same-sex attraction (SSA) is a wider term used here to encompass both HS and BS, as well as many heterosexuals who may feel attracted towards members of the same sex, for instance during an adolescent phase or as a repressed urge in adult life. There is confusion and potential bias in much of the literature caused by differing definitions of homosexuality.

An internet Google search using the terms *homosexuality* and *biology* produced 141,000 hits – an unmanageably large number that includes many repetitions and irrelevancies, as well as innumerable unsubstantiated postings and allegations. Amid this welter of online information – what is actually trustworthy? – scientists take a more conservative approach by searching mainly in the published scientific literature, where reports of original research findings have all been subjected to a rigorous process of peer review by experts in the field. These reviewers will ask whether the experimental findings are adequate to justify the conclusions, whether the methods used are appropriate and well described, and whether alternative interpretations have been carefully excluded. Only after passing through such scrutiny (and often several revisions) will the report finally get published. Although this does not guarantee that all aspects of every paper are necessarily correct, it does ensure that most are well grounded in verifiable fact. Where errors and oversights do creep in, they are usually corrected fairly rapidly when fellow scientists attempt to repeat or to build on the original findings (see above).

When starting to write this review, I used the broader search terms *biology** and *homosexual** to look at how often they appeared together in the titles and/or abstracts of articles published over the past five years in the biological literature, using the abstract service from BIOSIS Previews. This gave only 455 hits, of which the majority (310) were medical in theme, reporting, e.g., higher disease incidence amongst homosexuals as compared to other groups. Whilst not germane to my theme here, this preponderance underlines the fact that certain homosexual lifestyles (especially risk-taking promiscuous behaviour) can carry a heavy health cost. Amongst other major themes identified, 27 papers dealt with HS in animal systems (which are *not* reviewed here), and 55 focused mainly on psychosocial factors (discussed elsewhere). Ten papers dealt with various aspects of sociology in relation to HS, several criticizing the 'genomania' and even pseudo-science which surrounds this issue.[58] Whilst it is true that media stories about 'genes for HS' tend to over-simplify the underlying science and lead to a biased view of *all* HS as innate or inborn, we should not fall into the opposite trap of rejecting this science as a mere social construct pandering to Western liberal views. A total of 66 papers dealt with suggested biological mechanisms that might explain or contribute to HS, and most of these are reviewed below, together with key papers from the earlier (pre-2002) literature.

2. A brief primer on DNA and genetics

We are all aware of sharing certain traits and characteristics with our parents, since half of our genes derive from mother and half from father. Every one of our cells contains a double (*diploid*) set of genes. One set of genes comes from the mother's egg and a second set from the father's sperm. Each of these single sets is termed *haploid*, and results from a halving of the number of gene-sets (*meiosis*) during the maturation of both sperm and eggs. When sperm and egg fuse during fertilization, their respective gene-sets unite to restore the normal diploid number in the fertilized egg (*zygote*). All of the billions of cells in a human body result from cell division (*mitosis*), during which this diploid gene-set is copied exactly. All genes are composed of DNA, comprising two long intertwined strands in the famous double-helix structure proposed by Watson and Crick in 1953. Just four chemical base-units (or *nucleotides*, abbreviated A, G, C and T) are strung together in series (termed the *sequence*) along each DNA strand, and the double helix is held together by weak cross-links, such that A is always paired with T, and C is paired with G. When the two strands separate, each of them can direct the formation of a matching (*complementary*) strand, with C attracting G, T attracting A, and so on. This results in two double-helical pieces of DNA which are *identical* in sequence to each other and to the parent helix. This process of *DNA replication* ensures that every cell in our body (except for sperm or eggs) receives an *exact* copy of the diploid gene-set present in the fertilized egg. Thus our genetic identity was forged at fertilization, and (aside from accidental changes) does not alter during our individual lifetime.

In higher organisms, thousands of genes are contained within enormously long pieces of DNA known as *chromosomes*. The human diploid gene-set consists of 46 chromosomes, the haploid set (in sperm or eggs) of 23. During the development of our mother's egg, both of her parents' chromosome-sets became partially scrambled. The same thing happened during sperm development in our father. This means that we do not receive any one of our four grandparental chromosome-sets intact, but rather a mixture of both maternal grandparents' gene-sets through our mother, and of both paternal grandparents' gene-sets through our father. This mixing-up process (*recombination*) occurs only during meiosis, and confers a unique and unrepeatable genetic identity upon each one of us (with the notable exception of identical twins; see below). As a result, each one of us shares 50% of our diploid gene-set with each parent, but only 25% with each of our four grandparents. On average, we also share 50% of our gene-set with full brothers and sisters (from the same parents), but only 25% with half brothers or sisters (one parent the same, but not the other). In genetic terms, non-identical or *dizygotic* (DZ) twins share only 50% of their gene-set with each other (just like ordinary siblings), because such twins result from two separate fertilization events, each involving a different sperm and egg; they are therefore no more closely related than full brothers or sisters. However, DZ twins also share the same womb environment prior to birth, the importance of which will emerge later. By contrast, identical or *monozygotic* (MZ) twins arise when an early human embryo splits into two fragments during the first 15 days after fertilization. Each fragment is able to develop subsequently into a complete individual (very late splitting results in conjoined twins). Because both fragments originate from the same zygote and thus from the same fertilization event, MZ twins share 100% of their genes; they are genetically identical.

A *gene* is a stretch of DNA that encodes a specific *protein*, and proteins are the functional building blocks of all living organisms. Some proteins are structural, like actin and myosin in muscle; some speed up chemical reactions inside cells (enzymes), such as those which convert glucose into energy; some transport vital materials around the body, such as haemoglobin carrying oxygen in the blood; yet others break down toxic chemicals, or recognize invading microbes (antibodies). The details of how genetic information encoded in DNA is translated into protein need not detain us here. In essence, proteins provide the readout that links DNA information (genes) to recognizable traits such as eye colour or facial features.

If the DNA sequence of a gene becomes altered accidentally (through *mutation*), this usually causes a small change in the protein specified, which can sometimes lead to malfunction or even disease. A good example is the altered form of haemoglobin protein (termed β^s) that causes sickle-cell anaemia. If you are a carrier (*heterozygote*), inheriting one copy of the β^s gene plus one normal copy (β^A) from your parents, then your blood is able to carry oxygen efficiently but you also show increased resistance to malaria. This is termed *heterozygote advantage*, and probably accounts for the high prevalence of the β^s gene in West African populations. But if you inherit two copies of the β^s gene (*homozygote*), one from each parent, then your haemoglobin is unable to transport oxygen effectively and you will suffer from sickle-cell anaemia – a debilitating and usually fatal disease. This is a so-called *single-gene disorder* or genetic disease. Genetic factors also contribute to many commoner diseases (such as diabetes and heart disease), but usually these involve several disease-associated genes – none of which is sufficient on its own to cause that disease. Sometimes one or more genes may confer a predisposition towards developing a particular disease (such as BRCA–1 mutations linked to breast cancer), but environmental factors are also required to trigger the disease process (e.g. exposure to chemicals or viruses). These are termed *multi-gene disorders*, and their patterns of inheritance in affected families are always much more complex than those seen with the simple single-gene disorders outlined earlier. This is relevant to the present review because the available genetic evidence (in sections 4 and 5) suggests that multiple genes might influence HS.

Before moving on to the substance of this review, it is worth noting that humans possess a lot of DNA but relatively few genes – ~20,000 according to latest estimates[74] – around the same number as a simple millimetre-long roundworm! In humans, barely 1% of our DNA specifies proteins, and much of the rest performs complex regulatory functions, allowing very precise control over which proteins are produced when, in what quantity, and in which types of cell. Although simplified accounts assume that one gene should specify just one protein, there is increasing evidence that a single gene often gives rise to a small family of related proteins. This is because genes in higher organisms are organized into protein-coding (*exon*) and non-coding (*intron*) sections, and different combinations of exons can be used to specify several variant versions of the final protein. Thus the total number of functional human proteins may be larger than our modest gene tally might suggest!

3. Sex, gender, hormones and sexuality in humans

The 46 chromosomes in all diploid human cells fall into two classes; 44 are autosomes (with one copy of each from the sperm and one copy from the egg), while the other two are sex chromosomes. Female cells contain two copies of the X chromosome, whereas male cells contain one X chromosome (always derived from the mother's egg) and one much smaller Y chromosome (always from the father's sperm). Thus females are chromosomally XX and males XY. Broadly speaking, genes carried on the Y chromosome impose male sexual identity upon a default female state. For most people, this sex-chromosome-dependent mechanism of sex determination operates faultlessly. However, there are a number of genetic mutations and other abnormalities that can result in sex reversal or an intermediate state that is neither wholly male nor female (*intersexes*). A helpful review of human sex-determination, sexuality and intersexes is given by Hare.[43] The master-gene controlling male sexual identity, called *SRY*, is carried on the Y chromosome. Mutation or deletion of the *SRY* gene can result in an apparent female who is chromosomally male (XY). The explanation is simple; in the absence of *SRY* gene function, male sexual development cannot be initiated, and female development occurs instead by default. Not only can male-determining genes become inactivated in 'female' XY intersexes, but it is also possible for active versions of these genes to become transferred (*transposed*) onto other chromosomes, resulting in 'male' intersexes who are chromosomally female (XX). Insertion of the equivalent mouse gene (*Sry*) into chromosomally female XX mice results in male development.[56] These examples show that a person's apparent gender (technically, their sexual *phenotype*) can be at odds with their chromosomal sex (XX or XY). However, in genetic terms, it is the possession of active copies of the male-determining genes (such as *SRY*) that specifies whether male or female sexual development will ensue. The early embryonic gonad is *bipotential* – capable of developing either into a testis or an ovary. The choice between these options depends on a transient phase of *SRY* gene activity; if this happens, the male path of development is followed; but if not, female development is the default option.[24, 29, 72]

A second tier of control influencing human sexual development is exerted by sex hormones (mainly androgens such as testosterone in males, and oestrogens in females), which first appear in large amounts at the time of puberty. Androgens trigger the development of male secondary sexual characteristics (including facial hair etc.), whereas oestrogens trigger menarche (the onset of monthly periods) and breast development in females. However, it is important to realize that all females produce some androgens as well as oestrogens, and similarly all males produce oestrogens as well as androgens. Depending on the relative and absolute amounts of these hormones, individual humans vary enormously across a spectrum from masculine to feminine characteristics (in behavioural as well as physical terms). Moreover, the biochemical pathways that produce these hormones in the body are closely related; for instance, a single protein (the *aromatase* enzyme) can convert testosterone into oestrogens. The possible influence of androgens (especially) on HS is considered separately in section 7 below. Note that androgen production is essential for most aspects of male development, whereas much of female development can proceed even in the absence of oestrogens.

For more than half a century, human sexual orientation has commonly been assessed using the Kinsey scale,[53] with exclusively heterosexual behaviour ranking 0 and exclusively homosexual behaviour ranking 6. Bisexuality (BS) thus falls around the middle of this scale, tacitly assuming that bisexuality is in some sense intermediate between heterosexuality and homosexuality (HS). James[50] criticized these rankings as simplistic, pointing out that many homosexual partnerships are characterized by 'active' versus 'passive' roles that do not necessarily arise from the same biological or psychosocial factors. Active HS roles in both sexes may be associated with exposure to high testosterone levels (pre- and/or postnatally), and this in turn may be linked to risk-taking behaviour and bisexuality ('experimenting' sexually with partners of both sexes). On this basis, BS should not be viewed as an intermediate behaviour. More pertinent to the present debate, most current studies make no distinction between 'active' and 'passive' HS roles. If these do indeed arise from different biological and psychosocial causes (possibly differing also between men and women), then statistical evidence relating to one such factor will be weakened by the inclusion of HS (or indeed BS or SSA) groups in which that same factor plays no important role. However, classifying homosexuals into unambiguous categories is likely to prove far from simple!

4. The Nature/Nurture debate and the importance of twin studies in the HS debate

Although many simple traits are determined by our genes (e.g. our eye colour, or whether we suffer from sickle-cell anaemia), in many others our environment and/or upbringing also play a role. Height is a good example; children of tall parents are often tall themselves (suggesting strong genetic influence), but they sometimes grow even taller thanks to improved nutrition not available during their parents' childhood. Post-traumatic stress disorder (PTSD) is clearly triggered by unpredictable environmental causes – but the way in which we respond to such trauma is likely to show genetic influences. While musical tastes are obviously conditioned by our culture and upbringing, both genetics and training can affect our ability to discern complicated musical patterns. In most cases, genes and environment *together* help to mould who we are. So to what extent are complex human traits determined by our genes (Nature), and to what extent by our upbringing, environment or culture (Nurture)? Genetic determinists would have us believe that most human characteristics are specified precisely by our genes (a view sometimes criticized as genomania[58]). Conversely, others see the human person as a blank slate, inscribed largely by environmental and cultural factors. Arguably, we are neither slaves to our genes nor flotsam in an ocean of cultural crosscurrents, but something greater than either. 'Nature/Nurture' is thus a false dichotomy; in his review of this long-running debate, Robinson[79] suggests that 'both–and' is more appropriate than 'either–or'. As applied to the vexed issue of homosexuality (HS), this question can be restated as follows: 'Is HS determined genetically or by other early-acting biological factors (Nature), or does it result from a mixture of social, cultural or familial factors in the environment (Nurture)?' Broadly speaking, we might expect human choice (sinful or otherwise) to play a more significant role if HS is largely explicable in terms of Nurture. However, this does not deny the possibility that individuals may choose to suppress or override their innate inclinations (those determined by Nature, e.g. genetic factors). It is conversely possible that Nurture explanations may not be open to choice, e.g. if HS inclinations are linked to childhood sexual abuse.[49]

Studies of twins can provide a window onto this question. If a particular trait (e.g. eye colour) is wholly determined by our genes, then identical MZ twins will always share that characteristic – because they are genetically identical. Conversely, nonidentical DZ twins and ordinary siblings will share that characteristic, on average, in only 50% of cases. If that trait is also partly influenced by the womb environment experienced prior to birth, then DZ twins might show greater similarity than ordinary full siblings. Degrees of similarity are described by the term *concordance*, where MZ twins would be 100% concordant for a purely genetic trait. If concordance for MZ twins is higher than that for DZ twins, this difference can be used to estimate the extent of genetic influence on the trait under study. This in turn suggests how far the variability observed in human populations for a given trait can be explained by heritable genetic factors (*heritability*; i.e. Nature) and how much by environmental factors (Nurture). Some confusion arises from the use of two different concordance calculations; pair-wise concordance rates treat each pair of twins as a single unit, whereas proband-wise concordance rates count each individual twin as a unit. In a review of classical twin studies, Boomsma *et al.*[23] summarize current knowledge for several complex behavioural traits (including depression, risk-taking, anxiety, neuroticism, and multiple measures of intelligence), where at least 50% of the observed variation appears to be heritable, suggesting a strong genetic influence. Most estimates for the heritability of HS are lower than this, as shown by the proband-wise concordance rates listed in Table 1 below. However, all such figures should be treated with a degree of caution.

Table 1. Published twin-study estimates of proband-wise concordance rates for HS

Source of information	Prevalence of HS in general population	MZ twins – concordance for HS	DZ twins – concordance for HS	Limitations of study
Bailey & Pillard, 1991[2]	11% of men based on HS among adoptive brothers [n = 57]	52% (male only) [n = 56]	22% (male only) [n = 54]	Confined to male HS; also study group bias – recruited via adverts in homophile publications
Whitam et al., 1993[86]	Not stated	66% [n = 38]	30% [n = 23]	Study group bias – recruited via adverts in homophile publications
Bailey et al., 1993[3]	6% of women (only) based on adoptive sisters' HS [n = 35]	48% (female only) [n = 71]	16% (female only) [n = 37]	Confined to female HS; also study group bias – recruited via adverts in homophile publications
Kendler et al., 2000[51]	~8% based on DZ twins of opposite sex [n = 192]	32% [n = 324]	~13% for DZ twins of the same sex [n = 240]	US twin registry data; low statistical power due to relative rarity of HS in general twin population
Bailey et al., 2000[5]	Not stated explicitly	20–38% for men [n = 260] vs. 24–30% for women [n = 539]*	0–11% for men [n = 146] vs. 11–30% for women [n = 293]*	Australian twin registry; low statistical power due to relative rarity of HS in general twin population

*Range here reflects stricter or looser definitions of heterosexuality using the Kinsey scale. Sample numbers (number of twins in each category) are given as [n =] in square brackets.

In most such studies, concordance rates for MZ twins (sharing 100% of their genes) are much higher than for DZ twins (sharing the same womb and family environment, but only 50% of their genes). This implies that genetic factors *are* important.[2, 3, 5, 51] However, since concordance rates for MZ twins never approach 100%, environmental factors must also play a crucial role. In one earlier study,[52] much lower concordance rates were found amongst 46 mainly male MZ twins who were homosexual. Another more recent study of SSA found little difference between concordance rates for MZ and for DZ twins.[7] A plausible explanation for these contradictory findings comes from sampling bias in some earlier studies, since participants recruited through advertisements in homophile publications will skew the sample towards exclusive HS (Kinsey scale 6) and exclude those in the BS/SSA categories. More recent studies using national twin registries give lower estimates of the genetic contribution towards HS. Although many hundreds of MZ and DZ twins can be accessed from these registries, in only a small proportion of cases (1–5%) will one or both twins be homosexual, resulting in quite small sample numbers that can easily become distorted by a handful of extra (or fewer) cases. This results in low statistical power; i.e. the conclusions are far from definitive. Moreover, not all of the twins approached actually respond to questionnaires, and it is possible that those where both twins are homosexual may choose to respond more often than those where this is not the case (introducing another type of sample bias). Two large twin registry studies are not included in Table 1 because they quote estimates of HS heritability rather than twin concordance rates. One of these (also based on the Australian twin registry data)[55] suggests that additive genetic effects result in 50–60% heritability for female HS, but only 30% heritability for male HS. This broadly confirms an earlier study[44] estimating HS heritability at 24% among male MZ twins (although this was not significantly different from zero!) and at 60% among female MZ twins (significantly different). Overall, current evidence suggests a significant genetic contribution towards female HS, but less towards male HS, and little towards SSA.[7] However, childhood gender non-conformity (CGN, i.e. effeminate behaviour in boys or tomboy behaviour in girls) appears to be heritable in both sexes, and is also strongly predictive of later homosexual inclinations.[5] But this is open to the common criticism of all such retrospective correlations: homosexual respondents are likely to recall or even exaggerate CGN as a rationale for their subsequent HS. Independent evidence confirming CGN from parents or childhood associates is rarely available. Nevertheless, it is possible that certain types of male HS are strongly influenced by genetic factors, but that other types are not.

Very recently (April 2007), the distinguished geneticist Francis Collins concluded that the heritability of HS may be as low as 20%.[26] This may underestimate the genetic contribution to female HS, at least. But it is worth quoting Collins' conclusions from this estimate: 'Yes, we have all been dealt a particular set of [genetic] cards . . . But how we play the cards is up to us.' I would not demur from this statement – except to note that there are two ways of interpreting Collins' 20% HS heritability estimate. One is that this 20% estimate applies (with minor variations) to *all* homosexuals, implying an ~80% influence from environment and upbringing that could include personal choices at varying points in an individual's psychosocial development. But the other is that this average figure of 20% heritability might actually vary widely, and could even constitute the predominant factor underlying HS in certain individuals. On balance, in view of the evidence for multiple causative factors in HS, this latter possibility cannot be excluded.

Two further points arise from these studies. The first concerns the frequency of HS in the general population. Estimates based on the families of homosexuals recruited to the earlier studies seem unduly high, and only indirect estimates are available from twin registry data (either from data on adoptive siblings, or from DZ twins of the opposite sex). In general, the numbers quoted in the second column of Table 1 all tend to over-estimate the prevalence of HS. Several large-scale studies have addressed this question specifically, and (unsurprisingly) the resultant figures depend on how strict a definition of HS is used: typical numbers are in the range 0.5–2% for exclusive HS (Kinsey 6), but 3–10% if BS and SSA are included.[35, 36, 44] All such studies report more men than women in the non-heterosexual categories.

A second issue relates to concordance rates for same-sex DZ twins, which are usually lower than those for MZ twins (consistent with genetic influences) but higher than those for ordinary same-sex siblings.[4] Across three different samples of homosexuals, HS prevalence among their siblings was estimated at only 7–10% for brothers and 3–4% for sisters.[4] This implies that same-sex DZ twins may be more similar for HS than would be expected – given their 50% genetic similarity (the same as ordinary siblings), which might in turn reflect their shared environment. Where studies have looked at concordance rates for HS among DZ twins of the opposite sex, these are usually lower than for DZ twins of the same sex and differ little from ordinary full siblings. Thus factors that influence HS within the womb environment may affect DZ twin foetuses differently according to their gender. Such differential effects could be caused either by prenatal exposure to sex hormones (especially androgens), or by maternal antibodies (especially those raised against 'foreign' male-specific proteins). Once again, however, there are contradictions in the published literature. One large study of non-identical DZ twins showed that SSA is twice as frequent among males whose twins were female, but this effect disappears in families with an older brother;[7] furthermore, the incidence of female SSA among such twins was lower than expected. This argues against a role for androgen exposure in female SSA, since the female twin foetus would be exposed to elevated testosterone levels from the accompanying male twin foetus. The converse possibility, that this testosterone effect might be diluted for the male foetus by the presence of an accompanying female twin – perhaps leading to SSA in the male twin – is also unlikely, since the increased incidence of male SSA among opposite-sex DZ twins disappears in families with an older brother. Overall, this suggests a role for childhood gender role models, and argues against genetic or hormonal influences on SSA. Overall, these twin data can be interpreted in a variety of different ways, and do not prove any single cause for HS, let alone for SSA.

5. 'Genes for' homosexuality

This is a controversial topic – indeed the title I have (deliberately) used reflects a gross over-simplification of the evidence as presented in the popular media. The previous section adduced evidence for a heritable genetic contribution to HS, perhaps stronger in female than in male HS. If this is the case, there should be telltale genetic differences between homosexual individuals and the rest of the population. But how do we go about pin-pointing such genetic differences? The analogy of human genetic diseases can be helpful here, though properly we should not prejudge the core issue under discussion by comparing HS to a disease. Since heritability among MZ twins is nowhere near 100%, HS is unlikely to be caused by a single variant gene (similar to a single-gene disorder). Instead, the situation may be more similar to multi-gene disorders, where a variant gene (or a combination of such genes) may confer susceptibility to that condition, dependent on interactions with environmental factors, and indeed other genes. Such a multi-gene/susceptibility model would help to explain both the low concordance for HS among MZ twins and the undoubted importance of environmental factors in HS. However, finding relevant HS-associated genes among a total of 20,000[74] in the human *genome* is very much like seeking the proverbial needle in a haystack.

Efforts to identify genes contributing to HS began in the 1990s, long before completion of the human genome *sequence* (which specifies the precise order of As, Ts, Cs and Gs along the entire length of DNA in the human gene-set[47]). To simplify this huge task, Hamer and colleagues[42] decided to focus on a subtype of male HS that appears to be inherited maternally – i.e. through the mother only. This means that all homosexual relatives (uncles, cousins etc.) are on the mother's side of the family and not on the father's. In genetic terms, such exclusively maternal inheritance most likely points to a gene or genes carried on the X chromosome, since all men receive their single X chromosome from the mother. This narrowed down the amount of DNA that needed to be searched (essentially down from 23 to just 1 chromosome), but even so there are some 1100 genes on the X chromosome. The approach used by Hamer *et al.*[42] was essentially the same as that used in searching for disease-associated genes, comparing DNA samples from the selected homosexual group against control samples from the heterosexual population. Any consistent DNA differences between these two sets of samples might point to HS-associated variant genes (technically known as *alleles*, just as β^S is a mutant allele of β^A). It would be far too time-consuming and expensive to sequence the entire X chromosome from every participant in both groups, so instead Hamer *et al.*[42] used a form of DNA fingerprinting – similar to that used in forensic science for linking suspects to DNA evidence left at a crime scene. Put simply, this depends on the presence of short repetitive sequences known as microsatellite DNA (one example would be AGGGTTCC–AGGGTTCC–AGGGTTCC-, where the dashes delineate repeats of the same sequence). These microsatellite repeats are highly variable (*polymorphic*) in number between individuals, and can be used to identify criminals, trace family histories or help identify disease-associated genes. Note, however, that these variable repeats (termed *polymorphic microsatellite markers* or PMMs) do not usually occur within genes (such repeats rarely specify a protein). Rather, PMM patterns act like signposts at intervals along the chromosome, and particular variant patterns may point to an unusual allele of a nearby gene. This can be used to home in on chromosomal regions containing disease-associated genes. By extension, the same approach could identify candidate genes linked to HS.

Hamer *et al.*[42] found a variant version of a specific region of the X chromosome (Xq28) that seems to be strongly associated with HS in this particular group of male homosexuals showing maternal inheritance. Though interesting, this does *not* identify a 'gay gene' – indeed it does not actually identify a variant gene-allele at all, but only an unusual pattern of PMMs that *may* be associated with such an allele. Further work by the same group found that this variant-Xq28 association extends only to maternally inherited male HS, and not to female HS.[46] Several groups have attempted to replicate this finding, but with mixed success. For instance, Rice *et al.*[78] failed to find any evidence for an Xq28 association with HS, even though their study was also restricted to homosexual males showing maternal inheritance. More recently, Mustanski *et al.*[71] have used a genome-wide scan (covering all of the human chromosomes) to search for genes associated with maternally inherited male HS. Using accepted criteria for significant degrees of association (as used in studies of multi-gene disorders), none of the variant PMM patterns identified in HS individuals quite reached the required level of significance, although several closely approached this value (at 7q36, 8p12 and 10q26 – respectively on chromosomes 7, 8 and 10).

Interestingly, the Xq28 variant did not show a significant association in this study, although a re-analysis of Hamer's HS group using an X-chromosome-specific PMM set confirmed his original findings.[42] This is potentially quite important; the genome-wide PMM markers used by Mustanski et al.[71] are widely spaced across the human genome, a bit like a blurry low-resolution digital photograph. By contrast, the X-chromosome-specific PMM set is more closely spaced (since it represents only one chromosome) and therefore gives a higher-resolution picture of any variants present. Future work along these lines – perhaps using PMM sets specific to chromosomes 7, 8 and 10 – may confirm that some or all of these gene variants are indeed significantly associated with maternally inherited male HS.[71] Equally, these links may turn out to be statistical flukes on closer investigation. Bearing in mind that this is only one narrowly defined subtype of male HS (already with four candidate gene-regions!), the sheer scale of the search for HS-associated alleles becomes evident. We are still very much at the start of such a quest, although the impetus for pursuing this line of research has lessened with the weakening of genetic links to HS implied by recent twin studies (reviewed above). Finally, even if variant PMM patterns can be linked unambiguously to particular types of HS, it will still be necessary to sequence the DNA around those variant sites. This will determine: (a) whether recognizable genes exist in that region, (b) whether the variant PMM pattern identifies an unusual allele of one such gene, and (c) whether that unusual allele encodes an altered protein which might plausibly function in determining sexual orientation. Perhaps prematurely, Mustanski et al.[71] note that the DNA region around their strongest candidate (at 7q36) includes a peptide hormone-receptor gene and a gene essential for patterning the early embryo, while the 8p12 region includes 2 genes associated with regulating the production of sex steroid hormones. These are intriguing candidates, but as yet there is no clear evidence that variant alleles of these genes are linked to HS. Many in the gay community are uneasy about the emphasis on genetic research in relation to HS, fearing that identification of 'genes for' HS ('gay genes' in media parlance) may lead to calls for genetic testing and possible abortion of unborn foetuses that *might* show some genetic predisposition towards HS.[30]

Finally, if such variant alleles are indeed influential in predisposing individuals towards HS, why are more than 50% of MZ twins (who share 100% of their genes) discordant in regard to HS? Part of the resolution to this paradox may involve differential genetic *imprinting*, which has been described in other instances where MZ twins are discordant for a genetically determined trait.[85] Indeed, discordant imprinting may arise during the lifetime of an MZ twin.[37] Imprinting can alter the *activity* of genes (i.e. whether they are switched on or off), for instance by changing the local pattern of DNA methylation – a process which does not alter the fundamental DNA sequence. This is because methyl groups are only added onto C residues in CG sequences; despite this, the methylated Cs still attract only Gs during DNA replication. Usually, any gene which is heavily methylated becomes inactive, whereas a gene which remains unmethylated is more active and gives rise to a corresponding protein product. A notable case of wholesale gene inactivation involves one copy of the entire X chromosome in female (XX) cells. Normally, this happens randomly during early development, so that some of a woman's cells retain one version of the active X and some the other. However, recent evidence suggests that X inactivation is highly skewed (>90% of cells retaining the *same* active X) in the mothers of men with maternally inherited HS.[16] To what extent this might help to explain such maternal inheritance of HS remains to be seen.

6. Hormonal influences on HS

The influence of sex hormones (androgens such as testosterone in males, or oestrogens in females) on human sexual development was outlined at the end of section 3 above. These hormones act by entering cells and switching on sets of genes responsive to that hormone – a process that requires the mediation of a specific hormone *receptor* protein. Whilst the details of hormone-regulated gene expression need not detain us here, it is important to reiterate that women produce some androgens (as well as androgen receptors) in addition to oestrogens, and men produce some oestrogen (plus oestrogen receptors) in addition to androgens. There is thus a gradation in human sexual phenotypes from androgen-dominated (aggressively male) to oestrogen-dominated (female), which are correlated loosely with psychological and behavioural traits. If HS arises at the male end of the female range and at the female end of the male range, then unusually high androgen exposure might plausibly play a role in female HS, and unusually low androgen exposure a role in male HS. This basic hypothesis was forwarded some 20 years ago,[34] but evidence in its favour still remains somewhat sparse.[70]

Two rare medical conditions suggest that androgen exposure may indeed make an important contribution towards female HS. In congenital adrenal hyperplasia (CAH), the foetal adrenal glands secrete androgens instead of cortisol, resulting in masculinization of female babies. This condition can be fully corrected by surgery and subsequent postnatal treatment with cortisol, such that CAH women are anatomically and genetically female. Nevertheless, the incidence of female HS is about five times higher among CAH women, suggesting that prenatal exposure to androgens has indeed influenced their later sexuality.[68] Conversely, there is a much lower incidence of HS among people with androgen insensitivity syndrome (AIS). AIS is an inherited inability to respond to androgens which is often seen in chromosomally XY but phenotypically female intersexes. The prevalence of female HS is therefore increased by CAH and decreased by AIS,[68] correlating with the influence exerted by androgens (prenatally, in the case of CAH) in both conditions. An admittedly small study[83] showed that boy-like behaviour was more pronounced in girls with the more severe forms of CAH, though links to adult HS were not investigated. Moreover, CAH affects gender identity in women but not in men.[45] However, Gooren and Kruijver[41] have emphasized that other (as yet unidentified) factors can override androgen influence. Indeed, even in severe cases of CAH (i.e. those most strongly 'masculinized' by androgens before birth), girls still identify themselves as female despite showing masculine behavioural traits.[66] It is over-simplistic to suggest that androgens *impose* a masculine sexual identity on the human brain. A broadly similar conclusion is reached by Gooren,[40] in a review of the complex relationships between gender identity, gender-role behaviour and prenatal/perinatal hormone exposure, based on evidence from a range of clinical conditions where hormone levels are abnormal. At least in some cases, these hormonal influences clearly do *not* dictate an individual's sexuality. Some CAH women are homosexual, but many are not – and there are rare cases of HS even among those with AIS. Even so, it is clear that androgens exert a powerful masculinizing influence on psychosocial as well as physical development. However, as noted earlier (section 4), a large-scale study of opposite-sex DZ twins argues against any influence of androgen exposure on SSA in either twin.[7]

In section 3, it was noted that testosterone can be converted into oestrogens through the action of the enzyme aromatase. Counter-intuitively, brain aromatase activity in males produces oestrogens that act (via oestrogen receptors) to reinforce masculine and suppress feminine characteristics. If brain aromatase activity is low, the excess testosterone can be converted by a different pathway into another potent androgen (dihydrotestosterone – DHT), and this may cause certain masculine traits to become over-developed. Paradoxically, the net result can be a mixture of feminized (due to *low* oestrogen!) and hyper-masculinized (due to *high* DHT) characteristics, both of which are found among some male homosexuals.[77] Note that this correlation does not prove a hormonal cause for male HS in humans, although there is direct evidence linking male HS with low brain aromatase activity in sheep, where some rams are exclusively homosexual.[69]

Maternal hormone (including androgen) levels are not routinely monitored during pregnancy – and in any case, this could not exclude local factors affecting the intra-uterine environment. It is therefore difficult to establish any retrospective correlation between prenatal hormone exposure and sexual orientation (e.g. HS), which may not become apparent until many years after birth. For this reason, there is much interest in possible 'surrogate indicators' that show a close correlation with such exposure. One widely discussed surrogate measure is the ratio between the lengths of the index (second) and ring (fourth) fingers (henceforward the 2D:4D ratio). This ratio is markedly lower in men (XY) than in women (XX), a difference that extends across different racial groups.[63] Because this 2D:4D difference is clearly detectable by 2 years of age, it is likely to reflect prenatal factors. The 2D:4D ratio is lower (more masculine) in CAH females, suggesting some influence from prenatal androgen exposure. This has been directly confirmed by correlating the 2D:4D ratios of 2-year-old infants with the ratio of androgens to oestrogens in amniotic fluid samples obtained during pregnancy;[60] the higher the level of androgen, the lower the 2D:4D ratio. Curiously, these gender differences in 2D:4D ratio are stronger for the right hand than for the left, and there are also differences between ethnic groups.

If prenatal androgen exposure can influence HS as well as the 2D:4D ratio, then one would expect there to be a clear relationship between HS and 2D:4D ratio. Unfortunately, different studies have come up with contradictory answers, partly reflecting inconsistencies as to how the ratio was measured, and on which hand (left or right). In a re-analysis of five such studies, McFadden *et al.*[65] concluded that 2D:4D ratios were fairly uniform among homosexuals across different white Caucasian study populations, whereas 2D:4D ratios in the corresponding heterosexual groups showed much wider variation. This was true for both males and females, and argued against any consistent relationship between HS and 2D:4D ratio. More recent studies have shown that female HS is associated with a lower (more masculine) 2D:4D ratio[57] – reinforcing the suggestion (above) that prenatal androgen exposure in females may predispose them towards HS. Overall the evidence suggests a stronger correlation between HS and 2D:4D ratio in females as compared to males.

7. HS and the brain: neuroanatomy and pheromone responses

The brain is not a static organ, fixed in size and capabilities. One classic study established that a region of the brain associated with navigational skills (the posterior hippocampus) is larger in London taxi drivers than in the general population, and furthermore this difference increases with length of experience. The more you learn about how to find your way around the London streets, the larger your posterior hippocampus grows.[62] A number of studies have identified anatomical differences between the brains of men and women (*sexual dimorphism*), and a few have gone further to claim that the brains of homosexual men show greater anatomical similarities to those of women than to those of heterosexual men.[58] This claim is much disputed,[25] and there is little agreement even in regard to the precise identity of the brain structures (*nuclei*) under discussion. However, even though the basic brain *structure* (*neuroanatomy*) may differ little between homosexuals and heterosexuals, it is nonetheless clear that there must be differences in brain *function* regarding sexual attraction. By definition, heterosexuals are attracted to members of the opposite gender, whereas exclusive homosexuals are attracted to members of the same gender. Such responses can be visualized in terms of real-time brain function using magnetic resonance imaging techniques, as shown in a recent study comparing homosexual and heterosexual men.[80]

In many insects and mammals, volatile chemicals termed *pheromones* act as sexual attractants. Male moths can detect females of the same species at distances of more than a kilometre, because a specific pheromone emitted by females interacts (at extremely low concentrations) with highly sensitive detectors present in the antennae of males. In domestic pets and livestock, all males are well aware of which females are 'on heat' at any given time. Although visual (and tactile) stimuli play a major role in human sexual attraction, it has long been speculated that there might also be some involvement of pheromone-like odour cues – despite the fact that modern humans often go to great lengths to cover up their natural odours! A critical review of the status of human pheromone research[73] notes that genuine pheromone responses could easily be modified or overlaid by other factors that may be contextual or learned.

Several candidates for human sex pheromones have emerged in recent years; not surprisingly, androgen derivatives (e.g. AND) seem to act as male-generated sexual attractants, whereas oestrogen derivatives (e.g. EST) may act as female-generated attractants. Using positron emission tomography (PET) scanning to monitor brain function in real time, heterosexual men were found to respond to EST in brain areas associated with sexual arousal, and a similar response of heterosexual women to AND was also demonstrated.[81] Both of these candidate pheromones were also perceived as odours in both sexes. However, homosexual men responded sexually to AND but not to EST,[81] and similarly homosexual (lesbian) women responded to EST but not to AND.[8] While these studies strengthen the position of both AND and EST as candidate human pheromones, they tell us nothing about homosexuality that we did not know already – namely that male homosexuals are attracted to men but not women, and vice versa for lesbians. However, they do open up some fascinating questions for further research. Do bisexuals respond equally to both AND and EST? In cases where homosexuals have undergone therapy to mitigate or even cure SSA,[84] do their responses to AND and EST also change accordingly? Since Spitzer[84] concedes that such therapies succeed more often in cases where HS is not firmly fixed, is it possible that some or most of these therapeutic 'successes' are in reality bisexuals whose choices have been modified but whose underlying responses have not necessarily changed? This raises a further fundamental question: are these pheromone responses hard-wired (i.e. laid down during early development and thereafter immutable), or do they remain plastic and open to change during the course of an individual's life? It is possible that studies in animals may shed light on this issue, but ethical considerations would rule out any investigation of AND or EST responses in human infants, pre-pubescent children or teenagers. With regard to both the effectiveness of therapy[84] and the role of choice in HS, this question of 'hard-wired' versus 'plastic' responses to sexual stimuli is at the very heart of the HS debate. The taxi-driver story at the start of this section[62] reminds us that the brain remains plastic even in adult life, hence the possibility that sexual orientation might change over time cannot be dismissed. As elsewhere in this review, we should allow for the ambiguity of 'both–and', rather than a clear 'either–or' answer.

8. Fraternal birth order and male HS

So far, the evidence for unavoidable biological factors affecting HS (e.g. genetic inheritance or prenatal hormone exposure; see sections 4, 5 and 6 above) seems stronger for female than for male HS. We turn now to an association that holds true for male homosexuals only: namely that the chances of a male child becoming homosexual seem to increase in line with the number of older brothers (but not sisters) within the family.[11, 13] In a recent meta-analysis of 14 separate studies, Blanchard[9] concluded that this fraternal birth order (FBO) effect is statistically robust – in other words it is a real trend, whatever its underlying mechanism. There are also associations of FBO with both height and parental age,[21, 22] though not with several commonly used markers of HS.[75] Another association involving FBO and HS is right/left-handedness, although this too is a rather complex relationship.[10, 14, 20] Leaving these complications aside, the likelihood of HS in a younger brother increases by roughly one third for each older brother in the family. If the mean prevalence of male HS is about 3% (see 4 above), then the probability of a second brother becoming homosexual is increased to roughly 4%, for a third brother to just over 5%, and so on. From this, one can calculate the proportion of male homosexuals who might owe their HS trait to the FBO effect. One paper[28] estimated a figure of 15% from a Canadian sample, whereas another[12] calculated a higher figure of 29%, albeit with wide confidence intervals (15–48%). For men with 3 or more older brothers, this FBO effect would outweigh all other causes of HS combined. The probability of male HS increases by about 38% for each older brother, but for female HS there is no such effect of sibling number (either brothers or sisters).[13, 17] However, if a much broader definition of HS is used (essentially, that of SSA as used here), then both male and female SSA are correlated with sibling birth order.[64] This implies that the underlying mechanism might be social rather than biological, at least within this broader SSA category. But for strictly defined HS, the FBO effect remains limited to men. One surprising exception to this general rule emerges from a large study of Danish people in heterosexual marriages as compared to homosexual civil partnerships (which have been legal in that country since 1989). Several interesting correlations with childhood experiences were observed, but notably the FBO effect was absent among those homosexual men who had chosen civil partnerships.[38] There is no obvious reason for this disparity, since homosexual men choosing civil partnerships presumably fall into the HS rather than BS or SSA categories.

Several mechanisms have been suggested to explain the FBO effect. Within families with multiple older bothers, younger boys might (sometimes) adopt more feminine characteristics as a way of establishing their sense of being different from older brothers (*sex typing*). In a large sample of homosexual and heterosexual men, there was no detectable association between the number of older brothers and sex typing, undermining this suggestion.[18] Another possibility is homosexual abuse by older brothers leading to HS among their younger brothers, since this situation would predict an obvious FBO effect.[48, 49] There is some evidence for similar FBO effects among men convicted of sexual offences,[61] including paedophilia. Childhood homosexual abuse perpetrated by older brothers (for whom this might represent a transient phase of SSA) could predispose younger brothers towards becoming largely or permanently homosexual. Although this is a postnatal psychosocial explanation for HS, it is clearly not a matter of choice for the younger brother, who would most likely be subjected to coercion. Against this, however, Bogaert[19] has recently shown that the FBO effect for HS holds true only for biological older brothers (sons of the same parents), and breaks down in the case of adopted brothers. This would imply a biological rather than psychosocial explanation. Once again, we should beware of possible confounding factors – such as the boy's age at the time of adoption; ideally, attention should be focused on those who were adopted as infants. Similarly, becoming aware of a brother's homosexuality does not seem to influence the onset or incidence of HS in families with two or more gay brothers.[31]

As discussed in section 7, there is evidence linking HS with prenatal androgen exposure at unusually low or high levels. However, this link is stronger for female than for male HS, and in any case the linkage may be weakened by other factors: high maternal androgen levels are associated with bearing sons, and postnatal androgen production often reflects prenatal exposure. It is therefore difficult to disentangle cause from effect here. In the specific context of the FBO effect, it seems difficult to explain any progressive change in maternal androgen levels with each successive male pregnancy.[48] A somewhat more plausible explanation involves progressive immunization of the mother against some male-specific protein(s) with each successive male pregnancy. Because the father's genes specify proteins that are often different from those specified by the mother's genes, an unborn foetus is in some ways comparable to a 'foreign organism' within the mother's body. Usually, the immune system mounts a powerful antibody response against foreign proteins (antigens), particularly if it has been primed by prior exposure. Several mechanisms combine to ensure that this does not happen in pregnant women, but on occasion these fail. One example of a maternal immune response against her foetus is seen in the so-called Rhesus (*Rh*) syndrome. In an *Rh*-negative mother, the first *Rh*-positive foetus (after fertilization by a *Rh*-positive father) causes few if any problems. However, during pregnancy and especially during birth, some of the *Rh*-positive foetal cells (carrying Rhesus antigen proteins) enter the mother's circulation. Because these *Rh*-positive cells are perceived as foreign (since the mother is *Rh*-negative), the mother's immune system will produce antibodies against the Rhesus antigens. So-called *immunological memory cells* ensure that the ability to produce anti-*Rh* antibodies at short notice is retained for many years (vaccination also relies on this principle). Therefore, if a second *Rh*-positive pregnancy is established, the mother rapidly produces anti-*Rh* antibodies which can cross the placenta and attack blood cells in the unborn foetus, causing haemolytic anaemia. The second baby may survive this, but a further influx of *Rh*-positive foetal cells into the mother's blood-stream will act like a booster vaccination. This means that a third *Rh*-positive pregnancy will provoke a much more serious immune attack (involving high levels of anti-*Rh* antibodies) by the mother, usually resulting in foetal death. Once this problem has been identified, blood transfusions to the foetus and/or prompt treatment of the *Rh*-negative mother with anti-*Rh* antibodies (to mop up any foetal Rhesus antigens and so stop the mother mounting an immune response against them) can usually prevent the most severe outcomes.

The take-home message here is that a mother can sometimes mount an immune response against her unborn foetus. We know that male cells differ from female cells because they express so-called H-Y antigens, which are specified by genes carried on the Y chromosome. It is therefore possible that mothers might produce anti-H-Y antibodies during a male pregnancy, and that this anti-H-Y response would become stronger with each successive male pregnancy (on the same principle as booster vaccinations).[67] If these anti-H-Y antibodies can somehow interact with androgen responses or with genetic systems that might predispose men towards HS, then a role for such antibodies in the FBO effect is plausible. However, actual evidence supporting such a mechanism remains extremely weak.[48] Nonetheless, the telltale FBO pattern is difficult to explain otherwise, particularly if future research confirms Bogaert's recent finding[19] that adoptive brothers do not contribute to the FBO effect. This would rule out most of the obvious psychosocial explanations and favour the maternal immunization hypothesis. Further discussion of this issue is provided by Blanchard,[9] who points out that the Y chromosome carries more protein-coding genes, and foetal cells enter the mother's circulation to a much greater extent, than was previously suspected. (Note that genetic tests for foetal abnormalities can now be carried out on maternal blood samples.[87])

9. What evolutionary rationales might account for HS?

Though unpopular in some Christian circles, Darwin's theory of evolution through natural selection is the mainstay of modern biology, without which very little of it makes any sense. However, the existence of gene-variants (alleles) associated with HS would seem at first sight to present a paradox. Exclusive homosexuals (Kinsey scale 6) presumably have fewer children than heterosexuals, so why have HS-promoting alleles persisted (and possibly even spread) in the human population? Is there some concealed advantage in possessing such alleles (similar to heterozygote advantage, outlined in section 2) that might account for their apparent prevalence? For the sake of simplicity, I shall summarize the available evolutionary rationales as if there were a single 'gene for' HS; however, the same form of argument can equally be extended to a larger gene-set contributing to HS or indeed to multiple gene-sets each contributing to a different type of HS. Rahman and Wilson[77] review a range of suggested evolutionary mechanisms that might help explain this paradoxical prevalence of HS.

The kin selection hypothesis assumes that most homosexual men are at the feminine end ('effeminate') of a male behavioural spectrum, and that most homosexual women are at the male end ('tomboy') of a female behavioural spectrum.[67] If we can accept these caricatures as having *some* validity, what advantages would accrue from the presence of such individuals in an extended family group or clan? The argument is perhaps most easily made for male HS, since aggressively heterosexual male ('macho') behaviour is likely to be socially disruptive, even if large numbers of offspring (from different female partners) result. By contrast, homosexual men showing feminine characteristics (sensitivity to others, nurturing and caring) would help to promote social cohesion in the group and so improve its overall reproductive 'fitness', even if they themselves produce few if any offspring. (It is noteworthy that churches often select male candidates for ordination on the basis of these same empathic qualities.) This model predicts that homosexuals should manifest greater-than-average generosity towards relatives and family. However, two independent tests of this prediction have failed to provide any clear evidence supporting it.[15, 76] Thus the kin selection model – at least in its original form – is not supported by the available data. It is also possible that male HS may help to strengthen social bonds between men, and may indeed serve very different functions from heterosexuality[32] – a view first proposed by Freud.

An intriguing variant involving group (rather than kin) selection has been proposed by Kirby.[54] He noted that many homosexuals (perhaps better categorized as BS or SSA) do in fact reproduce heterosexually. In several plausible scenarios, the reproductive success of BS/SSA males could actually be greater (i.e. more offspring reared successfully) than that of more macho heterosexual males. This could arise, for instance, if extreme macho behaviour tends towards rivalries or conflicts leading to violence and death (whether of macho males, their partners or their offspring). The fact that many women consider supposedly 'feminine' qualities (empathy, nurturing, etc.) to be attractive in a male partner[33] could also play a role, since such partnerships might offer a safer and more secure environment for child-rearing. But the overall prevalence of HS, BS and SSA could remain high, or possibly increase, even if it were true that homosexuals on average have fewer children than heterosexuals. In situations where a social group splits into subgroups that are, for the most part, congenial with regards to sexuality (i.e. mainly HS/BS/SSA versus mainly heterosexual), paradoxical consequences can ensue where the HS/BS/SSA subgroup actually shows better reproductive success than the heterosexual subgroup! The mathematical basis of this counter-intuitive finding would take too long to explain here; interested readers are referred to the original paper.[54] Moreover, this group selection model neither requires a genetic basis for HS, nor predicts that homosexuals should be any more altruistic or generous to their kin than heterosexuals.

Notably, in these models men in the SSA and BS categories would be employing a very different reproductive strategy from that used by heterosexual macho males. Each strategy offers distinct advantages and disadvantages under different conditions (group size, resource availability, etc.). On this view, exclusive HS could be seen as an evolutionary dead-end for those at one extreme of a spectrum of homosexual behaviours. Characteristics that may work to the reproductive advantage of BS and SSA males would virtually preclude reproduction for exclusively homosexual men, who (by definition) beget few if any children. Though maladaptive in evolutionary terms, this small HS minority would not necessarily negate the advantages accruing to a much larger group of men whose sexuality falls into the BS or SSA categories. It is now well established that mice and other animals can exhibit very different reproductive strategies depending on their social position within a group.[6] In fact, numerous instances of homosexual behaviour have been described in animals,[1] though rather few of these seem to involve exclusive HS. Descriptions of homosexual behaviour as unnatural therefore do not stand up to scrutiny. Everything we know about the genetics of animal behaviour points to a complex interplay between genes and the environment (or Nature and Nurture) – where neither is sufficient on its own.

Alternative evolutionary explanations also have some limitations. Alleles promoting HS may exist in a so-called *balanced polymorphism*, where some clear reproductive advantage is conferred on heterozygotes (one non-HS plus one HS-variant copy of the gene), even though homozygotes (with two HS-variant copies) are at a reproductive disadvantage because they are homosexual and produce fewer offspring. As mentioned above, supposedly feminine characteristics in men – such as empathy, sensitivity and verbal skills – are rated as attractive by many women, which may enhance the reproductive success of male heterozygotes.[33] An alternative idea is that alleles which promote HS in men may also confer a reproductive advantage on female relatives (and perhaps vice versa for alleles promoting female HS?). This model predicts that female relatives of homosexual men should have more children than average, and there is some evidence in support of this idea.[27] A strong form of this 'fertile female' model proposes that the gene(s) involved would be carried on the X chromosome – of which women have two (XX) to men's one (XY). Although one X chromosome becomes inactivated randomly in women's cells, the reproductive advantage to women who carry this gene could still be greater than the disadvantage to homosexual men with fewer offspring. Thus evidence pointing to HS-variant alleles on the X chromosome (e.g. Xq28)[42] assumes considerable theoretical importance. Most of these evolutionary models can be readily extended from a single 'HS allele' to multiple contributory alleles, or to hormonal mechanisms underlying HS (since hormone levels also have a genetic basis, determined by the underlying patterns of gene activity).

These questions can be tackled instead from the standpoint of theoretical population genetics, and the rival models can be formulated mathematically such that their predictions can be tested quantitatively.[39] Whether or not the real-life quantitative data will clearly support any one of these models is another matter – but at least the questions can now be posed more precisely. Savolainen and Lehmann[82] point out that such models can account for the maintenance and even spread of alleles contributing to HS in the human population, and furthermore they predict that bisexuality (BS) should be widespread. If a broad definition of BS and SSA is adopted (including transient phases or inclinations towards either), then this is arguably the case; however, the relatively low incidence of consistent BS might argue otherwise. Perhaps societal constraints act to restrict same-sex expression of BS? In the absence of clear evidence favouring one model over another, these suggestions remain little more than *post hoc* Darwinian rationalizations of the fact that HS is so common, given the paradox that exclusive HS has a detrimental effect on reproductive success.

10. Implications

Biology is complex; therein lies its perennial fascination. If nothing else, this should teach us to beware of simplistic explanations and over-generalizations. In the areas of genetics and animal development with which I am most familiar, 'redundancy' is almost the norm. Many genes exist in several copies with related or overlapping functions. Often, two embryonic pathways can each independently direct the development of the same structure. This kind of redundancy makes biological systems unusually robust, despite their enormous complexity and consequent fallibility. So-called reserve pathways (or genes) provide a fail-safe in case the primary system breaks down, which can ensure a more-or-less normal outcome in spite of major system failures. In relation to HS, all of the evidence cited earlier points to a multiplicity of redundant and often overlapping mechanisms. Homosexuals are not a single category of people who can be pigeonholed for convenience – they are as varied and as complex as the heterosexual majority. Some choose to conceal their HS, others to express it openly. Some opt for therapy, but others refuse this on principle. Homosexual behaviours range from faithful, long-term, loving partnerships to risky promiscuity (a range mirroring that seen among heterosexuals). As for causation, some may perhaps choose HS, but for some it is most likely innate. Finally, homosexual inclinations (SSA, whether repressed or overt) can change over time for some individuals, but clearly not for all.

There is clearly a great deal that we do not yet know about the biology of HS. As Bonhoeffer warns us (in his *Ethics*), we must choose to act in a Christ-ward direction 'over an abyss of not knowing'. Current evidence implies that most of the mechanisms reviewed above *do* play some role in HS in at least some individuals. Certain mechanisms may apply only to specific subtypes of HS, and part of the ambiguity in this field may result from a conflation of different HS categories, each involving different (combinations of) mechanisms. In many (perhaps most?) cases, multiple causes are likely to combine, and the relative proportions of these elements in the overall mixture will vary from one individual to another. Only a complex and highly variable *mixture* of underlying mechanisms – some biological, as well as some psychosocial – seems adequate to explain the reality of HS in human society, and no single mechanism can claim to hold the key to HS. This is the biological reality with which theologians must grapple.

References

1   B. Bagemihl (1999). Biological exuberance. Profile Books, London.
2   J. Bailey et al. (1991). *Arch Gen Psychiat* 48, 1089–96.
3   J. Bailey et al. (1993). *Arch Gen Psychiat* 50, 217–23.
4   J. Bailey et al. (1999). *Behav Genet* 29, 79–86.
5   J. Bailey et al. (2000). *J Personal Soc Psychol* 78, 525–36.
6   C. Barnard et al. (2006). In: *Micro mammals and macroparasites.* (eds S Morand et al.), 475–514; Springer Verlag, Berlin.
7   P. Bearman et al. (2002). *Amer J Sociol* 107, 1179–205.
8   H. Berglund et al. (2006). *Proc Natl Acad Sci USA* 103, 8269–74.
9   R. Blanchard (2004). *J Theor Biol* 230, 173–87.
10 R. Blanchard (2007). *Arch Sexual Behav*, in press (published online Dec 22nd 2006).

11 R. Blanchard et al. (1996). *Amer J Psychiat* **153**, 27–31.

12 R. Blanchard et al. (2004). *Amer J Hum Biol* **16**, 151–7.

13 R. Blanchard et al. (1998). *J Bioso Sci* **30**, 511–9.

14 R. Blanchard et al. (2006). *Hormones Behav* **49**, 405–14.

15 D. Bobrow et al. (2001). *Evol Hum Behav* **22**, 361–8.

16 S. Bocklandt et al. (2006). *Hum Genet* **116**, 691–6.

17 A. Bogaert (2003a). *J Pers Soc Psychol* **84**, 644–52.

18 A. Bogaert (2003b). *Arch Sexual Behav* **32**, 129–34.

19 A. Bogaert (2006). *Proc Natl Acad Sci USA* **103**, 10771–4.

20 A. Bogaert (2007). *Neuropsychol* **21**, 141–8.

21 A. Bogaert et al. (2004). *J Biosoc Sci* **36**, 19–37.

22 A. Bogaert et al. (2006). *J Biosoc Sci* **38**, 811–9.

23 D. Boomsma et al. (2002). *Nature Rev Genet* **3**, 872–82.

24 J. Brennan et al. (2004). *Nature Rev Genet* **5**, 509–21.

25 W. Byne (1994). *Sci Amer* **270** (May 1994), 26–31.

26 A. Byrd (2007). http://www.narth.com/docs/nothardwired.html

27 A. Camperio-Ciani et al. (2004). *Proc Roy Soc, Biol Sci, Ser B* **271**, 2217–21.

28 J. Cantor et al. (2002). *Arch Sexual Behav* **31**, 63–71.

29 C. Cederroth et al. (2007). *Mol Cell Endocrinol* **265/266**, 3–9.

30 Council for Responsible Genetics Position Paper (accessed June 2007). http://www.gene-watch.org/programs/privacy/gene-sexuality.html

31 K. Dawood et al. (2000). *Arch Sexual Behav* **29**, 155–63.

32 A. De Block et al. (2004). *Philosoph Psychol* **17**, 59–76.

33 C. Dewar (2003). *Med Hypoth* **60**, 225–32.

34 L. Ellis et al. (1987). *Psychol Bul* **101**, 233–58.

35 L. Ellis et al. (2005). *Arch Sexual Behav* **34**, 569–81.

36 D. Fergusson et al. (1999). *Arch Gen Psychiat* **56**, 876–80.

37 M. Fraga et al. (2005). *Proc Natl Acad Sci USA* **102**, 10604–9

38 M. Frisch et al. (2000). *Arch Sexual Behav* **35**, 533–47.

39 S. Gavrilets et al. (2006). *Proc Roy Soc, Biol Sci, Ser B* **273**, 3031–8.

40 L. Gooren (2006). *Hormon Behav* **50**, 589–601.

41 L. Gooren et al. (2002). *Mol Cell Endocrinol* **198**, 31–40

42 D. Hamer et al. (1993). *Science* **261**, 321–7.

43 J. Hare (2007). In: *An acceptable sacrifice?* (eds. D Dormor et al.), 98–111. SPCK, London.

44 S. Hershberger (1997). *J Sex Res* **34**, 212–22.

45 M. Hines et al. (2004). *J Sex Res* **41**, 75–81.

46 S. Hu et al. (1998). *Nature Genet* **11**, 248–56.

47 IHGSC (2001). *Nature (Lond)* **409**, 860–921.

48 W. James (2004a). *J Biosoc Sci* **36**, 51–9.

49 W. James (2004b). *J Biosoc Sci* **36**, 61–2.

50 W. James (2005). *J Biosoc Sci* **37**, 555–67.

51 K. Kendler et al. (2000). *Amer J Psychiat* **157**, 1843–6.

52 M. King et al. (1992). *Brit J Psychiat* **160**, 407–9.

53 A. Kinsey et al. (1948). *Sexual behavior in the human male.* WB Saunders, Philadelphia.

54 J. Kirby (2003). *Biol Philosoph* **18**, 683–94.

55 K. Kirk et al. (2000). *Behav Genet* **30**, 345–56.

56 P. Koopman et al. (1991). *Nature (Lond)* **351**, 117–20.

57 B. Kraemer et al. (2006). *Neuropsychobiol* **53**, 210–14.

58 R. Lancaster (2006). *Identities – Global Stud Cult Power* **13**, 101–38.

59 S. LeVay et al. (1994). *Sci Amer* **270** (May 1994), 20–5.

60 S. Lutchmaya et al. (2004). *Early Hum Develop* **77**, 23–8.

61 S. MacCulloch et al. (2004). *Arch Sexual Behav* **33**, 467–74.

62 E. Maguire et al. (2000). *Proc Natl Acad Sci USA* **97**, 4398–403.

63 J. Manning (2002). *Digit ratio*. Rutgers University Press, New Brunswick, USA.

64 N. McConaghy et al. (2006). *J Homosexual* **51**, 161–74.

65 D. McFadden et al. (2005). *Arch Sexual Behav* **34**, 341–51.

66 H. Meyer-Bahlburg et al. (2004). *Arch Sexual Behav* **33**, 97–104.

67 E. Miller (2000). *Arch Sexual Behav* **29**, 1–34.

68 J. Money et al. (1984).. *Psychoneuroendocrinol* **9**, 405–14.

69 J. Morris et al. (2004). *Endocrinol* **145**, 475–7.

70 B. Mustanski et al. (2002). *Ann Rev Sex Res* **13**, 89–140.

71 B. Mustanski et al. (2005). *Hum Genet* **116**, 272–8.

72 M. Noordam et al. (2006). *Curr Opin Genet Develop* **16**, 225–32.

73 B. Pause (2004). *Physiol Behav* **83**, 21–9.

74 E. Pennisi (2007). *Science* **316**, 1113.

75 Q. Rahman (2005). *Biol Lett* **22**, 393–5.

76 Q. Rahman et al. (2005). *Arch Sexual Behav* **34**, 461–7.

77 Q. Rahman et al. (2003). *Personal Individ Differ* **34**, 1337–82.

78 G. Rice et al. (1999). *Science* **284**, 665–7.

79 G. Robinson (2004). *Science* **304**, 397–9.

80 A. Safron et al. (2007). *Behav Neurosci* **121**, 237–48.

81 I. Savic et al. (2005). *Proc Natl Acad Sci USA* **102**, 7356–61.

82 V. Savolainen et al. (2007). *Nature (Lond)* **445**, 158–9.

83 A. Servin et al. (2003). *Develop Psychol* **39**, 440–50.

84 R. Spitzer (2003). *Arch Sexual Behav* **32**, 403–17.

85 R. Weksberg et al. (2002). *Hum. Molec Genet* **11**, 1317–25.

86 F. Whitam et al. (1993). *Arch Sexual Behav* **22**, 187–206

87 Y-H. Yang et al. (2006). *Fetal Diagn Ther* **21**, 125–33.

Acknowledgements

I would like to thank the many people who have read and commented upon this review in its draft stages, in particular Phil Groves, Dr Francis Gilbert and Professors Glynn Harrison, Sjoerd Bonting, Jerzy Behnke and John Armour. Most of their suggestions have been incorporated – and the text has been greatly improved thereby. Remaining infelicities and inaccuracies are the author's own. This review is dedicated to the memory of Professor Chris Barnard, from whom I learnt that there is always more to behaviour (both animal and human!) than meets the eye.

PART 2:
UNWANTED SAME-SEX ATTRACTIONS: CAN PASTORAL AND COUNSELLING INTERVENTIONS HELP PEOPLE TO CHANGE?

Glynn Harrison

Executive Summary

1. In this review we ask whether it is possible for people with unwanted same-sex attraction (SSA) to experience significant changes in their sexual feelings and desires. Specifically, we investigate the effectiveness of Christian ministries and professional clinical approaches that are designed to help people change. As we gather the evidence, we listen to the voices of people who say they have experienced benefits from attempts to help them in this way. And we pay attention to those who say that they have been harmed or who object to these ministries in principle. We review the evidence from psychological studies that have been carried out in this area, and we listen to what various professional organizations have to say on this matter.

2. Homosexuality is not a mental illness, and stigmatizing concepts of pathology and disorder have played a critical role in the sometimes inhumane treatment and social exclusion of people with SSA. So our first task is to ask what, precisely, might be 'changed' by these approaches? Although labels such as 'homosexual' and 'heterosexual' have become popular in Western cultures over the last century, they have been the subjects of growing criticism in recent years. Professionals disagree about how such labels should be defined, and attempts to identify and validate different 'orientations' on the basis of underlying biological factors have not been successful. Also, there is considerable evidence to challenge concepts of sexuality that view sexual attractions in terms of fixed and enduring categories.

3. Patterns of sexual attraction can be understood in terms of differences of feelings and desire, types of behaviour, the different labels that people choose to apply to themselves, or by some combination of all three. Studies suggest that there are cultural variations in the way these differences are expressed and conceptualized. And in Western cultures estimates of the proportion of people with SSA differ, sometimes markedly, depending upon what particular concept of 'orientation' is being used.

4. Even when studies have attempted to use broadly comparable definitions of 'orientation', rates of SSA in different populations appear to vary. This may be due to unreliable methods used to measure SSA, or because of real differences caused by social, cultural and biological factors; we do not know. Overall, however, studies suggest that significant numbers of people from Western populations, around 10–15% of men and 20–30% of women, experience some degree of SSA at some time in their lives. A much smaller proportion appear to be 'predominantly' same-sex attracted, probably about 2.0–2.5% of men and 1.5–1.75% of women. Prevalence rates of SSA in non-Western populations have not been reported reliably, but

ethnographic studies report varying patterns of cultural expression of same-sex behaviour and desire.

5. Whilst some people report a relatively stable experience of SSA from adolescence, others report mixed same-sex and other-sex attractions, occurring at different points in their life course. For some this mixed patterning of sexual desire is confined to their adolescent years, whereas others experience it throughout adult life. There is also evidence to suggest that patterns of reported SSA can change over time, with some individuals reporting first experiences of same- or other-sex attraction in later adult life. However, whilst this experience of flexibility of sexual desire applies to some people with SSA, it would be wrong to think that it applies to all people, and more and better research is needed in this area.

6. There is considerable anecdotal evidence from people with unwanted SSA who believe that they have experienced change as a result of some form of religious ministry or professional therapy. There is also considerable anecdotal evidence from those who believe that they have been harmed by their involvement in these approaches. It is difficult to evaluate these claims objectively because of problems in carrying out high quality research in this area. Most studies suffer from weaknesses in the way that subjects have been identified and the methods used to measure change. Studies have also tended to group the many different types of interventions together, when in fact they range from psychological techniques delivered by professionals, through various 'Ex-Gay' ministry approaches, to informal prayer and support offered by ministers and lay people. There are few data available to help differentiate between the relative 'effectiveness' of these approaches.

7. Research on individuals who have been willing to participate in studies suggests that the outcomes achieved by these interventions can be classified into 3 broad groups. The first group (approximately 10–15% of men, and 15–30% of women) report marked degrees of change in both feelings and behaviour. In this group, 'change' involves both diminution of SSA and significant growth of heterosexual desire and functioning. A second group (approximately 30–50%) includes more mixed outcomes, with varying degrees of diminished SSA and increased heterosexual interest. The changes reported in this group are expressed predominantly in terms of behavioural and psychological adjustment, rather than marked increases in heterosexual attraction and functioning. In other words, the outcome is focused on satisfaction in learning to live with the persisting residue of SSA, even if this means valuing a life of celibacy. A third group, approximately 35–55%, report little or no change in their patterns of sexual attraction as a result of participating in one of these interventions.

8. Because of weaknesses in the methodology of these studies we cannot apply these percentage findings to *all* people with SSA who may wish to enter a similar programme. In other words the outcomes are not readily generalizable. All we can say is that there is reasonable evidence that, following some form of intervention (which can take the form of psychotherapy, counselling, or participation in an Ex-Gay ministry programme), *some* individuals with SSA experience significant degrees of

change. The proportion achieving marked degrees of change in both inner sexual desire and behaviour is likely to be modest but a range of 'intermediate' outcomes are possible. A significant proportion will report no change at all. We know very little about which factors may contribute to the different outcomes.

9. Studies suggest that a proportion of participants in these ministries and interventions report that they have been harmed in some way as a result of participation. Reports based upon case series of participants suggest that the proportion is relatively small, whereas studies employing different case-finding techniques have suggested the problem may be on a larger scale. It is difficult to evaluate these conflicting claims because of the methodological problems outlined in [6] above. We do not know what proportion of individuals in the wider population with SSA would suffer harm as a result of engaging with one of these interventions (assuming that they wished to do so) and it is not possible to determine whether some types of intervention may be associated with greater risk of harm than others. All we can conclude is that some individuals report various types of harm as a result of taking part in these interventions.

10. Professional organizations, including those of psychiatry, psychology, counselling and social work, have expressed varying degrees of reservation about interventions for unwanted SSA. These concerns must be taken seriously, especially where they are focused upon the potential for causing harm, and the risk that such interventions may lead to further stigmatization and prejudice toward people with SSA.

11. However, there is no evidence to suggest that psychologists, psychiatrists or other secular professionals have special skills in determining whether, or in what circumstances, the expression of erotic sexual desires should be given priority over conflicting religious and moral values. Deciding between different value systems is a moral, ethical and theological matter, not a 'scientific' enterprise. Concerns about potential harm as a result of participation in one of these interventions need to be balanced against the individual's right to bring their feelings and behaviour into line with their religious and moral values if that is their choice. Whilst some professional organizations do acknowledge that religious values are important in psychological development and health, it is critical that all secular professionals recognize that individuals have a right to decide that their religious identity is the preferred organizing principle for them. This right should be defended even if it means learning to live with sexual feelings that the individual does not value and does not wish to nurture.

12. There is currently insufficient objective and reliable evidence of harm to justify a general proscription of religiously motivated programmes for unwanted SSA or to discourage their further development. However, reports of harm, and examples of poor standards of practice, require that a number of safeguards should be implemented in both ministry-centred and clinical programmes.

13. All organizations and ministries offering interventions for unwanted SSA should adopt guidelines to ensure that potential participants give extended informed consent. These should be based upon conservative estimates of the likelihood of change toward a comprehensive heterosexual function, and clear recognition of the potential for harm if these expectations are unrealistic. Guidelines should seek to respect the statements of professional associations regarding the importance of sexual diversity *and* religious diversity. They should set out explicit requirements for defining the goals of the ministry or counselling, in line with client autonomy and choice, and encompass issues of informed consent, therapist capability and other ethical obligations.

14. These developments will help ensure that appropriate ministry and counselling can be provided for those who seek support in bringing their sexual attractions into line with their religious worldview. As we have noted, adjudication between different religious values does not fall within the expertise of psychiatrists, psychologists or professional counsellors. Questions about the Divine intention for the ordering of human relationships are theological and ethical issues that the Church must discern for itself.

1. The Aims of This Review

Our task in this review is to consider whether (and if so to what extent) it is possible for people with unwanted same-sex attraction (SSA) to experience significant changes in their sexual feelings and desires. In addressing this issue, we shall listen to the voices of people with SSA, including those with both negative and positive experiences of attempts to change their 'orientation'. We shall also review the research evidence as to whether specifically designed interventions to help people change have been found to 'work' and whether these interventions might cause harm to those who use them.

In pursuing our task, we will briefly describe the different types of interventions, and the theories (if any) that lay behind them. We will review the different approaches critically in terms of their stated objectives, and the methodological rigour and appropriateness of the studies used to support their claims.

It is important to note that we do not attempt to carry out a 'systematic review'.[1] Systematic reviews are methodologically standardized and rigorous processes of evidence sifting. By using replicable methodologies, often involving complex statistical techniques of meta-analysis, systematic reviews can reduce bias and produce balanced inferences. Such an approach is outside the scope of the current Listening Exercise, especially given the difficulties of combining the many different types of evidence we need to consider. Instead, for the purposes of this overview, we shall attempt to locate and summarize the main sources of research evidence and then supplement the data with personal/experiential narratives. Finally, we shall also review various position statements that have been issued by professional bodies on the subject of 're-orientation' therapies.

Throughout this review, although it will not be possible to set aside the reviewer's own views, our primary purpose will be to give readers the appropriate critical tools to assess the different types of 'evidence' for themselves.

2. Terminology

When we discuss issues in human sexuality, language and labels are important. Labels can be recruited as tools to caricature and misrepresent. By over-simplifying and exaggerating arguments, we can use labels to denude our opponents' views of nuance and qualification. And when labels are used to pathologize people as being in some way psychologically disordered, they become instruments of power and control. So in this review we shall attempt to use language, and labels, with care.

The use of the term sexual 'orientation' poses problems for some people because it presumes the existence of fixed compartments of sexual experience with clear points of discontinuity. In their view, the use of the term 'orientation' pre-empts the possibility of change, especially when it is read as capturing an immutable core of 'who we are'. The term 'sexual preferences' arouses similar objections on the other side of the debate: a 'preference' seems to imply that sexual attraction is consciously determined, allowing people to choose freely among the objects of their desire.

The term 'reparative therapy', which is sometimes used to describe attempts to change one's pattern of sexual attractions, raises similar objections. It seems to pre-empt discussion by presuming the presence of a disorder or a dysfunction, something about an individual that is broken and in need of repair. Words such as 'therapy', 'healing' and 'treatment' convey similar notions of disorder and pathology.

So how should we approach this review? None of the terminology we shall use is free of such difficulties. We shall sometimes need to speak of 're-orientation' to describe the concept of changing one's patterns of sexual desire. And where the context seems appropriate, we shall occasionally need to use categorical labels such as 'homosexual', 'lesbian' and 'gay' etc. Generally, however, we shall use the term 'same-sex attractions' (SSA) to describe patterns of behaviour and desire that focus upon members of one's own sex. And we shall use the relatively neutral descriptor of 'interventions for SSA' for the variety of pastoral and clinical approaches that have been used to help people who want to change.

3. Prevalence and Causes of SSA

3.1 The Problem of Definition

Over the last century, it has become conventional to divide the world into the categories of 'heterosexual' and 'homosexual'. Indeed, the question of whether homosexuals can 're-orientate' into heterosexuals presumes that such distinct populations already exist. We have come to think of sexual 'orientation' as a psychological entity that is present from birth (either because of genetics or hormones), and part of the natural variation of human existence. In the popular imagination (and much scientific discourse) we speak of the 'homosexual' and 'heterosexual' binary as though they are naturally occurring human 'kinds'.[2]

But the idea that sexual 'orientation' exists in fixed and unalterable categories has been the subject of increasing criticism in recent decades. Objections have been raised from a diverse range of theoretical perspectives, including labelling theory, life-course developmental theory and evolutionary psychology.[2-4]

Much of the debate has focused on the problem of definition[2] and lack of consensus over what 'orientation' actually is: does it describe *observed* (that is, objectively measured) patterns of behaviour; *self-reported* narratives of interior experience (e.g. romantic attraction, fantasies etc.); *self-ascribed identity* in terms of current social conventions ('gay', 'lesbian' etc.); or some combination of all three? And how do we deal with different combinations being reported at different stages of the life-course?

Surveys that attempt to determine the prevalence of different sexual 'orientations' illustrate the problem. As we shall see below, depending on which definition is being used, surveys[3, 5-8] report wide variations in rates of SSA. Similarly, cross-cultural ethnographic studies[9-14] have demonstrated diverse patterns of sexual expression and behaviour, both across time, and between cultures.

Sexual taxonomies developed over the last two centuries have thus been variously conceptualized in binary, bipolar or multi-dimensional terms,[2] but there are few empirical data to help adjudicate between them. The hope that scientific research would uncover some kind of biological validity for these categories has proved illusory. Further, it has become clearer that our scientific models do not, and cannot, stand independently of the cultures in which they have been conceived. Sexual categories constructed in popular and scientific discourse are as likely to be products of Western social forces that shape concepts of what is normative in sexual behaviour, as evidence of 'nature at work'.[15]

Because of these complexities, there have been various attempts to move away from fixed categories of 'orientation', with Kinsey's dimensional model among the best known. On the basis of their interviews, the Kinsey researchers developed a classification (effectively a seven-point scale) based on the 'relative amounts of heterosexual and of homosexual experience or response in each history'.[16] In 1998 the American Psychological Association also attempted to reflect a more dimensional approach, describing sexual orientation as 'an enduring emotional, romantic, sexual or affectional attraction to [(an) other person(s)] . . . that ranges from exclusive homosexuality to exclusive heterosexuality and includes various forms of bisexuality'.[17] In this definition, sexual desires are conceptualized dimensionally: one person may have 25% SSA and another 75% SSA, with these variations presented as 'enduring' features of personality.

But how strong is the evidence that these different vectors of attraction are in fact 'enduring'? Anecdotal data suggests otherwise.[a] And advocates from within the gay and lesbian community have also argued for the essential plasticity of sexual attraction.[b] Research studies, including data reported from representative samples of adolescents and adults,[3, 8, 18, 19] have found that many individuals with SSA report experiencing other sexual attractions, at different times and to different degrees. And a range of qualitative and quantitative studies[3, 20-23] have found evidence of shifts in patterns of attraction over the life-course. Discontinuities between behaviour, attractions and self-labelled identities may also be relatively common.

Because of these difficulties, many theorists have come to view sexual orientation as inherently flexible, an evolving interplay between instinctive desire, experience, and the influence of cultural context, with transitions occurring across the life-span. If this perspective proves durable in the light of further emerging evidence, we may indeed conclude, as Kinsey famously cautioned,[16] that 'the world is not to be divided into sheep and goats'.

3.2 The Problem of Calculating Prevalence

The evidence of instability of same-sex attraction, behaviour and identity presents a number of dilemmas for researchers.[3,24] The impact becomes clearer as we turn to examine prevalence studies in more detail. For example, the proportion of people who are prepared to label themselves as gay/bisexual appears far smaller (by as much as a factor of at least one half) than the proportion that report that they engage in same-sex behaviours. Laumann et al.,[8] who carried out some of the best known work in this area, based upon the US National Health and Life Survey, found that whereas the incidence of lifetime SSA was 7.7% for men and 7.5% for women, the rate at which men identified themselves as gay was 2.8% and 1.4% for lesbians. Similarly, Black et al.[6] found that rates varied greatly depending on how SSA was defined. For example, 4.7% of their large population sample had had at least one same-sex sex partner since age 18, but only 2.5% had engaged in exclusively same-sex sex over the previous year and a similar proportion over the previous five years. 1.6% had had same-sex *and* opposite-sex partners over the past five years.

We should note that response rates in surveys of sexual behaviour are sometimes poor and the reliability of responses to intimate questioning remains open to question. Overall, however, the data from several surveys suggest that the prevalence of those reporting *predominantly or exclusively* same-sex behaviours is about 2.5% of men and 1.75% of women.[6,8,25,26] If the definition is broadened to include those with some degree of same-sex attraction and/or those who enter into sexual behaviour with both sexes, then the proportion of 'same-sex attracted' individuals can be expanded up to 15–20% of the population, depending on the study methodology and where it was carried out. In a Norwegian study,[7] for example, 16% of adolescents had experienced some degree of same-sex attraction, 7% some same-sex behavioural contact, but only 3% labelled themselves as 'gay' or 'bisexual'. In the US survey of adults[8] referred to above, 8% reported some degree of SSA, and 7% reported at least one incident of same-sex behaviour since puberty. There was little difference between the sexes in terms of reported *behaviour/self-labelling*, but there were marked differences in reported rates of sexual/romantic *attractions*, with females in the range 14–21%, compared with rates in males of 5%.

In a representative study[26] carried out on a birth cohort in New Zealand, 1.2% of women and 1.4% of men reported 'currently' predominant or exclusive same-sex attractions, but in the previous year 3.2% of women and 3.5% of men had had sexual contact with a same-sex partner. Studies also suggest that the same individuals may not necessarily be in the same group when surveyed a month, year or decade later. In the New Zealand cohort study,[26] for example, the proportion of males reported as ever having had at least occasional SSA increased (from 4.4% to 5.6%) between age 21 and 26, and rates in females increased from 9.3% to 16.1% over the same period. By age 26, 10.7% of men and 24.5% of women reported having being attracted to their own sex *at some time*. This dropped to 5.6% of men and 16.4% of women who reported 'some' *current* same-sex attraction. Interestingly, occasional same-sex attraction was more common among the 'most educated'. Between age 21 and 26, slightly more men moved away from an exclusive heterosexual attraction (1.9% of all men) than moved towards it (1.0%), while for women, many more moved away (9.5%) than towards (1.3%) exclusive heterosexual attraction. These findings suggest that much same-sex attraction is not exclusive and that it is unstable in adolescent and early adulthood, and possibly beyond.

What can we conclude? First, most men (c.85–90%) and most women (c.70–80%) report only ever having been attracted to members of the opposite sex. Second, a significant minority, 10–15% men and 20–30% of women, experience same-sex desires at some time in their life. And third, a much smaller group, about 2.5% of men and 1.75% of women, understand themselves to be 'predominantly' same-sex attracted in terms of desire and behaviour. Of these, some report SSA as a continuous experience since childhood whereas others report a more gradual realization.

3.3 The Problem of Establishing Causation

The debate about 'causes' of SSA has tended to be polarized between 'essentialist' and 'social constructionist' schools of thought. In the former, categories of sexual experience are important because they are held to describe something 'deep' about a person, an inner essence or 'core' of their personality. Essentialists speak of sexual orientation in the same terms as they speak of gender or race. They defend the notion of an inner 'core' of sexual orientation by dismissing instances of fluidity of sexual attractions as 'situational' or somehow irregular to the norm.

Social constructionists, on the other hand, argue that our categories of homo- and heterosexual are relatively modern inventions and cite the evidence of cross-cultural and within-individual variations in behaviour. They posit that people tend to think of themselves as heterosexual, homosexual and bisexual because these categories have become socially reified, determining expectations and roles. Thus, constructionists expect that different environments kindle different patterns of sexual experience and regulate sexual behaviour according to culturally determined value systems.

Where is the balance of the evidence? As we have noted, research into biological and social causes of sexual attraction continues to be frustrated by problems of definition. With so many definitions, it is difficult to make valid comparisons between studies and to arrive at general inferences. So can these different perspectives be reconciled? Although the evidence is inconclusive, and often conflicting, there are good reasons for considering a more integrationist perspective between the biological evidence (reviewed in a previous section) and social/experiential factors. Here, we understand the development of sexual desires in terms of multiple trajectories of sexual experience resulting from a complex interplay of biological, social and personal factors. This approach, based upon gene to environment interactions, is the most widely accepted model for understanding the development of other complex behaviours, and there seems little reason to believe that sexual development should be different. In this paradigm, the possibility of choice is not excluded; but choice or preference are held to play a contributory role within a complex web of impulse, desire and response that both reflects, and constructs, the architecture of human personality.

4. Interventions for Unwanted SSA: Can People Change?

Having reviewed difficulties in our conceptual understandings of SSA, we are now in a position to appreciate the complexity of the question of whether people with SSA can change. The answer will depend upon how we define 'SSA' and the different patterns of SSA we may wish to consider. The situation is clearly different for a young man in his early twenties who has experienced exclusive same-sex attractions as long as he can remember compared with a mature university academic who views her journey into lesbianism (from being a 'happy heterosexual') as part of an evolving feminist narrative. The answer will also depend upon whether the individual wants to change, how much they wish to change, what 'change' would actually mean for them, and how long the change must be sustained before we are prepared to declare the whole venture a 'success'. For some, it is quite possible that attempts to effect change may result in more distress or even some form of psychological harm. And finally, if we believe the evidence from studies that suggest a degree of plasticity in sexual attraction, then some people will experience change regardless of whether they seek 'therapy' or not. If there is a degree of instability in patterns of sexual attraction then, by definition, people can change.

4.1 The Marketplace of Interventions for SSA

Interventions that have been used for SSA embrace an eclectic group of techniques and methodologies, ranging from psychoanalytically based therapy, through behavioural approaches, 'prayer ministry', to 'spiritual direction'. Even the more specific forms of 'reparative therapy' offered by professional counsellors and psychologists recruit a variety of psychological approaches with differing theoretical stances.

Unfortunately, studies often lump these different approaches together. For example, in a recent study of outcomes of 'reparative' therapies, Spitzer[27] included any individual who reported change in SSA for at least 5 years because of '*some kind of therapy* . . .'; the great majority (90%) of the participants reported using more than one type of therapy. Less than half (47%) reported that seeing a professional (most commonly a psychologist or a pastoral counsellor, with psychiatrists rarely involved) was the only or most helpful kind of therapy. About one third (34%) of the participants reported that the 'only or most helpful type of therapy' involved attending an 'Ex-Gay' ministry or some other religious support group. The remainder of the participants (19%) reported that the only or most helpful type of 'therapy' included such things as repeated meetings with a heterosexual role model, 'bibliotherapy' (e.g. reading a self-help book) or, rarely, on their own, 'changing their relationship with God'.

Ex-Gay Ministries

Interventions for SSA are often associated with various 'Ex-Gay' ministries[28, 29] linked with different Christian denominations or faiths. Exodus International is one of the largest Christian organizations, providing referrals to a range of member agencies and organizations. Exodus claims to have grown to include over 120 local ministries in the USA and Canada and to be linked with other regions outside of North America, totalling over 150 ministries in 17 countries.

Exodus is a non-profit, interdenominational Christian organization promoting the message of freedom from homosexuality through the power of Jesus Christ. Since 1976 . . . within both the Christian and secular communities, Exodus has challenged those who respond to homosexuals with ignorance and fear, and those who uphold homosexuality as a valid orientation. These extremes fail to convey the fullness of redemption found in Jesus Christ, a gift which is available to all who commit their life and their sexuality to Him.[c]

'Redeemed Lives Ministries' claims to have a growing influence internationally, offering a variety of courses and resources:

Redeemed Lives is a pastoral course designed to help all people recover from the fall-out of the sexual revolution. It has helped thousands of people overcome sexual issues (including homosexual attractions), identity confusion and relational difficulties. RL integrates insights from Biblical theology, Christian spiritual formation, depth psychology and classical Christian philosophy.[d]

JONAH, an international Jewish organization, is 'dedicated to educating the world-wide Jewish community about the prevention, intervention, and healing of the underlying issues causing same-sex attractions'.[e] Muslims can seek support through 'Eye on Gay Muslims'.[f] COURAGE, a Catholic organization, has '110 Chapters and contact people world-wide, over 1500 persons participating . . . and hundreds of persons per week receiving assistance from the main office and website'. Catholic Courage does not offer interventions aimed at changing or re-ordering SSA but suggests that 'by developing an interior life of chastity, which is the universal call to all Christians, one can move beyond the confines of the homosexual identity to a more complete one in Christ'.[g]

Other organizations that deal with SSA within a religious framework include the 'Powerful Change' ministry group for African Americans, 'One by One' (Presbyterian) and 'Evergreen International' (affiliated to the Church of Latter Day Saints). Most of these organizations have been subsumed into the PATH ('Positive Alternatives to Homosexuality') coalition of religious and non-religious organizations. The PATH organization states:

Collectively, our organizations have worked with thousands of men, women and youth who are finding peace and fulfilment by resolving their SSA feelings in ways that are emotionally healing, gender-affirming, congruent with their deeply held values and beliefs, and supportive of their individual life goals.[h]

In the United Kingdom, True Freedom Trust (TFT) is probably the longest serving organization (since 1987) offering support to people 'who accept the Bible's prohibition of homosexual practice and yet are aware of homosexual tendencies, or struggle with other sexual and relational issues'. Although TFT was a founding member of Exodus International, the organization resigned from Exodus in 2000. Whilst maintaining its commitment to a conservative interpretation of Scripture in relation to homosexual practice, and affirming that change is possible, TFT no longer seeks to raise expectations of change but rather emphasizes the positive role of celibacy. In

2001, UK Courage (not to be confused with the Catholic organization of the same name), founded in 1988, underwent a fundamental shift to recognize that 'God supports and blesses sincere committed relationships between gay people (for whom a heterosexual relationship is inappropriate)' and disaffiliated from Exodus International. Living Waters,[i] affiliated to Desert Streams International, continues to offer interventions using a variety of techniques, including 'Journey into Manhood' weekends and group support and intervention.

In addition to these religiously based ministries, several non-religious international organizations such as 'People can change' and the 'International Healing Foundation' offer varying theoretical models of how people change and seek to address underlying causes of SSA through therapy or group initiatives.

Professional Organizations

The most widely cited professional psychological organization interested in interventions for unwanted SSA is the US National Association for Research and Therapy of Homosexuality (NARTH). NARTH's 'primary goal is to make effective psychological therapy available to all homosexual men and women who seek change'.[j] With a specific membership category for professional psychotherapists and counsellors, NARTH provides scientific and psychological resource materials on SSA, supports professionals assisting people with SSA and campaigns for the rights of individuals who seek to bring their unwanted SSA into line with their values. The organization is not explicitly religious, although much of the material provided draws upon the religious experiences and the values of many of its members.

4.2 Psychological Models Used in Interventions for Unwanted SSA

We have noted that organizations and individuals offering interventions for SSA appear to draw upon a variety of techniques and approaches. We now consider these in more detail.

Approaches Linked to Medicine

In the earlier parts of the last century, interventions were largely offered within the secular professions of psychiatry and psychology. Psychiatrists attempted a variety of physical treatments, including castration, implanting testicular tissue, brain surgery and hormone therapy.[30, 31] None of these biological interventions was particularly 'successful' and many would have caused significant and irreversible harm. Of course, these kinds of interventions in the history of psychiatric medicine were not confined to sexual 'disorders'; a wide variety of conditions, including psychotic disorders, were sometimes subject to brutal physical treatment methods with comparable adverse outcomes.

Approaches Linked to Psychoanalysis

From the perspective of psychological treatments, the two most influential and widely used treatments have been psychoanalysis and behaviour therapy. Sigmund

Freud, the father of psychoanalysis, came to believe that homosexual attractions resulted from disturbances in the 'normal' trajectory of psychosexual development. In his classic 'Oedipal' theory,[32] Freud delineated the process of 'normal' heterosexual development. In this model, the male child relinquishes mother as an object of sexual desire, identifies with father, and replaces mother with other women. Male homosexuality is understood to result from a subversion of this process, often in the context of an over-involved mother and/or a cool, emotionally distant father.

Variations on the Oedipus theory created the foundations for the pathologization[k] of homosexuality that held sway in psychoanalytic circles for much of the twentieth century, especially in the United States.[33] Psychoanalytic theory spawned a variety of developmental theories of homosexual development, all of which viewed the relationship with one's parents as crucial in some way to determining SSA.[34-36] The work of Elizabeth Moberly[34] was especially influential in underpinning various elements of interventions for SSA, many of which are now used both professionally and in Ex-Gay ministries.

Moberly suggested that adversity in the relationship with the same-sex parent creates a defensive emotional detachment, not only from the parent but also from their gender identity. She believed that the resulting yearning for same-sex affirmation then becomes sexualized in early adolescence. The homosexual love-need is viewed as essentially a search for same-sex parenting. Various 'cut-down' versions of Moberly's theory have provided the intellectual stimulus for approaches such as 'Growth into Manhood'[37] and other interventions aimed at rebuilding a sense of belonging (identification) with the individual's same-gender group. Other variations of 'early experience' models involve Daryl Bem's 'exotic becomes erotic' theory[38] and the parent manipulation theories advanced by some sociobiologists.[39]

Therapists, pastors and counsellors have used these various models to try to help their clients develop insight and understanding about how they came to feel the way they do, and to open up the possibility of developing alternative patterns of relating and identification.

But what is the evidence that the development of SSA is connected with early childhood experiences? Much of the psychoanalytic theorizing on sexuality falls foul of the critical treatment that has been meted out to psychoanalysis in general.[40] In its harshest expression, critics have portrayed psychoanalytic theory as speculative generalization, based upon the findings of small case series of unrepresentative individuals, reported by potentially biased practitioners. And from within psychoanalysis itself, critics have emerged who view SSA as 'constitutional' in origin rather than the product of severe developmental disturbances.[41] A more balanced critique might recognize the valuable insights provided by some psychoanalytic theory, whilst remaining somewhat sceptical about inflated claims for the effectiveness of psychoanalytic therapy itself.

To be convinced of an association between SSA and early childhood experiences, we would need empirical evidence derived from objective studies that compare individuals with SSA with 'controls' without SSA. Retrospective comparisons are relatively easy to carry out but because subjects are asked to recall childhood experiences their responses are likely to be biased by memory deficits and the distortions of a personal 'search for meaning'. Retrospective studies are also subject to sampling biases, often relying upon advertisements in newspapers and 'gay' literature. People who respond to such advertisements are unlikely to be representative of the population of same-sex attracted individuals as a whole.

Prospective studies, which follow groups of individuals from childhood through to adulthood, are more methodologically robust because they measure different patterns of parenting before the identification of adult SSA. However, these studies are difficult to carry out because of high rates of attrition, problems of small sample size and measures of sexual attraction that rely upon subjective self-report. These and numerous other methodological problems in this kind of research have been reviewed elsewhere.[1,2]

In one of the most comprehensive retrospective studies,[42] the authors surveyed 686 gay men, 293 lesbians, 337 heterosexual men and 140 heterosexual women living in San Francisco. The study has been criticized on various grounds, not least sampling biases (gay subjects were recruited through advertisements in various gay subcultures), but it remains one of the most useful in this area. The researchers found no significant differences between the groups in terms of their attachments to their mothers, but there was (weak) evidence of correlations between adult SSA and unfavourable relationships with their fathers in early childhood. The authors also found associations between gender non-conformity[1] in childhood and early homosexual experience. An overview[43] of 48 such studies in which adults were asked to recall their childhood behaviours concluded that people with SSA reported substantially more gender-atypical behaviour in childhood and that such children grew up to experience an estimated 12-fold increase in adult SSA among males and a 4-fold increase in females.

The most frequently cited prospective study[44] found an association between adult SSA and gender non-conformity in childhood. Further, this study found that those with adult SSA reported decreased father–son shared contact time when they were aged between two and five years old. A much larger prospective study[45] that utilized the Danish Civil Registration System analysed homosexual and heterosexual 'marriages' in over 2 million persons born in Denmark between 1952 and 1983 (Denmark was the first country to legalize same-sex marriage in 1989). This study was based upon a complete national data set, with childhood family information available for all 18–49-year-old men who entered same-sex marriage. The authors found that for men, homosexual marriage was associated with having older mothers, divorced parents, absent fathers, and being the youngest child (although they found no evidence for a fraternal birth order effect). For women, maternal death during adolescence, and being the only or youngest child or the only girl in the family, increased the likelihood of homosexual marriage.

This study is important because of its size, and the independent nature of the childhood measures. It suffers however from identifying homosexual 'marriage' as the dependent variable rather than SSA per se. Because of this, the main findings may be related to factors that influence the decision to enter into civil partnerships rather than the development of SSA itself. Nevertheless, the authors uncovered convincing evidence that same-sex parental absence appeared to be more common among boys and girls who later enter into same-sex unions.

A small but methodologically robust birth cohort study[46] of nearly 1000 individuals, followed prospectively from birth to age 21, also found that gay, lesbian and bisexual subjects had experienced more frequent changes of parents during childhood, primarily as a result of parental separation and/or divorce and remarriage. And in their analysis of 3-wave interview data from a large nationally representative study of adolescents conducted in 1994–5, Bearman and Bruckner (2002)[47] showed that adolescent males who are opposite-sex twins are twice as likely to report SSA, suggesting that less-gendered socialization in early childhood and pre-adolescence may shape subsequent same-sex romantic relationships. The authors' theory was strengthened by a further observation that the greatest probability of SSA was observed in those families that had other-sex twins without an older same-sex sibling.

Taken together, these data suggest that experiences associated with being a gender non-conforming child are significantly associated with later SSA. They also provide some evidence of a more general association between unstable childhood experiences and adult SSA, especially where the experience relates to the same-sex parent. However, the methodological weaknesses of all these studies caution against dogmatic conclusions. Correlation does not mean causation; fathers may simply spend less time with a son because of his non-gender conformity. And evidence of an association between gender non-conformity and later SSA may simply reflect a common underlying (biological?) process. The association between unstable childhood experience and adult SSA may also reflect some common, as yet unidentified causal factor.

The lack of conclusive evidence for a causal association between childhood family patterns and adult SSA does not however mean that such an association does not exist under certain circumstances or in specific instances. Also, as Stein[2] points out, the lack of robust evidence for the role of family factors, and the lack of evidence generally in the sphere of psychosexual development, should not surprise us. Evidence for the role of family dynamics in the development of personality in general is notoriously difficult to unravel. What factors, for example, lead people to pursue certain careers? Biological factors will play a significant role (contributing to intelligence, temperament, etc.) but a variety of family and social/cultural experience (parents, teachers, adult role models, etc.) are likely to mould and shape career choices. In addition, different patterns of interaction between these factors will be crucial for different people.

It is likely that sexual desires and attractions are shaped and moulded in ways similar to other complex human behaviours, as biologically determined differences of temperament and personality interact with the familial and social environment. As Byne and Parsons[48] have suggested, because such traits may be heritable or developmentally influenced by hormones, the model will indeed predict a degree of heritability for homosexuality. But this does not require that either genes or hormones *directly* influence sexual orientation per se. They may, for example, be causally related to gender non-conforming behaviours that only develop into adult same-sex desire in certain family and social environments. We may conclude therefore that the absence of irrefutable evidence of causal connections between childhood environment and adult SSA is not evidence that such relationships do not exist. Our overview suggests there is evidence of general associations and further research in this area is justified.

Approaches Linked to Behaviour Therapy

Based on the work of Pavlov and Skinner, behaviour therapy approaches are essentially agnostic about inner psychic processes. They focus instead on techniques that modify external behaviour. Whilst such disregard for inner human experience can appear almost inexplicable to the casual observer, as a pragmatic approach to psychological disorders, behavioural models (and particularly modern cognitive behaviour therapy) enjoy the most robust evidential base.

Historically, behavioural approaches, particularly those using the classical techniques of re-conditioning and re-enforcement, were among the most widely used for SSA. Attempts were made to re-align behaviours linked to sexual arousal with heterosexual stimuli, using a variety of association techniques and punishment/reward paradigms.[49] For example, a patient may be administered an electric shock as he views sexually arousing (same-sex) imagery. In more sophisticated paradigms, 'orgasmic re-conditioning' was used to substitute heterosexual imagery just before orgasm during masturbation. In this approach, more 'appropriate' (i.e. heterosexual) imagery was substituted earlier each time until it made up the sole content of the masturbatory experience.[50] The behaviourist Martin Seligman initially reported favourable results for such techniques[51] but later characterized the data as flawed because of uncertainties regarding the number of 'bisexuals' and other 'uncertain categories' that were included in his studies.

Byrd and Nicolosi[52] synthesized treatment outcomes from numerous studies using a meta-analytic technique. One hundred and forty-six studies evaluating treatment efficacy were identified but only 14 met inclusion criteria and provided statistics that could be used in a meta-analysis. These 14 outcome studies were published between 1969 and 1982 and used primarily behavioural interventions. Analysis indicated that treatment for homosexuality was significantly more effective than alternative treatments or control groups.

With growing concern about the superficial nature of these techniques their use declined significantly after the removal of homosexuality from the American Psychiatric Association's Diagnostic and Statistical Manual[53] (DSM) classification of psychiatric disorders in 1973.[54] It is difficult to assess how far these behavioural techniques are currently used in professional 're-orientation' approaches and 'Ex-Gay' ministries, although it is the author's impression that aversion techniques are now uncommon. Anecdotal evidence suggests that some Ex-Gay ministries continue to use techniques involving cognitive re-structuring and auto-aversive techniques (the often cited 'elastic band on the wrist') as part of an eclectic package, but it appears that these are used mainly to supplement other approaches.

4.3 Position Statements Issued by Professional Organizations

In 1998 the Board of Trustees of the American Psychiatric Association (APA) issued a Position Statement outlining its opposition to 'any psychiatric treatment, such as "reparative" or "conversion" therapy, which is based upon the assumption that homosexuality per se is a mental disorder or based upon the a priori assumption that the patient should change his or her sexual homosexual orientation'.[55] In doing so the APA joined many other professional organizations in the United States, including the American Academy of Pediatrics, the American Medical Association, the American Psychological Association (APsA), the American Counselling Association, and the National Association of Social Workers. The emphasis appeared to be concern that these therapies imply that homosexuality is an illness or a disorder, and concern about the implication that individuals with SSA *should* seek such interventions.

The Lesbian and Gay Special Interest Group of the Royal College of Psychiatrists has also provided a submission[m] to the Listening Exercise stating that 'although there is now a number of therapists and organizations in the USA and in the UK that claim that therapy can help homosexuals to become heterosexual, there is no evidence that such change is possible' and that 'this can be deeply damaging'.

These authoritative position statements are of considerable importance and require careful analysis. There is a remarkable uniformity of approach across a range of professional organizations including psychologists, psychiatrists, social workers and counsellors. Their statements underline the relative marginalization of professionals who offer 'reparative' therapy and Ex-Gay ministries in terms of the secular mainstream. It is therefore important to be clear about what precisely these statements are saying and the evidence base that supports them.

We should note that in the year 2000, the APA's 'Commission on Psychotherapy by Psychiatrists' issued a further statement[55] that noted that 'to date there are no scientifically rigorous outcome studies to determine either the actual efficacy or harm of reparative treatments'. The APA committee re-affirmed its 1973 position that homosexuality per se is not a diagnosable mental disorder and asserted, 'recent publicized efforts to re-pathologize homosexuality by claiming that it can be cured are often guided not by rigorous scientific or psychiatric research, but sometimes by religious and political forces opposed to a full civil rights for gay men and lesbians'. Further, it stated, 'until there is such research available, APA recommends that ethical practitioners refrain from attempts to change individuals' sexual orientation, keeping in mind the medical dictum to "first, do no harm"'. The report also commented that there was 'an increasing body of religious thought arguing against traditional, biblical interpretations that condemn homosexuality and that underlie religious types of reparative therapy'. The authors proceeded to cite a number of theological sources that reflected these views. Finally the APA committee encouraged and supported further research to determine the risks versus the benefits of 'reparative therapy'.

So must we conclude that these professional organizations have effectively proscribed interventions for SSA? A statement of the American Psychological Association (APsA) (as opposed to the American *Psychiatric* Association [APA]), issued in 1997, stopped short of recommending that practitioners refrain from attempts to change individuals' sexual orientation. Instead, the APsA set out a number of principles emphasizing that 'in their work-related activities, psychologists do not engage in unfair discrimination based on . . . sexual orientation'. They further set out a number of guidelines for obtaining informed consent, including a requirement that practitioners should not inflate evidence of effectiveness and that they should consider each person's 'preferences and best interests'. It has recently been announced that these guidelines are to be reviewed by a specially convened working party.[n]

We have noted that in their 2000 elaboration of their earlier 1998 position statement, the APA went somewhat further than the APsA, recommending that ethical practitioners 'refrain from attempts to change individuals' sexual orientation'. They did so without qualification as to the wishes of those seeking help or therapy or the personal values of those clients who seek change. This recommendation rested upon three areas of concern.

First, the statement took the view that *any* offer of 'treatment' or therapy necessarily implies that there must be a disorder present to be treated, effectively re-pathologizing homosexuality and turning back the clock in terms of public stigma and opprobrium. Thus, therapy for SSA was seen as implicitly reversing the 'landmark' decision of the APA to remove homosexuality from the American DSM classification in 1973. Second, the statement pointed to the lack of evidence of effectiveness, and the anecdotal nature of much of the research. 'Ethical' practitioners, it suggested, desist from proffering therapies that do not have a robust evidence base. Third, the statement highlighted the issue of potential harm and the cautionary constraint upon ethical practitioners to 'first do no harm'. In the mind of this particular APA committee, these three issues conspired to provide a compelling ethical constraint upon professionals and would-be 'Ex-Gay' practitioners.

These issues merit careful consideration and analysis. First, much has been made of the decision to remove homosexuality from the DSM classification of mental disorders in 1973. However, in public and scientific discourse the relatively limited role played by science, as opposed to politics, in arriving at this decision tends to go unnoticed.[56] Robert Spitzer, an eminent psychiatrist widely credited as the architect of the 1973 APA decision, recollects how he came to change his own views at that time: 'Now, how much of that [change in his own thinking that led to the 1973 decision] was a result of true scientific logic? I would like to think part of it was that. But certainly a large part of it was just a feeling that they [gay activists] were right! That if they were going to be successful in overcoming discrimination, this clearly was something we had to change.'[57]

This quotation illustrates the need to recognize how cultural and political contextual influences operate more generally in the development and construction of psychiatric diagnoses.[58] Although defining the boundaries of 'normality' is a problem for medicine in general, this issue is of unique importance in the field of psychiatry. Psychiatric diagnoses are rarely constructed on the basis of straightforward correlations with some underlying biological abnormality. They reflect the social, political and cultural imperatives of their time.[58] Around the time of the removal of homosexuality from DSM, the 'anti-psychiatry movement', associated with intellectuals such as R. D. Laing, and popular writers such as Thomas Szasz,[59] was offering a cogent intellectual critique of psychiatric labelling as a process of 'social control'. These views were implanted in the popular imagination by the release of the film *One Flew Over the Cuckoo's Nest* in 1975. This, together with evidence of abuse of psychiatry in certain totalitarian regimes, heightened awareness of its potential for controlling social deviance. This discourse continues, with recent proposals for the development of 'values based classifications'[58] which explicitly recognize the cultural and social values that shape our notions of psychological abnormality.

Recognizing the significance of this debate, the APA's Diagnostic and Statistical Manual (4th edition) (DSM–4) now states, 'although this manual provides a classification of mental disorders, it must be admitted that no definition adequately specifies the precise boundaries for the concept of mental disorder'.[53] DSM–4 explicitly recognizes the contextual dependence of psychiatric concepts and categories: 'Mental disorders have . . . been defined by a variety of concepts . . . each is a useful indicator for a mental disorder . . . and different situations call for different definitions'. The World Health Organization's International Classification of Diseases (10th edition) (ICD–10)[60] also attempts to discriminate between what are 'natural' variations in human experience and behaviour and what are categories of 'disorder' by imposing a requirement of subjective distress or disability: 'social deviance or conflict alone, without personal dysfunction, should not be included in mental disorder as defined here'.[60] Similarly, the DSM defined a 'disorder' as being a form of psychological deviance that is 'associated with present distress . . . or disability . . . or significantly increased risk of suffering death, pain, disability, or an important loss of freedom'.[53]

If we bear in mind these strictures about the nature and limitations of psychiatric diagnoses, we are in a better position to judge the significance of the de-classification of homosexuality as a 'disorder'. As social mores and values were changing in the 1960s and 1970s, the criteria of 'personal dysfunction' or 'distress' were no longer being satisfied in the case of homosexuality. Many individuals were saying that they were happy with their sexuality. Thus, as Western society came to view different sexual practices as part of the broad tapestry of human variation, and people with SSA asserted their acceptance and embrace of a 'gay' identity, it was almost inevitable that, sooner or later, homosexuality would lose its status as a psychiatric 'disorder'.

There have been further revisions across a range of other 'disorders'. In 1999, a DSM–4[53] revision introduced an additional requirement for the presence of 'marked distress or interpersonal difficulty' in the diagnosis of a variety of so-called sexual 'dysfunctions'. So, for example, prior to 1999 'Female Sexual Arousal Disorder' would have been considered to be present regardless of whether the individual complained of it or not. A year later, such an individual would no longer be considered to have the disorder if they were content with their life experience. The 'science' had not changed, simply the consensus among diagnosticians about where to draw the boundaries for 'clinical' purposes.

There is a growing lobby[61] for the removal of certain 'paraphilias' from DSM on the same grounds. The term 'paraphilias' identifies a range of fantasies, urges or behaviours that 'involve non-human subjects or the suffering or humiliation of oneself or one's partner' (for example sadomasochism). Critics are pursuing a similar class of arguments as were used for the removal of homosexuality. They contend that such disorders simply reflect values about what is 'normal' sexual behaviour that vary from culture to culture. Moser et al.[61] make the point that 'nymphomania, satyriasis and erotomania [are already] not included in the current DSM for the same reasons that homosexuality was removed' and suggest that it is time to move further with other 'paraphilias' as societal values and mores continue to change.

In the light of these developments, we may view the APA decision to remove homosexuality from DSM as a political and social development, rather than a critical turning point in the march of scientific discovery. And when the APA strayed into theological debate by publicly endorsing the views of a selected group of theologians, as it did so clearly in the 2000 position statement, we may have further cause to doubt the 'scientific objectivity' of this enterprise.

None of this should deflate the importance of the decision in terms of reducing prejudice and discrimination, and allowing people to make up their own minds about their sexual desires. But there is a distinct impression that the APA is functioning within a particular secular and ideological worldview that excludes the interests of many people in faith communities. In 2002, Nicholas A. Cummings, a former President of the APsA, publicly expressed his concerns about a 'disconnect' between the underlying philosophic assumptions and values of influential members of the APsA and many 'ordinary Americans' and cited unusually low rates of religious affiliation among psychologists compared with other professional groups.° It is likely that some faith groups have experienced a similar 'disconnect' between their own ethical and theological worldview and that of the APA, at least in terms of the statement issued in 2000.

The second concern cited in the 2000 APA position statement was the lack of scientific evidence of effectiveness. We shall consider the evidence of effectiveness in detail below, but as Spitzer has commented, the answer depends on what we mean by 'scientific evidence': 'if "scientific evidence" requires a study with randomized assignment of individuals to a treatment condition, reliable and valid assessment of target symptoms before treatment, when treatment is concluded, and at follow up, then it is certainly true that there are no such studies of reparative therapy. However the same can be said about many widely used types of psychotherapy, including gay affirmative therapy, whose efficacy has never been subjected to rigorous study.'[27, 62]

Kenneth J. Zucker, editor of the research journal *Archives of Sexual Behaviour* nand President (2005–6) of the International Academy of Sex Research, has made a similar point about the lack of empirical evidence for many other psychological treatments: 'without such data it is difficult to understand how professional societies can issue any clear statement that is not contaminated by rhetorical fervour . . . '.[63]

4.4 Research Evaluations of Interventions for SSA

We turn to consider the evidence for the effectiveness of interventions to help people change unwanted SSA. We should note first of all that personal testimonials for the benefits of useless treatments abound. Some people genuinely believe that crystals healed their arthritis or garlic cured their cancer. In the mind of the believer, the placebo effect, spontaneous recovery and self-deception all work to construct the illusion of causation.

Over the past two decades the 'evidence based medicine' movement has made substantial progress in agreeing standards of evidence when trying to decide whether or not medical and psychological interventions 'work'.[64, 65] The 'Randomized Controlled Trial' (RCT) remains the 'gold standard' of evaluation. Here, subjects are randomly allocated to treatment or non-treatment (controlling for non-specific components that may exert a placebo effect) comparison groups, and results are assessed independently and objectively. Ideally, the subject, the treating therapist, and those measuring the results are all 'blind' to which subject is in which group.

Unfortunately, whilst it is relatively easy to evaluate drug treatments with RCTs (for example by comparing blue capsules with active ingredient versus blue capsules that contain an inert substance), more complex interventions can be difficult to evaluate in this way, because of difficulties in either maintaining blind conditions or ensuring appropriate controls. For example, how does one maintain perfect control conditions if one is attempting to evaluate whether prayer 'works'? It is difficult to prevent prayers being offered for individuals assigned to the control condition. Or if one is evaluating an approach to help people who present in desperate emotional crisis, can one ethically assign them to a control (e.g. waiting list) condition? Because of these logistic and ethical issues, many counselling and psychotherapeutic interventions that are routinely used in clinical settings have a questionable evidence base, at least in terms of the gold standard of the RCT. So what evidence is available for the effectiveness of interventions for SSA?

Anecdotal Evidence of Effectiveness

By the time I was eighteen, I lost all hope of finding help or healing, went to university and entered into the gay lifestyle in New York City . . . the turning point in my life came when, a few months later, I repented of homosexuality and received the forgiveness of sins . . . the Lord used psychological insights to address my lack of affirmation in my identity as a man and fears related to men and women. I came to see how I misperceived manhood in myself. I grew to accept the unique ways God has created me to be a man and masculine. Through healthy friendships with men, I began to accept myself as a man among men . . . as I continued growing in the Lord so did my desire for marriage and family. Concurrently, so did my attraction to women . . . in 1996 I married Nancy and since then we have had five children . . . I may always be weak and vulnerable in my sexuality. But through His power working in me, I can be obedient. Even though same-sex attractions occasionally revisit me, they no longer have the power to define who I am . . . I am a Christian, a husband, father and a priest.[p]

God has continued to work in my marriage. Now I really enjoy the physical part of my relationship with Vicki, no longer needing homosexual fantasies for stimulation. My struggles with homosexual lust are virtually gone. I'm not afraid of temptation when it comes; I've learned how to successfully deal with it. For so many years I struggled to deal with my homosexuality between just me and the Lord. Then I discovered that, all along, He had wanted to bring me healing by means of His people. I praise God that He led me to two loving Christians who were willing to be His instruments of healing and change.[q]

The initial period in counselling and support groups was agonizing. At times, I felt like giving up. I felt it was impossible for me to change, and sometimes none of the things I did for recovery made any sense at all . . . I was used to meeting my craving for the tangible, warm, loving touch of another woman with lesbian contacts. Learning to allow my needs to be met in a healthy, nonsexual way was very challenging . . . the time finally came when He removed the piercing pain in my heart that I had carried over my former girlfriend . . . I now understand that my lack of maternal bonding as well as the negative male role model and lack of affirmation from my father were the major roots in my struggle. That does not mean that I blame my parents. It does mean that I am now able to stand tall and accept who I am . . . slowly but surely, my mindset has changed as I have learned to replace my faulty habits and be in touch with and express my long lost emotions. I realize that God came into my life when I first asked Him, and this gave Him permission to do His work in my wretched life. Indeed, He has a good plan and purpose for my life.[r]

I'm post-gay because I chose to leave 'gay' behind. I chose to no longer accept 'gay' as an explanation of who I was and instead to begin a journey away from it. For some of us that journey involves changes in our sexual orientation, perhaps marriage and kids. For others they see no change in their sexual attractions, but they have left behind the place of false-identity, of seeing themselves as 'gay' . . . what's interesting in my case is that I only walked the first of those two possibilities above after having reconciled myself to the second (change and celibacy). I remember on my post-gay journey reaching a point where I was seeing no change in my attractions and was getting angry with God about it. Wasn't this ex-gay choice meant to work? Shouldn't God be doing something about it? God challenged me over the course of a few days with a clear message – 'If I want you to stay like this for my purposes, why can't I do that? Will you follow me wherever I take you, not just only to the places you want to go?' That night I surrendered my sexuality and future to God, reconciled to a life of celibacy but not a life of 'gay'. It was only in the surrender to God's path for me that I then later saw him taking me on the journey to where I am now happily married.[s]

These personal narratives are important and illustrate the range of spiritual and psychological insights that may be brought to bear upon unwanted SSA, and the varied pathways of experience toward 'change'. However, critics[29] have pointed to the fact that many of these anecdotes are supplied by people who are now in full-time 'Ex-Gay' ministries themselves, with a vested interest in advocating their cause and developing their business.[t] And, as we have noted, anecdotal evidence does not prove that specifically designed interventions 'work'. So we turn to consider the available research data more critically.

Research Evidence of Effectiveness

There is an extensive research literature on interventions for SSA.[28, 66–69] As we have noticed, none meet 'gold standard' conditions of proof. These studies are vulnerable to methodological objections such as selection bias, lack of controls, assessment bias and reliance upon self-reports. Crucially, there is often poor specification of what precisely is claimed to have 'changed' (e.g. self-identity, subjective attractions or behaviour). Socarides,[67] for example, reported that 20 (44%) of 45 of his patients in long-term psychoanalytic therapy developed 'full heterosexual functioning' but did not provide detailed information as to what precisely this meant in terms of behaviour and/or patterns of attraction/self-identity.

The largest evaluation of Ex-Gay ministries (in terms of number of subjects) has been conducted by Nicolosi *et al.*,[70] with 882 recruits drawn from various ministries. The survey methodology encompassed a mixture of 'interventions', including those delivered by professional counsellors, pastoral counsellors, and informal help from family and friends. 'Outcomes' were not stratified by intervention type, but of 318 respondents who rated themselves 'exclusively homosexual' prior to the interventions, after therapy 11.6% rated themselves unchanged, 11.3% as almost entirely homosexual, 24.2% as more homosexual than heterosexual, 6.9% as equally homosexual and heterosexual, 11.6% as almost entirely heterosexual, and 17.6% as exclusively heterosexual. Thus the outcomes break down very approximately into 1/3 little or no change, 1/3 some change and 1/3 substantial change. Importantly, 7.1% rated themselves as being worse after intervention than before, leading the authors to conclude that 'conversion therapy is not appropriate for all clients'. This survey suffered from potential sampling biases, heterogeneity of interventions, lack of controls, and incomplete specification of outcomes.

A study by Schaeffer et al.[71, 72] compared 105 participants who affirmed their Lesbian/Gay identity with a 'matched' sample of participants in the Ex-Gay ministry of Exodus International. Compared with the gay-affirming group, the Ex-Gay group was more religious, reported less good mental health, and described a significantly more dysfunctional relationship with their parents. It is possible that those seeking 're-orientation' interventions are more likely to have early childhood relational problems, compared with those who achieve satisfaction and acceptance of their gay identity. However, as Throckmorton[28] points out, it may be that each group simply interpreted their experiences in terms of the causal models presented to them in therapy. In other words the participants in Exodus may have experienced a need to reinterpret and exaggerate their early childhood struggles whilst the gay-affirming group may have experienced a need for better-than-actual portrayal of their childhoods to avoid fitting the traditional stereotype. We noted these problems of 'searching after meaning' associated with retrospective assessments earlier. But bearing in mind these caveats, we should nevertheless note that in their follow-up study[72] the same authors found that nearly 61% of male and 71% of females in the Ex-Gay ministries said that they had abstained from any same-sex sex behaviours in the previous year and there were also movements in favour of greater heterosexual orientation on the more broadly rated 'Kinsey scale'.

The Spitzer Study

A significant development in Ex-Gay research in recent years was a study by Robert Spitzer published in 2003.[27] As we have noted, Spitzer is credited with initiating the process that led to the removal of homosexuality from DSM in 1973. His decision to investigate the effectiveness of re-orientation therapies many years later attracted both criticism and acclaim. Some respected professionals viewed the resulting work as fundamentally flawed to the extent that it should not have been published[73] whilst others[74] hailed it as a long overdue recognition of the rights of a disenfranchised minority.

Interestingly, as the following quotation illustrates, in terms of its political and personal context, Spitzer's decision to undertake his study of re-orientation outcomes in 2003 bore a number of similarities to his decision to take homosexuality out of the DSM in 1973:

It's funny because in some ways there are interesting parallels. I got into the original 1973 controversy because I . . . started to talk to the people breaking up a meeting [pro-gay advocacy groups]. [Later,] in 1999, there was a protest at the

APA annual meeting by some Ex-Gay groups . . . I started talking to one of these guys, and he tried to tell me how he had changed . . . I got the idea 'Gee, well maybe it's not so open and shut about changing sexual orientation'.[57]

The research study that ensued from this conversation was published, after peer review, in the authoritative journal *Archives of Sexual Behaviour*. Because of the political importance of the work, the editor took the unusual step of calling for additional peer commentaries, and published 26 of these alongside the main research findings.

Spitzer justified his work as a response to the 2000 APA Position Statement: 'APA encourages and supports research . . . to further determine "reparative" therapy's risks versus its benefits.' He formulated the hypothesis to be tested as follows:

Some individuals whose sexual orientation is predominantly homosexual can become predominantly heterosexual following some form of reparative therapy (which can take the form of psychotherapy, counselling, or participation in an ex-gay ministry program).

The method used to investigate the hypothesis involved a structured interview, via telephone, of 200 participants (143 men and 57 women), selected on the basis that they 'report that their sexual orientation had been predominantly homosexual, but who now report that because of some kind of therapy they have sustained for at least 5 years some change to a heterosexual orientation'. Participants were recruited over a 16-month period; 43% learned of the study through Ex-Gay ministries and 23% from the National Association for Research and Therapy of Homosexuality (NARTH). These two organizations sent repeated notices to their members; the remaining third were recruited via other participants or via therapists providing re-orientation therapy.

Despite being conducted by telephone, the assessment method advanced those used in most previous studies by adopting a structured, multi-dimensional assessment of 'orientation' across a range of measures including strength of subjective attraction; self-identity; severity of being distressed by homosexual feelings; frequency of homosexual activity; frequency of yearning for romantic intimacy with a same-sex partner; 'lustful' fantasies; percentage of masturbation occasions associated with same-sex fantasy; and use of gay pornography. There were similar measures of heterosexual desire and function.

The results showed that 11% of males and 37% of the females reported complete or near complete change on all of the sexual orientation measures. A significant proportion of participants achieved intermediate degrees of change. Prior to the interventions, 99% of males and 98% of females affirmed that they had same-sex sexual fantasies, whereas afterwards only 31% of men and 5% of women reported the same type and intensity of fantasies. A yearning for romantic emotional involvement with same-sex partners among 78% of men and 88% of the women changed to 8% of men and 4% of the women. Most of those who achieved lesser degrees of change reported some benefit from the intervention(s). The proportion reporting homosexual sex 'at least a few times a month' fell from 50% before the intervention to 1% in males and from 56% to 0% among females. Conversely, the criteria for 'good heterosexual functioning' were met in none of the females before intervention, and only 2.1% of males, but in 44% of females and 66% of males afterwards. The vast majority of participants reported that religion was 'extremely' or 'very' important in their lives.

Spitzer interpreted his findings in a carefully worded conclusion:

> Some gay men and lesbians, following reparative therapy, report that they have made major changes from a predominantly homosexual orientation to a predominantly heterosexual orientation, and that changes were not limited simply to behaviour and self-ascribed identity.

Bearing in mind the methodological issues raised previously in relation to other studies, it is clear that this study also suffered many weaknesses. These have been dissected at length and in detail in the 26 commentaries published at the same time. Weaknesses included biased sample selection, retrospective study design, use of telephone interviews, and insufficient reporting of the findings.[73, 75, 76] Given well recognized issues of demand characteristics and cognitive dissonance theory, the study's reliance upon self-reports came in for particular scrutiny.[77] How do we know the respondents were not simply deceiving themselves? Other critics commented on the slow selection process, which relied upon 'repeated' notices to Ex-Gay organizations. Others highlighted the fact that participants were clearly not blind to the study purpose and most, if not all, had compelling personal reasons to provide data that would prove the hypothesis correct.[78] On the other hand, several commentators,[63, 79-81] by no means all supportive of the ethics and rationale of the study, noted significant improvements in the methodology compared with previous research. They commented upon the impressive sample size, use of multi-dimensional assessments and the favourable effects of these interventions compared with many other psychotherapeutic treatments in routine use in clinical settings, including gay-affirmative therapy.

It should be noted that few of the commentators raised methodological limitations that were not already recognized by Spitzer:

> It is unclear how many gays and lesbians in the general population would want to change their sexual orientation or how representative the study sample is of those who would be interested in therapy with that goal . . . obviously, this study cannot address the question of how often sexual reorientation therapy actually results in the substantial changes reported by most of the participants in this study.

Spitzer recognized that the absence of a control group was a major limitation but argued that this would involve serious logistical and ethical challenges; potential subjects wishing to change their sexual orientation would be unlikely to agree to being assigned to a control group that would not provide therapy for several years, and it would be difficult to prevent them seeking 'informal' assistance elsewhere.

Although Spitzer recognized the limitations of his study, he believed that his findings were sufficiently robust to challenge the conventional view that desire for therapy to change sexual orientation is always succumbing to societal pressure and internalized homophobia, asserting that 'for some individuals changing sexual orientation can be a rational, self-directed goal'. Further, he asserted that the APA 2000 Position Statement that 'ethical practitioners refrain from attempts to change individuals' sexual orientation' was based on a double standard 'by implying that it is unethical for a clinician to provide reparative therapy because there is inadequate scientific evidence of effectiveness, whereas it assumes that it is ethical to provide gay affirmative therapy for which there is also no rigorous scientific evidence of effectiveness and for which, like reparative therapy, there are reports and testimonials of harm'.[82]

The Jones and Yarhouse Study

The most comprehensive study to date was published in 2007 by Jones and Yarhouse:[83] *Ex-Gays: A Longitudinal Study of Religiously Motivated Change in Sexual Orientation*. The authors acknowledge that Exodus International funded their work, and the findings are published in a book, through a Christian publisher, rather than in peer-reviewed journals. Nevertheless, the outcome data are presented in considerable detail and allow detailed analysis of the findings. The authors are academics with a track record in psychological research. They take care to recognize the limitations of their methodology as well as highlighting the advances over previous work.

The authors aimed to answer two questions: 'Is change of sexual orientation possible?' and 'Is the attempt to change sexual orientation harmful?' This is a prospective study that followed participants from the beginning of their involvement with an Ex-Gay ministry programme. In other words, measures were carried out before, during, and at completion of the programme. This is a considerable advance on previous studies (such as Spitzer), which asked people to remember change experiences that had happened in the past. Because the study was prospective, the researchers did not have to rely upon (possibly faulty and biased) accounts from memory.

Other strengths of the study included the use of standardized measures of self-report, including the Klein Sexual Orientation Grid, Kinsey scales and the Shively De-Cecco scales.[84] The latter measure, for example, separates homosexual and heterosexual attractions on two independent scales, with the zero axis representing asexuality.

The sample size was 98, including 72 men and 26 women. Over time, as always happens in work of this kind, there were dropouts, either because people left the therapy programme or because they declined to participate further in the study itself. The original sample eroded from 98 subjects at Time 1 assessment to 85 at Time 2 and 73 at Time 3, which is a Time 1 to Time 3 retention rate of 74.5%.

Overall, there were significant levels of decrease in the measures of same-sex attraction between times 1 and 3, and significant increases in the measures of other-sex attraction over this time. These changes were judged to be meaningful in terms of the objectives of the study, as well as significant in statistical terms. However, it should be noted that the changes were larger for movement away from homosexuality than towards heterosexuality.

These outcomes can be grouped in various ways. Among the 75% of the original sample who completed the study, ratings for 'self-identity' at stage 3 were as follows:

- 33 people (45%) reported significant change (moving from homosexual, bisexual or other at Time 1 to heterosexual at Time 3; or from homosexual at Time 1 to bisexual or other at Time 3)
- 8 (11%) reported 'negative change' (moving from heterosexual, bisexual or other at Time 1 to homosexual at Time 3; or from heterosexual at Time 1 to bisexual or other at Time 3)
- 3 (4%) reported uncertain change (moving from bisexual to other, or the reverse)
- 29 (40%) reported no change

The authors reported: 'Changes on the Shively and DeCecco rating scales [used to measure homosexual and heterosexual attractions on different dimensions] for all three dimensions of our analysis followed a stable pattern . . . We see that change away from homosexual orientation is consistently about *twice* the magnitude of changes toward heterosexual orientation'. Thus, it appeared that it was easier to decrease homosexual attraction than to increase heterosexual attraction.

A common criticism of such studies is that those who report change are probably 'bisexual' to some degree when starting the change process. To test that theory, Jones and Yarhouse created a subpopulation from their sample that they dubbed 'The Truly Gay':

. . . To be classed as truly gay, subjects must have reported above average homosexual attraction and homosexual behaviour and reported past embracing of a gay identity. We would emphasize that these were much more rigorous standards than are typically employed in empirical studies to classify research subjects as homosexual. Using this method, 45 out of our total 98 subjects were classed as 'Truly Gay', just less than half the population sample. We expected that the results of change for the Truly Gay subpopulation would be less positive, as these individuals would be those more set and stable in their sexual orientation. This is not what we found. Rather the change reported by the Truly Gay subpopulation was consistently stronger than that reported by others.

The researcher also classified outcomes on the basis of a series of interviews that relied upon qualitative methods and then provided quantitative data for each group. These groups were as follows:

- 'Success: Conversion' (15%) These were subjects who reported that they felt their change to be successful and reported substantial reduction in homosexual desire and growth of heterosexual attraction and functioning. Subjects showed large, meaningful and statistically significant shifts on the scaled outcomes.
- 'Success: Chastity' (23%) These were subjects who reported that their change was successful in terms of resolving SSA; subjects reported homosexual attraction to be present only incidentally or in a way that did not seem to bring about distress, allowing them to live happily without overt sexual activity. They did not report statistically significant or meaningful growth in heterosexual attraction.
- 'Continuing' (29%) These persons may have experienced modest decreases in homosexual attraction, but were not satisfied with their degree of change and

remained committed to the change process. Quantitative measures of change were not, with one exception, significant.

- 'Non-response' (15%) These people experienced no significant change. They had not given up on the change process, but may be confused or conflicted about which direction to turn next.
- 'Failure: Confused' (4%) These persons had experienced no significant change and had given up on the change process but without yet embracing gay identity.
- 'Failure: Gay identity' (8%) These persons had given up on the change process and embraced a gay identity. (The remaining 6% were not classifiable due to failures in the qualitative assessment procedures.)

Outcomes for Harm

Jones and Yarhouse administered the System Check List–90-Revised (SCL), a standardized measure of psychological distress. 'Normative' scores are available for general population and psychiatric outpatient populations that can be used for comparison. At baseline, the average score for participants fell midway between what would be obtained in a general population sample and a psychiatric outpatient sample. In those who remained in the study, there was no evidence of worsened psychological functioning as a result of participating in the programme. Indeed, some measures (especially intensity of symptom distress) showed improvement. Sub-group analysis did not reveal exceptions to these findings, either in the 'truly gay' sample or those with equivocal outcomes classified finally as 'continuing'. There was no evidence of decline or adverse outcomes on measures of spiritual well-being and maturity.

Strengths and Limitations of this Study

We have noted the prospective nature of the study, use of standardized measures and fair and cautious interpretation of the study findings. The sample size is disappointing (the authors originally hoped to recruit 300–400 people) and because of recruitment problems the period of prior involvement was lengthened to up to three years for 41 of the participants (reducing the prospective impact of the study and potentially biasing the sample). There are the usual problems of 'representativeness' – the mean age was 37, somewhat older than might be expected, although one might expect that this would militate against the chances of positive outcome.

There is an issue of bias: both authors are known for their evangelical affiliations (although the same problem of bias applies to many other studies in terms of public 'gay affirming' stances of the researchers involved, including members of secular professional boards making various pronouncements in this area).

Relatively little information is available on those lost to follow-up and it would have been preferable to have reported base-line data for dropouts. The authors give examples of one individual who said he had dropped out because he decided to accept his gay orientation and another who believed herself 'cured and healed' and had married. The remainder were either uncontactable or refused consent to further participation. It should be noted that problems of recruitment and attrition are common in longitudinal studies of this nature, not least in such a sensitive and personal area.

But both factors compromise the representativeness of the study findings, and if we were to assume that all the dropouts had negative outcomes, then rates of harm could be higher and rates of 'success, conversion' would reduce further to 11%.

Some critics continue to insist that only psycho-physiological measures of sexual arousal, such as penile plethysmography, would provide incontrovertible evidence of change. The authors explain the logistical and ethical hurdles to incorporating these measures into their methodology, and provide a detailed and plausible critique of the validity of plethysmography, which remains of uncertain status as a 'lie detector'.

Overall, this study provides convincing evidence that some individuals can achieve levels of diminution of homosexual attraction and sufficient heterosexual attraction to be considered as examples of very good outcomes in terms of the objectives of the study. And a larger proportion can achieve a satisfactory outcome in terms of diminished same-sex attractions and adjustment, even where this means reconciling to a life of celibacy. Over half reported little or no change. We cannot know how many individuals in the general population would achieve similar outcomes because of problems of generalizability. Importantly, there was little evidence of harm as a result of participation in these interventions, with the caveat of lack of information on the 25% who did not complete the study.

General Conclusions from Studies of Interventions for Unwanted SSA

So what can we reasonably conclude from this overview of studies of interventions for SSA?

- There is reasonable evidence that some individuals with unwanted SSA may, during the course of interventions for SSA, successfully align their experience and their behaviour with their values in ways that they find helpful and satisfying.
- A significant proportion of participants in these studies report transitions in favour of heterosexual function (in the range of 45–66%) on at least *some* dimensions of sexual experience. However, change across *all* dimensions of sexuality appears to be much smaller – of the order of 10% in males and up to 30% in females. For most participants, changes are greater for diminution of same-sex attraction than for increases in other-sex attractions. For this group, satisfaction and psychological adjustment to coping with the residue of SSA appear to be the main outcome. The group with the 'best' outcomes, that is those achieving diminution of homosexual attractions *and* marked growth of heterosexual attraction and function, appears to be 10–15% of men and up to 30% of women.
- Because of selection biases, we cannot know whether these outcomes would be achieved in a random sample from the general population. Outcomes could be better or worse. The same criticism applies to many other counselling interventions for emotional and psychological issues, including 'gay-affirmative' therapy.
- Although there is evidence of a temporal correlation between the interventions and the reported outcomes, because there were no controls in these studies we cannot know whether the reported changes are causally related to the specific interventions or to some other non-specific factors. The same criticism applies to

many other counselling interventions for emotional and psychological issues, including 'gay-affirmative' therapy.

- The studies suggest that there is potential for harm, especially where expectations are raised or if there is a degree of coercion. Because of selection biases, it is not possible to estimate the potential for harm if applied to a general population of individuals with SSA. The levels of harm reported in these studies casts doubt, however, on prevailing notions that intervention is *always* harmful or unhelpful, and they caution against negative generalizations.

- There is sufficient evidence of benefits, and potential for harm, to provide a scientific rationale for further investigations of both the benefits and harm that might result from interventions for SSA.

- Provided that full and informed consent is obtained that emphasizes uncertainties about the potential effect size and the risks of disappointment and unfulfilled expectations, the evidence does not support the case for proscribing such approaches, especially where personal choice remains a desirable component of client autonomy and self-determination.

4.5 Evidence that Intervention for Unwanted SSA Causes Harm

For many years, counselling journals[85–87] and the media have reported anecdotal accounts of harm caused by interventions for SSA. However, there was no large-scale systematic study with the specific goal of documenting harm before Shidlo and Schroeder[88] published their findings from a survey of 202 consumers of 'sexual conversion interventions' in 2002.

In this survey, the majority of participants failed to change sexual orientation, and many reported that they had experienced harm. 'Harm' was documented in terms of self-reported depression; suicidal ideation and attempts; self-esteem problems linked with 'internalized homophobia'; intrusive imagery; sexual dysfunction, especially in those undergoing behaviour therapy methods; social and interpersonal harm, such as social isolation and interference with intimate relationships; and 'spiritual harm' such as loss of faith, sense of betrayal and anger at clinicians.

Some attributed these negative effects to being told by the therapist – and their believing – that they had chosen their sexual orientation:

I've felt more depressed after I did the therapy. The negative aspect was that I really felt it was all up to me, the choice I had made, and because of that choice I was condemned to being in this pain for ever. This need for unnatural affections.

Other participants said that they tried not to be homosexual, but when they failed to change they became depressed and/or suicidal:

I wanted to die. I felt as though I would never change and be 'killed'. It harmed my self-esteem very much. I wanted to die. I felt as though it took away who I was.

Another female participant described her experience:

I attempted suicide with pills. I just wanted to die. Part of it had to do with the feeling that I was dying already because of what the Nun [conversion therapist] was doing to me. It felt like she was killing me, trying to get rid of my lesbian self.

A group of participants who underwent cognitive behaviour therapies, especially those who had aversive conditioning, reported long-term harm indicated by the intrusion of disturbing images formed in conversion therapy. They experienced aversive conditioning as punitive and degrading, and they responded with fear and shame:

It was a pretty humiliating experience. I was sitting in somebody's office . . . unzip your pants and strapped to electrodes. And [then] walk out to the waiting room with burn marks in my arms . . .

Some respondents spoke about an increase in worrying that they appeared 'gay acting', reporting hyper-vigilance to displaying incongruous gender traits, resulting in an increase in paranoid-like worries and fears that they would not 'pass' as being heterosexual.

Many participants spoke of experiencing significant harm in their relationships with families. Participants spoke of anger, alienation, hatred and other negative emotions toward their parents as a result of the conversion therapy:

I really wanted to believe . . . so, for a while, it added to my hatred of my father . . . during that period I broke off relationship with my father to get away from that influence.

Many participants complained of experiencing social isolation and loneliness:

[The conversion therapy] made me feel like a freak. Made me feel about it even worse than I did before. Consequently, I couldn't reach out to anyone about it . . . I had no one to talk to, and didn't feel I could be open with the therapist.

Some male participants reported that conversion therapy created in them fear of becoming a child abuser and interfered with their relationships with children:

It really screwed me up, because these thoughts were put in my head that I was attracted to little boys, and I'm not. I was very angry at that . . . I have very few nephews, I was afraid to be around them, afraid to play with them.

Spiritual harm was also described:

God became this very punishment. In church you get homophobia twice a year, in therapy it was every week. God was a punishing, phobic figure, and I became an evil sinner . . .

These anecdotes can be supplemented with similar experiences reported in Europe. For example, a carefully executed (but relatively small) survey[89] of Ex-Gay ministries in the UK included narratives describing 'harm' from several participants in different forms of ministry:

> When I reflect on my experiences, I am bitterly aware that in seeking to meet my spiritual needs I was encouraged to deny any aspect of my life over which I had no control. Furthermore, my desire to be 'normal' led me to allow other people to abuse me when I was in a vulnerable state. I am still attempting to come to terms with the consequences of this in relation to my feelings of self esteem and self-worth.

> [Practitioners of an Ex-Gay ministry] work on fear and make you feel worthless, sick and perverse if you are gay. The mind is left confused and obsessed with blocking out alleged evil thoughts that come naturally to gay people. It also appeared that [they] considered homosexuality to be a choice . . . and that the mind was programmed incorrectly with data like a computer which they could 're-program to normal' – this is what they said.

The survey raised concerns about unethical and exploitative practices among 'Ex-Gay' therapists, an issue that has been highlighted elsewhere.[29, u]

This anecdotal evidence is important. The personal narratives include examples of intense suffering and provide plausible accounts of unprofessional behaviour on the part of some counsellors, pastors and therapists. The potential for harm as a result of unrealistic marketing and over-inflated claims of success is self-evident. However, when we attempt to interpret these anecdotal data to establish the scale of the problem, or the conditions likely to increase (or reduce) the risk of harm, we find ourselves grappling with similar methodological issues to those encountered in the effectiveness studies.

The Shidlo and Schroeder study[88] had a reasonably large sample size and the qualitative interviews were conducted in considerable detail and reported carefully. However, although the authors used semi-structured interviews they were unable to report frequency responses because of time constraints and the qualitative nature of their methodology. There were no objective measures of mental health problems alleged to have been caused by the intervention. Further, subjects had participated in a variety of clinical, psychotherapeutic, counselling and pastoral religious interventions and the authors were unable to distinguish between them in terms of their potential for harm. As in the Spitzer study, recruitment was extremely slow, with interviews being conducted over a five-year period, and there were serious sampling biases. For example, the authors recruited the first 10% of their subjects with an advertisement headed 'Homophobic Therapies: Documenting the Damage' that continued 'have you gone through counselling and therapy where you were encouraged to become heterosexual or ex-gay? The National Lesbian and Gay Health Association wants to hear from you.' When, after the first 20 interviews, the authors discovered that some participants reported being helped as well as harmed, they changed the project title to be more inclusive and neutral: 'Changing Sexual Orientation: Does Counselling Work?'[88] However, it appears that the majority of participants continued to be recruited from gay and lesbian websites and email lists, advertisements in the gay press, friends and media.

The study methodology does not allow us to determine whether the interventions actually caused the reported harm. For example, when the authors attempted to quantify episodes of deliberate self-harm among the participants reporting such attempts, 25 took place *before* the re-orientation therapy, 23 during and 11 afterwards. Further studies of mental health problems among gay and lesbian people in the general population (as opposed to studies of those who have been through some kind of intervention for SSA) show higher rates of suicidal behaviour and self-harm independently of participation in re-orientation therapy.[90] For example, a prospective birth cohort study[46] in New Zealand reported a 5-fold increase in suicidal ideation and a 6-fold increase in self-harm among those with SSA. Whatever the causes of these increased rates, the Shidlo and Schroeder study simply establishes an association between participating in an intervention and subject complaints of harm, not a causal link. The same applies to other mental health problems identified in this study. Given the several-year time spans involved, there is no way of knowing whether the incidents during and after therapy were not simply part of an ongoing pattern of mental health problems.

It is important to note that the authors fully recognized, and documented, the limitations of their study:

> Our results therefore focus on the meanings of harm attributed by clients, and the accuracy of these attributions remains to be determined by future process-and-outcome research . . . The data presented in this article do not provide information on the incidence, and the prevalence of failure, success, harm, help or ethical violations in conversion therapy. The qualitative data obtained can serve to develop rigorous quantitative measures to be validated in future studies.

Thus, like the Spitzer study, this work provides sufficient evidence to justify further research, but cautions against making sweeping generalizations.

Case Series in Outcome Studies

We have noted that outcome studies of interventions for SSA utilizing case series report relatively modest rates of 'harm': Nicolosi[70] reported subjective harm in about 7%, while Spitzer[27] and Jones and Yarhouse[83] reported no cases of significant harm. In the latter study, standardized measures of psychological distress showed no deterioration as a result of participation in Ex-Gay ministries, and indeed improvement in some areas, although information is lacking on the 25% who dropped out of follow-up.

What can we reasonably conclude from these reviews of harm?

- There is evidence that some individuals with SSA may, during the course of interventions for SSA, experience adverse life events and mental health problems that they attribute to the adverse effects of intervention.
- Participants have reported harm across several domains, including mental health and well-being, social relations, and spiritual health. Some individuals report severe degrees of depression and suicidal ideation. Some find their experience to be demeaning, oppressive and a negation of their sense of dignity.
- Because of problems of representativeness, selection biases, and frequent lack of

standardized measures of 'harm', it is not possible to generalize the chances of 'harm' to all individuals who may be considering entering some form of ministry or clinical intervention, although the case series studies suggest this is small.

- We cannot determine causal attributions with certainty. Because the studies do not have control groups, we do not know whether these reported mental health problems are greater than would be expected in a population of lesbian and gay people who are not taking part in some form of intervention.

- It is not clear how experience of harm is related to participants' expectations, motivation or other factors not connected with the intervention itself. Outcomes may vary markedly depending upon the attitudes and readiness of participants.

- There are reported incidents of poor practice on the part of some individuals offering interventions for SSA that raise serious questions about training and supervision. These include prejudice, over-simplification, and attempts to 'force' interpretive frameworks upon participants that may lead to distressed family relationships.

- It appears that there is insufficient evidence to support the case for banning such interventions where personal choice remains a desirable component of client autonomy and self-determination. It is mandatory, however, that fully informed consent is obtained, emphasizing uncertainties about the potential effect size of such interventions and the potential risks of disappointment and unfulfilled expectations.

- More research is justified in this area.

5. Ethical Issues

We have seen that the research evidence is inconclusive regarding both the scale of potential benefits and the potential for harm resulting from interventions for SSA. However, we need to consider whether even preliminary evidence of harm provides sufficient grounds to support calls for their withdrawal. There are, in addition, wider political and philosophical issues that require attention. Are such interventions justi-fied if they imply the existence of a mental disorder and promote a resurgence of negative prejudice and stigma against gay and lesbian people? And what, on the other hand, are the rights of individuals whose experience of SSA conflicts with their personal value system, and who wish to bring their attractions into line with their values, rather than the reverse? As Haldeman has suggested,[91] giving an individual's attractions and erotic desires a higher priority than her religious values is a value judgement that is in itself a product of one internalized socially constructed meaning system among many.

The balance of the evidence supports the current position of most professional organizations that more research is needed to understand both the potential for harm and the relative effectiveness of these interventions. However, it is difficult to see how the evidence of harm reviewed here could justify a call for a complete pro-scription of such interventions and Ex-Gay ministries. Such a proposal would indeed support claims of the application of double standards,[27] especially if the potential risks of 'gay-affirmative' therapies for those with conflicting personal and religious values goes unchallenged and under-researched. While more research is undertaken, there are clearly risks of harm that arise from poorly trained and supervised counsellors who work to rigid explanatory models that create unrealistic expectations of change. This may be addressed by the development and careful implementation of guidelines for those offering interventions for SSA, as we shall discuss further below.

Many critics of interventions for SSA believe that their acceptance will result in the 're-pathologization' of homosexuality and encourage a resurgence of stigma and prejudice. This is an important issue because of outrageous examples of prejudice and abuse in the social history of attitudes toward people with SSA. Even today, many Christians continue to hold views that betray extraordinary levels of ignorance and malice. This needs to be recognized, owned and combated at every level of church life. But there is no compelling reason to believe that attempts to support people who wish to bring their attractions and desires into line with their values must inevitably lead to the re-pathologization of these people; there are many counselling and 'therapeutic' interventions for a range of 'problems in living' that do not imply that the client is ill or somehow 'disordered'. The fact that support for people who wish to modify their same-sex attractions risks 're-pathologizing' SSA is part of a larger issue connected to the way we use labels and stigmatize people who are different from ourselves. The solution is to challenge the labelling, not the support. There is a difference between moral evaluation of behaviours and implacable prejudice against another in terms of their race, sex or, indeed, reported pattern of SSA.

Those who hold 'essentialist' biological views of human sexual variation may fear that interventions for SSA seek to undo 'nature' by imposing socially constructed constraints. And by placing their categorical views of sexuality alongside other differences of race and sex they ask, for example, whether one would encourage the development of interventions that successfully altered skin tones if patients demanded it? But the problem with such essentialist views, as we have seen, is the lack of evidence for a biologically validated stratification of human sexual desires; most complex human behaviours result from an interaction of genetic and environmental factors, mediated through complex webs of causation that also involve human exigency and choice.

In pursuing this argument further, we may argue that a putative biological basis for behaviour is not equivalent to ethical legitimacy. It is likely, for example, that biological factors will be identified that influence different patterns of sexual sensation seeking that lead to promiscuity, or different patterns of preference for passivity and dominance that are observed in both heterosexual and homosexual behaviours. This does not mean that the individuals are unable to exercise choice in managing these impulses and pre-dispositions. Even gay-affirming theorists such as Edward Stein discriminate between *experience* and *behaviour* in terms of their capacity for moral evaluation:

> Even if one's sexual orientation is primarily biological and not a choice, much of what is ethically relevant about being lesbian or a gay man is not biologically based and is not determined . . . For example, even if homosexuality were genetic, engaging in sexual acts with a person of the same sex-gender, identifying as a lesbian or a gay man, and deciding to establish a household with a person of the same sex-gender are choices, choices that each . . . might well not have made (for example, he or she could have decided to be celibate, closeted, and companionless).[v]

6. Respecting Individual Autonomy and Self-determination

Given the present state of the evidence, who is to say that erotic sexual desires deserve higher priority than religious or other personal value systems? Adjudication between these value systems is a moral, ethical and theological issue, not a scientific enterprise.[92] A number of researchers and commentators have recently suggested a more thoughtful and reasoned approach that attempts to de-polarize the debate over conservative religious values and issues of SSA. They have sought to do so by emphasizing a person-centred approach[93-95] with a more explicit emphasis upon the individual's rights to autonomy and self-determination.[96]

Some gay-affirming practitioners have also come to recognize that diversity of religious views is a legitimate expression of human diversity on a par with other expressions of human diversity such as sexual attractions. For example Haldeman:[93]

> Honoring religious experience as a legitimate aspect of identity is the duty of all who work with conflicted clients. Those who have spoken out on behalf of the rights of LGB [Lesbian/Gay/Bisexual] individuals for competent and ethical treatment insist that therapists in the religious world refrain from pathologizing their LGB clients. So, too, should gay-affirmative practitioners refrain from overtly or subtly devaluing those who espouse conservative religious identities.

In order to capture this balance of views, Throckmorton and Yarhouse[v] have produced a 'Framework and Recommendations for Practice', effectively a guideline, for those professionals working with clients who experience conflict between their personal values and sexual attractions, and who desire therapeutic support. The authors describe their work as follows:

> These guidelines do not stigmatize same-sex eroticism or traditional values and attitudes. The emergence of a gay identity for persons struggling with value conflicts is a possibility envisioned by the recommendation . . . thus, some religious individuals will determine that their religious identity is the preferred organizing principle for them, even if it means learning to live with sexual feelings they do not value. Conversely, some religious individuals will determine that their religious beliefs may become modified to allow integration of same-sex eroticism with their valued identity. We seek to provide therapy recommendations that respect these options.

The approach of 'sexual identity management' worked out in these guidelines seeks to respect the statements of professional associations regarding both sexual diversity *and* religious diversity.[w] They set out explicit requirements for defining the goal of treatment in line with client autonomy and choice, advanced informed consent, and the issue of therapist capability and ethical obligations.

7. The Church and Interventions for SSA

Where the Church adopts a conservative theological stance in relation to expressions of same-sex attractions, it is crucial that those offering practical and pastoral support to people conflicted over their SSA are aware of the complexities of the issues surrounding Ex-Gay ministries and therapies promising re-orientation. The Church may wish to consider the development of standards recommending that such organizations explicitly address issues of:

- Advanced informed consent that includes realistic estimates of the benefits of interventions and balanced warnings about the potential for harm.
- The Church's right to teach its understanding of the Divine intention for the ordering of sexual relationships balanced against its responsibility to ensure that those who seek pastoral support and counselling do not encounter an atmosphere of shame and coercion.
- The priority of client autonomy and self-determination in setting goals for the intervention.
- Accreditation and competencies of pastoral counsellors and volunteers.
- Arrangements for the supervision and oversight of those offering counselling and minimum standards of experience and training.
- Explicit commitment to combating prejudice and stigma against people with same-sex attractions.

8. Conclusions

The crowded marketplace of opinions on interventions for SSA contains a commingling of facts, theories and assertions by proponents on all sides of the debate. All claim to have science on their side.

We have attempted to survey copious amounts of empirical data, and have concluded that there is evidence that some individuals can achieve significant changes in patterns of unwanted SSA. It is difficult to estimate the proportion of people with unwanted SSA who may achieve *marked* degrees of change and it would be advisable to adopt a conservative estimate of around 10–15%, possibly higher for women. However, a larger proportion may achieve satisfaction in bringing their unwanted SSA into line with their values, even if this implies long-term commitment to cognitive and behaviour disciplines (including sexual abstinence) in the face of a persisting mix of sexual attractions.

We have noted that there is a risk of harm, especially where those offering interventions make unrealistic claims. So we have recognized the need for minimum standards that set out requirements for informed consent and that ensure the safety of vulnerable clients. These developments would help ensure that appropriate pastoral and counselling space can be provided for those who seek help in bringing their sexual attractions into line with their religious worldview.

Finally, we have recognized the potential significance, and the pivotal organizing principle, of religious beliefs and values in human mental life. We have noted the way secular values shape and inform the practice of many therapists and counsellors, and we have welcomed more explicit recognitions among some professionals of their need to respect the religious values of their clients. Questions about the nature of those beliefs, and the Divine intention for the ordering of human relationships, must be answered outside of the counselling room. These are theological and ethical issues for which science and psychology have no privileged insights.

Notes

a   Sue Wilkinson, Professor of Feminist and Health Studies at Loughborough University, UK, is quoted as saying: 'I was never unsure about my sexuality throughout my teens or 20's. I was a happy heterosexual and had no doubts. Then I changed, through political activity and feminism, spending time with women's organizations. It opened my mind to the possibility of a lesbian identity.' <http://women.timesonline.co.uk/tol/life_and_style/women/relationships/article2002552.ece>

b   Peter Tatchell, a UK gay rights campaigner: 'It is, therefore, not in the interest of lesbians and gay men to maintain sexual difference. Our liberation is irrevocably bound up with the dissolution of separate, mutually exclusive, rival orientations and identities.' <www.petertatchell.net/queer%20theory/beyond.htm>.

     See also: Peter Tatchell: <http://commentisfree.guardian.co.uk/peter_tatchell/2006/06/born_gay_or_made_gay.html>. 'If we are all born either gay or straight, how do they explain people who switch in mid-life from fulfilled heterosexuality to fulfilled homosexuality (and vice versa) . . . In an enlightened, gay-affirming society, more people might be inclined to explore same-sex desire.'

c   <www.exodus-international.org/>.

d   <http://74.1.174.242/redeemedlives/index.asp>.

e   <www.jonahweb.org/>.

f   <http://gaymuslims.wordpress.com/about/>.

g   <http://couragerc.net/>.

h   <www.pathinfo.org/>.

i   <www.living-waters-uk.org/>.

j   <www.narth.com/index.html>.

k   It is interesting to note that Freud, whilst viewing homosexuality as a disorder of psychosexual development, did not consider that homosexuals were 'sick'. In his 'Letter to an American mother' he wrote, 'Homosexuality is assuredly no advantage, but it is nothing to be ashamed of, no vice, no degradation, it cannot be classified as an illness . . . '

l   A gender-atypical child fails to conform to the behavioural stereotypes associated with his or her sex-gender in their particular culture. For example, in certain Western cultures, such boys would be less likely to play sports involving rough physical contact or play games pretending to be soldiers.

m   <www.rcpsych.ac.uk/college/specialinterestgroups/gaylesbian.aspx>.

n   <www.advocate.com/news_detail_ektid47311.asp>.

o   In an address delivered to the APA convention, New Orleans, 2006, Dr Cummings stated: '60% of physicists and chemists on college faculties profess a religious affiliation, while only 10% of their counterparts in psychology do. Religion is regarded as unscientific [by psychologists]. Are physicists less scientific . . . or are they less concerned with political correctness? Almost 90% of Americans express a belief in God. Is this disconnect causing more Americans to distrust psychotherapy and to ask for religiously affiliated counsellors, resulting in a rapid proliferation of faith-base counselling centers?' APA, New Orleans.

p   Mario Bergner, Submission to Listening Process.

q   John's story, New Direction Ministries, Canada.

r   Mabel's story, <http://exodus.to/content/view/256/148/>.

s   Peter Ould, <www.peter-ould.net/2007/04/19/you-and-me-together/>.

t   The reluctance of large numbers of individuals to 'come forward' and air their personal sexual narratives in public may not be all that surprising, however.

u   'Beyond Ex-Gay, an online community for those who have survived Ex-Gay ministries' contains further personal narratives: <www.beyondexgay.com/>.

v   <http://wthrockmorton.com/wp-content/uploads/2007/04/sexualidentitytherapyframeworkfinal.pdf>.

w   Guidelines for psychotherapy issues by the American Psychological Association in 2000 include statement that 'psychologists are encouraged to recognise how their [personal] attitudes and knowledge about lesbian, gay and bisexual issues may be relevant to assessment and treatment and encourage its members to make appropriate referrals when indicated. With regard to respecting religious diversity, a division of the American Counselling Association has adopted competencies for counsellors which state: 'the professional Counsellor is sensitive to and receptive of the religious and/or spiritual themes in the counselling process as befits the expressed preference of each client' and 'the professional counsellor uses a client's religious and/or spiritual beliefs in the pursuit of the client's therapeutic goals as befits the client's expressed preference'.

Works Cited

1   CRD report 4 (March 2001). Centre for Reviews and Dissemination York.
2   E. Stein (1999).The Mismeasure of Desire. Oxford University Press.
3   J. Savin-Williams et al. (2007). *Arch Sex Beh* **36**, 385–94.
4   R. Baumeister (2000).*Psych Bull,* **26**(3), 347–74
5   M. Eskin et al. (2005). *Arch SexBeh* **34** *(2)*, 185–95.
6   D. Black et al. (2000). *Demography.***37** *(2)*, 139–54.
7   L. Wichstrom et al. (2003). *J Abnl Psychy* **112**, 144–51
8   E. Laumann et al. (1994). The Social Organisation of Sexuality. Chicago Press
9   R. Troiden (1988) Gay and Lesbian Identity. General Hall, New York.
10 B. Risman (1988) *Annual Review of Sociology* **14**, 125–47.
11 G. Herdt (1996). Sexual Orientation: Toward Biological Understanding. Praeger.
12 B. Kumar et al. (1991) *Int J STD and AIDS* **2**, 442–4.
13 Naz Foundation (2000). London.
14 A. Sanders (1997). *J African Law* **41**, 100–8.
15 M. Wainberg et al. (2003). *Arch Sex Beh* **32**(5), 455–7.
16 A. Kinsey et al. (1948) Sexual Behavior in the Human Male. Philadelphia.
17 APA (1998). Answers to Your Questions. Washington, DC.
18 S. French et al. (1991). *International Journal of Eating Disorders* **2**, 119–26.
19 R. Garofalo et al. (1999). *Arch Ped Adol Me* **153**(5), 487–9
20 J. Stokes et al. (2004). *Arch Sex Beh* **26**, 383–97.
21 L. Diamond (2000). *DevPsych* **36**(2), 241–50.
22 M. Rosario et al. (1996). *J Sex Res* **33**, 113–26.
23 P. Rust (1992). *Social problems* **39**(4), 386.
24 K. Kinnish et al. (2005). *Archs Sex Beh* **34**(2*)*, 173–8.
25 R. Sell et al. (1995). *Arch Sex Beh* **24**(3), 235–48.
26 N. Dickson et al. (2003).*Social Science & Medicine.56(8)*, 1607–15,
27 R. Spitzer (2003). *Arch Sex Behav* **32**, 403–17.
28 W. Throckmorton (2002). *Prof Psych: Res and Pract* **33**: 242–8.
29 W. Besen (2003). Anything but Straight. Harrington Park Press, NY.
30 J. Gonsiorek et al. (1991) Homosexuality. Sage, CA.
31 M. King et al. (1999). *Br J Psych* **175**, 106–13.
32 S. Freud (1905).Three Essays on the Theory of Sexuality. Basic Books, NY.
33 I. Bieber (1962). Homosexuality: A Psychoanalytic study. Basic Books, NY.
34 E. Moberley (2006).Homosexuality: A New Christian Ethic. Lutterworth, Camb.
35 K. Lewes(1988).Psychoanalysis & Male Homosexuality. Simon and Schust, NY.
36 C. Socarides (1979). *Am JPsychoth* **33**, 506–20.
37 A. Medinger (2000). Growth into Manhood. Random House.
38 D. Bem (1996). *Psych Rev* **103**, 320–35.
39 M. Ruse (2007). Homosexuality: a Philosophical Enquiry. Blackwell, NY.
40 R. Webster (1995).Why Freud Was Wrong. Harper Collins/Basic Books.
41 R. Isay (1989).Being Homosexual: Gay Men and their Development.Collins, Can..
42 A. Bell et al. (1981). Sexual Preference. Bloomington Indiana University Press.
43 M. Bailey et al. (1995). Dev Psych **31**, 43–55.
44 R. Green (1987). The 'Sissy Boy' Syndrome. Yale University Press, New Haven.

45 M. Frisch et al. (2006). *Arch Sex Beh* **35**, 533–47.
46 D. Fergusson et al. (1999). A*rch GenPsych* **56**, 876–80.
47 P. Bearman et al. (2002). *Am J Soc* **107**, 1179–1205.
48 W. Byne W et al. (1993). *Arch Gen Psychy* **50**, 228–39.
49 S. Gold et al. (1965). *Behav Res & Therapy* **3**, 201–4
50 M. Herzen. (1978) Progress in Behavioural Modification. Academic Press, NY.
51 M. Seligman (1994). What You Can Change and What You Can't. Knopf.
52 A. Byrd et al. (2002). *Psych Reports* **90**, 1139–52.
53 Diagnostic and Statistical Manual (4th Edition) (2000). APA, Washington.
54 J. Bancroft (1975). *Journal Medical Ethics* **1**, 176–80.
55 APA. Position Statement (2000) *Am J Psych* **157**, 1719–21.
56 R. Bayer (1981) Homosexuality and American Psychiatry. Basic Books, NY.
57 J. Drescher (2007) Ex-Gay Research. Binghampton, NY.
58 K. Fulford et al. (2006) Oxford Textbook Philosophy and Psychiatry. Oxford
59 T. Szasz (2007) The Manufacture of Madness. Syracuse University Press.
60 WHO (1992). International Classification of Diseases (10th Edition). Geneva.
61 C. Moser et al. (2006) *J Psych & Human Sexuality* **17**, 91–109.
62 Bieschke K et al. (2000) In: Handbook of Counselling and Psychotherapy with Lesbian, Gay and Bisexual Clients. APA.
63 K. Zucker (2003). *Archives of Sexual Behavior.* **32**, 399–402.
64 J. Craig et al. (2001). http://www.mja.com.au/public/issues/174_05_050301/craig/craig.html
65 D. Sackett et al. (1996) http://www.cebm.net/?o=1014.
66 I. Bieber (1962) Homosexuality: A Psychoanalytic study. Basic Books, NY.
67 C. Socarides (1978) Homosexuality. Jason Aronson, NY.
68 H. Adams et al. (1977) *Psych Bull* **84**, 1171–88.
69 M. Schwartz (1984) *Am J Psych* **141**, 173–81.
70 J. Nicolosi et al. (2000). *Psychological Reports* **86**, 1071–8
71 K. Schaeffer et al. (2000) *J Psych and Christianity* **19**, 61–70.
72 K. Schaeffer et al. (1999). *J Psych Theol* **27**, 329–37.
73 L. Hartmann (2003). *Arch Sex Behav* **32**, 436–8.
74 M. Yarhouse (2003). *Arch Sex Behav* **32**, 462–3.
75 T. Sandfort (2003) *J Gay and Lesb Psych* **7**, 15–29.
76 G. Herek (2006) In: Ex-Gay Research. Binghampton, N.Y.
77 L. Beckstead (2003). *Arch Sex Behav* **32**, 421–3.
78 K. Cohen (2003). *Arch Sex Behav* **32**, 427–9.
79 S. Hershberger (2003). *Arch Sex Behav* **32**, 440.
80 B. Rind (2003). *Arch Sex Behav* **32**, 447–9.
81 R. Krueger (2003). *Arch Sex Behav* **32**, 443–44.
82 J. Gonsiorek (1982). *J Homosex* **7**, 9–20.
83 S. Jones (2007). Ex-Gays? A Longitudinal Study. IVP. Downers Grove, IL.
84 R. Sell (1997). *Arch Sex Behav* **26**, 643–58.
85 A. Shidlo et al. (2001). Sexual Conversion Therapy. Haworth Press.
86 D. Haldeman (1994). *J Consult& Clin Psych* **62**, 221–7.
87 D. Haldeman (2002).*J Gay and Lesb Psych* **5**, 119–32.
88 A. Shidlo et al. (2002). *Prof Psych: Res and Pract* **33**, 249–59.
89 T. Green et al. (1996). Not For Turning. Authors, Leeds, UK.
90 I. Meyer (2003). *Psych Bull* **129**, 674–97.
91 J. Wakefield (2003). *Arch Sex Behav* **32**, 457–9.
92 M. Yarhouse et al. (2002). *Psychotherapy* **39**, 66–75.
93 D. Haldeman (2004) *The Couns Psych* **32**, 691–715.
94 J. Lasser et al. (2004) *Prof Psych: Res Prac* **35**, 194–200.
95 A. Beckstead et al. (2004) *The Couns Psych* **32**, 651–90.
96 M. Yarhouse (2002) *Prof Psych: Res Pract* **33**, 235–41.

Acknowedgements

I am grateful to several colleagues who commented on earlier drafts, including Professors Andrew Sims and Richard Winter, Phil Groves and my colleague Dr David de Pomeroi, although of course the responsibility for the final text is mine alone. I am most grateful of all to the numerous people on all sides of this debate who have been willing to share their personal journeys with me, often at a deeply personal level. I never take for granted the privilege of sharing in the experience of another human being.